STRESS AND EMOTION

THE SERIES IN STRESS AND EMOTION:
ANXIETY, ANGER, AND CURIOSITY
(Formerly part of the Series in Clinical and Community Psychology)

CONSULTING EDITORS
Charles D. Spielberger and Irwin G. Sarason

STRESS AND EMOTION
Anxiety, Anger, and Curiosity

Volume 15

Edited by
Charles D. Spielberger
University of South Florida, Tampa, USA

Irwin G. Sarason
University of Washington, Seattle, USA

Guest Editors
John M. T. Brebner
University of Adelaide, South Australia

Esther Greenglass
York University, Toronto, Canada

Pittu Laungani
South Bank University, London, England

Ann M. O'Roark
Executive Consultant, St. Petersburg, Florida, USA

Taylor & Francis
Publishers since 1798

USA	Publishing Office:	Taylor & Francis 1101 Vermont Avenue, N.W., Suite 200 Washington, DC 20005-3521 Tel: (202) 289-2174 Fax: (202) 289-3665
	Distribution Center:	Taylor & Francis 1900 Frost Road, Suite 101 Bristol, PA 19007-1598 Tel: (215) 785-5800 Fax: (215) 785-5515
UK		Taylor & Francis Ltd. 4 John St. London WC1N 2ET Tel: 071 405 2237 Fax: 071 831 2035

STRESS AND EMOTION: Anxiety, Anger, and Curiosity, Volume 15

1 2 3 4 5 6 7 8 9 0   BRBR   9 8 7 6 5

This book was set in Times Roman by Harlowe Typography, Inc. The editor was Heather L. Jefferson. Cover design by Michelle M. Fleitz. Printing and binding by Braun-Brumfield, Inc.

A CIP catalog record for this book is available from the British Library.

∞ The paper in this publication meets the requirements of the ANSI Standard Z39.48-1984 (Permanence of Paper)

Library of Congress Cataloging-in-Publication Data
Advanced Study Institute on Stress and Anxiety in Modern Life, Murnau, Ger., 1973.

Stress and anxiety: [proceedings]/edited by Charles D. Spielberger, Irwin G. Sarason. Washington: Hemisphere Publ. Corp.
    v. :ill.: 24 cm. (v. 1–2: The series in clinical psychology
    v. 3–5: The series in clinical and community psychology)
    Includes bibliographies and indexes.
    1. Stress, (Psychology)—Congresses. 2. Anxiety—Congresses.
I. Sarason, Irwin G., ed.   II. Spielberger, Charles Donald, date, ed.
III. North Atlantic Treaty Organization. Division of Scientific Affairs.
IV. Title. [DNLM: 1. Anxiety. 2. Stress, Psychological. WM 172 S755a]
BF575.S75A38   1973   616.8′522   74-28292
                        MARC

BF
575
.S75
A38
v.15

ISBN 1-56032-284-5
ISSN 1053-2161

Contents

8   Occupational Stress and Informed Interventions   121
Ann M. O'Roark

IV
STRESS AND HAPPINESS

**9   Testing for Stress and Happiness: The Role of
      Personality Factors   139**
John Brebner and Maryanne Martin

Contributors

MICHAEL ARGYLE, University of Oxford, United Kingdom
CÉSAR AVILA, Jaume I University, Casteló, Spain
JOHN BREBNER, University of Adelaide, South Australia
IAN J. DEARY, University of Edinburgh, United Kingdom
SOLLY DREMAN, Ben Gurion University of the Negev, Beer Sheva, Israel
HANS J. EYSENCK, Institute of Psychiatry, University of London, United
    Kingdom
SHIRLEY FISHER, Centre for Occupational and Health Psychology,
    Strathclyde University, Glasgow, United Kingdom
BRIAN M. FRIER, Royal Infirmary of Edinburgh, United Kingdom
IMMACULADA GRANDE, Autonomous University of Barcelona, Spain
CHOK C. HIEW, University of New Brunswick, Canada
PITTU LAUNGANI, South Bank University, London, United Kingdom
RONALD F. LEVANT, Cambridge Hospital/Harvard Medical School, Cam-
    bridge, Massachusetts, USA
LUO LU, Institute of Behavioral Sciences, Eachsiung, Taiwan
MARYANNE MARTIN, University of Oxford, United Kingdom
JAVIER MOLTÓ, Jaume I University, Casteló, Spain
ANN M. O'ROARK, Executive Consultant, St. Petersburg, Florida, USA
DEREK ROGER, University of York, United Kingdom
JAN STRELAU, University of Warsaw and Silesian University, Warsaw and
    Katowice, Poland
SANDRA P. THOMAS, University of Tennessee, Knoxville, Tennessee,
    USA
RAFAEL TORRUBIA, Autonomous University of Barcelona, Spain

Foreword

The modern world, with its fast-changing social environments, inflicts considerable stress on most humans. Thus, the relationship between stress and illness is of great importance. The chapters in this volume analyze, comment on, and explicate the details of the relationships among various aspects of the individual's environment, including life events and stress, emotions, health, and illness.

Life events, such as the death of a loved one, divorce, the loss of a job, insults received in a job environment—in other words, any event that can be perceived as unfortunate because it causes the individual to feel powerless or the victim of the irresponsible or unjust behavior of others—do not affect every individual the same way. The way a life event is perceived and impinges on the individual depends on the temperament and personality of that individual, the extent to which that person is receiving social support, and cultural and gender factors.

Personality includes individual differences in how information is selected, processed, and interpreted. There are individual differences in emotional control, extraversion, and neuroticism that increase or decrease the impact of each life event. Persons with highly developed social skills can deal with debilitating life events, while those with few such skills experience the events as totally destructive of their lives. Those with high self-esteem are often protected from debilitating life events, while individuals with low self-esteem may find them devastating. Thus, the same life event can result in high or low levels of stress and its emotional consequences (anger, anxiety, and worry), depending on the individual.

The rich details describing the above relationships that can be found in this volume make these contributions important and, in some cases, invaluable additions to the literature on stress and illness. Most of these chapters were first presented at the 23rd International Congress of Applied Psychology, which took place in Madrid, Spain, on July 17–22, 1994. In that Congress, four symposia were presented. The editors of this volume have skillfully shaped these chapters into their present form.

The International Association of Applied Psychology (IAAP), sponsor of the Madrid Congress, has been organizing meetings that constitute excellent research forums for almost 75 years. Those congresses started with a relatively narrow psychotechnology focus. However, in recent years the focus has expanded to include symposia on industrial/organizational, environmental, educational, instructional, school, clinical, community, health, political, and sports psychology, as well as psychological assessment and evaluation, the psychology of national development, applied gerontology, psychology and law, and traffic and transportation psychology.

For many years, the IAAP focused on European and American science and its applications. The focus has now expanded to include data from all six inhabited continents. Thus, the IAAP Congresses are now articulating a broad outline for a universal psychology that includes Western (Euro-American) psychology as a special case, and that now embraces theory and research findings from all parts of the world.

At the Madrid IAAP Congress, the Senior Editor of this volume was elected President of the International Association of Applied Psychology; he will take office during the 1998 IAAP Congress in San Francisco. I am delighted to know that he will be at the helm of the organization during the period of change from one millennium to the other. Under his able leadership, amply demonstrated in this volume, many more symposia on this important theme are likely to be presented, which will help us to understand the relationships among stress, emotions, and illness much better.

Harry C. Triandis
President, 1990–1994
International Association of Applied Psychology

Preface

This volume marks the 20th anniversary of the series on *Stress and Anxiety*, which was established to facilitate the dissemination of research presented at international scientific institutes and conferences. The first volume, published in 1975, was based on papers presented in June 1973 at an Advanced Study Institute, on Stress and Anxiety in Modern Life, sponsored by the Scientific Affairs Division of the North Atlantic Treaty Organization (NATO). The congenial setting of this institute, held at Murnau-am-Staffelsee, West Germany in the foothills of the Bavarian Alps, provided an ideal context for the communication of new and exciting findings presented by leading contributors to stress-related theory and research.

The continuing international interest in research on stress and anxiety in the 1970s, perhaps heightened by the cold war, stimulated the editors to organize a series of NATO Advanced Study Institutes, which were held in Norway, Italy, and England. The papers presented at these NATO institutes were published in Volumes 2–7 of this series. Volumes 8–12 and Volume 14 reported theoretical advances and research findings based on papers presented at international conferences held in Israel, The Netherlands, Poland, and Hungary. Publication of the papers presented at these conferences has helped bring advances in stress-related theory and research to the attention of social, behavioral, and medical scientists.

During the 1980s, the series on *Stress and Anxiety* continued to reflect the rapid growth in research in behavioral medicine, and in stress-related research on personality, social, and health psychology. The 1980s also witnessed numerous investigations of the Type A behavior pattern, anger and hostility, and their effects on the etiology of hypertension and cardiovascular disorders. Research on the contributions of psychosocial and personality factors to the etiology and progression of cancer also greatly increased. The importance of family and social support as moderators of the effects of stress on physical and emotional disorders was investigated and recognized as well.

The evolution of theory and research on emotional reactions to stress has required broadening the title of this series to encompass anger, anxiety, and other emotions. Volume 13 was primarily based on papers presented in two symposia on "Stress and Emotions" at the 24th International Congress of Psychology convened in Sydney, Australia, in 1988. These symposia also reflected a trend toward encompassing more in-depth coverage of specific research areas at international congresses. Beginning with Volume 14, this broader interest in stress-related phenomena contributed to changing the name of the series to *STRESS and EMOTION: Anxiety, Anger, and Curiosity*, and to its establishment as an independent series, separate from the Hemisphere

Publishing *Series in Clinical and Community Psychology*, where it previously resided.

Volumes 15 and 16 of this series on *STRESS and EMOTION* are primarily based on papers presented in four stress-related symposia at the 23rd International Congress of Applied Psychology in Madrid, Spain, in July 1994. These symposia were organized by the guest editors of these volumes: John M.T. Brebner of the University of Adelaide, South Australia; Esther Greenglass of York University, Toronto, Canada; Pittu Laungani of the South Bank University, London, England; and Ann M. O'Roark, Executive Consultant, St. Petersburg, Florida. The guest editors also contributed chapters based on their own research, and assisted participants in developing the chapters for this volume.

Volume 15 consists of five main parts, each with a major theme. There is, however, substantial overlap in the topics and methodologies considered in the individual chapters. Part I examines the effects of stress, life-change events, and personality on risk factors for disease, and on the specific contributions of these variables to the etiology and progression of diabetes, cancer, and coronary heart disease. Part II examines causes, manifestations, and consequences of stress-related violence in the family and, specifically, the effects of violence and anger on women and children.

Part III reports findings with regard to the causes and consequences of occupational stress in the workplace, and provides insights on the development of effective stress-reducing interventions. A relatively new area of research—the relationship between stress and happiness—is examined in Part IV. The three chapters in this part report recent studies of the influence of cognitive, social, personality, and biological factors on coping and happiness. Part V presents findings from studies of stress, temperament, and coping in Poland, the United Kingdom, and India. Similarities and differences in reactions to stress in Eastern and Western cultures are also noted in the final chapter.

The contents of this volume should be of substantial interest to social, behavioral, and medical scientists concerned with stress-related phenomena. The complex, interrelated effects of stressful circumstances, personality, and emotions on violence, disease, family relations, and happiness are especially relevant to behavioral medicine and health psychology, and to the development of effective treatment and preventive interventions. Although the thoughtful reader can identify emerging theoretical integrations of these complex phenomena, a true synthesis requires continuing to build on the promising research findings reported, developing more precise research methods, and establishing a comprehensive, integrated theoretical framework.

The series editors take pleasure in expressing their appreciation to the guest editors who organized the symposia for the IAAP Congress in Madrid, and for their contributions to this volume. We would also like to express our gratitude to Virginia Berch, Diane Gregg, Staci Martin, Jennifer Pagnotta, Eric Reheiser, and Karen Unger of the University of South Florida for their assistance in preparing the manuscript for publication.

Charles D. Spielberger
Irwin G. Sarason

I

STRESS, PERSONALITY, AND DISEASE

1

The Causal Role of Stress and Personality in the Aetiology of Cancer and Coronary Heart Disease

H. J. Eysenck
Institute of Psychiatry, University of London, England

ABSTRACT

In recent years, a large body of evidence has been produced in support of the 2000-year-old theory of a cancer-prone and heart disease-prone personality. Stress imposed on these types of personalities has been shown to play an important part in causing cancer and coronary heart disease (CHD), and prospective studies have demonstrated the ability of personality-based tests to accurately predict mortality. There are also theories concerning the way personality and stress can act in a causal manner to produce these diseases. Finally, it has been shown that psychological treatment can largely prevent cancer and CHD, and can prolong life in persons already suffering from these diseases. Research in this area is of exceptional scientific interest, and has high social value.

Theories concerning psychosocial causes of cancer and coronary heart disease (CHD) have been promoted and accepted by medical practitioners since the days of Hippocrates (Greer, 1983; Mettler & Mettler, 1947; Rosch, 1979; Temoshok & Dreher, 1992). As Sir William Osler (1906) said: "It is many times much more important to know what patient has the disease than what kind of disease the patient has" (pp. 758–759). Cancer-prone persons were believed to: (a) suppress emotions like fear and anger, and present a bland surface toward other people; and (b) make inappropriate and ineffectual reactions to stressful circumstances, leading to feelings of hopelessness, helplessness, and depression. Early workers in this field provided observational evidence in favour of these views (e.g., Bahnson, 1969; Greene, Young, & Swisher, 1956; Le Shan, 1966). Surveys of many of these early studies are given by Temoshok and Dreher (1991). Typical are studies like those of Le Shan, who claimed to have found "loss of hope" in 70%–80% of his cancer patients, but in only 10% of his control group. Criticisms of these early studies include: investigators knew the composition of their samples, used subjective methods of investigations, employed inappropriate control groups or none at all, confounded possible differences between people suffering from different types of cancer, and so on.

Regarding CHD, Friedman and Rosenman (1974) publicized the concept of a Type A personality predisposing a person to die of CHD. But it has been found that this "type" has no real existence. The parts of it that predict CHD are anger, hostility, and aggression, linked with heart disease long before Type A saw the light (Eysenck, 1990). Thus, there are two different theories relating stress, coping behaviour, and personality to cancer or CHD (Eysenck, 1991). The evidence for these theories is descriptive, derived from comparisons of cancer patients, CHD patients, and control groups, as well as experimental (Kneier & Temoshok, 1984), and may be said to give strong support to the theories outlined.

PREDICTIVE STUDIES

The most impressive studies, of course, are predictive studies, in which healthy people are studied by means of ratings, interviews, or questionnaires, and then followed up for many years. With these procedures, it is possible to test the validity of theories linking personality/stress with disease. The oldest of these studies was started by Thomas, who studied and followed up groups of students for 40 years (Shafer, Graves, Swank, & Pearson, 1987). It was found that people who were "loners" and suppressed their emotions "beneath a bland exterior" had the highest risk of cancer; in fact, the loners were 16 times more likely to develop cancer than those who vented their emotions. This figure should be compared with the comparable figure for smoking, comparing smokers with nonsmokers: it is 2.1 for cancer and 1.7 for CHD. Even for cancer of the lung, it is only 11.3 (i.e., much less than for personality; Doll & Peto, 1981). In other words, psychological factors are about eight times as predictive of cancer and CHD as is smoking. On the basis of independent studies, Eysenck (1988) arrived at a figure of personality/stress being six times as important as smoking in predicting disease.

These figures are not strictly correct because they assume independence of personality/stress and smoking. Rather, the evidence points strongly to a synergistic interaction between the two (Eysenck, 1994a); their effects seem to multiply rather than add. This, indeed, seems to be a general feature of many different risk factors for cancer and CHD (Doll & Peto, 1981). Furthermore, there are genetic links between personality and smoking (Eysenck, 1980; Kendler et al., 1993). These factors are usually disregarded in estimates of smoking-related deaths, but they are crucial in any scientific estimate of causality.

The Thomas study is not the only prospective study to give positive results. Kaplan and Reynolds (1988), Shekelle et al. (1981), Persky et al. (1987), and Dattore, Shantz, and Coyle (1980) also offered support to the general theory (Eysenck, 1994b). The largest set of prospective studies was contributed by Grossarth-Maticek, whose work has been summarized in book form by Eysenck (1991). Grossarth-Maticek has published three large follow-up studies, using a wealth of interviewer-administered questionnaires of his own de-

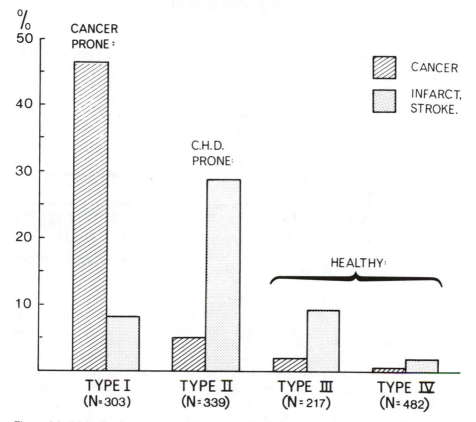

Figure 1.1 Mortality from cancer and coronary heart disease of different personality types—
Yugoslav study (Eysenck, 1991).

vising, and following up the samples in question for 10 years. One of the
samples came from his native Yugoslavia, the others from the German town
of Heidelberg. He used "type" questionnaires, with Type 1 being cancer-
prone, Type 2 CHD-prone, and Type 4 self-regulatory, autonomous, and fun-
damentally healthy. (Type 3 is also healthy, but of no particular interest here.)
Figures 1.1, 1.2, and 1.3 show the results of a 10-year follow-up. They clearly
support his theories.

One of the Heidelberg groups was normal (on a random selection basis),
and the other was stressed (being nominated as such by friends and family
members). Clearly, the stressed group had much higher mortality, resembling
that of the Yugoslav group, despite that the Heidelberg group was 10 years
younger than the Yugoslav one on average. Because of certain criticisms of the
original studies, the two Heidelberg groups were followed up for another 4.5

HEIDELBERG STUDY
(normal group)

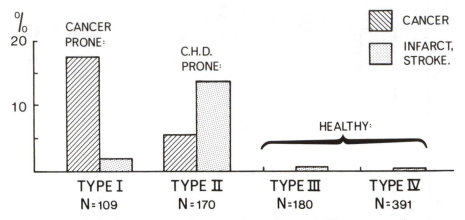

Figure 1.2   Mortality from cancer and coronary heart disease of different personality types—
Heidelberg normal sample (Eysenck, 1991).

years, with similar results (Eysenck, 1993). Figure 1.4 shows that results continued to be positive, with Type 1 persons dying of cancer, Type 2 persons dying of CHD, and Types 3 and 4 continuing healthfully. Many independent replications have supported the validity of Grossarth-Maticek's theories. A list is given by Eysenck (1995). It is important to realize that the method of questionnaire administration can make an important difference (Grossarth-Maticek, Eysenck, & Barrett, 1993). It is not enough to simply hand out questionnaires; one must establish *trust* and provide answers to questions concerning the meaning of various items.

RECENT STUDIES

More recent work has concentrated on the nature of psychological health (i.e., a closer scrutiny of Type 4). Grossarth-Maticek created a 105-item questionnaire expanding the contents of the Type 4 concepts, which is now named *self-regulation*. This term denotes a person who is not governed by his or her emotions, is autonomous of other people, and is functional in his or her behaviour. The inventory has high reliability, and has proved its validity in predicting mortality from cancer and CHD. Figures 1.5 and 1.6 show the results of administering the questionnaire to 3,108 male and 2,608 female subjects, none of whom suffered from serious illness. The subjects were selected on a random basis from official records in Heidelberg. Fifteen years later, cause of death was established from death certificates for all those who had died. Scores

HEIDELBERG STUDY
(stressed group)

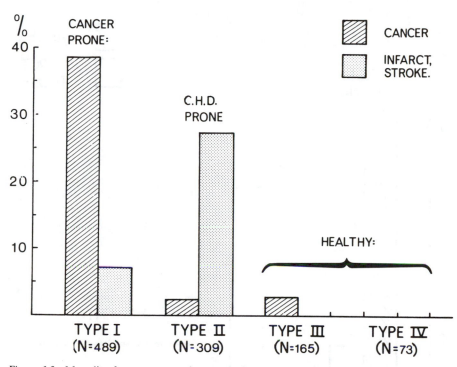

Figure 1.3 Mortality from cancer and coronary heart disease of different personality types—Heidelberg stressed sample (Eysenck, 1991).

were turned into six categories from *low* (1) to *high* (6). The distribution of scores is reasonably normal.

The figures clearly show that there is a monotonic relation between score and mortality—least steep for cancer, roughly equal for CHD and other causes of death. A fairly clear-cut break is evident; high scores (4, 5, 6) show little difference for cancer and CHD. However, when scores are below the mean, this lack of self-regulation increases the death rate. For other causes of death, the regression is much more linear, although the causes of this difference are not known. It is clear that personality is closely related to mortality (i.e., the greater a person's self-regulatory behaviour, the less likely he or she is to die at an early age).

The data given so far are essentially correlational; can they be interpreted as having a causal nexus? Intervention studies, using methods of behaviour therapy and stress management in healthy Type 1 and Type 2 persons to avoid their contracting cancer or CHD, have been highly successful (Eysenck & Grossarth-Maticek, 1991; Grossarth-Maticek & Eysenck, 1991), whether using

HEIDELBERG STUDY
(1982-1986)

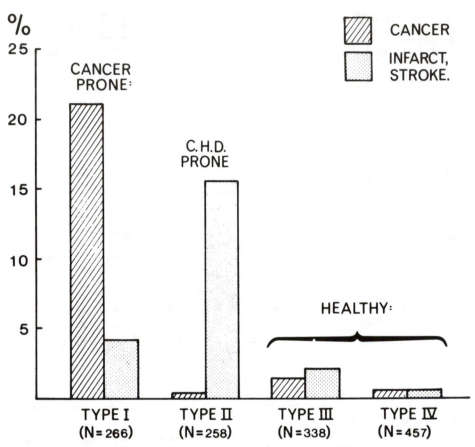

Figure 1.4   Mortality from cancer and coronary heart disease of different personality types: Follow-up of studies in Figures 1.2 and 1.3 for a further 4.5 years (Eysenck, 1993).

individual or group autonomy training. This suggests quite strongly that the personality–disease relation is causal, rather than purely statistical.

The self-regulation test was administered to 662 cancer patients; some accepted, but others rejected offers of operations, chemotherapy, or radiotherapy. Members of each group were subdivided into good or poor self-regulators on the basis of their scores. The acceptors and refusers were matched as closely as possible on the basis of their age, sex, diagnosis, and treatment. Survival in years was the outcome criterion. There was little difference in survival time according to acceptance or rejection of treatment: 5.1 years for rejectors, 5.7 years for acceptors. In both groups, survival times were much higher for those

Prospective 1973-1988 Study: Males (N=3,108)

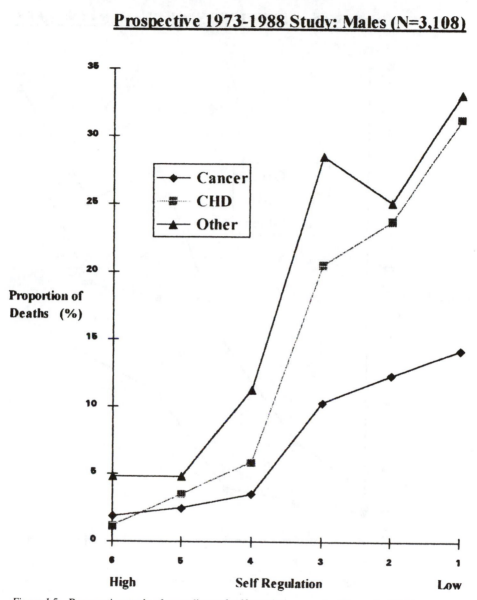

Figure 1.5   Prospective study of mortality and self-regulation—males (Eysenck, 1994b).

with high self-regulation scores than for those with poor self-regulation scores. For those who refused therapy, survival times were 2.9 and 6.5 years; for those who accepted therapy, survival times were 3.7 and 13.8 years. It is clear that a person's degree of self-regulation is much more important for his or her survival than acceptance or rejection of orthodox medical therapy.

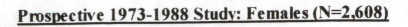

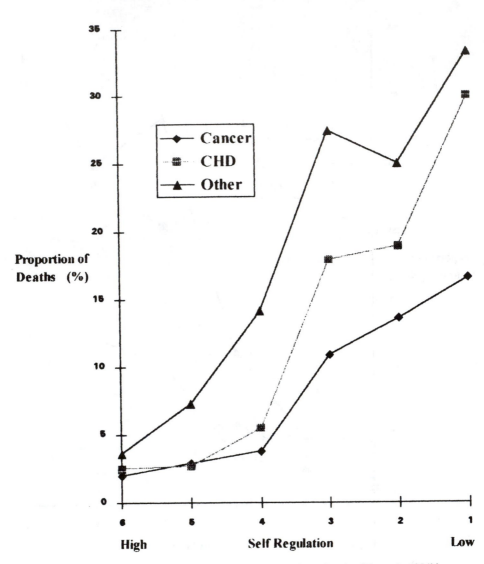

Figure 1.6   Prospective study of mortality and self-regulation—females (Eysenck, 1994b).

CONCLUSION

It is clear that stress and personality are important factors in a person's liability to cancer and CHD, and his or her power to survive before succumbing to either disease. It is important to treat personality and stress together because a person's reaction to objective stressors is the crucial element in the strain, which is the product of stress, coping, and personality (Eysenck, 1994a). It is this combination of personality and stress that is characteristic of Grossarth-Maticek's definition of the Type 1 and Type 2 personalities, and autonomous, self-regulating Type 4 (Grossarth-Maticek, Eysenck, & Boyle, 1994). The inclusion of these psychosocial risk factors for cancer and CHD, and the widespread use of behaviour therapy in the prevention of both, seem to be the most likely sources of improvement in the present way of dealing with these diseases.

REFERENCES

Bahnson, C. B. (1969). Psychophysiological complementarity in malignancies: Part work of future writers. *Annals of the New York Academy of Sciences, 164*, 319–332.

Dattore, P., Shantz, R., & Coyle, L. (1980). Premorbid personality differentiation of cancer and non-cancer groups: A test of the hypotheses of cancer proneness. *Journal of Counseling and Clinical Psychology, 43*, 380–384.

Doll, R., & Peto, R. (1981). *The causes of cancer.* Oxford: Oxford University Press.

Eysenck, H. J. (1980). *The causes and effects of smoking.* London: Maurice Temple Smith.

Eysenck, H. J. (1988). The respective importance of personality, cigarette smoking and interaction effects for the genesis of cancer and coronary heart disease. *Personality and Individual Differences, 9*, 453–464.

Eysenck, H. J. (1990). Types of behaviour and coronary heart disease. The third stage. *Journal of Social Behaviour and Personality, 5*, 25–44.

Eysenck, H. J. (1991). *Smoking, personality and stress: Psychosocial factors in the prevention of cancer and coronary heart disease.* New York: Springer-Verlag.

Eysenck, H. (1993). Prediction of cancer and coronary heart disease mortality by means of a personality inventory: Results of a 15-year follow-up study. *Psychological Reports, 72*, 499–516.

Eysenck, H. J. (1994a). Synergistic interaction between psychosocial and physical factors in the causation of lung cancer. In C. Lewis, C. O'Sullivan, & J. Barraclough (Eds.), *The psychoimmunology of cancer* (pp. 163–178). Oxford: Oxford University Press.

Eysenck, H. J. (1994b). Cancer, personality and stress: Prediction and prevention. *Advances in Behaviour Research and Therapy, 16*, 167–215.

Eysenck, H. J., & Grossarth-Maticek, R. (1991). Creative novation behaviour therapy as a prophylactic treatment for cancer and coronary heart disease: II. Effects of treatment. *Behaviour Research & Therapy, 29*, 17–31.

Friedman, M., & Rosenman, R. (1974). *Type A behavior and your heart*. New York: Knopf.

Greene, W., Young, I., & Swisher, S. N. (1956). Psychological factors and reticuloendothetical disease: II. Observation on a group of women with lymphomas and leukemias. *Psychosomatic Medicine, 18*, 284–303.

Greer, S. (1983). Cancer and the mind. *British Journal of Psychiatry, 143*, 535–543.

Grossarth-Maticek, R., & Eysenck, H. J. (1991). Creative novation behaviour therapy as a prophylactic treatment for cancer and coronary heart disease: I. Description of treatment. *Behaviour Research and Therapy, 29*, 1–16.

Grossarth-Maticek, R., Eysenck, H. J., & Barrett, P. (1993). Prediction of cancer and coronary heart disease as a function of method of questionnaire administration. *Psychological Reports, 73*, 943–959.

Grossarth-Maticek, R., Eysenck, H. J., & Boyle, G. J. (1994). An empirical study of the diathesis-stress theory of disease. *Australian Journal of Stress Management, 1*, 3–18.

Kaplan, C., & Reynolds, R. (1988). Repression of cancer mortality: Prospective evidence from the Alameda County Study. *Journal of Behavioural Medicine, 11*, 1–13.

Kendler, K., Neale, M., MacLean, C., Heath, A., Eaves, L., & Kessler, R. (1993). Smoking and major depression. *Archives of General Psychiatry, 50*, 36–73.

Kneier, A. W., & Temoshok, L. (1984). Regressive coping reactions in patients with malignant melanoma as compared to cardiovascular disease patients. *Journal of Psychosomatic Medicine, 28*, 145–155.

Le Shan, L. (1966). An emotional life-history pattern associated with neoplastic disease. *Annals of the New York Academy of Sciences, 125*, 780–793.

Mettler, C. C., & Mettler, F. A. (1947). *History of medicine*. Philadelphia: Blakiston.

Osler, W. (1906). *Aequanimitas*. New York: McGraw-Hill.

Persky, V., Kempthorne-Rawson, J., & Shekelle, D. (1987). Personality and risk of cancer: 20-year follow-up of the Western Electric Study. *Psychosomatic Medicine, 49*, 435–449.

Rosch, P. J. (1979). Stress and cancer: A disease of adaptation? In J. Tache, H. Selye, & S. B. Day (Eds.), *Stress and cancer* (pp. 187–212). New York: Plenum.

Shaffer, J. W., Graves, P. L., Swank, R. T., & Pearson, T. A. (1987). Clustering of personality traits in youth and the subsequent development of cancer among physicians. *Journal of Behavioral Medicine, 10*, 441–447.

Shekelle, R., Raynar, W., Ostfield, A., Garron, D., Biolanskas, L., Liu, S., Maliza, C., & Paul, O. (1981). Psychological depression and 17-year risk of death from cancer. *Psychosomatic Medicine, 43*, 117–125.

Temoshok, L., & Dreher, H. (1992). *The Type C connection: The mind-body link to cancer and your health*. New York: Penguin Books USA.

2

Stress, Life Change, Contexts, and the Risk of Disease

Shirley Fisher
Centre for Occupational and Health Psychology,
Strathclyde University, Glasgow, Scotland

ABSTRACT

Life circumstances, marital status, life events, and gender are factors that influence the risk of disease. Perhaps distress and loss of control are mediating factors. Historical research has identified the distress factors associated with migration, and more recent research has identified the stressors associated with moves, even for upwardly mobile situations. This chapter discusses the variables that increase the risk of ill health, including cognitive factors associated with loss of control, social disruption, and single status. Being alone and having tendencies toward depressed thinking and excessive worry may be linked to specific hormone patterns that, if persistent across time, raise the risk of antigen proliferation and somatisation, leading to chronic disease. Unmitigated worry has the theoretical capacity to enhance the disease process.

A variety of social and situational conditions have long been believed to be associated with the risk of disease and shorter life expectancy. Evidence on the effects of conditions such as single marital status and events such as job loss, bereavement, divorce, financial crisis, and so on has indicated a relationship with ill health. In addition, low social class, as defined by income and education, is a risk factor (see Fisher, 1989).

Historically, investigations of the relationship between life experiences and disease formed the basis of psychosomatic medicine (Weiner, 1982). In contrast, traditional medical science focused on the role of constitutional and genetic factors. More recently, the research balance has shifted toward understanding the impact and role of psychogenic factors. What used to be part of psychosomatic medicine is now becoming central to modern medical science.

LIFE CHANGE UNITS: STRESS AND DISEASE

Studies by Holmes and Rahe (1967), arising from clinical observations that life events such as job loss, divorce, and bereavement seemed to feature in the life history protocols of patients at a naval base in the United States, led to the construction of a scale designed to assess and quantify the impact of life events. This consisted of a spectrum of personal, social, and occupational life events generated by cohorts of normal, healthy Americans. A quantitative weighting scale was then developed: Normal judges were provided with a list of 42 life changes, one of which—marriage—was nominated as the standard for comparing other life changes and was given the value of 500. Subjects were asked to provide a rank order of relative life change units (LCUs) for the rest of the life events: Death of a spouse, divorce and marital separation, death of a close family member, and detention in jail ranked high in terms of perceived stressful qualities.

Early retrospective studies (e.g., Holmes & Rahe, 1967) showed that there was a cumulative increase in LCUs in the first 2 years prior to illness. The effect was nonspecific and did not predict the type of illness. The studies also provided a quantitative index: With LCU values below 150, there was no reason to expect ill health, whereas with values between 150 and 300, approximately half the individuals reported an illness in the following year. For values of 300 LCU, 70% of subjects were affected. A later study involving 2,500 U.S. Navy officers (see Rahe, 1972) identified a buildup of LCUs prior to illness. However, following the illness, LCU totals remained elevated.

Holmes and Rahe (1967) hypothesised that the cumulative LCU scores index stress levels in terms of the amount of adjustment required by change. The power of this scale to predict the risk of major illness, both prospectively and retrospectively, has been given recent detailed consideration by Rahe (1988), where a particularly robust relationship between cumulative LCUs and sudden cardiac death syndrome was reported. However, Connolly (1975) provided a more circumspect view, arguing that the power to predict illness in general is weak and the power to predict specific forms of illness is extremely low.

Specific attempts to determine the impact of life events, both positive and negative, have indicated that distress reactions are important. The reaction to change could provide important clues concerning the process by which illness is an outcome.

MIGRATION AND DISEASE

The research literature indicated a positive relationship between relocation and migration and poor mental and physical health. However, the interpretation of the research findings is difficult because the causal directions cannot be identified. This consideration is important because, although there is a tendency to attribute the causes of ill health to the geographical transition, self-selection factors may be operative (those who move away may be those who are poor or discontented with a previous environment).

A number of early studies focused on the health of migrant communities, compared with that of the indigenous population. For example, Odegaard (1932) reported greater rates of hospital admissions for mental disorders, such as depression and schizophrenia, among Norwegian immigrants to Minnesota than for the native-born of Minnesota or Norway. Malzberg and Lee (1940) reported a similar result for populations in New York when age, race, and gender were taken into account. These studies, although not devoid of the previously stated methodological difficulties, point to the vulnerability of the migrant group. The reasons for the effect remain unclear: There may have been exposure to adverse environments, mediating behaviours may increase the risk of ill health, general poverty factors may weaken resources through poor nutrition, and so on.

However, there is also evidence that undermines the hypothesis of migrants' enhanced vulnerability with regard to mental disorder. Kleiner and Parker (1963) demonstrated the greater prevalence of psychoneurotic and psychosomatic symptoms in native-born individuals migrating within the United States. There was some evidence of greater discrepancy between educational aspiration and achievement for the native-born group, which underlines the possible importance of circumstantial factors.

Perhaps the most quoted work is that of Faris and Dunham (1939), who, using home ownership as an index of life stability and rental status as an index of mobility in the city of Chicago, found a negative association between mobility and mental health. However, the mobile areas of cities were also the most socially disorganised and the most likely to be associated with poverty. The conclusion that social location causes psychopathology epitomises the main difficulties of interpretation; those with poor mental health may become incompetent and drift down to ghetto areas of cities. Equally, the stress of life in these areas may create the nurturent conditions for psychopathology.

The picture is much the same with physical health. Research evidence during the last 60 years has demonstrated the vulnerability of migrant populations to physical ill health. In particular, cardiovascular disease, gastric disorders, and infectious illnesses such as tuberculosis have been found to be more prevalent in migrant populations than in the "initial" or "receiving" communities (see Christenson & Hinkle, 1961; Cruze-Coke, Etcheverry, & Nagel, 1964; Medalie & Kahn, 1973; Wolff, 1953).

More insight into the type of adverse effects created by moving was provided in a longitudinal prospective study by Fried (1962), who examined inhabitants of Chicago who were moved to new housing as part of slum-clearance schemes. Although family ties were preserved, the city environment remained familiar, and the move was to better housing, major effects akin to grief life reactions were found in many of the residents.

Pre- and postrelocation data show that a large number of those who moved reported intense, overwhelming emotions and grief for the old (slum) premises: "I felt as if the heart was taken out of me." The results show that objects in the old home retained symbolic importance. People made visits back to the old home to look at sentimental features and objects. Situation and status defined by occupational, educational, and income factors were positively associated with good adjustment.

Syme (1967) described the process of undergoing changes as "cultural mobility," and envisaged the result as enhancing the disease risk. An interesting outcome occurred in a longitudinal study on the effects of relocation to a new job (Stokols, Schumaker, & Martinez, 1983). Although mobility might be fashionable for a vigorous, modern economic nation, moving may have negative implications. The study involved 242 adult employees, 121 of whom completed a follow-up study of emotional and physical well-being 3 months after a move to a new job in a new location. The authors obtained self-report data on mobility history, and reported that frequent relocation was associated with a greater number of illness-related symptoms and reduced satisfaction. The study indicated the adverse effect of moving on those with "low exploratory tendency"; this was described in terms of lack of exploration of various aspects of the psychosocial environment.

Fisher, Murray, and Frazer (1985; see also Fisher, 1990) examined the effect of moving in situations where a young person leaves home for the first time to take up a place at a university or college. Increased levels of depression, anxiety, and obsession were apparent. Homesickness and negative emotional impact were evident for 70% of students in the sixth week of the first term. Prolonged distress may be a precursor of disease if maintained long enough. This is discussed in later sections of this chapter.

SOCIOECONOMIC STATUS AND DISEASE

Again in historical perspective, the vulnerability of those in low socioeconomic positions has been an issue of interest. Carroll, Niven, and Sheffield (1993) remarked that, even as far back as the 15th century, effects of significance were noted. Morrison, Kirshner, and Molha (1977) examined the records of dowry investments in Florence (1925–1442). When the magnitude of the dowry sum was compared with age at death, a gradient of increased mortality was found to be associated with smaller dowries.

More recent data confirm this tendency of poor socioeconomic groups to die young. Carroll et al. (1993) showed a relationship between height of obelisk in a Victorian cemetery in Glasgow and age at death. This was true for both genders. Carroll et al. argued that self-selected drift down to low social status is less useful as an explanation because of a mismatch between the years when mobility commonly occurred and those characterised by ill health. Thus, in terms of arguments on mobility, causes of ill health may be one factor, but not the only factor, in disease. Interpretation needs to be circumspect. In general, the migration studies support the relationship between mobility and ill health.

When factors such as smoking and alcohol consumption are held constant, occupational/class status factors are still influential (Marmot, Shipley, & Rose, 1984). One of the most important features of work on health statistics and class is that the class effects are not confined to the poverty/low-class zones; the effect continues in groups that are not deprived. Carstairs and Morris (1991) looked at class effects for different postal codes indicating different socioeconomic benefits; a continuous gradient of mortality risk from least to most affluent was found to exist. Perhaps the concept of *demoralisation*, or *lack of perceived power and status*, is the underlying construct that should be examined. Perhaps this, in turn, can be hypothesised as operating via human distress.

Figure 2.1 illustrates a conceptualisation of processes by which the experiences of life situation and change might increase the risk of infectious or chronic disease. First, the life event might create adverse prevailing conditions (poverty, overcrowding, etc.), resulting in more encounters with existing or new types of antigens. Low social class may create constant poor prevailing conditions, thus raising the frequency of stress experience. The second possibility is that the individual's behaviour changes as a response to the stress of new places, and that the risk of bodily malfunction or antigen encounter changes as a result. Finally, irrespective of the nature of the life event, the mental and physical states of the individual may change as a function of the stress of a move: A person may become more biologically aroused or more worried and preoccupied, thus increasing the potential for prolonged arousal. This could adversely affect hormone levels for a longer period of time.

GENDER, MORTALITY, AND MORBIDITY

As illustrated in Fig. 2.2, epidemiological evidence has already established that a number of psychosocial factors influence the risk of ill health. For example, single marital status is a risk factor in illness. The single and divorced are more at risk for various forms of ill health and aberrant behaviours compared with the married. This finding alone underlines the possible importance of psychosocial mediators in the risk of illness, although the causal direction is unclear.

Epidemiological results that are largely descriptive show that the effect of marriage is protective; but this may be more true for males than females, which raises some interesting questions. Perhaps because lowered disease risk in females creates smaller samples, there is a "floor effect" and the marital status factor does not materialise. An alternative explanation is that the effect of marriage is social, and females do not obtain the level of support in marriage compared with males. Self-selection into marriage provides another alternative: Maybe only robust males marry.

National health records traced by Connolly (1975) identified the vulnerability of widowers. Those over 55 years of age have mortality rates 40% above the expected rate for aged-matched married men, and there is a vulnerable period 6 months postbereavement. Common diseases experienced by widowers are cancer and heart disease (Parkes, 1965).

Taken collectively, both gender and marital status effects indicate the importance of considering psychological factors in ill health. The effect may be genetically determined, but may combine with marital status factors. However, the explanation must include protective social factors and the role of the lonely. Recent research by Fisher and Bailey (1995) has established single marital status in young males as a significant factor in railroad suicides in the United Kingdom.

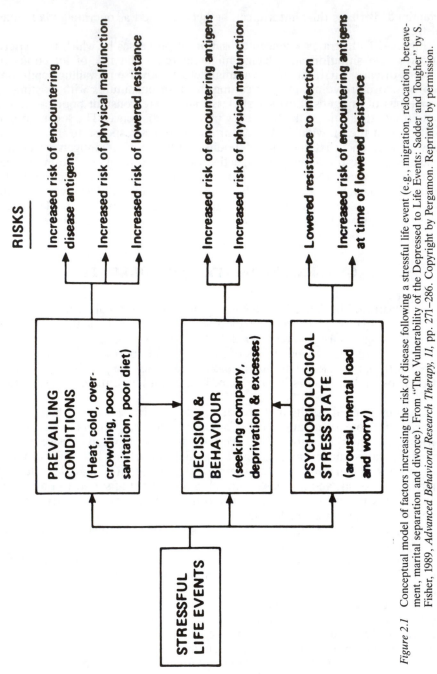

Figure 2.1 Conceptual model of factors increasing the risk of disease following a stressful life event (e.g., migration, relocation, bereavement, marital separation and divorce). From "The Vulnerability of the Depressed to Life Events: Sadder and Tougher" by S. Fisher, 1989, *Advanced Behavioral Research Therapy, 11,* pp. 271–286. Copyright by Pergamon. Reprinted by permission.

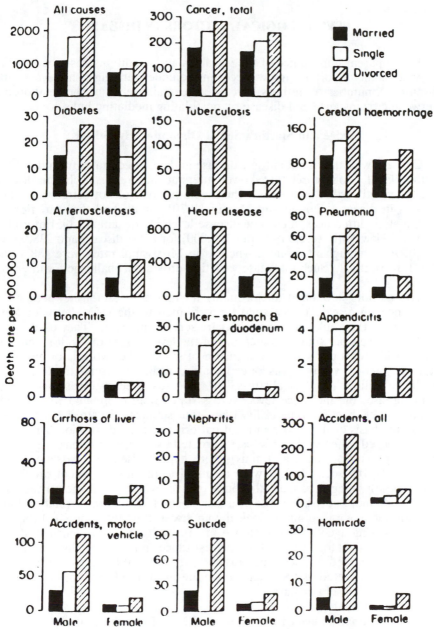

Figure 2.2 Standardized death rates for different causes of death in the United States. Data redrawn from Berkson (1962) with the permission of the American Medical Association. From *Stress and Strategy* (p. 221) by S. Fisher, 1986, London: Lawrence Erlbaum Associates. Copyright 1986 by Lawrence Erlbaum Associates. Reprinted by permission.

PSYCHOLOGICAL FACTORS IN DISEASE

The apparent importance of the variables and conditions described earlier provides some important jigsaw pieces in the understanding of life events and disease. A number of authors have tried to make sense of the relationship between circumstance and disease by postulating mediating links.

Dodge and Martin's Social Disruption Hypothesis

Concern with the rise of chronic disease in the United States from the 1950s to the 1980s led to research that showed interstate differences in chronic disease and provided further evidence of the mediating role of both stress and class factors in disease. Dodge and Martin (1970) established the statistics for within-state differences in chronic disease levels. For example, 1951 mortality rates for New York were 938.5 (per 100,000) for heart disease and 238.9 (per 100,000) for malignant disease, whereas in Mississippi rates were 488.4 and 163.3, respectively. Such interstate variation provides a challenge for interpretation.

The authors developed an ingenious technique to establish whether the differences in disease levels could be attributed to the stress levels or were functions of the availability of health care services per state. They used infant mortality levels per state as a measure of the level of general health facilities, and suicide rates per state as a measure of stress. The two sets of mortality statistics then provided a basis for explanation of chronic disease levels in terms of "health milieu" or "social stress." In the cases of heart disease and malignant disease, the incidence levels across states were correlated with suicide levels, rather than infant mortality rates, thus supporting a stress hypothesis.

On the basis of these correlational patterns, a social disruption hypothesis was proposed. Life experiences, partly created by living conditions (e.g., competitive pressures, goals, and aims), were hypothesised to impose stress on individuals, but social factors were assumed to dictate the extent of effects. Thus, poorly integrated marital groups (single, widowed, divorced) were argued to be more at risk because of a lack of stable and durable relationships. The authors envisaged an etiological complex of three elements: (a) the disease-provoking agent, (b) the nature of the environment in which host and agent are brought together, and (c) the resistance and susceptibility of the host in turn determined by social integration level. Thus, the marital status factor could be interpreted as the important buffering variable that attenuates the effect of stress level per state.

Totman's Social Consistency and Rule Breakdown Model

The theoretical position taken by Totman (1979) has common features with the Dodge and Martin theory (because of the emphasis on social breakdown and disharmony following life changes). Totman argued that social factors exert a protective influence on health. The individual becomes at risk for illness when social mobility or status incongruity occur. Totman proposed a structural theory that assumes that people make sense of each other's actions in terms of social rules and conventions. Thus, each individual is equipped with a set of prescriptive rules. For these rules to exist, they must be resistant to change, although some clarification or refinement can occur as the result of social interactions. Social change is assumed to create a situation of rule breakdown. Exits, losses, and marital disruption could all be seen in terms of the breakdown of rules, and will create periods of instability and demoralisation.

Fisher's Control Model

Fisher (1984, 1986) proposed that life events create changes in the level of demand together with reduction of control. Reduction of control occurs when a person feels unable to produce a set of actions that will restore perceived discrepancy between reality and aims or ambitions. In this context, change creates discrepancies and, because of novelty, decreases the level of socioenvironmental control a person experiences.

Studies of animals and people suggest that power or mastery over the environment is likely to have an ameliorating effect on threat. In laboratory studies, animals provided with the instrumental means to avoid punishment generally show fewer signs of distress and less evidence of stomach lesions and ulcers than paired, yoked, and helpless controls who receive the same amount of punishment (Mowrer & Viek, 1948). The evidence supports the concept of perceived control over punishment as a significant factor in response. The studies by Brady, Porter, Conrad, and Mason (1958) on ulcers in "executive monkeys," although weakened by a poor design (in that the monkeys were not assigned at random to helpless and executive conditions), showed that the results could be reversed if the monkeys had to press a switch continuously to avoid shock. The helpless monkeys benefited from not having control. However, Fisher (1989) termed the situation *control by avoidance*, and argued that it had special properties because the executive animals never obtained appropriate coping feedback, and therefore sustained more signs of ill health.

In a study by Haggard (1943) involving human beings, the situation was more complex. Up to one third of a sample of subjects did not choose to have direct control over administered electric shock. However, Ball and Vogler (1971) showed that those who chose not to have control provided reasons that suggested their targets for control are different (Fisher, 1986). In a study where subjects could choose between self-shock and external shock, a small proportion persisted with external shock, even when punished for doing so by having to accept double shock. Yet it may be that what appears like loss of control may in fact be a powerful form of control. Accepting double shock may indicate a wish to thwart the experimenter or prove bravery.

The role of perceived control at work has been identified by Karasek (1979), who reported that job strain in working environments can be defined with respect to two dimensions: demand (or workload) and discretion (control). Job strain is reported when demand is high and control is low. Perceived challenge is a more likely perception when demand and control are both high.

On this analysis, a major life event might be argued to create a personal job strain environment. For example, the bereaved person has to cope with the strain of living a life without the help and protection of a spouse. Perhaps this is part of the reason for demoralisation and distress associated with some of the circumstances described previously.

THE MECHANISMS OF PSYCHOSOCIAL FACTORS IN DISEASE

There are now a number of possible linking pieces in the jigsaw, although none of the evidence is conclusive. The gender and class effect, the marital status effect, the apparant role of LCUs as partial and sometimes robust predictors of ill health, and the apparently profound effects of major moves and the resultant negative change in mental state, all seem to provide important pointers. Moreover, the effects of low social class and single marital status underline the importance of long-term situational factors as negative or positive determinants of health.

Perhaps superordinate common denominators can be identified, such as anxiety and distress. Loss of control, social disruption, and major changes may all create conditions where a person feels "out of kilter," unanchored, or out of control. Perhaps this, in turn, creates the state of mental turmoil and distress that affects other bodily processes. If the origins of disease are to be understood, it is necessary to find the links with biological states that support ill health. For example, the finding that bereavement increases the risk of cancer and heart disease by up to 400% in the first 6 months (Parkes, 1965) must eventually be interpreted in biological terms.

The methodological problems are considerable because, as is frequently argued, there is no way to time-lock the occurrence of a cancer cell to a particular life state. Many forms of cancerous disease may have origins up to 20 years before manifestation.

Selectivity in Biological States of Stress

To understand how an individual's psychological states might influence the risk of antigens becoming established or chronic diseases developing, links between stable psychological states and biological states must be explicit. Psychological states are rich and varied, and they link with biological activity in such a way as to raise the risk of particular structural diseases. Biological states once thought to be characterised only in terms of an intensity dimension are now increasingly understood to be selectively affected by the environment, including social conditions, as well as by personality traits.

In historical perspective, the effect of stress on biological activity was first described in terms of a unitary state of increased arousal, implying that any number of different kinds of stressful experience (e.g., bereavement, failure, surgical operations, public speaking, illness, job loss) would be associated with nonspecific arousal effects (Selye, 1956). Cannon (1932, 1936) was one of the first to make sense of the biological state, which accompanied the experience of stress in terms of the need to restore equilibrium. The biological response to the disequilibrium produced by environmental stressors was assumed to provide the power to restore the balance. However, this did not change the basic assumption of the nonspecificity of the biological state. The question of why one person reacts to stress with ulcers and another with heart disease (Malmo & Shagass, 1949) provided an early challenge to this assumption, which for a considerable time was never considered and has still not been resolved today.

Perhaps the attempt to link even physiological states to disease proclivities must remain fanciful. Weiner (1982) pointed out that, in any population, some individuals are at risk for disease but the illness never materializes. One example is the presence of elevated levels of pepsinogen isoenzyme, which is a biological marker for peptic duodenal ulcer. Such a marker can occur in persons who remain well. Weiner concluded that some individuals are programmed for disease by a multitude of predisposing markers and psychological sensitivities.

However, it might be possible to probe the medium in which markers exist. The recent acknowledgment of helicobactor as a factor in disorders of the gut might suggest that antigen personality profiles be biological risks. Perhaps the person with a biological marker or antigen favouring a peptic ulcer remains well unless creating or encountering stresses, which produce changes in gastric activity. A risk model based on compatibility and synchrony of biological and psychological patterns might be the answer. Also, existing biological markers that should predispose toward illness might be created and sustained by stressful life experiences. It then requires a further life event to create the synchronous existence of sufficient risk factors for a particular kind of illness. This is perhaps close to the analogy of a road accident, where many single factors converge to produce a critical event.

There has been an increasing realization that physiological responses are capable of producing rich patterning that may reflect the features of the stress (fear-provoking, anger-provoking) or the idiosyncrasies of the individual (self-blaming, external blaming). On the basis of drug and ablation studies, Lacey (1967) even suggested that biological arousal is rarely a uniform state; "temporal parallelism" exists between cortical, autonomic, and behavioural arousal states, and fractionation of states is possible.

Important work by Frankenhauser and colleagues identified direct environmental or personal circumstances on the balance of the main hormones that mediate stress (Frankenhauser & Johansson, 1982). From studies in a saw mill, workers who were restricted in work posture were likely to experience states of irritability and show a preponderance of noradrenaline. By comparison, workers who were submitted to externally paced assembly line work were more likely to have raised anxiety and raised levels of adrenaline. Thus, the possibility of idiosyncrasy in hormone states exists.

The suggestion of a selective balance in hormone ratios dictated by the external environment, or even by personality traits as in Type A behaviour pattern (Rosenman, 1982), might provide a vital element in understanding the risk of disease.

Somatisation, the process by which a person's functional biological activity eventually creates structural damage, is assumed to create sufficient conditions for illness risk. For example, a person who experiences the same irritability in the work environment for 40 hours a week may perhaps, by analogy with "grooves in a record," create an increasing tendency to become structurally determined in that mode. If one imagines different prevailing hormone balances, the implications for structural patterns and selective wear and tear could be important.

This provides an important role for work environments and other social environments. It may selectively tune specific hormone states, and thus refine consequent structural risk. A person demoralised by lack of control at work may constantly experience an adverse feeling, with accompanying selective hormone states, day after day until it becomes part of his or her personality. The hormone patterns would carry the underlying structural damage.

Stress and the Sympathetico-Medullary Route

The autonomic nervous system provides the basis of a complex system that controls the release of the catecholamines adrenaline and noradrenaline via the adrenal medulla. Raised sympathetic activity is associated with increased cardiac output, vasoconstriction, changes in gastric motility, reduction of bodily secretions, increased muscle tension, changes in respiratory rate, mobilization of glycogen, and release of fats, cholesterol, and fatty acid into circulation.

Chronic, elevated levels of catecholamines can create structural changes in systems. In the cardiovascular system, cholesterol and fatty acid deposits decrease the lumen of blood vessels. Therefore, stresses that are frequent or prolonged, perhaps because they relate to uncontrollable problems, are likely to create conditions that might prepare for structural changes leading to chronic disease. Dietary fat may raise serum cholesterol levels, hence stress-related behaviour leading to obesity may be another risk factor in cardiovascular disease. Yet Japanese immigrants in the United States who eat high-fat diets but maintain a traditional way of life are less prone to heart disease than those who do not (Marmot & Syme, 1976). Thus, the effects of stress and dietary fat may be interactive as well as independent risk factors in cardiovascular disease.

In an analysis of the underlying causes of heart disease in the Western world, Carruthers (1974) examined a high-risk group of race-car drivers. High levels of noradrenaline during and after a race led to the idea that an "arousal jag" is actively sought by drivers. Because of lack of physical activity, elevated levels of cholesterol and fats, together with constriction of the cardiovascular system at a time of raised cardiac output, were argued to increase the risk of morphological damage. Therefore, work, leisure, and general life environments may provide perfect nurturant conditions for prolonged stress experience, as well as for hormone states that create structural change. The paradox of prolonged exercise is that it is a stress and, at high duration levels, may be damaging.

Stress and the Corticoid Hormone Route

The production of corticoid hormones is more likely to be associated with the distress associated with severe acute or chronic stress, and is triggered by the production of adrenocorticotrophic hormone (ACTH), which is released in the brain and acts on the adrenal cortex. Selye (1956) concentrated on the corticoid response pattern in rodents exposed to chronic low-temperature stress. An early alarm phase, accompanied by increased cortisol and high discharge of fat granules on first exposure, was followed by a period of resistance in which the adrenal glands were found to be laden with hormones and fat. By the third exhaustion phase, these resources were depleted and the animals were not able to survive further stress. The important aspect of this finding is that hormone states persist, but depend on further adrenal resource, and may interact at different phase positions with incoming events.

Cortisol and Immunosuppression

There is evidence that the cortisol response directly suppresses the immune response. Amkraut and Solomon (1975) showed that ACTH injected into animals increased the risk of antigen infection. Moreover, the vulnerability of animals distressed by electric shock, constraint, or loud noise (120 dB) was well demonstrated by Rassmussen (1957), who demonstrated susceptibility to a wide range of infectious agents in prestressed animals, and who specifically reported an increased risk of herpes simplex, poliomyelitis, coxsackie B, and polyoma virus infections. The effect was attributed to increased cortisol level.

The precise mechanisms by which raised cortisol levels might have immunosuppressant consequences are currently being explored. An analysis of the consequences of acute physical stress (Nieburgs et al., 1979) showed that there may be a decrease in the number of small lymphocytes and an increased level of committed medium-sized lymphocytes in circulation. One possibility is that acute physical stress activates immature lymphocytes, and so the number of committed cells is small and insufficient to cope with the range of possible specific viruses.

However, it has also been shown that chronic stress can have immunofacilitatory properties: When food availability to animals was limited to 2 hours per day for a week, there was enhanced T-cell-dependent immune response (Solomon & Amkraut, 1979). More interestingly, exposure to chronic noise caused facilitation in T- and B-cell systems; but when the noise was acute, the effect was one of immunosuppression. One important implication is that the timing and features of the stress may be determinants of reaction (Sklar & Anisman, 1979, 1981).

The importance of the timing of stress occurrence and antigen occurrence was further confirmed. Immunological suppression to the antigen flagellin was only apparent if the stress occurred at the time of flagellin inoculation (see Monjan & Collector, 1977). The explanation that makes sense is that cortisol precipitates the commitment of the bodily defense system in advance. If this occurs prematurely without the necessary cues for specificity, the population of lymphocytes may be wasted. However, if this occurs at the appropriate time, the defenses could be efficiently committed to prevent attack. There could be survival advantages to a system that allowed stressful conditions to have access to bodily defense mechanisms in this way.

Other influences of cortisol on the immune response have been identified. They include thymus involution, as well as reduction of spleen and lymph modes; there also may be reduction of natural killer (NK) cells, which are believed to provide challenge to developing malignancies (Riley, 1979; Riley, Spackman, McClanahan, & Santisteban, 1979). The surveillance capacity of the body, once reduced, could act as an enhancer of disease risk.

AN ASSUMPTIVE MODEL OF STRESS AND DISEASE

Perhaps the unifying variables that drive the hormone levels and facilitate illness provide an important risk base. Low socioeconomic class, single marital status, and life events, which even if positive cost in terms of periods of worry and distress, may provide important links to ill health.

Figure 2.3 illustrates a possible theoretical basis for differentiation of health effects in terms of the availability of personal control: Where control is possible, the individual is assumed to engage the problem and experience effort and anxiety in the process, but in the end achieve the rewards of success. In such a situation, the source of the stress is attenuated. The cost in terms of hormone levels will be raised, with implications for current or future health. As already argued, the workplace often provides ideal conditions for enhancing the risk of ill health. A 40-hour, high-strain week that is conducive to constant high levels of stress hormones and that increase with longer hours of the working day could be argued to provide biological memories that predict the risk of disease.

Figure 2.3 also illustrates a situation where control is low and success is unlikely. In such an environment, successive struggle produces no success; the result is cortisol levels that, as argued previously, can suppress the immune sytem and the NK cells believed effective in cancer surveillance. Because effort is still involved, the risk of the strain associated with effort is added to the strain associated with distress and helplessness. Thus, there is more risk of functional abuse of bodily systems, as well as increased risk of infectious disease and neoplasms. Maintenance of biological state associated with low control may continue to protect neoplastic processes and aid the more serious development of metastases.

STRESS AND DISEASE:
THE SLOT MACHINE ANALOGY

From the previous hypothesis—namely, that ill health can be a direct result of selective patterns of stress hormones—it is possible to think of different risk

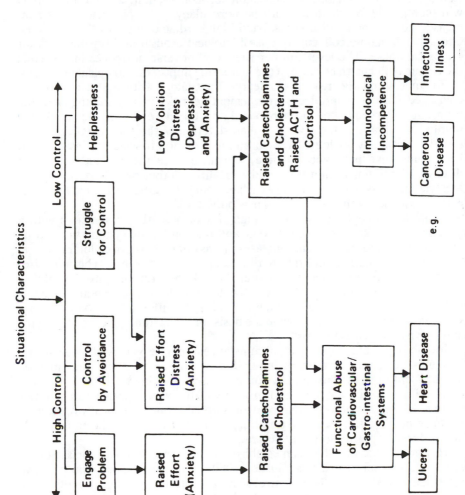

Figure 2.3 Map of possible routes—from cognitive factors in perception of control to mental disorder and physical illness.

profiles evolving as a function of both work experience and life events. A person constantly irritated at work by restricted conditions may be characterised by high noradrenaline with constant vasoconstriction, whereas the person with continuous overload at work is more likely to be characterised by increased adrenaline cardiac arousal and high cardiac output. Both noradrenaline and adrenaline collectively raise biological arousal and set the risks for biological abuse. The level and persistence of adverse hormones may predict the timing of ill health because of the increasing impact on biological processes.

To understand the risk more clearly, an analogy with a slot machine is envisaged. Just as a prefixed arrangement of risks in a gambling machine program will predict the probability of the target (e.g., four lemons), the number of occasions the lever is pulled determines the time it takes for the target to occur. By analogy, the wear and tear on bodily systems is assumed to have cumulative properties in time, which enhance the risk and timing of disease. The timing of morbidity and mortality can thus be determined by the lifestyle and personality factors (wear and tear). In terms of the analogy, this is the frequency with which the lever is pulled.

Thus, for example, cancer is at high risk of occurring if someone with a genetic risk smokes tobacco; the wear and tear on bodily systems created by tobacco, tars, and carcinogens increases the risk of turnover of cellular material and influences the risk and timing of a neoplastic occurrence. The more frequently the person smokes, the greater the risk that, during a fixed period of time, a neoplasm will occur. The selective forms of hormone response to stress linked by Frankenhauser and Johansson (1982) to different environments and selective hormone patterns provide the basis for understanding both the origins and survival of disease factors.

In summary, life events and circumstances operate via psychological and biological processes to raise or lower disease risk across time. This may be independent of stress-linked behaviours, such as smoking or drinking of alcohol, and may be best understood in terms of the way experiences are interpreted. Those who perceive that control is possible and realistically operate to enhance positive features may gain both by reduced selective hormone levels and reduced exposure to the life event.

However, it has already been established that depression is associated with realistic appraisal of evidence (Fisher, 1989). Therefore, those who perceive realistically lowered levels of control may be more likely to set in motion the hormone patterns that engender ill health because they perceive low control in a wider variety of situations. The human propensity to worry in advance and in retrospect, while having certain benefits in problem-solving situations, may nevertheless create prolonged periods of distress or demoralisation, which enhance the risk of somatisation from selective hormone balances and increase the risk of reduced surveillance due to immunoincompetence.

The Sick Computer Program

It might be useful to consider the previous issues by analogy with the programming of a computer to become ill. One would need to provide intractable life events with low control over outcome, a state of single marital status (not married to any other computer), maleness, and low socioeconomic class. Then one would like an unsettled and lonely lifestyle and prolonged experience in work environments that are perceived as unpleasant. Finally, a program with depressive realism (seeing the negative side of events) and a "worry" style of coping would rapidly achieve the base risk. All that is needed is an antigen or neoplastic event and the computer response receptively. Perhaps those who deny person problems and who cannot express emotion continue to run personal "worry programmes." To be truly ill quickly, it would be desirable that the computer has no outlets for its symbolic emotional states and is a worrier so that the programmes' hormone levels are sustained by daily preoccupations and ruminations.

REFERENCES

Amkraut, A., & Solomon, C. F. (1975). From the symbolic stimulus to the pathophysiologic response immune mechanisms. *International Journal of Psychiatry in Medicine, 5*, 541–563.

Ball, T. S., & Vogler, R. E. (1971). Uncertain pain and the pain of uncertainty. *Perceptual Motor Skills, 33*, 1195–1203.

Brady, J. V., Porter, R. W., Conrad, D. G., & Mason, J. W. (1958). Avoidance behaviour and the development of gastroduodenal ulcers. *Journal of the Experimental Analysis of Behaviour, 1*, 69–72.

Cannon, W. B. (1932). *The wisdom of the body* (2nd ed.). New York: Norton.

Cannon, W. B. (1936). *Bodily changes in pain, hunger, fear and rage*. New York: Appleton-Century-Crofts.

Carroll, D., Niven, C. A., & Sheffield, D. (1993). Gender, social circumstances and health. In C. A. Niven & D. Carroll (Eds.), *The health psychology of women*. Chur, Switzerland: Harwood.

Carruthers, M. (1974). *The western way of death*. London: Davis-Poynter.

Carstairs, V., & Morris, R. (1991). *Deprivation and health in Scotland*. Aberdeen: Aberdeen University Press.

Christenson, W. W., & Hinkle, L. E. (1961). Differences in illnesses and prognostic signs in two groups of young men. *Journal of the American Medical Association, 177*, 247–253.

Connolly, J. (1975). Circumstances, events and illness. *Medicine, 2*(10), 454–458.

Cruze-Coke, R., Etcheverry, R., & Nagel, R. (1964, March 28). Influences of migration on blood pressure of Easter Islanders. *Lancet*, pp. 697–699.

Dodge, D. L., & Martin, W. T. (1970). *Social stress and chronic illness. Mortality patterns in industrial society*. London: University of Notre Dame Press.

Faris, R. E. L., & Dunham, H. W. (1939). *Mental disorders in urban areas*. Chicago: University of Chicago Press.

Fisher, S. (1984). *Stress and the perception of control*. London: Lawrence Erlbaum Associates.

Fisher, S. (1986). *Stress and strategy*. London: Lawrence Erlbaum Associates.

Fisher, S. (1989). The vulnerability of the depressed to life events: Sadder and tougher. *Advanced Behavioral Research Therapy, 11*, 271–286.

Fisher, S. (1990). The causes and control of anxiety. *The British Journal of Hospital Medicine, 44*(3), 194–197.

Fisher, S., & Bailey, C. (1995). *Posttraumatic stress disorder in train drivers and crew*. Manuscript submitted for publication.

Fisher, S., Murray, K., & Frazer, N. (1985). Homesickness and health in first-year students. *Journal of Environmental Psychology, 5*, 181–195.

Frankenhauser, M., & Johansson, J. (1982, July). *Stress at work: Psychobiological and psychosocial aspects*. Paper presented at the 20th International Congress of Applied Psychology, Edinburgh.

Fried, M. (1962). Grieving for a lost home. In L. J. Duhl (Ed.), *The environment of the metropolis*. New York: Basic Books.

Haggard, E. A. (1943). Experimental studies in affective processes: I. Some effects of cognitive structure and active participation on certain autonomic reactions during and following experimentally induced stress. *Journal of Experimental Psychology, 33*, 257–284.

Holmes, T. H., & Rahe, R. (1967). The social readjustment rating scale. *Journal of Psychosomatic Research, 11*, 213–218.

Karasek, R. A. (1979). Job demands, job decision latitude and mental strain: Implicated for job redesign. *Administrative Science Quarterly, 24*, 43–48.

Kleiner, R. J., & Parker, S. (1963). Goal-striving and psychosomatic symptoms in a migrant and non-migrant population. In M. B. Kantor (Ed.), *Mobility and mental health*. Springfield, IL: Charles C Thomas.

Lacey, J. (1967). Somatic response patterning and stress: Some revisions of the activation theory. In M. H. Appleby & R. Turnbull (Eds.), *Psychological stress: Issues in research*. New York: Appleton-Century-Crofts.

Malmo, R. B., & Shagass, C. (1949). Physiologic study of symptom mechanisms in psychiatric patients under stress. *Psychosomatic Medicine, 11*, 25–29.

Malzberg, B., & Lee, E. S. (1940). *Migration and mental disease: A study of first admissions to hospital for mental disease*. New York: Social Science Research Council.

Marmot, M. G., Shipley, M. J., & Rose, G. (1984). Inequalities in health-specific explanations of a general pattern? *Lancet, i*, 1003–1006.

Marmot, M. G., & Syme, S. L. (1976). Acculturation and coronary heart disease in Japanese-Americans. *American Journal of Epidemiology, 104*(3), 225–247.

Medalie, J. H., & Kahn, H. A. (1973). Myocardial infarction over a five-year period: I. Prevalence, incidence and mortality experience. *Journal of Chronic Diseases, 26*, 63–84.

Monjan, A. A., & Collector, M. I. (1977). Stress-induced modulation of the immune response. *Science, 196*, 307–308.

Morrison, A. S., Kirshner, J., & Molha, A. (1977). Life cycle events in 15th century Florence: Evidence from Glasgow graveyards. *British Medical Journal, 305*, 1554–1557.

Mowrer, O. H., & Viek, P. (1948). An experimental analogue of fear from a sense of helplessness. *Journal of Abnormal and Social Psychology, 43*, 193–200.

Nieburgs, H. E., Weiss, J., Navarrete, M., Strax, P., Teirstein, A., Grillione, G., & Siedlecki, B. (1979). The role of stress in human and experimental oncogenesis. *Cancer Detection and Prevention, 2*, 307–336.

Odegaard, O. (1932). Emigration and insanity: A study of mental disease among the Norwegian born population of Minnesota. *Acta Psychiatrica et Neurologica* (Suppl. 1–4).

Parkes, C. M. (1965). Bereavement and mental illness. *British Journal of Medical Psychology, 38*, 1–26.

Rahe, R. (1972). Subjects' recent life changes and their near future illness reports. *Annals of Clinical Research, 4*, 250–265.

Rahe, R. (1988). Recent life changes and coronary heart disease: 10 years' research. In S. Fisher & J. Reason (Eds.), *The handbook of life stress cognition & health* (pp. 317–331). Chichester, England: Wiley.

Rassmussen, A. F. (1957). Emotions and immunity. *Annals of the New York Academy of Sciences, 254*, 458–461.

Riley, V. (1979). Cancer and stress: Overview and critique. *Cancer Prevention and Detection, 2*, 163–195.

Riley, V., Spackman, D., McClanahan, H., & Santisteban, G. A. (1979). The role of stress in malignancy. *Cancer Detection and Prevention, 2*, 235–255.

Rosenman, R. H. (1982). Role of Type A behavior pattern in the pathogenesis and prognosis of ischaemic heart disease. In H. Denolin (Ed.), *Psychological problems before and after myocardial infarction*. Basel: S. Karger.

Selye, H. (1956). *The stress of life*. London, New York, Toronto: Longmans Green.

Sklar, S. L., & Anisman, H. (1979). Stress and coping factors influence tumor growth. *Science, 205*, 513–515.

Sklar, S. L., & Anisman, H. (1981). Stress and cancer. *Psychological Bulletin, 89*(3), 369–406.

Solomon, G. F., & Amkraut, A. A. (1979). Neuroendocrine aspects of the immune response and their implications for stress effects on tumour immunity. *Cancer Detection and Prevention, 2*, 197–223.

Stokols, D., Schumaker, S. A., & Martinez, J. (1983). Residential mobility and personal well being. *Journal of Environmental Psychology, 3*, 5–19.

Syme, S. L. (1967). Implications and future prospects. In S. L. Syme & L. G. Reeder (Eds.), *Social stress and cardiovascular disease*. Milbank Memorial Fund Quarterly.

Totman, R. (1979). *Social causes of illness*. London: Souvenir Press.

Weiner, H. (1982). The prospects for psychosomatic medicine: Selected topics. *Psychosomatic Medicine, 44*(6), 491–517.

Wolff, H. G. (1953). *Stress and disease*. Springfield, IL: Charles C Thomas.

3

Personality, Stress, and Diabetes

Ian J. Deary
University of Edinburgh, United Kingdom

Brian M. Frier
Royal Infirmary of Edinburgh, United Kingdom

ABSTRACT

The influence of personality, stress, and coping styles on illness-related fear is examined in patients with diabetes. Associations among these variables with reference to current theories of stress and illness behaviour are described in the context of diabetes mellitus and its treatment with insulin. Hypoglycaemia, a common complication of insulin treatment, is much feared by diabetic patients. The Hypoglycaemia Fear Survey (HFS), which measures patients' worries about hypoglycaemia and the precautions they take to avoid it, has been found to be significantly correlated with neuroticism, trait anxiety, and patients' awareness of the onset of hypoglycaemia attacks. In the present study, 141 diabetic patients were assessed with the HFS, the "Big Five" dimensions of personality, and illness-related coping strategies; they were also asked about the severity of their diabetes. Neuroticism, Emotion-Oriented Coping, HFS Worry and Behaviour, and illness severity ratings were significantly intercorrelated. These intercorrelations were tested using two structural equation models: The first was based on the transactional model of stress, and the second was a negative affectivity model. Although both models had adequate fit statistics, the negative affectivity model was superior.

The discipline of health psychology is burgeoning. There is much interest in the idea that psychological factors might influence the susceptibility to or expression of illness (Adler & Matthews, 1994). The psychological effects of illness and the psychological strategies used to cope with illness are also increasingly studied (Endler, Parker, & Summerfeldt, 1992). However, the contribution that psychology can make to these endeavours is limited by the validity of the psychological constructs involved and the adequacy of the theories that attempt to explain the relationships between psychology and health–illness.

The authors thank Linda Hunter for data collection and compilation.

Among the psychological constructs with putative associations to objective health outcomes, the most prominent are personality dimensions or traits. Some of the most studied traits are Type A/B Behaviour Patterns (in fact, this has been studied from dimensional and typological perspectives), Hostility/Anger, Hardiness, Neuroticism, Locus of Control, and trait anxiety (Adler & Mtthews, 1994; Friedman & Booth-Kewley, 1987; Marshall, Wortman, Vickers, Kusulas, & Hervig, 1994; Smith & Williams, 1992). Despite the large number of studies that have examined personality variables in concert with health measures, there are few robust associations between personality and objective health outcomes. Possible exceptions to this are the associations between Hostility/Anger and atherosclerotic disease (Deary, Fowkes, Donnan, & Housley, 1994; Matthews, 1988), and between conscientiousness and longevity (Friedman, Tucker, Tomlinson-Keasey, Schwartz, Wingard, & Criqui, 1993).

However, by contrast with objective outcomes (such as mortality or verified myocardial infarction), stronger and more consistent relationships have been reported between personality variables and illness self-reports. Personality traits such as Negative Affectivity and Neuroticism are related to scores derived from physical symptom inventories and other subjective health measures (Watson & Pennebaker, 1989). Indeed, the intercorrelations among different symptom scales are frequently similar in magnitude to the correlations between these symptom scores and personality trait variables like Neuroticism. As a consequence, there is a tendency to view illness self-reports more sceptically than has been done in the past, with some researchers urging that a latent personological trait, such as Negative Affectivity or Somatopsychic Distress, might account for tendencies to have negative emotions and to report physical symptoms (Watson & Pennebaker, 1989). Thus, for some, the idea of an illness-prone personality has been recast as a distress-prone personality, reflecting that there are few objective illness criteria that correlate with personality measures (Stone & Costa, 1990). However, others have counseled that scepticism concerning health–illness self-reports has been taken too far. They argue that concepts like *negative affectivity* and *somatopsychic distress* cannot explain all of the covariance between personality and illness; ergo, there must be some true personality–illness associations (Adler & Matthews, 1994; Antonovsky, 1990). The provocative hypothesis of negative affectivity (i.e., that associations among illness reports, personality, and other related variables can be accounted for by a single latent construct—*somatopsychic distress*) is addressed in the present study.

By contrast with the theory of negative affectivity, the present study also examines the same data set using a transactional model of human stress and illness. In this view, a number of separate, albeit correlated, constructs must be considered to achieve a full description of personality–illness relationships (Cox, 1978; Lazarus, 1990). The transactional model recognises variables of at least three distinct types (viz. antecedent, mediating, and outcome; Jerusalem, 1993). Antecedent variables are typically personality and environmental variables. Mediating variables are usually mental processes, such as those related to coping with and appraising stressors. Outcome variables are commonly mental and physical health indices. The transactional model explains intercorrelations among these various concepts in a different manner to that of the negative affectivity hypothesis. In the transactional model, one might expect personality, coping, and, say, reports of illness to be correlated because they form part of a process, with each variable partly caused by its antecedent in the chain of cause and effect. The transactional model contains an implicit belief in the independent existence of concepts such as *neuroticism, emotion-oriented coping* (Endler & Parker, 1990), and *illness self-reports* (Cooper, Kirkaldy, & Brown, 1994). This contrasts with the negative affectivity model, which views these putatively distinct variables as expressions of the same latent variable.

Therefore, the present study gathered data to test these two hypotheses of personality–illness relationships competitively. Patients with diabetes mellitus were chosen as the target population. Although this is a chronic condition, most patients with diabetes feel well most of the time. As such, it provides a better subject sample than the normal population, where illness reports pertain to mild everyday symptoms, and other illness groups, where pain or discomfort are more prominent and might affect personality and other types of self-report data. Moreover, because the diabetic patient plays a major role in the everyday control of the illness (through testing glucose, injecting insulin, altering insulin doses, and regulating diet and exercise), the concept of coping with this illness is highly relevant—more so, perhaps, than in other illnesses that are more acute or in which the patient is less involved. Additionally, insulin treatment of diabetes brings with it the threat of hypoglycaemia if too much insulin is injected. Therefore, there is a stressor related to this illness that is shared by all sufferers and that might be used to examine patients' appraisals of illness-related stress.

The variables assessed in this study were those that might reasonably be considered relevant to both the negative affectivity and transactional models. Therefore, personality, illness-related coping, illness-related stress appraisals (i.e., worry), illness severity reports, and illness-related behaviours were measured. Before describing the present study in more detail, the basic facts of diabetes mellitus and hypoglycaemia are introduced, as is previous research on fear of hypoglycaemia and its personality associations.

DIABETES MELLITUS

Diabetes mellitus is a clinical syndrome characterised by hyperglycaemia and caused by an absolute or relative deficiency of insulin. It affects the metabolism of carbohydrate, fat, and protein, and can alter the metabolic balance of water and electrolytes. Acute metabolic decompensation can occur, such as diabetic ketoacidosis, which may be fatal if untreated. The long-term effect of chronic hyperglycaemia and disturbed metabolism is permanent and irreversible changes in various tissues, particularly the vascular system, leading to the development of diabetic complications that particularly affect the eye (retinopathy), the kidney (nephropathy), and the nervous system (neuropathy).

The two primary types of diabetes are insulin-dependent (Type 1) diabetes mellitus (IDDM) and noninsulin-dependent (Type 2) diabetes mellitus (NIDDM), which are separate metabolic disorders with different aetiologies. IDDM results from auto-immune destruction of the pancreatic beta cells that secrete insulin; it requires treatment with the exogenous administration of insulin, usually by subcutaneous injection. Patients with NIDDM, most of whom are overweight and have insulin resistance, are usually treated with dietary measures and oral hypoglycaemic drugs.

In humans, insulin is a major anabolic hormone that promotes glucose transport into muscle and adipose tissue, so lowering blood glucose. It also promotes storage of glucose in the liver as glycogen and inhibits the release of glucose from the liver into the circulation. Despite refinements in insulin delivery systems and formulations for the use of diabetic patients, insulin replacement therapy is still far removed from the pattern of endogenous insulin secretion. Devoid of the complex homeostatic mechanisms that normally maintain blood glucose within a narrow physiological range, blood glucose concentrations can fluctuate widely in the diabetic patient. As a consequence of a mismatch among the action of insulin, the ingestion of food, and energy expenditure, blood glucose can fall to within a subnormal range and thus provoke acute hypoglycaemia (a low blood glucose level). Although various counterregulatory mechanisms operate to restore blood glucose to normal, the transient clinical effects of aute hypoglycaemia may be profound.

HYPOGLYCAEMIA

Hypoglycaemia is very common in diabetic patients treated with insulin. Most episodes are mild, being detected at an early stage by the patient, and are self-treated. However, severe episodes of hypoglycaemia, defined by the need for external assistance for resuscitation (and not solely by the development of coma), may have serious morbidity and has a recognised mortality of 2%–4% in insulin-treated patients (Tattersall & Gale, 1993). About 30% of an insulin-treated diabetic population experiences one or more episodes of severe hypoglycaemia per annum, at a rate of 1.6 episodes per patient per year (MacLeod, Hepburn, & Frier, 1993). Recurrent severe hypoglycaemia is very disruptive to the lives of patients and their immediate families, and infringes on all aspects of activity, including employment, driving, and sport. Hypoglycaemia is the most important factor that limits the maintenance of strict glycaemic control.

The classical symptoms of hypoglycaemia can be subdivided into *autonomic* symptoms, resulting from acute activation of the autonomic nervous system (e.g., sweating, trembling, pounding heart, anxiety, and hunger), and *neuroglycopenic* symptoms, the direct effect of glucose deprivation on the brain (e.g., confusion, drowsiness, inability to concentrate, incoordination, and difficulty with speech; Deary, Hepburn, MacLeod, & Frier, 1993). The symptoms of hypoglycaemia are idiosyncratic and differ from individual to individual. They normally commence when the blood glucose falls below 2.5 mmol/l, but the glycaemic threshold for the onset of symptoms is dynamic in insulin-treated patients and varies with the quality of glycaemic control. IDDM patients with strict control do not develop symptoms until the blood glucose is much lower than normal; this may lead to hypoglycaemia unawareness, which is a problem with perception of the onset of hypoglycaemia and which renders patients more susceptible to an increased frequency of severe hypoglycaemia.

In addition to intensive insulin therapy and hypoglycaemia unawareness, other risk factors for severe hypoglycaemia include a long duration of diabetes and a previous history of severe hypoglycaemia and sleep, during which the perception of symptoms is obtunded (Frier, 1993). The causes of hypoglycaemia are numerous and may be multiple in causing a particular episode. The principal causes include excessive dose of insulin (or sulphonylurea), inadequate or delayed ingestion of food, and sudden or sustained exercise; however, a specific cause can only be determined in about one third of all episodes. Errors of judgment by the patient (or the physician) in daily management of diabetes and superimposed psychological or social problems may contribute to the induction of unexpected hypoglycaemia.

The morbidity of hypoglycaemia is often underestimated by physicians, but diabetic patients and their relatives view the trauma and disruption of severe hypoglycaemia from a different perspective. Because the brain is dependent on a continuous supply of glucose as its principal energy source, cognitive function deteriorates rapidly as a result of neuroglycopenia. In addition to coma and convulsions, neurological abnormalities such as transient ischaemic attacks and hemiplegia may occur, and myocardial ischaemia and cardiac arrhythmias have been reported. Hypoglycaemia-induced convulsions and accidents may provoke fractures, joint dislocations, and soft-tissue injuries, and hypoglycaemia can cause or contribute to driving accidents. Recurrent exposure to severe hypoglycaemia over a period of years may cause cumulative impairment of cognitive function (Deary, 1993).

The inherent desire to achieve strict glycaemic control in the diabetic patient must be counterbalanced by the threefold risk of increased severe hypoglycaemia (The Diabetes Control and Complications Trial Research Group, 1993) and the potential morbidity that this may incur. The development of intermittent severe hypoglycaemia is unlikely to be eradicated with the therapeutic regimes of insulin in current use, and the potential risks of strict glycaemic control provoking severe hypoglycaemia must be acknowledged.

FEAR, WORRY, AND STRESS IN DIABETES

Because severe hypoglycaemia may present in a dramatic and potentially dangerous manner, it is the therapeutic hazard that is most feared by patients, who rate severe hypoglycaemia with the same degree of anxiety as the development of advanced diabetic complications, such as sight-threatening diabetic retinopathy (Pramming, Thorsteinsson, Bendtson, & Binder, 1991). The prominence of the threat that hypoglycaemia constitutes in the lives of insulin-dependent diabetic patients has been recognised by researchers who devised the Hypoglycaemia Fear Survey (HFS; Cox, Irvine, Gonder-Frederick, No-wacek, & Butterfield, 1987). The HFS is a psychometric instrument composed of two subscales related to patients' concerns about hypoglycaemia (viz. Worry and Behaviour). The 17 questions in the Worry subscale ask patients how frequently they worry about hypoglycaemia-related matters (e.g., "No one being around me during a reaction," "Feeling dizzy or passing out in public," "Having seizures or convulsions," etc.). The Behaviour subscale has 10 questions and asks patients to report the frequency with which they perform actions to avoid low blood sugar levels (e.g., "Eat large snacks at bedtime," "Reduce my insulin when I think my blood sugar is too low," "Carry fast acting sugar with me," etc.). Both subscales' items are ranked on a 5-point scale with the following response options: *never, rarely, sometimes, often*, and *very often*.

In three studies, the internal consistency (Cronbach's alpha) of the HFS Worry subscale was .89, .90, and .96, and that of the HFS Behaviour subscale was .60, .69, and .84, respectively (Irvine, Cox, & Gonder-Frederick, 1994). However, the Worry subscale appears to be related to more general aspects of stress and worry. Irvine, Cox, and Gonder-Frederick (1992) reported a correlation of .31 and .22 (both $p < .05$) between anxiety scores from the Symptom Check List–90 (SCL–90) and HFS Worry and Behaviour scales, respectively. They also reported a significant association between scores on the Perceived Stress scale and the HFS Worry scale.

Polonsky, Davis, Jacobson, and Anderson (1992) undertook a more extensive investigation of the psychological and somatic associations of fear of hypoglycae-mia. In a study of 169 Type I diabetic patients, they found that HFS Worry correlated .42 ($p < .001$) with trait anxiety levels (Taylor Manifest Anxiety Scale) and .39 ($p < .001$) with trait fear levels (Fear Survey Schedule). Trait anxiety and fear correlated .38 ($p < .0005$). More anxious patients reported greater frequencies of hypoglycaemia in the previous month ($r = .18, p < .05$) and had greater difficulty discriminating hypoglycaemic symptoms from anxiety symptoms ($r = -.33, p < .0005$). In a multiple regression analysis of these data, it was found that trait anxiety, trait fear, hypoglycaemia frequency, and symptom discrimination ability all made significant contributions to the prediction of hypoglycaemia fear, as measured by the HFS Worry score.

Fear of hypoglycaemia, therefore, is a prominent, constant stressor in the lives of diabetic patients. A measure of the strain produced by this stressor may be assessed by the HFS, especially the Worry subscale. However, the degree of worry caused by fear of hypoglycaemia is related to patients' tendencies to be anxious generally, and to their prior experience of hypoglycaemia. In an extension of the findings of Polonsky et al. (1992), further exploration of the clinical and personological associations of fear of hypoglycaemia was carried out by Hepburn, Deary, MacLeod, and Frier (1994). They recruited 302 insulin-treated adult diabetics attending a hospital diabetic clinic. Information was obtained about the dimensions of Neuroticism and Extraversion (using the short version of the revised Eysenck Personality Questionnaire), HFS Worry, and HFS Behaviour. Each patient rated the number and intensity of hypoglycaemic symptoms they experienced in a typical episode of hypoglycaemia, and these data were divided into separate scores for autonomic and neuroglyco-penic symptoms. Patients were asked to indicate whether they were fully aware of the onset of hypoglycaemic attacks or whether they had reduced awareness. Finally, patients were asked to indicate the number of episodes of severe hypoglycaemia they had experienced in the previous 12 months.

A covariance matrix was constructed using the scores of the variables mentioned previously. Models of the variable interrelationships were tested using structural equation modeling. Bentler's (1989) EQS package was used, and the generalised least squares method was employed to test the fit of the model. The model with best fit to the data is shown in Fig. 3.1. All the pathways it contains make significant contributions to the successful fit of the model, and many of them confirm causal relationships hypothesised within clinical diabetes research. The model shows that reduced awareness of the onset of hypoglycaemia is associated with a greater number of hypoglycaemic episodes. Also, as expected, reduced awareness is associated with reduced experience of autonomic symptoms (the usual warning symptoms of hypoglycaemia) and increased neuroglycopenic symptoms. Reduced awareness of hypoglycaemia had a direct effect on HFS Worry: Those who reported being less aware of the onset of hypoglycaemia were, understandably, more worried about hypoglycaemia.

HFS Worry was significantly affected by Neuroticism scores: Those patients with higher Neuroticism scores worried more about hypoglycaemia, confirming the results of Polonsky et al. (1992). The study by Hepburn et al. (1994) also confirmed the Polonsky et al. finding that frequency of severe hypoglycaemia increased HFS Worry. Neuroticism was associated with increased reporting of autonomic symptoms, at a level that was greater than that for neuroglycopenic symptoms. (This specific association between neuroticism and autonomic reactivity supports Eysenck's hypothesis with respect to the biological basis of neuroticism.) The only direct associate of HFS Behaviour was HFS Worry. In other words, worrying about hypoglycaemia affected the actions taken in an effort to avoid it.

In their discussion of the possible causal mechanisms that might explain the associations among fear of hypoglycaemia and trait anxiety and fear, Polonsky et al. (1992) proposed two contrasting models. First, they suggested that trait anxiety might be a cause of fear of hypoglycaemia. Second, they suggested that some patients might operate a response bias such that they admit to a wide range of fears and anxiety, including trait fear, trait anxiety, and fear of hypoglycaemia. The first of their suggestions is a causal model. Like a section of the transactional model of stress, it posits a number of independent constructs that have causal effects on each other. Their second suggestion resembles the negative affectivity/somatopsychic distress model, in that it suggests that the covariance among the variables might arise from a single latent trait, which they dubbed *response bias*, but which might easily be called *negative affectivity*. The present study uses trait anxiety (neuroticism), HFS Worry, and other health-related variables to test the Polonsky et al. models formally, using structural equation modeling techniques.

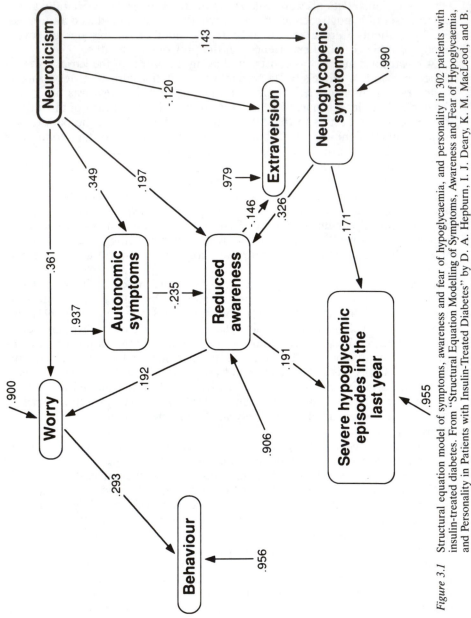

Figure 3.1 Structural equation model of symptoms, awareness and fear of hypoglycaemia, and personality in 302 patients with insulin-treated diabetes. From "Structural Equation Modelling of Symptoms, Awareness and Fear of Hypoglycaemia, and Personality in Patients with Insulin-Treated Diabetes" by D. A. Hepburn, I. J. Deary, K. M. MacLeod, and B. M. Frier, 1994, *Diabetes Care*. Copyright by American Diabetes Association. Reprinted with permission.

TRANSACTIONAL THEORY VERSUS NEGATIVE AFFECTIVITY

The present study examined insulin-treated patients attending a diabetic outpatients' clinic. It extended the investigation of the antecedents and outcomes of fear of hypoglycaemia and illness-related stress.

Subjects

One hundred and forty-one insulin-treated diabetics (61 men, 80 women) were studied. Their mean age was 35.8 years (SD = 14.4), they had a mean duration of diabetes of 13 years (10.4), and they had been on insulin therapy for 12 (10.5) years. Sixty-five were single, 68 married, 4 divorced, 3 separated, and 1 widowed. Patients' social class was assessed by occupational status and classified into five groups. In each group, from professional to unskilled, there were 13, 62, 48, 14, and 4 subjects, respectively.

Measures

Personality variables studied were the so-called "Big Five" dimensions: Neuroticism (N), Extraversion (E), Openness (O), Agreeableness (A), and Conscientiousness (C). These dimensions were measured by the NEO-Five Factor Inventory (Costa & McCrae, 1992). Measures of coping styles were included as putative mediators between personality variables and the experience of stress. From previous research, it was hypothesised that emotion-oriented coping styles would be an especially important mediator between neuroticism and illness self-reports. Coping styles were measured using the Coping with Health, Injuries, and Problems scale (CHIP; Endler, Parker, & Summerfeldt, 1992). This inventory indexes individual differences in four types of coping: Emotion-Oriented, Instrumental, Palliative, and Distraction.

Stress related to hypoglycaemia was measured by the HFS Worry and Behaviour scales. In addition, patients were asked to note the most troublesome, frequent, and recent problems associated with their diabetes. Their responses were unprompted. They were asked the following question: Overall, how severe do you rate the problems associated with your diabetes? Patients answered on a 5-point scale ranging from *not at all* to *extremely*.

Results

Hypoglycaemia was nominated by 30.5% of the patients as the most troublesome problem related to their diabetes. Others reported no particularly troublesome problems (22%), retinopathy (7.1%), weight gain (7.1%), infections (5%), mood swings (2.1%), and diet restrictions (2.1%). An additional 21 problems were reckoned to be most troublesome by either one or two subjects in the sample. Sex and marital status (single vs. married) had no

Table 3.1 Correlations between diabetes-related stress and personality and coping variables[a]

Variable	Severity of diabetic problems	HFS Worry	HFS Behaviour
HFS Worry	.20*	—	
HFS Behaviour	.13	.43**	—
Neuroticism	.33**	.27**	.03
Extraversion	−.24** (−.13)	.04	.04
Openness	−.01	.15	.21*
Agreeableness	−.13	−.05	.11
Conscientiousness	−.24** (−.15)	−.03	.08
Distraction	−.01	.16	.18
Palliative	.12	.18* (.12)	.15
Instrumental	.20*	.15	.22**
Negative Emotion	.29** (.19*)	.24** (.15)	.12

Note. Values in parentheses are partial correlation coefficients controlling for Neuroticism scores.

[a]$N = 141$.

*p < .05. **p < .01.

significant effects on rated severity of diabetic problems (two-way analysis of variance [ANOVA]). Social class (one-way ANOVA) and age (Pearson's $r = .04$, ns) did not affect self-reported ratings of diabetic problems.

The mean Worry score was 39.2 (13.3), and the mean Behaviour score was 29.5 (5.9). These are similar to levels reported in several previous studies (Irvine, Cox, & Gonder-Frederick, 1994). Sex and marital status (single vs. married) had no effect on either subscale (two-way ANOVA). Social class had no significant effect on Worry or Behaviour scales (one-way ANOVA). Age was correlated $-.28$ ($p < .01$) with HFS Behaviour and $-.17$ ($p < .05$) with HFS Worry; older people engaged in less of both with respect to hypoglycaemia. Hypoglycaemia-related Worry and Behaviour were significantly positively correlated ($r = .43, p < .01$). Patients' reports of severity of diabetic problems were significantly associated with HFS Worry ($r = .20, p < .05$), but not with HFS Behaviour.

Because demographic factors had little effect on the main outcome variables, all 141 patients were treated as a single group for the purposes of the present analyses. Table 3.1 shows the correlations between personality and coping variables and the three hypoglycaemia- and diabetes-related variables. Patients reporting more severe problems with their illness tended to have higher Neuroticism levels ($r = .33, p < .01$), and lower Extraversion ($r = -.24, p < .01$) and Conscientiousness ($r = -.24, p < .01$) scores. Such patients also tended to use more Emotion-Oriented ($r = .29, p < .01$) and Instrumental ($r = .20, p < .05$) Coping. HFS Worry scores were associated with high Neuroticism ($r = .27, p < .01$) and Negative Emotion Coping ($r = .24, p < .01$). The highest correlates of HFS Behaviour scores were Openness ($r = .21, p < .05$) and Instrumental Coping ($r = .22, p < .01$).

Table 3.2 Correlations among the NEO-Five Factor Inventory personality dimension scores[a]

Dimension	Neuroticism	Extra-version	Open-ness	Agree-ableness	Conscien-tiousness
Neuroticism	—				
Extraversion	− .39**	—			
Openness	.03	.16	—		
Agreeableness	− .04	.03	.12	—	
Conscientiousness	− .33**	.18*	− .04	.13	—

[a]N = 141.
*p < .05. **p < .01.

It was noted earlier that patients' reports of severity of diabetic problems were significantly correlated with Neuroticism, Extraversion, and Conscientiousness. However, scores on these three personality dimensions were significantly intercorrelated, as shown in Table 3.2. In particular, the correlations among Neuroticism, Extraversion, and Conscientiousness are greater than .3 and highly significant. Therefore, the correlations among Extraversion, Conscientiousness, and severity of diabetic problems were recomputed, controlling for Neuroticism. The resulting partial correlations are nonsignificant, as shown in parentheses in Table 3.1.

Table 3.3 shows the correlations between personality and coping variables. The strongest association was between Neuroticism and Negative Emotion Coping ($r = .38, p < .01$). Neuroticism was significantly associated with Palliative Coping ($r = .26, p < .01$). Extraversion correlated significantly with Distraction ($r = .29, p < .01$) and Instrumental Coping ($r = .25, p < .01$). Agreeableness and Conscientiousness had significant, but low, correlations ($p < .2$) with Instrumental Coping.

There were significant correlations among Neuroticism, Negative Emotion Coping, and severity of diabetic problems. Therefore, the association between Negative Emotion Coping and severity of diabetic problems was recomputed, controlling for Neuroticism. The partial correlation of .19 ($p < .05$; Table 3.1, in parentheses) was significant, indicating that the effect of coping style on rated illness stress was not due entirely to Neuroticism variance. However, the

Table 3.3 Correlations between personality and coping variables[a]

Variable	Distraction	Palliative	Instrumental	Negative Emotion
Neuroticism	.00	.26**	− .06	.38**
Extraversion	.29**	− .16	.25**	− .13
Openness	.08	.04	.12	− .11
Agreeableness	.14	.16	.19*	− .14
Conscientiousness	.09	.08	.17*	− .11

[a]N = 141.
*p < .05. **p < .01.

significant correlations between Palliative and Negative Emotion Coping and HFS Worry scores did fall to nonsignificant levels when Neuroticism levels were controlled (Table 3.1, in parentheses).

In summary, Neuroticism differences are significantly related to patients' reports of illness severity, worries about hypoglycaemia, and Negative Emotion and Palliative Coping styles. Openness and Instrumental Coping were associated with hypoglycaemia prevention-related behaviours. Extraversion was significantly correlated with an Instrumental Coping style.

Structural Equation Modeling

To understand these multivariate associations more clearly, structural equation models were constructed and tested. Competing models related to: (a) the transactional model of stress, and (b) the negative affectivity hypothesis were compared. The variables used in these analyses were NEO-FFI Neuroticism, CHIP Negative Emotion, HFS Worry and Behaviour, and patients' ratings of severity of diabetic problems.

The transactional model assumed that neuroticism influenced negative emotion coping and worry. In turn, it was assumed that negative emotion coping and worry about hypoglycaemia influenced severity ratings. It was assumed that worry about hypoglycaemia influenced behaviours aimed at avoiding hypoglycaemia. The negative affectivity model made the simpler assumption that all reports were surrogates for a latent variable of negative affectivity, with the exception that HFS Behaviour was influenced only by HFS Worry.

Models were tested by the EQS structural equations program (Bentler, 1989), using the method of maximum likelihood. The transactional model specified previously had poor fit statistics and was modified to achieve satisfactory fit statistics. Figure 3.2a shows the best-fitting transactional model. The chi-square for the model is 7.0 (5, $p = .22$), the average of the off-diagonal absolute standardised residuals is .05, the Bentler-Bonett Normed Fit Index is .921, the Bentler-Bonett Non-Normed Fit Index is .948, and the Comparative Fit Index is .974. All of the parameters in the model had significant Z-test scores, and the addition of further paths would not have improved the fit of the model. Therefore, the transactional model has comprehensively acceptable fit statistics.

Figure 3.2b shows the negative affectivity model, as specified earlier. Latent variable F1 is hypothesised to underlie the variance shared by self-reported neuroticism, negative emotion coping, severity of diabetic problems, and HFS Worry. The chi-square for the model is 2.5 (5, $p = .76$), the average of the off-diagonal absolute standardised residuals is .02, the Bentler-Bonett Normed Fit Index is .972, the Bentler-Bonett Non-Normed Fit Index is 1.063, and the Comparative Fit Index is 1.000. All of the parameters in the model had significant Z-test scores, and the addition of further paths would not have improved the fit of the model. Therefore, the transactional model has comprehensively acceptable fit statistics, all of which are superior to the transactional model.

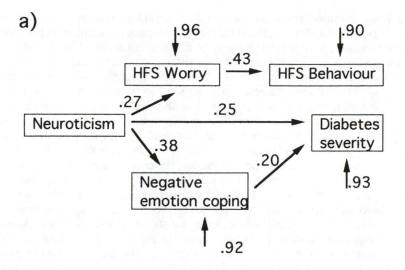

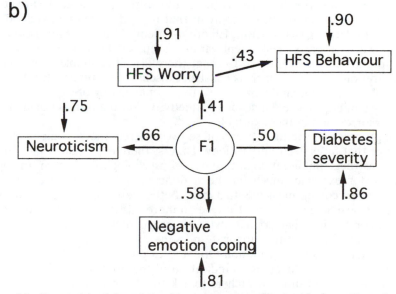

Figure 3.2 Two models of the relationships among personality, coping, fear of hypoglycaemia, reports of illness severity, and actions taken to avoid hypoglycaemia: (a) transactional model, and (b) negative affectivity model.

DISCUSSION

The present study examined personality, coping, stress appraisal, illness severity reports, and illness-related behaviours in diabetes mellitus. This illness provides a suitable setting for the study of these phenomena: The illness is life long, the patients are heavily involved in their own treatment, and there are major illness- and treatment-related effects that constitute recognised stressors. Thus, patients with diabetes may be said to be constantly coping with their illness and its dangers without, most of the time, actually feeling unwell.

The main target variables—Neuroticism, Emotion-Oriented Coping, illness severity reports, hypoglycaemia-related fear, and hypoglycaemia-related behaviours—were substantially intercorrelated. Two theories of such intercorrelation were tested in parallel. The first theory, the transactional model of stress, supposes a flow of causation from antecedent through mediating to outcome variables. The second theory, that of negative affectivity, hypothesises that most of the covariance among the variables has its source in a general tendency toward distress—be it emotional, somatic, or social. These were tested using structural equation modeling. Models constructed from both theories, each with five degrees of freedom, had acceptable fit statistics. The negative affectivity model had better fit statistics, although it is not possible to say that these are significantly better.

However, in addition to generally better fit statistics, the negative affectivity model has the advantage of economy in that it posits only one psychological construct underlying Neuroticism, Emotion-Oriented Coping, HFS Worry, and illness severity reports. This latent variable's highest loadings were for Neuroticism and Emotion-Oriented Coping; therefore, it resembles the negative affectivity/somatopsychic distress construct discussed by others. By the criterion of William of Occam's razor (i.e., that of parsimony of explanatory constructs) we might choose the negative affectivity over the transactional view of the intercorrelation of these variables.

The process of deciding between these two different models emphasises the challenge that faces health psychology. That is, there is a need to validate the many constructs that are used in this area of psychological research. In coping research, for example, much has been done to obtain general coping and illness-related coping measures that have better psychometric characteristics than those available previously. However, a more difficult job will be the definitive demonstration that coping styles (because they are long lasting and, therefore, traitlike) are not surrogate personality measures. The correlation between Neuroticism and Emotion-Oriented Coping is particularly high. This should not simply be taken as an indication of the predictive validity of Neuroticism. It should cause researchers to ask the more difficult question: Are the two constructs distinct in any useful way, or is Emotion-Oriented Coping a mere surrogate Neuroticism measure?

Apart from the theoretical interest of the present study, the results have practical implications as well. As was shown previously, illness self-reports are influenced by personality factors. Therefore, because health professionals seeing patients in the diabetic clinic often use self-report data as the bases for clinical decision making, the present results emphasise the influence that personological factors have on these reports. One positive result is that worry about hypoglycaemia appears to lead to action to avert further episodes of hypoglycaemia. However, that self-reports of such behaviours correlate with fewer episodes of objectively recorded hypoglycaemia has yet to be demonstrated.

REFERENCES

Adler, N., & Matthews, K. (1994). Health psychology: Why do some people get sick and some stay well? *Annual Review of Psychology, 45*, 229–259.

Antonovsky, A. (1990). Personality and health: Testing the sense of coherence model. In H.S. Friedman (Ed.), *Personality and disease* (pp. 155–177). New York: Wiley.

Bentler, P. (1989). *EQS: Structural Equations Program Manual.* Los Angeles, CA: BMDP Statistical Software, Inc.

Cooper, C. L., Kirkaldy, B. D., & Brown, J. (1994). A model of job stress and physical health: The role of individual differences. *Personality and Individual Differences, 16*, 653–655.

Costa, P. T., & McCrae, R. R. (1992). *Revised NEO Personality Inventory and NEO Five Factor Inventory. Professional manual.* Odessa, FL: Psychological Assessment Resources, Inc.

Cox, D., Irvine, A., Gonder-Frederick, L., Nowacek, G., & Butterfield, J. (1987). Fear of hypoglycaemia: Quantification, validation, and utilization. *Diabetes Care, 10*, 617–621.

Cox, T. (1978). *Stress.* London: Macmillan.

Deary, I. J. (1993). Neuropsychological manifestations. In B. M. Frier & B. M. Fisher (Eds.), *Hypoglycaemia and diabetes: Clinical and physiological aspects* (pp. 337–346). London: Edward Arnold.

Deary, I. J., Fowkes, F. G. R., Donnan, P. T., & Housley, E. (1994). Hostile personality and risks of peripheral arterial disease in the general population. *Psychosomatic Medicine, 56*, 197–202.

Deary, I. J., Hepburn, D. A., MacLeod, K. M., & Frier, B. M. (1993). Partitioning the symptoms of hypoglycaemia using multi-sample confirmatory factor analysis. *Diabetologia, 36*, 771–777.

Endler, N. S., & Parker, J. D. A. (1990). Multidimensional assessment of coping: A critical evaluation. *Journal of Personality and Social Psychology, 58*, 844–854.

Endler, N. S., Parker, J. D. A., & Summerfeldt, L. J. (1992). *Coping with health problems: Developing a reliable and valid multidimensional measure* (Tech. Rep. No. 204). York University, Canada, Department of Psychology Research.

Friedman, H. S., & Booth-Kewley, S. (1987). Personality, Type A behavior, and coronary heart disease: The role of emotional expression. *Journal of Personality and Social Psychology, 53*, 783–792.

Friedman, H. S., Tucker, J. S., Tomlinson-Keasey, C., Schwartz, J. E., Wingard, D. L., & Criqui, M. H. (1993). Does childhood personality predict longevity? *Journal of Personality and Social Psychology, 65*, 176–185.

Frier, B. M. (1993). Hypoglycaemia in the diabetic adult. In J. W. Gregory & A. Aynsley-Green (Eds.), *Hypoglycaemia. Ballières clinical endocrinology and metabolism, 7*, 757–777.

Hepburn, D. A., Deary, I. J., MacLeod, K. M., & Frier, B. M. (1994). Structural equation modelling of symptoms, awareness and fear of hypoglycaemia, and personality in patients with insulin-treated diabetes. *Diabetes Care, 17*, 1273–1280.

Irvine, A., Cox, D., & Gonder-Frederick, L. (1992). Fear of hypoglycaemia: Relationship to physical and psychological symptoms in patients with insulin-dependent diabetes mellitus. *Health Psychology, 11*, 135–138.

Irvine, A., Cox, D., & Gonder-Frederick, L. (1994). Development of a scale measuring fear of hypoglycaemia in individuals with diabetes mellitus. In C. Bradley (Ed.), *Handbook of psychology and diabetes* (pp. 133–155). Chur, Switzerland: Harwood.

Jerusalem, M. (1993). Personal resources, environmental constraints, and adaptational processes: The predictive power of a theoretical stress model. *Personality and Individual Differences, 14*, 15–24.

Lazarus, R. S. (1990). Stress, coping and illness. In H. S. Friedman (Ed.), *Personality and disease* (pp. 97–120). New York: Wiley.

MacLeod, K. M., Hepburn, D. A., & Frier, B. M. (1993). Frequency and morbidity of severe hypoglycaemia in insulin-treated diabetic patients. *Diabetic Medicine, 10*, 238–245.

Marshall, G. N., Wortman, C. B., Vickers, R. R., Kusulas, J. W., & Hervig, L. K. (1994). The five-factor model of personality as a framework for personality-health research. *Journal of Personality and Social Psychology, 67*, 278–286.

Matthews, K. A. (1988). Coronary heart disease and Type A behaviors: Update on and alternative to the Booth-Kewley and Friedman (1987) quantitative review. *Psychological Bulletin, 104*, 373–380.

Polonsky, W. H., Davis, C. L., Jacobson, A. M., & Anderson, B. J. (1992). Correlates of hypoglycaemic fear in Type I and Type II diabetes mellitus. *Health Psychology, 11*, 199–202.

Pramming, S., Thorsteinsson, B., Bendtson, I., & Binder, C. (1991). Symptomatic hypoglycaemia in 411 type 1 diabetic patients. *Diabetic Medicine, 8*, 217–222.

Smith, T. W., & Williams, P. G. (1992). Personality and health: Advantages and limitations of the five factor model. *Journal of Personality, 60*, 395–423.

Stone, S. V., & Costa, P. T. (1990). Disease-prone personality or distress-prone personality? The role of neuroticism in coronary heart disease. In H. S. Friedman (Ed.), *Personality and disease* (pp. 178–200). New York: Wiley.

Tattersall, R. B., & Gale, E. A. M. (1993). Mortality. In B. M. Frier & B. M. Fisher (Eds.), *Hypoglycaemia and diabetes: Clinical and physiological aspects* (pp. 190–198). London: Edward Arnold.

The Diabetes Control and Complications Trial Research Group. (1993). The effect of intensive treatment of diabetes on the development and progression of long-term complications in insulin-dependent diabetes mellitus. *New England Journal of Medicine, 279,* 977–986.

Watson, D., & Pennebaker, J. W. (1989). Health complaints, stress and distress: Exploring the central role of negative affectivity. *Psychological Review, 96,* 234–254.

II

STRESS AND ANGER IN WOMEN AND THE FAMILY

4

Women's Anger: Causes, Manifestations, and Correlates

Sandra P. Thomas
University of Tennessee, Knoxville, USA

ABSTRACT

Societal prohibitions, causes of anger arousal in everyday life, and selected correlates of women's anger are examined, drawing primarily from the data of the Women's Anger Study (Thomas, 1993). Subjects were 535 women, ages 25–66, recruited from worksites and community groups. Most were married and working outside the home. The test battery included: Spielberger's Trait Anger Scale, The Framingham Scales, the Cognitive-Somatic Anger Scale, the Perceived Stress Scale, Rosenberg's Self-Esteem Scale, the Beck Depression Inventory, the Current Health Scale from Ware's Health Perceptions Questionnaire, Norbeck's Social Support Questionnaire, and a questionnaire assessing health indicators and demographics. Open-ended questions were asked about situations that triggered anger, how and to whom it was (or was not) expressed, and how long it lasted. Three pervasive themes (powerlessness, injustice, irresponsibility) were found in the qualitative analyses of anger precipitants. Women's anger was very relational, generated within their closest relationships. Demographic comparisons revealed age, education, and occupational differences in anger proneness and expression styles. Perceived stress was strongly related to trait anger, cognitive anger, and somatic anger symptoms; vicarious stress was the predominant type of stressor (i.e., arising from events in the lives of others, rather than personal events).

These are the voices of women, excerpts from tape-recorded interviews. Their discomfort with the emotion of anger is evident.

I believe that I have been socialized to not acknowledge anger as a valid human emotion. The result of this socialization is that I have not always known when I am angry nor do I have many effective ways of expressing anger. I often feel powerless when I am angry. I feel hopeless. I feel foolish. I feel afraid. Feeling angry can scare me.

I would like to acknowledge the following members of the research team: Kaye Bultemeier, Gayle Denham, Madge Donnellan, Patricia Droppleman, June Martin, Mary Anne Modrcin-McCarthy, Sheryl Russell, Pegge Saylor, Elizabeth Seabrook, Barbara Shirk, Carol Smucker, Jane Tollett, and Dorothy Wilt.

It takes me a long time to get angry—too long, because by the time I decide I'm mad, the incident is past and the offender is out of reach. Then I feel like a fool and I just get mad at myself.

I guess I'm afraid that if I express anger I will be rejected because I'm expressing myself and my needs and I feel like if I do express needs at all . . . I'll be rejected.

I don't talk to my husband when I'm mad at him. I just do what my mother did. I ice up. He never even knows I'm mad, even if it's something important.

Anger is such a tricky emotion for me . . . . Anger has often been disguised as something else. In my life it is often mistaken for fear, weakness, embarrassment, shame, regret, guilt, and/or remorse and many other uncomfortable feelings.

This chapter explores societal prohibitions of women's anger, causes of anger arousal in the natural settings where women enact their social roles, and selected correlates of anger. Data from the Women's Anger Study (Thomas, 1993) are summarized.

THE TABOO ON WOMEN'S ANGER

Why is women's anger often aborted, suppressed, or turned against the self? Women's anger is contrary to the ethos of "women's world" (Bernard, 1981), with its prescription that women care for others. The most pervasive function of women, according to Bernard, is "stroking," which means helping, agreeing, complying, understanding, and passively accepting. Expressing anger is inconsistent with agreeing, complying, and passively accepting. Women's anger does not conform to the feminine ideal of the selfless, ever-nurturing "perfect mother" (Bernardez, 1987), and it creates fear of rejection or disruption in relationships that women consider vital to their well-being. Powerful societal forces converge to prohibit its direct and forthright expression. Lerner (1985) went so far as to say that women's anger is taboo in American culture.

Although some theories emphasize biology, genetics, primitive drives, and other determinants of emotional behavior (Thomas, 1990), social-cognitive formulations are more useful for explaining these constraints. As Averill (1982) persuasively argued, emotions are socially constituted syndromes that cannot be understood without consideration of the social context. In a society where women have lower status, power, and sense of self-worth than men, they must depend on men and others who are more powerful for approval. Consequently, women are highly sensitive to nonverbal cues, and hide their own negative emotional reactions to avoid antagonizing those in positions of dominance over them (Bernardez, 1987; Miller, 1976, 1983). In the words of Fiske (1993), "The powerless attend to the powerful who control their outcomes" (p. 621).

Angry women clearly threaten the status quo. Miller (1983) stated, "Obviously any subordinate is in a position which constantly generates anger. Yet this is one of the emotions that no dominant group ever wants to allow in subordinates" (p. 2). All of the labels for women's anger in the English language are pejorative—*bitch, virago, shrew, harpy, nag, scold, castrator*, and so forth (Lerner, 1985). Female anger is labeled *unfeminine* and *unattractive*. In one recent experiment (MacGregor & Davidson, 1994), videotapes of male and female actors portraying verbal and physical hostility were shown to subjects. Subjects rated females as *more hostile* even though the behavior of the male actors was identical, indicating that viewers' perceptions are actually distorted when women violate gender role expectations.

How Does It All Begin?
Gender Differences in Socialization of Children

From infancy on, boys' anger is treated differently than girls'. Parents apply different contingencies to the behaviors of sons and daughters, showing more acceptance of anger expression by sons than by daughters (Birnbaum & Croll, 1984). Mothers emphasize anger more frequently when generating stories for their preschool sons than for their daughters (Greif, Alvarez, & Ulman, 1981). Boys are actually stimulated to aggressive action by their fathers from ages as young as 1½–2 years (Miller, 1983), although the expression of emotions such as fear and sadness is discouraged. In contrast, girls are permitted to be more emotional, as long as they are nonaggressive (Block, 1973). Television and other powerful socialization agents reinforce parental childrearing practices, with male characters showing significantly more anger than female characters (Birnhaum & Croll, 1984). Children begin to understand that there are specific display rules that regulate emotional expression in their culture (Saarni, 1979). By preschool age, happiness, sadness, fear, and general emotionality are more evident in girls, whereas anger and aggression are more characteristic of boys (Brody, 1985).

Experiences on the playground continue the shaping of children's emotion behaviors. During their school years, boys learn through competitive, aggressive, rough-and-tumble games that life is a contest in which males have to stay one-up. Meanwhile, girls, through cooperative activities with good friends, learn that community is important (Tannen, 1990). Boys' games involve frequent quarrels, which do not terminate their play, whereas girls' games are terminated when quarrels occur (Lever, 1976).

During adolescence, traditional sex-typed expectations of girls by their parents, teachers, and peers become even more pronounced. A phenomenon called *invalidation* can be a powerful mechanism in discouraging girls' anger expression. Their anger is trivialized, ignored, or labeled as inappropriate. Consequently, they feel misunderstood; their emotion has been denied. A group of female Australian theorists recently provided compelling examples of such invalidation (Crawford, Kippax, Onyx, Gault, & Benton, 1990).

Harvard researchers Brown and Gilligan (1992) attributed teenage girls' loss of ability to express anger to enormous pressure to be "perfect girls" who were always quiet, calm, and kind. During their 5-year study of the transition from girlhood to adolescence, 100 girls were interviewed annually. At younger ages, like 7 and 8, the girls spoke openly about their anger and other feelings; their voices were clear and honest. However, in adolescence, the girls (with

few exceptions) stopped expressing their real feelings, especially anger, because they wanted to be popular. According to Gilligan, "The coming of age
of girls in this society is accompanied by a falling away of self" (cited in Moses,
1990, p. 26).

Gender Differences in Anger of Adults:
An Abbreviated Review of Literature

Emotional development continues throughout life, and obviously some
women transcend the restrictions of their gender role socialization. However,
little is known about when, how, or why some women achieve a diverse repertoire of emotion behaviors, enabling them to be clear and direct with their
anger when it is appropriate to do so. As a matter of fact, very little is known
about the anger of adult women due to the paucity of studies. After two early
investigations (Anastasi, Cohen, & Spatz, 1948; Gates, 1926) involving small
samples of female college students, there was a long hiatus in the literature.
An upsurge of interest in anger and other emotions in the 1970s was fueled by
the discovery of a link between the anger-prone Type A personality and coronary heart disease (CHD). Subsequent behavioral medicine research activity
was vigorous, focusing almost exclusively on men. Male samples were used in
the Western Collaborative Group Study, the Multiple Risk Factor Intervention
Trial, the French-Belgian Cooperative Heart Study, the Honolulu Heart Program, and many other well-known studies (Fischman, 1987).

When studies of anger variables included women as well as men, quite often
the researchers' hypotheses were not supported for the female participants.
The discrepant findings were dutifully noted, but rarely discussed in the articles. Here is an example of this tendency. In a recent book, Smith and Christensen (1992) reviewed several studies that examined hostility (assessed by the
Cook–Medley Hostility [Ho] scale) in both men and women. The following
statements were made (italics added):

- "Interestingly, Ho scores were only *weakly* related to overt behaviors and
  reported affect among wives" (p. 37).
- "Ho scores of the wives were *unrelated* to blood pressure reactivity in either
  condition" (p. 39).
- "Hostile persons also report interpersonal conflict at work, in their families
  of origin, and in their marriages, *although the latter effect has been found for
  men but not women*" (p. 40).

In their summary, there was no further mention of gender differences, nor any
suggestion for further study of women. Smith and Christensen should not be
singled out for criticism; their work is just one example of a phenomenon that
is all too prevalent in the literature.

In addition to the behavioral medicine studies, literature search reveals two
other sources of information about women's anger: (a) clinical articles written
by psychotherapists about their patients, and (b) reports of laboratory experiments conducted by college professors on their undergraduate students. There

are limitations to both of these approaches to knowledge development about women's anger. With regard to the former, many women in therapy have suffered devastating traumas, such as rape, incest, battering, abandonment, or other life-shattering events. As a consequence, they have deep-seated anger and rage. Although the clinical literature pertaining to these serious problems is of great value, it does not deal with the anger of ordinary women in their typical daily experiences. With regard to the latter, such experiments involve contrived conditions of provocation, insult, or challenge that lack relevance to the realities of women's lives. Eagly and Steffen (1986) pointed out that laboratory studies of short-term encounters with strangers have little ecological validity.

Averill's (1982) study more than a decade ago is one of the few investigations conducted on nonstudent community samples of men and women. He found that women got angry as often as men, as intensely as men, for much the same reasons as men, and that women expressed anger as openly as did the men. Subsequent studies supported Averill's finding that females and males did not differ in general propensity to experience anger (Stoney & Engebretson, 1994), but there is conflicting evidence about their ways of expressing it.

In early research on anger expression, a unidimensional conceptualization dominated; anger expression was depicted on a continuum, with low scores indicating anger-in and high scores indicting anger-out. This depiction is evident in articles by Funkenstein, King, and Drolette (1954); Harburg, Erfurt, Hauenstein, Chape, Schull and Schork (1973); and Gentry, Chesney, Gary, Hall, and Harburg (1982). However, subsequent research by Spielberger, Johnson, Russell, Crane, Jacobs, and Worden (1985) demonstrated that anger-in and anger-out are independent. Other studies have supported the independence of these dimensions; correlations between anger-in and anger-out were essentially zero for both males and females in studies of mid-life subjects (Thomas, 1989) and college students (Thomas & Williams, 1991). Some researchers have found women more likely than men to suppress their anger (Haynes & Feinleib, 1980), whereas others found no gender difference (Greenglass & Julkunen, 1989) or found men scoring higher on anger-in (Spielberger et al., 1985). In addition to anger-in and anger-out, researchers have begun to investigate anger-control (being calm and patient while angry; Spielberger, Krasner, & Solomon, 1988), anger-discussion (getting anger off one's chest by talking about the incident with a supportive listener; Haynes, Levine, Scotch, Feinleib, & Kannel 1978), and anger-symptoms (expression of anger via somatic symptoms such as headache; Haynes et al., 1978).

One rather consistent finding is females' greater propensity to discuss their anger. Less is known about this mode of expression because of its omission from most questionnaires, but it appears to be a healthy choice that deserves greater attention. In research on boys and girls in the 4th, 8th, and 12th grades, Brondolo (1992) found that girls of all ages were more willing than boys to confide their angry feelings in another person. This remains true in later life. In my own studies of adults ages 18–60 (Thomas, 1989; Thomas & Williams, 1991), as well as studies by other researchers (Riley & Treiber, 1989; Weidner, Istvan, & McKnight, 1989), women scored higher on anger-discussion than men. In Averill's (1982) community sample, women more often than men (62% and 40%, respectively) reported that they wanted to talk about the anger incident with the instigator and/or a neutral third party. Along the same lines, Harburg, Blakelock, and Roeper (1979) described a reflective anger coping style that was more characteristic of the women in their sample than of the men. Women said they used this style to handle an angry boss; after he cooled down, they would talk to him about the unfair attack.

Research also consistently shows that men are more likely than women to behave aggressively (Barefoot et al., 1991; Deffenbacher, 1994; Eagly & Steffen, 1986). Campbell (1993), who has studied aggression for 20 years, contended that aggression feels good to men because it confers the reward of control and power over others. In contrast, aggression does not feel good to women because it means failure of self-control and guilt about the distress of the person who got the brunt of their attack. Furthermore, women are concerned about placing themselves in danger; their aggression may result in retaliation (e.g., sexual or physical assault; Eagly & Steffen, 1986).

In summary, available evidence suggests that men and women do not differ in general propensity to be aroused to anger, but they do differ in ways of expressing it, with males having a more aggressive response when aroused. Males and females also differ in hostility (a more enduring attitude of antagonism and distrust), with males scoring higher in most studies (Barefoot et al., 1991; Scherwitz, Perkins, Chesney, & Hughes, 1991). There is still confusion and overlap in the literature among conceptualizations of *anger, hostility*, and *aggression*, and several investigators are seeking to clarify the distinctions among these concepts. Spielberger pointed out that angry behavior has both consistency over time (a traitlike element) and situational variability in intensity of arousal (state anger; Spielberger, Jacobs, Russell, & Crane, 1983). Suarez and Williams (1990) delineated distinctions between neurotic and expressed hostility. Some components are more pathological (i.e., more strongly associated with disease end points) than others, and thus receive greater attention from behavioral medicine researchers; this burgeoning literature is not reviewed here.

Our own program of research seeks to describe and understand women's anger; we delimit its boundaries, excluding hostility, aggression, and violence. Drawing from the literature, clinical experience, and the results of our research, we define *anger* as a strong, uncomfortable emotional response to a specific provocation that is unwanted and incongruent with one's values, beliefs, or rights. It pertains to events of greater significance than minor irritation or annoyance. It is less enduring and mean-spirited than hostility, and it is less destructive than aggression. An overview of the research conducted follows.

THE WOMEN'S ANGER STUDY

The Women's Anger Study (Thomas, 1993) is the first large-scale, comprehensive, empirical investigation of women's anger. The focus is on the anger women feel in their everyday home and work situations. In view of the paucity of extant research, the aim here is to describe what occurs in natural settings where women enact their social roles. Guided by a conceptual model derived from existential and cognitive-behavioral theories of emotion (Thomas, 1991), women's anger is examined in relation to their stress, self-esteem, social support, role responsibilities, and a variety of physical and mental health indicators. Findings of the study are reported elsewhere (Thomas, 1993); only highlights are presented here.

The Women's Anger Study was conducted by an all-female team of faculty and graduate students at the University of Tennessee, Knoxville, assisted by collaborators at several other universities. The project was framed within the research strategy that Coward (1990) described as *critical multiplism* (i.e., use of multiple stakeholders to develop the research questions, probes of many different types of issues within a single investigation, and multiple modes of data collection and analysis). Although the strategy has commonalities with triangulation, Coward contended that critical multiplism is more than triangulation. Benefits of the strategy include blending of quantitative and qualitative research methods, as well as ongoing dialogue among multiple data analysts with different perspectives.

A combination of network and purposive sampling was used to obtain subjects from a variety of community sources, such as worksites, educational settings, women's groups, and social clubs. Despite the main objective of describing anger experiences of "normal" or "average" women, it became apparent that comparisons with clinical groups would be useful. Therefore, permission was obtained from several health care providers in private practice to approach their clients regarding study participation, and access to women hospitalized in two inpatient psychiatric facilities was granted.

The resultant sample of 535 women was quite diverse, ranging in age from 25 to 66, years of education from 7 to 24, and number of children from 0 to 7. Most of the participants were married (69%) and working outside the home (full time 74%, part time 12.5%). Eighty-five percent of the sample was White and 13% was African American. Many occupations were represented, including professional and entrepreneurial ventures, but the preponderance of the women were in traditional female areas, such as teaching, nursing, and clerical work. Homemakers (10% of the sample) were perhaps slightly underrepresented, but the full-time homemaker is truly a vanishing breed.

Anger is a multidimensional construct, and the test battery contained tools for assessing cognitive, behavioral, and somatic dimensions. Spielberger's Trait Anger Scale was used to assess the general tendency to become aroused to anger (Spielberger, Jacobs, Russell, & Crane, 1983), the Framingham Scales measured four modes of expressive behavior (anger-in, anger-out, anger-discussion, anger-symptoms; Haynes, Levine, Scotch, Feinleib, & Kannel, 1978), and the Cognitive-Somatic Anger Scale (Contrada, Hill, Krantz, Durel, & Wright, 1986) assessed: (a) faulty cognitions such as obsessing, ruminating, and making incorrect attributions; and (b) physical manifestations, such as knots in stomach, heart pounding, and fists clenching. Other instruments were the Perceived Stress Scale (Cohen, Kamarck, & Mermelstein, 1983), the Rosenberg Self-Esteem Scale (Rosenberg, 1965), the Beck Depression Inventory

(Beck, Ward, Mendelson, Mock, & Erbaugh, 1961), the Current Health Scale from Ware's (1976) Health Perceptions Questionnaire, Norbeck's Social Support Questionnaire (Norbeck, Lindsey, & Carrieri, 1981), and a researcher-developed questionnaire assessing various health indicators and demographics. Information about these tools and their reliability and validity are reported elsewhere (Thomas, 1993). In addition to the structured tools, open-ended questions were asked about typical day-to-day experiences of anger (what situations or circumstances triggered it, how and to whom it was [or was not] expressed, and how long it lasted).

SELECTED FINDINGS

Precipitants of Women's Anger

In response to open-ended questions, women recalled situations, persons, places, and things that precipitated their everyday episodes of anger. Qualitative analysis, using the approach of Miles and Huberman (1984), was facilitated by use of the computer software program "Hyperqual" (see Denham & Bultemeier, 1993, for additional details). An umbrella theme of personal ideology emerged as the overriding pattern. Women held ideologies about roles and behavior involving themselves, their family and work interactions, and society in general. Anger was triggered when events were not congruent with their ideologies. More specifically, ideologies concerning power, justice, and responsibility were often incongruent with the events women encountered in their day-to-day experiences.

The most pervasive theme was the role of power, or lack thereof, in women's anger arousal; two thirds of the anger-producing situations involved women's powerlessness. Women were angry at (a) themselves when they were unable to do all that they expected of themselves, or lacked the necessary resources or power to change frustrating situations; (b) intimates (spouses, children, friends, and co-workers) whose behavior was not congruent with their ideation; and (c) unspecified people: "People using me," "When someone won't listen to me because I'm a woman," "When I'm minding my own business and some man says something harassing or threatening," or "When a person I talk with is always right and I'm wrong, or when I try to tell something that has happened that is really important to me and no one listens." Not being listened to is perhaps the epitome of powerlessness; the woman's views, preferences, and ideas are ignored as if she were invisible.

The theme of injustice included accounts of unfair or disrespectful treatment and betrayal of trust (e.g., lying by a loved one). Women's belief that family, friends, and colleagues should treat them with respect and dignity was violated. Typical responses were: "When boyfriend doesn't show up or call," "When my husband spends a lot of money without telling me," "When my children act hateful," "When my son tells lies," and "When my husband tells me 'There you go again' or compares me to my mother!" In this category, there were numerous examples of disrespect and disregard among co-workers: "Being unjustly accused of mistakes on the job," "Being put down or yelled at in front of a bunch of people," "Being blamed for something I didn't do," or "When someone talks down to me as if I were stupid." Some women wrote about the injustice of sexist behaviors or violence toward women. Anger was also produced when injustices occurred to others in the women's circle of intimates, especially their children: "When a child takes advantage of my child or hurts her in some way," "When my ex-husband mistreats my children," "Some teachers had misinterpreted my daughter and it really hurt her. And I was angry over that," or "My children being treated with insensitivity."

Irresponsible behavior of family, friends, and co-workers—behavior that was incongruent with women's ideologies of commitment and responsibility—comprised the third category of anger precipitants. Women described situations in which they gave to others but did not receive, needed support but did not get it, and were "left holding the bag" (in the words of one subject). Within the home, a frequent trigger of women's anger was the failure of husbands and children to do their share of household chores. In the words of one study participant:

> I felt like my weekends were spent cleaning the house while his weekends were spent playing, and I resented that. . . . Like I told him when I was angry, "You don't want to compare what you do and what I do because you'll lose, trust me. How many times do you do the laundry, and how many times do you fold and put up clothes, and cook the meals and run the kids?" He knows he doesn't do that. He knows I do most of it and he likes it that way and he wants to keep it that way.

At the workplace, women's ire was aroused by similar "acts of omission": "When others do not . . . take care of their 'fair share' of the day-to-day responsibilities," "When you've done your job and they put more work on you, while some others get away with doing nothing all day," or "When other people have 'bright ideas' for someone else (me) to do rather than doing it themselves."

Perhaps the two most striking aspects of these findings about anger precipitants are: (a) their location squarely within the interpersonal realm, mainly within a relatively small circle of intimates; and (b) their overall legitimacy and rationality. Given the provocations described by these women, their anger seems largely justifiable. It does not appear to be fueled by the irrational cognitions or unrealistic expectations that have been identified by Beck (1976), Ellis (1976), and others. Given the opportunity to write about their own experiences, instead of responding to questionnaires with predetermined lists of anger triggers, women seldom (in fact, almost never) describe triggers such as being caught in a slow-moving bank or supermarket line, waiting for a long time for an elevator, being stuck in a traffic jam, or being bumped by a stranger in a store—typical questionnaire items in *Anger Kills* (Williams & Williams, 1993). Although it is not disputed that delays or jostles from strangers may be momentarily irritating, frustrating, or inconvenient, one wonders whether most women would regard them as provoking anger. Women did not mention provocations of this type in response to this broad question: When are you likely to become angry? In other words, what situations or circumstances would usually trigger anger?

Precipitants of women's anger in the study were of deeper import, consistent with Solomon's (1976) view of anger as a judgment of personal offense—a substantive violation of one's values, morals, or principles that is more than simple annoyance or momentary irritation. Women were angry because significant others had let them down in significant ways. The anger was relational, generated in dyadic encounters (wife–husband, mother–child, friend–friend, colleague–colleague). The data support the theoretical formulations of Gilligan (1982); Miller (1976); Jordan, Kaplan, Miller, Stiver, and Surrey (1991); and others who emphasized women's embeddedness in caring relationships. Anger arises in these close relationships and "breaks the circle," in the words of one subject. Describing how she felt after angry conflict with her husband, she said, "I feel real uneasy . . . I don't feel like I'm really whole . . . as if my happy little circle with him is broken." In the words of another study participant, "The bottom line is not feeling loved." Although Solomon (1976) contended that anger includes a desire to punish the instigator, the data from the present study do not support this notion. Rather than a desire to punish, women want to "make right." Solomon also proposed that anger has a component of self-righteousness, but the data do not support this stance in women's anger experiences.

On the basis of this study alone, it cannot be confidently claimed that the subjects' responses were uniquely female, but there is some support in the literature for such a notion. For example, in an earlier study of adolescents, it was found that adolescent girls were more likely than adolescent boys to get angry when someone tried to take advantage of their friendship (Kollar, Groër, Thomas, & Cunningham, 1991). Likewise, in Stapley and Haviland's (1989) study of adolescents, females were angry because of interpersonal experiences, whereas males were angry in situations in which their performance was evaluated. In a college sample assessed by Lohr, Hamberger, and Bonge (1988), females became angry in one-sided intimate relationships ("People who do not give as well as take"), whereas males were provoked by obnoxious strangers ("Someone pretends to be something that he is not"). In another student sample, women reported that "condescending treatment" was the most anger-provoking behavior a peer could display toward them, whereas men's anger was triggered by physical and verbal aggression (Frodi; cited in Averill, 1982). Regardless of whether additional empirical evidence is forthcoming, it can be concluded that these gender differences in causes of anger are consistent with the literature on gender role socialization.

Demographic Comparisons

Women are not a monolithic, homogeneous group. Their life experiences differ according to their age, education, and a variety of other demographic characteristics. Therefore, various subgroups of the sample were examined to ascertain the effect of these characteristics on anger arousal and expression. Age was an important variable. Significant age differences were found on seven of nine anger dimensions using analysis of variance (ANOVA). Younger women were more frequently and overtly angry. Most striking was the incremental ordering of mean scores on Spielberger's Trait Anger Scale, with the youngest age group (age 34 or less) highest in anger proneness, followed by successively decreasing means for older women and the 55-or-older group scoring lowest of all. Similar patterns were observed for several other anger dimensions: Anger-Out was highest for the youngest women, as was Cognitive Anger; scores on both decreased as age increased. Conversely, women ages 55 and older scored highest on Anger-In.

There are several plausible explanations for these findings. It is reasonable to assume that the youngest and oldest cohorts had different socialization experiences. Women in their late twenties and early thirties at the time of the survey were born in the late 1950s and early 1960s, thus they were impressionable adolescents during the turbulent 1970s, when the feminist movement called attention to the devastating consequences of sex role stereotyping. In contrast, the women in the oldest group were born in the 1930s; they were adolescents during the conservative postwar period and probably learned to be "nice ladies."

However, lacking longitudinal data, it is not known whether older women scoring low on these anger dimensions in the 1990s are behaving much the same way they always have (decades of ladylike behavior?), or if they are in a life stage of "mellowing," no longer provoked to anger in their daily lives by recalcitrant children or thoughtless spouses. One also cannot conclude with confidence that the younger generation is fully liberated from constraints on anger expression. Consider the words of a 21-year-old woman interviewed as this chapter was being written:

I think that a lot of women my age are very very hesitant about, I don't think a lot of us feel worthy of, of being angry, and even when we are angry we're more afraid of, we want peace more than we want to actually express our anger and have somebody have to deal with it. Because then we have to deal with it too. And it's a lot easier just to suppress it and not make anybody unhappy. And not have to deal with a confrontation, which bothers me. Which makes me angry at myself.

Level of education makes a difference in the way women express their anger, although general anger proneness did not differ between groups (for these analyses, the upper and lower 25% of the sample in years of education were used to form the groups). Specifically, women with less education scored higher on Anger-Suppression and Anger-Symptoms than their better educated counterparts. It is likely that education level sorts women into different social roles with different rules for emotional expression. Occupational choices may also be influential. The anger of women in occupations grouped according to prestige, autonomy, and control was compared. Women in professional practice, female executives, and owners of their own businesses were placed in the "high" category. Teachers, nurses, social workers, and other human service workers were placed in the "middle" category. Clerical workers and homemakers constituted the "low" category (unfortunately, society accords little prestige to these vital occupations). On Spielberger's Trait Anger Scale, the human service workers scored highest on overall anger propensity and the Angry Reaction subscale, which contains items such as "I feel annoyed when I'm not given recognition for doing good work." Although they have somewhat more autonomy and prestige than the "low" group, human service workers must deal with the restrictions of bureaucratic organizations, the multifaceted needs of diverse clients, and other occupational frustrations. A common element is inadequate compensation and recognition for their work. Another factor in their high anger proneness could be an imbalance between giving and receiving. These women "give at the office" as well as at home, and they may be angry due to the lack of reciprocity or support. The burnout literature is supportive of this interpretation. Significant differences were also found between the three groups on the Anger-In dimension, with the "low" group of clerical workers and homemakers scoring highest on Anger-In. This group of women may be one of the most vulnerable in terms of health risk if their anger is chronically inhibited. In the Framingham study, clerical workers who had unsupportive bosses, heavy family responsibilities, and no outlet for their anger had a higher incidence of CHD (Haynes & Feinleib, 1980).

Interactions with children are a potential source of anger in the daily lives of women who are mothers, therefore scores on anger variables for mothers grouped according to the age of their youngest child were examined. There were 136 mothers of preschoolers (ages 5 or younger), 76 mothers of elementary school-aged children (ages 6–12), 75 mothers of adolescents (ages 13–18), and 120 mothers of adult children (older than 18 years). Overall propensity to be angry (trait anger) was higher in all groups of mothers with preadult children (< 18 years) than in the group of mothers whose children were older. Mothers of elementary school-aged children scored highest on the dimension of Anger-Out. Children in this stage of development frequently question parental authority and test limits as their social world enlarges and they begin to emulate peers. Consequently, their mothers are frequently provoked to anger and apparently vent it freely in a blaming way.

Relationships of Anger to Other Variables of the Study

Space does not permit exhaustive coverage of the correlational findings, but those of greatest utility to other researchers and clinicians are briefly reviewed. First, the correlates of trait anger are considered. In previous studies, researchers found relationships between trait anger and several other personal characteristics and health indicators. Trait anger was correlated with trait anxiety in studies by Spielberger's group (Spielberger et al., 1979) and by Israeli researchers (Ben-Zur & Zeidner, 1988). In a previous study of college women, higher trait anger was related to lower levels of optimism, purpose in life, self-efficacy, and life satisfaction, as well as to the belief that life's rewards are controlled by fate, chance, or luck (external locus of control) rather than by one's personal efforts (internal locus; Thomas & Williams, unpublished data). The present study contributes to this literature by its discovery of a strong link between higher trait anger and higher scores on the Contrada et al. (1986)

Cognitive Scale, which assesses a variety of faulty and irrational cognitions while one is "angry or furious." Individuals scoring high on this scale acknowledge that they have a very intense experience when angry ("I can't pay attention to anything else," "My mind seems to be caught up and overwhelmed with the feeling") and cannot easily let go of their anger ("I keep thinking about what happened over and over again"). They also think that the situations that evoke their anger are unfair, that they have been deliberately provoked, and that others should not behave that way. In the present study, trait anger was also significantly correlated with perceived stress, self-esteem, depression, insufficient social support, somatic anger symptoms, poorer health habits, and lower level of perceived health status. Later in the chapter, issues of women's stress and self-esteem are explored in more detail.

Anger-In was significantly correlated with physical anger symptoms, such as headaches, supporting Miller's (1983) proposal that women's suppressed anger is often expressed via somatic symptoms. However, Anger-Symptoms scores were also related to Anger-Out and every other anger variable except Anger-Discussion. Thus, anger symptoms are likely to occur when women vent anger outwardly, as well as when they inhibit its expression. At first, this finding appears paradoxical. One explanation hinges on the strong link between anger symptoms and unhealthy anger cognitions. Obsessing or ruminating about an incident can prevent termination of emotional arousal and complicate or delay the process of reconciliation with the offender. Another plausible explanation is that the physical symptomatology simply indicates intense arousal. Women in Averill's (1982) study reported greater tension than men during anger episodes, and some researchers (Fujita, Diener, & Sandvik, 1991) have proposed that women experience all emotions more vividly than do men. The somatic symptoms may be generated and/or maintained by the intensity of the emotion.

Anger-Discussion appears to be the most independent anger dimension, unrelated to Anger Cognitions, Anger-Out, or Anger-Symptoms, and only weakly related to trait anger. It is inversely related, predictably, to Anger-In. Women high on Anger-Discussion have less perceived stress, less depression, and better perceived health.

Women's Anger and Perceived Stress

Perceived Stress (a global assessment of the degree to which one feels overloaded and out of control) was strongly related to trait anger, Cognitive Anger, and Anger-Symptoms (higher stress associated with higher anger levels and intense resentful cognitions and physical complaints). These findings are consistent with the prediction, and remain unchanged when social support is controlled. What this study adds to the literature is identification of what women are stressed about. When given the opportunity to write responses to an open-ended question, women listed stressors that do not appear on most stress inventories.

When asked, What is your greatest stress right now?, the number one category of responses was vicarious stress (i.e., stress arising from women's concern for others and their need to care for others). Illustrative responses were:

- son's divorce
- grandson's illness
- nephew's car accident
- daughter's breast cancer
- turbulent adolescent son
- husband's unemployment
- daughter-in-law's mother terminally ill with cancer
- friend in jail
- parents' separation
- children's marital problems
- 8-year-old's difficulties at school
- aging parent's changing mental capacity

Although each woman was asked about her greatest stress, each answered by identifying events occurring to someone else—someone within her circle of intimates whose burdens she shoulders in addition to her own work stress and other personal burdens. Their stress becomes her stress due to her connectedness to them. A review of the nature of these events quickly impresses on the reader that they are essentially uncontrollable by the woman herself. The woman is helpless to take away her child's pain or "fix things." Another important aspect of vicarious stresses such as these is the probability of serious and long-term consequences for the woman and for others within her social network. She may have no one else to help care for ill family members or aging parents. Most traditional stress management modalities appear to be inadequate for dealing with such stressors. It seems likely that chronic stress will continue to fuel chronic anger.

This perspective (that anger is a reaction to overwhelming stress) is the converse of Smith and Pope's (1990) view of anger as a stress-engendering process. In their conceptualization, angry people create excess stress for themselves through their own thoughts and actions. Although this may be the case for the classic driven, hostile Type A male, it does not ring true for the woman whose stress derives from being stretched too thin to care for all those who depend on her. There is substantial evidence in the literature that women are more stressed than men (Cleary & Mechanic, 1983; Denton, 1993; Gannon & Pardie, 1989; Verbrugge, 1990) and receive less social support than they give to others (Belle, 1987; Turkington, 1985). Both men and women tend to rely on women for support because women are raised to be good listeners who respond with empathy and compassion (Turner & Avison, 1989). Some men rely solely on their wives for support.

It is true that women have larger social networks (creating the assumption that more support is available to them), but researchers are learning that involvement with more people may mean taking on even more vicarious stress. Many women can identify with Julie, who told psychologist Faye Crosby: "There's not enough of me. Everybody needs so much of me. I constantly feel as if one person or one group of people has one of my arms, and another group has the other arm, and they are pulling in different directions. And then two other groups have my feet. And then the phone rings" (Crosby, 1991, p. 27).

Abby, a participant in a study by Belenky and colleagues, was overloaded by her husband's needs after she became a mother:

> *Being married to him was like having another kid. I was his emotional support system. After I had my son, my maternal instincts were coming out of my ears. They were filled up to here! I remember the first thing I did was to let all my plants die. I couldn't take care of another damn thing. I didn't want to water them, I didn't want to feed anybody. Then I got rid of my dog. (Belenky, Clinchy, Goldberger, & Tarule, 1986, p. 78)*

In the new phase of the Women's Anger Study, many stories like those of Julie and Abby are heard in the phenomenological interviews. It seems evident that the stress drives the anger. Correlational analyses in the present study do not permit inferences regarding direction of the anger–stress association, but causal modeling could be undertaken in future investigations to resolve the chicken-and-egg issue.

Women's Anger and Self-Esteem

An inverse relationship between self-esteem and anger (the higher the self-esteem, the less the tendency to become angry) was found in this study, a finding of particular importance to women because they are more prone to low self-esteem than are men (Bardwick, 1971; Bush, Simmons, Hutchinson, & Blyth, 1978; Rosenberg & Simmons, 1975). Despite advances in the past two decades due to the women's movement, a recent survey sponsored by the American Association of University Women showed that today's high school girls have poorer self-images than do their male counterparts (cited in Saylor & Denham, 1993). Although 60% of girls were "happy the way I am" while in elementary school, by high school the percentage had dropped to 29%. This decline in self-esteem during adolescence is logically congruent with Brown and Gilligan's (1992) findings about the enormous pressure on girls to hide their honest emotions.

In one set of analyses, high and low scorers on the Rosenberg Self-Esteem Scale were compared on all of the anger dimensions. The two groups differed significantly on every anger variable. Study participants with low self-esteem had more frequent anger arousal (trait anger) and were more prone to suppress their anger or express it in an attacking, blaming way. On the Contrada Cognitive Scale, they endorsed specific irrational thoughts about their anger experience (i.e., that the situation was unfair, or people deliberately provoked them) and acknowledged replaying events in their mind to the point of obsession. Unfortunately, these ways of handling anger could potentially lower self-esteem even further.

Keeping anger in prevents problem solving and keeps women feeling powerless. Blaming and attacking may cause other people to avoid them (or to counterattack). Women with higher self-esteem were lower in trait anger and more likely to discuss their anger rationally (i.e., scored higher on Anger-Discussion). Because self-esteem has been shown to be a modifiable variable

(Sanford & Donovan, 1985; Watson & Bell, 1990), these findings have clinical implications.

CONCLUSIONS AND IMPLICATIONS FOR RESEARCH AND INTERVENTION

Despite societal efforts to silence women's anger, it is clear from the studies cited herein as well as those of other investigators that women still become very angry. Despite a widely circulated myth that women do not even know when they are angry, only six women in the study failed to complete the "typical anger experience" page of the questionnaire. Women do know when they are angry. In fact, anger proved to be the predominant emotion in a longitudinal study of important events, and the feelings generated by them, across 19 years of women's lives (Malatesta & Culver, 1984). However, evidence from this study indicates that, for some women, anger expression is still inhibited, especially those whose lack of education or occupational mobility (or other factors) keeps them in positions of low status and power. They are seething inside while maintaining the facade of the "nice lady." Solomon (1976) contended that emotions provide an avenue on which all that is meaningful in life surfaces. The emotion of anger is therefore a powerful way to express what is meaningful in a woman's life. Women who suppress their anger are depriving themselves of the power of their passionate feeling. Strong feeling can be a useful catalyst for correcting imbalances in the give-and-take ratios of primary relationships.

Much of women's anger seems to be reality based and justifiable, rather than irrational or pathological. It arises from interpersonal interactions in which other people deny them power or resources, treat them unjustly, or behave irresponsibly toward them. The offenders are intimates, not strangers. Nevertheless, the anger itself—if it is too intense, prolonged, or managed ineffectively—can contribute to health problems. Therefore, women, especially those with chronic stressors and/or high levels of trait anger and irrational cognitions, must be taught techniques for channeling anger into productive action and/or discharging it through vigorous physical activities or calming procedures (relaxation, meditation, etc.). Deffenbacher's work (Deffenbacher, Story, Brandon, Hogg, & Hazaleus, 1988; Deffenbacher, Story, Stark, Hogg, & Brandon, 1987) has demonstrated that trait anger, anger-suppression, and outward expression of temper can be successfully modified with behavioral interventions such as cognitive restructuring, relaxation therapy, and social skills training.

Suggestions for future research include the following. The most basic need is an in-depth examination of men's anger. If men were asked open-ended questions about anger provocations, would powerlessness be the number one theme? Probably not. No study has focused on men's everyday lived experiences. Continued efforts to refine and develop instruments should be given high priority. Many of the existing anger tools were developed by borrowing items from previously developed tools with questionable construct validity.

Many tools have a male bias. For example, hitting (a behavior more characteristic of men) is included in most anger instruments, whereas crying (a behavior more characteristic of women) is not. Similarly, rational discussion of anger, shown in several studies to be preferred by women, is not assessed by several of the most widely used questionnaires.

Further research is needed regarding ethnocultural influences on acquisition and maintenance of anger-expression styles. Too often, research samples are composed of predominantly privileged White subjects, such as middle- or upper-class college students. Much more needs to be done to examine disadvantaged individuals and members of minority groups, such as African Americans, Native Americans, Mexican Americans, or Asian Americans (and, of course, subgroups within these groups).

With regard to laboratory experiments, greater relevance to real-world experience can be obtained through use of anger-recall interviews (Lawler, Harralson, Armstead, & Schmied, 1993). In the experiments of Lawler et al. on cardiovascular reactivity, the subject is asked to recall an anger incident from his or her own life and discuss it. This procedure is quite effective in producing anger arousal in vivo. Some investigators are also bringing married couples into the lab and monitoring them during angry conflicts. Given that women's anger is more likely to be produced in interaction with intimates than strangers, such methodological improvements should yield more meaningful and accurate information.

Because the members of this research team are nurses and counselors, investigative work in the areas of anger propensity and anger expression in specific physical and mental disorders is of special interest. At this point, it is not known whether some anger patterns are precursors or by-products of disease. Many questions remain unanswered. For example, how do anger cognitions and behaviors change over the course of chronic, nonfatal conditions? Do fluctuations in anger levels correlate with disease exacerbations? What anger dimensions are most salient in diseases known to be more prevalent in women, such as arthritis, lupus erythematosus, and diabetes? If certain ways of handling anger seem to predispose women to conditions such as heart disease and cancer, what preventive interventions could be introduced? Much work remains before definitive recommendations for clinical practice with many subgroups of women can be made, particularly the understudied groups mentioned previously. This research team has taken women's anger as a serious phenomenon for study, but is fully cognizant that it has mapped only a portion of the vast territory yet to be explored. Other investigators must assist in finding answers to the questions that remain.

REFERENCES

Anastasi, A., Cohen, N., & Spatz, D. (1948). A study of fear and anger in college students through the controlled diary method. *Journal of Genetic Psychology, 73*, 243–249.

Averill, J. R. (1982). *Anger and aggression: An essay on emotion*. New York: Springer-Verlag.

Bardwick, J. M. (1971). *Psychology of women*. New York: Harper & Row.

Barefoot, J. C., Peterson, B. L., Dahlstrom, W. G., Siegler, I. C., Anderson, N. B., & Williams, R. B., Jr. (1991). Hostility patterns and health implications: Correlates of Cook-Medley Hostility Scale scores in a national survey. *Health Psychology, 10*, 18–24.

Beck, A. (1976). *Cognitive therapy and the emotional disorders*. New York: International Universities Press.

Beck, A., Ward, C., Mendelson, M., Mock, J., & Erbaugh, J. (1961). An inventory for measuring depression. *Archives of General Psychiatry, 4*, 561–570.

Belenky, M., Clinchy, B., Goldberger, N., & Tarule, J. (1986). *Women's ways of knowing: The development of self, voice, and mind*. New York: Basic Books.

Belle, D. (1987). Gender differences in the social moderators of stress. In R. C. Barnett, L. Biener, & G. Baruch (Eds.), *Gender and stress* (pp. 257–277). New York: The Free Press.

Ben-Zur, H., & Zeidner, M. (1988). Sex differences in anxiety, curiosity, and anger: A cross-cultural study. *Sex Roles, 19*, 335–347.

Bernard, J. (1981). *The female world*. New York: The Free Press.

Bernardez, T. (1987). Women and anger: Cultural prohibitions and the feminine ideal. *Work in progress, Stone Center for Developmental Services and Studies*. Wellesley, MA: Wellesley College, Stone Center.

Birnbaum, D. W., & Croll, W. L. (1984). The etiology of children's stereotypes about sex differences in emotionality. *Sex Roles, 10*, 677–691.

Block, J. (1973). Conceptions of sex role: Some cross-cultural and longitudinal perspectives. *American Psychologist, 28*, 512–526.

Brody, L. R. (1985). Gender differences in emotional development: A review of theories and research. *Journal of Personality, 53*, 102–149.

Brondolo, E. (1992, March). *Confiding versus confronting: Gender differences in anger expression among children and adolescents*. Paper presented at the meeting of the Society of Behavioral Medicine, New York City, New York.

Brown, L. M., & Gilligan, C. (1992). *Meeting at the crossroads: Women's psychology and girls' development*. Cambridge, MA: Harvard University Press.

Bush, D., Simmons, R., Hutchinson, B., & Blyth, D. (1978). Adolescent perception of sex roles in 1968 and 1975. *Public Opinion Quarterly, 41*, 459–474.

Campbell, A. (1993). *Men, women, and aggression*. New York: Basic Books.

Cleary, P., & Mechanic, D. (1983). Sex differences in psychological distress among married people. *Journal of Health and Social Behavior, 24*, 111–121.

Cohen, S., Kamarck, T., & Mermelstein, R. (1983). A global measure of perceived stress. *Journal of Health and Social Behavior, 24*, 385–396.

Contrada, R. J., Hill, D. R., Krantz, D. S., Durel, L. A., & Wright, R. A. (1986, August). *Measuring cognitive and somatic anger and anxiety: Preliminary report*. Paper presented at the meeting of the American Psychological Association, Washington, DC.

Coward, D. D. (1990). Critical multiplism: A research strategy for nursing science. *Image: Journal of Nursing Scholarship, 22,* 163–167.

Crawford, J., Kippax, S., Onyx, J., Gault, U., & Benton, P. (1990). Women theorizing their experiences of anger: A study using memory-work. *Australian Psychologist, 25,* 333–350.

Crosby, F. (1991). *Juggling.* New York: The Free Press.

Deffenbacher, J. (1994, August). *Anger does not equal aggression.* Paper presented at the American Psychological Association, Los Angeles, CA.

Deffenbacher, J., Story, D., Brandon, A., Hogg, J., & Hazaleus, S. (1988). Cognitive and cognitive-relaxation treatments of anger. *Cognitive Therapy and Research, 12,* 167–184.

Deffenbacher, J., Story, D., Stark, R., Hogg, J., & Brandon, A. (1987). Cognitive-relaxation and social skills interventions in the treatment of general anger. *Journal of Counseling Psychology, 34,* 171–176.

Denham, G., & Bultemeier, K. (1993). Anger: Targets and triggers. In S. P. Thomas (Ed.), *Women and anger* (pp. 68–90). New York: Springer.

Denton, L. (1993). Researchers hunt clues to solve stress mystery. *American Psychological Association Monitor, 24*(2), 28–29.

Eagly, A., & Steffen, V. (1986). Gender and aggressive behavior: A meta-analytic review of the social psychological literature. *Psychological Bulletin, 100,* 309–330.

Ellis, A. (1976, October). Techniques of handling anger in marriage. *Journal of Marriage and Family Counseling,* pp. 305–315.

Fischman, J. (1987). Type A on trial. *Psychology Today, 21*(2), 42–50.

Fiske, S. T. (1993). Controlling other people: The impact of power on stereotyping. *American Psychologist, 48,* 621–628.

Fujita, F., Diener, E., & Sandvik, E. (1991). Gender differences in negative affect and well-being: The case for emotional intensity. *Journal of Personality and Social Psychology, 61,* 427–434.

Funkenstein, D., King, S., & Drolette, M. (1954). The direction of anger during a laboratory stress-inducing situation. *Psychosomatic Medicine, 16,* 404–413.

Gannon, L., & Pardie, L. (1989). The importance of chronicity and controllability of stress in the context of stress-illness relationships. *Journal of Behavioral Medicine, 12,* 347–372.

Gates, G. S. (1926). An observational study of anger. *Journal of Experimental Psychology, 9,* 325–331.

Gentry, W., Chesney, A., Gary, H., Hall, R., & Harburg, E. (1982). Habitual anger-coping styles: Effect on mean blood pressure and risk for essential hypertension. *Psychosomatic Medicine, 44,* 195–202.

Gilligan, C. (1982). *In a different voice: Psychological theory and women's development.* Cambridge, MA: Harvard University Press.

Greenglass, E., & Julkunen, J. (1989). Construct validity and sex differences in Cook-Medley hostility. *Personality and Individual Differences, 10,* 209–218.

Greif, E., Alvarez, M., & Ulman, L. (1981, April). *Recognizing emotions in other people: Sex differences in socialization.* Paper presented at the biennial meeting of the Society for Research in Child Development, Boston, MA.

Harburg, E., Blakelock, E., & Roeper, P. (1979). Resentful and reflective coping with arbitrary authority and blood pressure: Detroit. *Psychosomatic Medicine, 41*, 189–199.

Harburg, E., Erfurt, J., Hauenstein, L., Chape, C., Schull, W., & Schork, M. (1973). Socio-ecological stress, suppressed hostility, skin color, and black-white male blood pressure: Detroit. *Psychosomatic Medicine, 35*, 276–296.

Haynes, S. G., & Feinleib, M. (1980). Women, work and coronary heart disease: Prospective findings from the Framingham Heart Study. *American Journal of Public Health, 70*, 133–141.

Haynes, S. G., Levine, S., Scotch, N., Feinleib, M., & Kannel, W. B. (1978). The relationship of psychosocial factors to coronary heart disease in the Framingham Study: I. Methods and risk factors. *American Journal of Epidemiology, 107*, 362–383.

Jordan, J. V., Kaplan, A. G., Miller, J. B., Stiver, I. P., & Surrey, J. L. (1991). *Women's growth in connection: Writings from the Stone Center*. New York: Guilford.

Kollar, M., Groër, M., Thomas, S., & Cunningham, J. (1991). Adolescent anger: A developmental study. *Journal of Child and Adolescent Psychiatric Nursing, 4*, 9–15.

Lawler, K., Harralson, T., Armstead, C., & Schmied, L. (1993). Gender and cardiovascular responses: What is the role of hostility? *Journal of Psychosomatic Research, 37*, 603–613.

Lerner, H. G. (1985). *The dance of anger*. New York: Harper & Row.

Lever, J. (1976). Sex differences in the games children play. *Social Problems, 23*, 478–487.

Lohr, J., Hamberger, L., & Bonge, D. (1988). The relationship of factorially validated measures of anger-proneness and irrational beliefs. *Motivation and Emotion, 12*, 171–183.

MacGregor, M., & Davidson, K. (1994, April). *Gender differences in the rating of hostility*. Paper presented at the fifteenth meeting of the Society of Behavioral Medicine, Boston, MA.

Malatesta, C., & Culver, L. (1984). Thematic and affective content in the lives of adult women: Patterns of change and continuity. In C. Malatesta & C. Izard (Eds.), *Emotion in adult development* (pp. 175–193). Beverly Hills: Sage.

Miles, M., & Huberman, A. (1984). *Qualitative data analysis*. Beverly Hills: Sage.

Miller, J. B. (1976). *Toward a new psychology of women*. Boston: Beacon.

Miller, J. B. (1983). The construction of anger in men and women. *Work in progress, Stone Center for Developmental Services and Studies*. Wellesley, MA: Wellesley College, Stone Center.

Moses, S. (1990). Teen girls can have "crisis of connection." *APA Monitor, 21*(11), 26.

Norbeck, J., Lindsey, A., & Carrieri, V. (1981). The development of an instrument to measure social support. *Nursing Research, 30*, 264–269.

Riley, W., & Treiber, F. (1989). The validity of multidimensional self-report anger and hostility measures. *Journal of Clinical Psychology, 45*, 397–404.

Rosenberg, F., & Simmons, R. (1975). Sex differences in the self concept in adolescence. *Sex Roles, 1*, 147–159.

Rosenberg, M. (1965). *Society and the adolescent self-image*. Princeton, NJ: Princeton University Press.

Saarni, C. (1979). Children's understanding of display rules for expressive behavior. *Developmental Psychology, 15*, 424–429.

Sanford, L., & Donovan, M. (1985). *Women and self-esteem*. New York: Penguin.

Saylor, M., & Denham, G. (1993). Women's anger and self-esteem. In S. P. Thomas (Ed.), *Women and anger* (pp. 91–111). New York: Springer.

Scherwitz, L., Perkins, L., Chesney, M., & Hughes, G. (1991). Cook-Medley Hostility Scale and subsets: Relationship to demographic and psychological characteristics in young adults in the CARDIA study. *Psychosomatic Medicine, 53*, 36–49.

Smith, T., & Christensen, A. (1992). Hostility, health, and social contexts. In H. S. Friedman (Ed.), *Hostility, coping and health* (pp. 33–48). Washington, DC: American Psychological Association.

Smith,T., & Pope, M. (1990). Cynical hostility as a health risk: Current status and future directions. *Journal of Social Behavior and Personality, 5*, 77–88.

Solomon, R. C. (1976). *The passions*. Garden City, NY: Anchor Doubleday.

Spielberger, C. D., Barker, L., Russell, S., Crane, R., Westberry, L., Knight, J., & Marks, E. (1979). *Preliminary manual for the State-Trait Personality Inventory (STPI)*. Tampa: University of South Florida Press.

Spielberger, C. D., Jacobs, G., Russell, S., & Crane, R. (1983). Assessment of anger: The State-Trait Anger Scale. In J. N. Butcher & C. D. Spielberger (Eds.), *Advances in personality assessment* (Vol. 2, pp. 161–189). Hillsdale, NJ: Erlbaum.

Spielberger, C. D., Johnson, E., Russell, S., Crane, R., Jacobs, G., & Worden, T. (1985). The experience and expression of anger: Construction and validation of an anger expression scale. In M. A. Chesney & R. H. Rosenman (Eds.), *Anger and hostility in cardiovascular and behavioral disorders* (pp. 5–30). New York: Hemisphere/McGraw-Hill.

Spielberger, C. D., Krasner, S. S., & Solomon, E. P. (1988). The experience, expression, and control of anger. In M. P. Janisse (Ed.), *Health psychology: Individual differences and stress* (pp. 89–108). New York: Springer-Verlag.

Stapley, J., & Haviland, J. (1989). Beyond depression: Gender differences in normal adolescents' emotional experiences. *Sex Roles, 20*, 295–308.

Stoney, C. M., & Engebretson, T. O. (1994). Anger and hostility: Potential mediators of the gender differences in coronary heart disease. In A. W. Siegman & T. W. Smith (Eds.), *Anger, hostility, and the heart* (pp. 215–237). Hillsdale, NJ: Erlbaum.

Suarez, E. C., & Williams, R. B. (1990). The relationships between dimensions of hostility and cardiovascular reactivity as a function of task characteristics. *Psychosomatic Medicine, 52*, 558–570.

Tannen, D. (1990). *You just don't understand*. New York: Ballantine Books.

Thomas, S. P. (1989). Gender differences in anger expression: Health impli-
    cations. *Research in Nursing and Health, 12*, 389–398.
Thomas, S. P. (1990). Theoretical and empirical perspectives on anger. *Issues
    in Mental Health Nursing, 11*, 203–216.
Thomas, S. P. (1991). Toward a new conceptualization of women's anger. *Issues
    in Mental Health Nursing,12*, 31–49.
Thomas, S. P. (Ed.). (1993). *Women and anger*. New York: Springer.
Thomas, S. P., & Williams, R. (1991). Perceived stress, trait anger, modes of
    anger expression and health status of college men and women. *Nursing
    Research, 40*, 303–307.
Turkington, C. (1985). What price friendship? The darker side of social net-
    works. *American Psychological Association Monitor, 16*, 38–41.
Turner, R., & Avison, W. (1989). Gender and depression: Assessing exposure
    and vulnerability to life events in a chronically strained population. *The
    Journal of Nervous and Mental Disease, 177*, 443–455.
Verbrugge, L. (1990). The twain meet: Empirical explanations of sex differ-
    ences in health and mortality. In M. G. Ory & H. R. Warner (Eds.), *Gender,
    health and longevity: Multidisciplinary perspectives* (pp. 159–199). New
    York: Springer.
Ware, J. E. (1976). Scales for measuring general health perceptions. *Health
    Services Research, 11*, 396–415.
Watson, W., & Bell, J. (1990). Who are we? Low self-esteem and marital
    identity. *Journal of Psychosocial Nursing, 28*(4), 15–20.
Weidner, G., Istvan, J., & McKnight, J. (1989). Clusters of behavioral coro-
    nary risk factors in employed women and men. *Journal of Applied Social
    Psychology, 19*, 468–480.
Williams, R., & Williams, V. (1993). *Anger kills*. New York: Times Books.

5

The Experience and Expression of Anger in Divorced Mothers: Effects on Postdivorce Adjustment in Children

Solly Dreman
Ben Gurion University of the Negev, Beer Sheva, Israel

ABSTRACT

This study investigated the effects of custodial mothers' anger on the adjustment of their adolescent children. High state anger (S-Anger) in these mothers, as measured with the Hebrew adaptation of Spielberger's State–Trait Anger Expression Inventory (STAXI), was related to good adjustment in sons, but poor adjustment in daughters. There was also a tendency for high Anger-Out scores to be related to poor adjustment in both sons and daughters, suggesting that the overt expression of anger by mothers with high Anger-Out scores is readily imitated by both boys and girls, which resulted in poor adjustment for children of both sexes. Factor analysis of the STAXI S-Anger items identified two state anger factors: Feeling Angry and feeling like expressing anger (Action Potential). Mothers with high Action Potential scores had sons with good adjustment, whereas their daughters displayed poor adjustment. It was hypothesized that the covert anger of mothers with high S-Anger Action Potential scores is expressed in increased maternal assertiveness and limit-setting with sons, thus explaining the good adjustment of boys. The poor adjustment of girls whose mothers were high in S-Anger may be explained by the greater sensitivity of these girls to their mothers' angry feelings—mothers serving as emotional role models for their daughters.

Although divorce research has extensively investigated the effects of interpersonal conflict on postdivorce adjustment (Camara & Resnick, 1988, 1989; Emery, 1982; Hauser, 1985; Johnson, Campbell, & Mayes, 1985; Kelly, 1982; Rutter, 1971; Wallerstein & Kelly, 1980), the effects of the personal emotional dimension, anger, have been ignored. The present chapter presents findings

The assistance of the Israel National Insurance Institute is gratefully acknowledged for their help in carrying out this research. I would also like to thank Ruth Fried of the Hebrew University for helping formulate some of the ideas for the study, and Ronit Zamir and Judy Auerbach of Ben Gurion University for their assistance with the statistical work-up and their helpful comments.

from a study in Israel that casts some light on how anger in divorced mothers affects their children's postdivorce adjustment.

Research shows that divorced women express more anger, disappointment, and dissatisfaction then do men, blaming the ex-spouse for the divorce even several years past the divorce event (Dreman & Aldor, 1994a; Kitson & Sussman, 1982; Wallerstein, 1986). Blaming and the failure to recognize one's own responsibility in the divorce process could hinder postdivorce cooperation. This may have important implications for children because parental cooperation has been shown to be an important factor in their postdivorce adjustment (Camara & Resnick, 1988).

Recent research on mothers' anger has shown that it may negatively influence parental cognitive processes such as memories and attributions, as well as action tendencies (Berkowitz, 1990; Dix, Reinhold, & Zambarano, 1990). For example, Dix et al. (1990) found that angry mothers judge children more negatively than mothers in a happy or neutral mood. These investigators proposed that anger may cause the mothers to scan the environment for negative cues. Such affect-related cognitive biases/attributions may influence parent–child interaction, adversely affecting children's adjustment. However, they did not present any findings related to adjustment outcomes.

Another factor that could influence children's adjustment is imitation, as postulated in social learning theory (Bandura, 1962). This theory predicts that an angry parent serves as a negative role model, adversely affecting children's adjustment. In the divorce situation, the probability of occurrence of such a negative role model is high.

In one of the few studies investigating parental anger and postdivorce adjustment in children, an inverse relationship was found between custodial mothers' state anger (S-Anger) and children's adjustment—mothers with high S-Anger having more poorly adjusted children (Dreman & Aldor, 1994b). The present study extends this earlier study. It investigates divorced mothers' experience of anger as measured by the S-Anger scale, and their expression of anger as measured by the Anger-Out and Anger-In scales of the State–Trait Anger Expression Inventory (STAXI), constructed by Spielberger (1988). The dependent variable is Children's Adjustment, as measured by the Externalizing, Internalizing, and General Adjustment scores of the Child Behavior Checklist (CBCL; Achenbach & Edelbrock, 1983) and the Youth Self-Report Form (YSRF; Achenbach & Edelbrock, 1987).

Mothers who were selected had been divorced at least 4 years to ensure that they had entered the postcrisis or "stabilization" phase of divorce (Herz Brown, 1988), where their level of functioning should be good and approximate to that of married women. The review indicated, however, that anger should continue to affect these women even several years past the divorce event. It was predicted that the children of mothers with high scores on S-Anger, Anger-In, and Anger-Out scales of the STAXI would have poorer Adjustment scores on the CBCL and YSRF. The effects of children's gender were also examined because previous research has shown that boys display poorer Adjustment scores in the postdivorce situation, particularly when they are in maternal custody (Zaslow, 1988, 1989).

METHOD

Subjects

The present study investigated the relation between the experience and expression of anger of 119 custodial mothers on the adjustment of one of their adolescent children. Mothers' mean time since divorce was 9 years 3 months, and their mean age 44 years 4 months. These mothers constituted a representative sample of divorced custodial mothers in Israel who receive regular child stipends from the National Insurance Institute. Mothers selected were at least 4 years past the date of the divorce decree. The "target" child was between the ages of 11–18, and thus was able to fill out the YSR, which constitutes a self-rating scale of child adjustment. The mean age of the child was 14 years 10 months.

Instruments

State–Trait Anger Expression Inventory. The STAXI (Spielberger, 1988) consists of 44 self-report items, rated on a 4-point scale, which form six scales: two scales measuring the experience of anger—State Anger (S-Anger) and Trait Anger (T-Anger)—and four scales measuring the expression of anger— Anger-In, Anger-Out, Anger-Control, and Anger-Expression. In the present study, divorced mothers' S-Anger, Anger-Out, and Anger-In were chosen as the independent variables, and their effect on postdivorce adjustment in children was investigated. Situationally linked S-Anger was chosen as one of the independent variables because a recent Israeli study showed that divorced mothers display higher S-Anger than divorced fathers even several years past divorce (Dreman & Aldor, 1994a). The investigators attributed this difference to such postdivorce factors as work overload, decreased economic standing, and diminished opportunities for social contacts in divorced women as compared with men.

The Anger-Out and Anger-In scales were also investigated because they were hypothesized to be related to externalizing and internalizing behavior problems of children as measured by the Child Behavior Checklist (see description later). Further support of the use of the S-Anger and Anger-Out scales is offered by the finding that divorced mothers demonstrated significantly more S-Anger and Anger-Out than a comparative population of married mothers (see Table 5.1) in the Hebrew Standardization of the STAXI (Dreman & Aldor, 1994c).

Child Behavior Checklist (CBCL): Custodial mothers' evaluation of children's behavior. The Hebrew adaptation of the original CBCL (Achenbach & Edelbrock, 1983), developed by Zilber, Auerbach, and Lerner (1994), was used to assess the custodial mothers' perception of their children's adjustment as reflected in the presence–absence of behavior problems. The mothers responded to 118 questions related to potential behavior problems. A 3-point Likert scale was used for each question, ranging from *not true of my child* to *somewhat true of my child* to *very true of my child*.

Table 5.1 Anger experience and expression scale means, standard deviations, and alphas for divorced and married mothers

Scale	Divorced mothers ($n = 191$)	Married mothers ($n = 132$)
S-Anger		
M	14.51	12.48
SD	7.17	4.17
Alpha	.95	.90
T-Anger		
M	19.16	18.37
SD	5.19	5.00
Alpha	.85	.86
Ax/Out		
M	15.07	13.50
SD	3.44	3.58
Alpha	.70	.79
Ax/In		
M	16.79	16.80
SD	4.36	3.74
Alpha	.73	.63
Ax/Con		
M	24.22	23.45
SD	4.88	5.22
Alpha	.87	.86

Ax/In = Anger-In; Ax/Out = Anger-Out; Ax/Con = Anger-Control.

Achenbach and Edelbrock (1983) factor analyzed responses to the CBCL items, and identified two wide-band dimensions: Externalizing and Internalizing Behavior Problems. Scales based on these two CBCL dimensions and on Total Behavior Problem scores were used as the dependent variables in the present study. The raw scores for each of these dimensions have been standardized separately for boys and girls by Achenbach and Edelbrock (1983), yielding sex-adjusted *T*-scores for American populations.

In the analyses of the present study, the Hebrew CBCL raw scores were converted into standard scores, with a mean of zero and a standard deviation of 1.00. To facilitate more clear-cut comparisons between the different subscales, this procedure was followed because the number of items in the CBCL and the YSR were unequal, and there were other technical difficulties that precluded the use of raw scores. The ratings on the CBCL can be compared with the scores on the YSR to evaluate the extent of the agreement between the custodial mother and child with respect to the ratings of the child's behavior problems.

Youth Self-Report Form (YSR): Children's evaluation of their behavior problems (Achenbach & Edelbrock, 1987). The YSR was used to evaluate children's perceptions of their adjustment, as reflected in the presence or absence of behavior problems. Children responded to 118 questions regarding how well they describe their behavior in the preceding 6 months. All items use a 3-point Likert scale ranging from *not true of me* to *somewhat true of me* to *very true of me*. YSR measures have been factor analyzed and have yielded two broad-band dimensions: Externalizing and Internalizing Behavior Problems, as well as an index of Total Behavior Problems. As with the CBCL, the raw scores on each of these scales were converted to sex-adjusted *T*-scores in the American standardization. In the present study, however, standard scores were utilized for reasons outlined in describing the CBCL. This scale was standardized on children 11 years of age and older (Achenbach & Edelbrock, 1987), which is the bottom limit of the age range of children sampled in the present study.

Procedure

For reasons of confidentiality, subjects selected were first contacted by mail through the National Insurance Institute. They were asked whether they were willing to participate in a research project studying single-parent families. Those who agreed were asked to sign a waiver of confidentiality and then were contacted by the research team. The response rate was 18.5%, which was considered quite adequate for mail surveys in Israel (Hornik & Meir, 1989). Parents who agreed to participate were mailed a structured questionnaire with measures of coping and adjustment. After completing the questionnaire, further testing was conducted by undergraduate psychology students at the home setting. At this time, a target child between the ages of 11–18 was also tested. The STAXI, CBCL, and YSR were administered to the mother and child at this time.

RESULTS

Custodial Mothers' Anger and Children's Adjustment

A 3 × 2 analysis of variance (ANOVA) factorial design was employed (mothers' anger levels [high, medium, low] × gender of child) to examine the effects of the different anger scales on the General Adjustment, Externalizing, and Internalizing scales of the CBCL and YSR. Mothers whose Anger scores were ½ standard deviation or more above the mean were classified as *high anger*, those within plus or minus ½ standard deviation from the mean as *medium anger*, and those ½ standard deviation or more below the mean as *low anger*.

Anger expression: Anger-out and anger-in of custodial mothers and children's adjustment. Although high levels of maternal Anger-Out were related to poor adjustment in children on the General Externalizing and Internalizing scales in both boys and girls, as predicted, these trends did not reach statisti-

Table 5.2 Custodial mothers' State Anger and children's General Adjustment scores (CBCL)

| | State Anger | | | |
	Low	Medium	High	Raw means
Boys	− .16	.41	− .28	.01
Girls	− .35	.05	1.00	.06
Column means	− .26	.24	.48	

cally significant levels. As for Anger-In, no consistent trends or significant effects were found in its relation to Children's Adjustment.

Anger experience: State anger of custodial mothers and children's adjustment. A significant interaction was obtained between mothers' S-Anger and children's gender on the CBCL General Adjustment scale $[F(2, 109) = 5.29, p < .006]$: High S-Anger resulted in relatively good adjustment in boys, whereas it was related to poor adjustment in girls (see Table 5.2). In the following tables (see Tables 5.2–5.10), lower mean scores represent better adjustment than higher mean scores on the different Achenbach scales.

An interaction approaching significance was obtained between maternal S-Anger and children's gender $[F(2, 72) = 2.54, p < .086]$ on the YSR General Adjustment scale. Boys of mothers with medium to high levels of S-Anger displayed relatively good adjustment, whereas girls of mothers with medium to high S-Anger displayed poorer adjustment (see Table 5.3).

An interaction between mothers' S-Anger and child's gender on Externalizing scores on the CBCL $[F(2, 100) = 3.382, p < .038]$ was also obtained. High S-Anger in mothers was positively related to good adjustment in boys, expressed in less externalizing, whereas girls displayed more externalizing behavior (see Table 5.4).

An interaction was again found between maternal S-Anger and children's gender on the Externalizing scale of the YSR $[F(2, 72) = 4.48, p < .015]$. Medium and high S-Anger levels in mothers led to less externalizing in boys, whereas these levels led to more externalizing and poorer adjustment in girls (see Table 5.5).

This is a unique finding. In developmental research, one rarely finds a relation between a parent-rated and a child-rated Adjustment variable like that

Table 5.3 Custodial mothers' State Anger and children's General Adjustment scores (YSR)

| | State Anger | | | |
	Low	Medium	High	Raw means
Boys	.39	− .31	− .02	.11
Girls	− .18	.12	.36	.03
Column means	.10	− .06	.17	

Table 5.4 Custodial mothers' State Anger and childrens' Externalizing scores (CBCL)

	State Anger			
	Low	Medium	High	Raw means
Boys	− .23	.78	− .22	.10
Girls	− .21	.11	.61	.08
Column means	− .22	.43	.27	

found between parental S-Anger and children's Externalizing. In addition, both parents' ratings (CBCL) and children's ratings (YSR) of children's Externalizing were related in a similar fashion to maternal S-Anger—boys of mothers with high S-Anger displaying better adjustment than girls. This finding adds external validity to the S-Anger scale because the Adjustment correlate, Externalizing, was rated similarly by multiple observers. With regard to the internalizing behavior, no main or interaction effects were found for mothers' S-Anger on Internalizing on either the CBCL or YSR.

S-Anger factors: Action Potential and Feelings. In view of the unpredicted relation found between high S-Anger in mothers and good postdivorce adjustment in sons, a secondary analysis was undertaken to explain these findings. Visual inspection of the S-Anger scale revealed two groups of items: those reflecting Action Potential, such as "I feel like yelling at someone," and those reflecting Feelings, such as "I am furious." A factor analysis employing a two-factor resolution with a varimax rotation on the S-Anger scale items yielded an Action Potential and a Feelings factor, in accordance with our observation. The Eigen values obtained were: Factor I—Action Potential = 7.22; Factor II—Feelings = 1.12. Factor I accounted for 72.2%, whereas Factor II accounted for 11.2% of the explained variance. The factor loadings were:

Factor I: Action Potential—State Anger
    Item 7. I feel like banging on the table (.889)
    Item 8. I feel like hitting someone (.867)
    Item 5. I feel like breaking things (.837)
    Item 10. I feel like swearing (.665)
    Item 4. I feel like yelling at someone (.531)*
    *This item also loaded .739 on Factor II

Table 5.5 Custodial mothers' State Anger and children's Externalizing scores (YSR)

	State Anger			
	Low	Medium	High	Raw means
Boys	.38	− .50	− .37	− .01
Girls	− .15	.26	.48	.13
Column means	.13	− .04	.06	

Table 5.6 Custodial mothers' State Anger Action Potential and children's General
            Adjustment scores (CBCL)

| | State Anger Action Potential | | |
	Low	High	Raw means
Boys	.04	− .19	.01
Girls	− .06	.58	.06
Column means	− .08	.29	

Factor II: Feelings—State Anger
  Item 2. I feel irritated (.880)
  Item 3. I feel angry (.878)
  Item 1. I am furious (.872)
  Item 6. I am mad (.851)
  Item 9. I am burned up (.740)

Custodial mothers were then divided into those with high scores (greater than 5) and those with low scores (5, which was the minimal score possible) on any given factor. Several 2×2 ANOVAs (factor score [high, low] $\times$ gender) were performed to investigate the differential effects of each factor, interacting with gender, on children's Adjustment scores. It was hypothesized that women displaying high scores on Action Potential items would engage in more effective limit-setting, thus promoting better adjustment in their sons. Daughters are more likely to imitate the anger experience of their mothers, who act as emotional role models for them. Thus, high Action Potential scores in mothers should adversely affect their daughters' behavior. Because no theoretical assumptions were entertained regarding the Feelings factor, its effect on children's adjustment was examined post hoc. The results are reported next.

State Anger: Action Potential

A significant interaction $[F(1, 111) = 4.28, p < .041]$ was found between Action Potential and gender on General Adjustment scores on the CBCL, with high Action Potential in mothers related to good adjustment in boys, but poor adjustment in girls, as predicted (see Table 5.6).

A significant interaction $[F(1, 81) = 4.28, p < .042]$ was again obtained between Action Potential and gender on General Adjustment scores on the YSRF, with high Action Potential in mothers resulting in good adjustment in boys, but not in girls (see Table 5.7).

No main or interaction effects were found on the Externalizing scale of the CBCL, although there was a tendency for boys to display good adjustment if mothers had high Action Potential. The opposite was true for girls (see Table 5.8).

A significant interaction $[F(1, 74) = 3.45, p < .021]$ was found between Action Potential and gender on the Externalizing scale of the YSR. Sons of

Table 5.7 Custodial mothers' State Anger Action Potential and children's General Adjustment scores (YSR)

| | State Anger Action Potential | | |
	Low	High	Raw means
Boys	.26	−.14	.11
Girls	−.18	.36	.03
Column means	.05	.10	

mothers with high Action Potential adjusted relatively well, whereas girls adjusted poorly (see Table 5.9).

Internalizing behavior was not significantly affected by mothers' Action Potential, although there was a trend for high Action Potential in mothers to be related to more internalizing in both boys and girls.

State Anger: Feelings

Main effects were found for mothers' Feelings of S-Anger, with high Feelings adversely affecting both boys' and girls' General Adjustment scores. Thus, high S-Anger Feelings were related to poorer adjustment on General Adjustment [$F(1, 114) = 12.05, p < .001$], Internalizing [$F(1, 93) = 5.17, p < .025$], and Externalizing [$F(1, 102) = 9.08, p < .003$] scores on the CBCL.

Mothers' Feelings scores on the S-Anger scale interacted less with gender than did their Action Potential scores. The only significant interaction found for the Feelings factor was on the Externalizing scale of the YSR [$F(1, 74) = 5.89, p < .018$], with boys affected positively by the maternal Feelings factor and girls affected negatively (see Table 5.10).

DISCUSSION

In Israel's traditional, family-centered society, divorced women face ongoing adversities that may result in chronic anger and bitterness. Divorced women are usually worse off financially, whereas divorced men usually maintain their

Table 5.8 Custodial mothers' State Anger Action Potential and children's Externalizing scores (CBCL)

| | State Anger Action Potential | | |
	Low	High	Raw means
Boys	.11	−.08	.10
Girls	.08	.36	.08
Column means	.01	.24	

Table 5.9 Custodial mothers' State Anger Action Potential and children's Externalizing scores (YSR)

| | State Anger Action Potential | | Raw means |
	Low	High	
Boys	.19	−.17	−.01
Girls	−.40	.64	.13
Column means	.01	.16	

standards of living postdivorce (Hetherington & Stanley-Hagan, 1986). In support of this, a recent Israeli study found that more custodial mothers than fathers receive welfare and are dependent on financial support from other sources to supplement their incomes (Dreman & Aldor, 1994b). In addition, divorced mothers are expected to devote the majority of their time to childrearing, whereas divorced fathers may pursue occupational goals and engage in new intimate relationships without undue sanction. Divorcees also experience difficulties maintaining relationships with married friends because they are perceived as a threat to the intact family (Katz & Pesach, 1985). These continuing material, occupational, and social difficulties may result in an enhanced experience and expression of anger, even several years past divorce, in divorced mothers. In support of this, the divorced mothers in this study, who were on the average over 9 years past the divorce event, had higher S-Anger and Anger-Out scores than a comparative group of married mothers (Means: S-Anger— 14.5 vs. 12.48; Anger-Out—15.02 vs. 13.50).

Custodial mothers' experience of S-Anger influenced children's postdivorce adjustment more than the expression of anger, represented by the Anger-Out and Anger-In scales of the STAXI. A possible explanation is that the S-Anger scale more accurately represents the cumulative stressors that divorced women experience after the divorce event. The author of the STAXI, in fact, defines *state anger* as follows: "Over time, the intensity of state anger varies as a function of perceived injustice, attack or unfair treatment by others, and . . . from barriers to goal-directed behavior" (Spielberger, 1988, p. 1). Anger expression is more like a trait or behavior style than a situationally determined

Table 5.10 Custodial mothers' Feelings of State Anger and children's Externalizing scores (YSR)

| | State Anger Action Potential | | Raw means |
	Low	High	
Boys	.38	−.01	−.01
Girls	−.44	.25	.13
Column means	.19	−.06	

variable. Hence, expression of anger may have a less differential impact on postdivorce adjustment than S-Anger, which is elicited directly by the post-divorce situation.

Maternal Anger and Children's Gender

High S-Anger in custodial mothers negatively influenced daughters' adjustment on the General Adjustment and Externalizing scales of the YSRF. This adverse effect on adjustment was expected because angry mothers may blame and not cooperate with the noncustodial parent, as well as make negative attributions toward their children, both of which contribute to children's negative adjustment. In addition, mothers with high S-Anger may serve as a negative role model for their daughters, adversely affecting their adjustment.

In contrast to our prediction, however, a positive relation was found between high S-Anger in custodial mothers and their sons' postdivorce adjustment. A possible explanation may be gleaned from recent divorce research, which suggests that custodial mothers have difficulty disciplining and setting limits, especially with sons (Hetherington, 1981; Hetherington, Cox, & Cox, 1985). Boys in maternal custody have been found to have the lowest levels of prosocial behavior and self-esteem, as well as display more aggression than girls (Camara & Resnick, 1989; Furstenberg, 1988). Boys living with fathers, however, are more independent and social than girls in this situation. These findings suggest that boys in maternal custody may be deprived of the limit-setting capacities usually associated with fathers, with this deficit adversely affecting their postdivorce adjustment. Hence, it might be hypothesized that custodial mothers, who are more capable of setting limits, should promote better adjustment in their sons.

The present study supports this hypothesis. Sons of mothers scoring high on the Action Potential factor of the S-Anger scale demonstrated better adjustment on the General Adjustment and Externalizing scales of the YSRF than sons of mothers scoring low on the Action Potential scale. The opposite was true for girls. Action Potential did not significantly affect children's internalizing, although there was a tendency for mothers with high Action Potential to have children who display more internalizing, perhaps hinting that higher Action Potential in mothers results in more suppression in children who already internalize. In summary, mothers with higher Action Potential more effectively set limits on their sons in relation to the overt behavior problems, expressed in the General Adjustment and Externalizing scales, thus resulting in good adjustment.

High scores on the Feelings factor, in contrast, were related to negative adjustment in both boys and girls, on both the General Adjustment and Internalizing scales. This might suggest a projection of mothers' negative feelings on their subjective ratings of children's adjustment.

No significant main or interaction effects were obtained between the maternal expression of anger as measured on the Anger-Out and Anger-In scales and children's adjustment. There was a trend, however, for high levels of

Anger-Out to negatively affect children's adjustment on the General, Externalizing, and Internalizing scales, irrespective of gender. These results are congruent with our prediction that high anger expression by custodial mothers will be related to poorer adjustment in both boys and girls.

In summary, sons' adjustment was positively influenced by high maternal S-Anger, whereas daughters' adjustment was negatively influenced by this anger experience. There was also a trend for the maternal expression of Anger-Out to negatively affect children's behavior, irrespective of gender. This suggests that the experience and expression of anger affect the adjustment of boys and girls in a different manner.

A possible explanation for the differential adjustment of boys versus girls rests on the fact that S-Anger items reflect the experience, rather than the overt expression, of anger. The experience of anger in the Action Potential factor (e.g., "I feel like banging on the table"; "I feel like swearing"), although not a direct expression of anger, may involve positive energy related to the intense anger experience. Such energy might, hypothetically, express itself in increased maternal assertiveness and an enhanced capacity to set limits on adolescent sons. This would explain the good adjustment of these boys in the high S-Anger condition of the present study. Daughters were negatively affected by their mothers' high S-Anger experience. It is suggested that daughters may be more sensitive to covert emotional cues and more likely to use the mother as an emotional role model than are sons. As a result, daughters are more likely to imitate the mother's S-Anger experience, which ultimately expresses itself in poorer adjustment in girls.

Maternal anger expression on the Anger-Out scale is more explicit and serves as a clear negative role model for both sons and daughters. Indeed, the items on this scale (e.g., "I say nasty things"; "I do things like slam doors") suggest implusiveness and loss of control, which could adversely affect children's adjustment.

Research and Intervention

Intervention should be designed to diminish those adverse factors, related to parental anger, that contribute to poor postdivorce adjustment. For example, emotional resolution that helps custodial mothers integrate the positive *and* negative aspects of the past should diminish anger and negative attributions, such as blaming the ex-spouse, thus promoting parental cooperation. This is important because postdivorce parental cooperation is related to good adjustment in children (Camara & Resnick, 1988, 1989). Similarly, diminished parental anger may prevent attributive processes that negatively affect parental judgments of children, parent–child interaction, and ultimately children's adjustment. Emotional resolution of anger would also diminish the possibility of parents serving as negative role models for their children.

This study suggests that the experience of anger may sometimes be useful, particularly in the interaction between custodial mothers and their sons. Hence, anger that promotes parental assertion and limit-setting by mothers in the postdivorce situation should not necessarily be dissipated. When making intervention decisions, clinicians must carefully consider whether a custodial mother or father is involved, as well as the child's gender. These factors affect decisions regarding how to deal effectively with parental anger.

Future research might systematically investigate how anger, acting through mediating variables such as cognitive appraisals and parent–child interaction, ultimately affects children's adjustment. Illustrative of such an approach is a study by Kline, Johnston, and Tschann (1991), which found that parental conflict most strongly affects children's postdivorce adjustment through its adverse effect on parent–child relationships.

REFERENCES

Achenbach, T. M., & Edelbrock, C. S. (1983). *Manual for the child behavior checklist and revised child behavior profile.* Burlington, VT: University of Vermont Press.

Achenbach, T. M., & Edelbrock, C. S. (1987). *Manual for the youth self-report and profile.* Burlington, VT: University of Vermont Press.

Bandura, A. (1962). Social learning through imitation. In M. R. Jones (Ed.), *Nebraska symposium on motivation* (Vol. 10). Lincoln, NE: University of Nebraska Press.

Berkowitz, L. (1990). On the formation and regulation of anger and aggression: A cognitive-neoassociationistic analysis. *American Psychologist, 45,* 494–503.

Camara, K. A., & Resnick, G. (1988). Interparental conflict and cooperation: Factors moderating children's post-divorce adjustment. In E. M. Hetherington & J. D. Arasteh (Eds.), *Impact of divorce, single-parenting, and stepparenting on children* (pp. 169–195). Hillsdale, NJ: Erlbaum.

Camara, K. A., & Resnick, G. (1989). Styles of conflict resolution and cooperation between divorced parents: Effects on child behavior and adjustment. *American Journal of Orthopsychiatry, 59,* 560–575.

Dix, T., Reinhold, D. P., & Zambarano, R. J. (1990). Mothers: Judgements in moments of anger. *Merrill-Palmer Quarterly, 36,* 465–486.

Dreman, S., & Aldor, R. (1994a). Work or marriage? Competence in custodial mothers in the stabilization phase of the divorce process. *Journal of Divorce & Remarriage, 22,* 3–22.

Dreman, S., & Aldor, R. (1994b). A comparative study of custodial mothers and fathers in the stabilization phase of the divorce process. *Journal of Divorce & Remarriage, 21,* 59–79.

Dreman, S., & Aldor, R. (1994c). *The experience and expression of anger in a stressful society: Standardization of the STAXI in Israel.* Unpublished manuscript.

Emery, R. E. (1982). Interparental conflict and the children of discord and divorce. *Psychological Bulletin, 92,* 310–330.

Furstenberg, F. F. (1988). Child care after divorce and remarriage. In E. M. Hetherington & J. Arasteh (Eds.), *Impact of divorce, single-parenting, and stepparenting on children* (pp. 245–261). Hillsdale, NJ: Erlbaum.

Hauser, B. B. (1985). Custody in dispute: Legal and psychological profiles of contesting families. *Journal of the American Academy of Child Psychiatry, 24,* 575–582.

Herz Brown, J. (1988). The postdivorce family. In B. Carter & M. McGoldrick (Eds.), *The changing family life cycle: A framework for family therapy* (pp. 371–398). New York: Gardner.

Hetherington, E. M. (1981). Children and divorce. In R. W. Henderson (Ed.), *Parent-child interaction: Theory, research, and prospects* (pp. 33–58). New York: Academic Press.

Hetherington, E. M., Cox, M., & Cox, R. (1985). Long-term effects of divorce and remarriage on the adjustment of children. *Journal of the American Academy of Child Psychiatry, 24,* 518–530.

Hetherington, E. M., & Stanley-Hagan, M. (1986). Divorced fathers: Stress, coping, and adjustment. In M. Lamb (Ed.), *The father's role: Applied perspectives* (pp. 103–134). New York: Wiley.

Hornik, Y., & Meir, N. (1989). Meta-analyses of non-response in mail surveys. *Megamot, 32,* 386–400. (In Hebrew)

Johnson, J. R., Campbell, L. E., & Mayes, S. B. (1985). Latency children in post-separation and divorce disputes. *Journal of the American Academy of Child Psychiatry, 24,* 563–574.

Katz, R., & Pesach, N. (1985). Adjustment to divorce in Israel: A comparison between divorced men and women. *Journal of Marriage and the Family, 47,* 765–772.

Kelly, J. (1982). Divorce: The adult experience. In B. Wolman & G. Stricker (Eds.), *Handbook of developmental psychology.* Englewood Cliffs, NJ: Prentice-Hall.

Kitson, G., & Sussman, M. (1982). Marital complaints, demographic characteristics, and symptoms of mental distress in divorce. *Journal of Marriage and the Family, 44,* 87–101.

Kline, M., Johnston, J. R., & Tschann, J. (1991). The long shadow of marital conflict: A model of children's postdivorce adjustment. *Journal of Marriage and the Family, 53,* 297–309.

Rutter, M. (1971). Parent-child separation: Psychological effects on the children. *Journal of Child Psychology and Psychiatry, 12,* 233–260.

Spielberger, C. D. (1988). *Manual for the State-Trait Anger Expression Inventory* (STAXI). Odessa, FL: Psychological Assessment Resources.

Wallerstein, J. S. (1986). Women after divorce: Preliminary report from a ten-year follow-up. *American Journal of Orthopsychiatry, 56,* 65–77.

Wallerstein, J. S., & Kelly, J. (1980). *Surviving the breakup: How children and parents cope with divorce.* New York: Basic Books.

Zaslow, M. J. (1988). Sex differences in children's response to divorce: 1. Research methodology and postdivorce family forms. *American Journal of Orthopsychiatry, 58,* 355–378.

Zaslow, M. J. (1989). Sex differences in children's response to divorce: 2. Samples, variables, ages, and sources. *American Journal of Orthopsychiatry, 59,* 118–141.

Zilber, N., Auerbach, J., & Lerner, Y. (1994). Israeli norms for the Achenbach Child Behavior Checklist: Comparison of clinically-referred and non-referred children. *Israel Journal of Psychiatry and Related Sciences, 31,* 5–12.

6

Male Violence Against Female Partners: Roots in Male Socialization and Development

Ronald F. Levant
Cambridge Hospital/Harvard Medical School
Brookline, Massachusetts, USA

ABSTRACT

This chapter discusses battering from the perspective of the new psychology of men. After reviewing data indicating the extent of the problem of battering and recent work on typologies of batterers, an overview of the gender strain perspective on male emotion socialization and development is presented. The chapter then discusses, in some detail, how certain facets of male socialization potentiate battering: the injunction to avoid all things feminine, emotion socialization (including the overdevelopment of anger, vulnerability transformation, and the Rubber Band Syndrome), and normative developmental traumas.

In the fledgling field of the new psychology of men, the problem of male violence is one of the thorniest. Thus, it is no accident that Betz and Fitzgerald (1993), in a broad overview of the work done in this area over the past decade, observed that: "Conspicuous by its absence is any sustained attempt to analyze and intervene in what can only be considered one of the most serious social problems of our age—male violence against women" (p. 361). Part of the problem is that, prior to recent attempts to deconstruct masculinity (Brooks & Silverstein, 1995; Levant, 1992, 1995; Levant & Kopecki, 1995), violence was considered one of the foundations of healthy manhood. For example, in Brannon's (1985; David & Brannon, 1976) model of masculinity, "Give 'em hell" (i.e., seek adventure and risk, and accept violence if necessary) is one of the four injunctions of traditional masculinity ideology. Furthermore, Rotundo (1993) noted that American culture has long considered youthful male violence, in the form of boys fighting with their peers, a positive way to build character. The modern-day equivalent is the requirement, known to every man,

These ideas were originally presented at the symposium, "Men, Anger and Aggression," at the 102nd annual convention of the American Psychological Association, Los Angeles, California, August 1994.

92   R. F. LEVANT

that: "When they were children and pushed down on the playground, it was their job to come up with a handful of gravel rather than [a faceful of] tears" (Grusznski & Bankovics, 1990, p. 209).

We are now in the midst of a major shift in the tectonic plates of gender relations. What was once excused with the cliche that "boys will be boys" is now being recognized for the serious problem that it is. Male-on-male violence is an enormous problem—one that is beyond the scope of this chapter. With regard to male violence against female partners, this phenomenon is not limited to physical aggression, but also includes a wide range of psychological violence, such as verbal harassment, restraint of normal activities, denial of access to resources, sexual coercion, and sexual assault (Brown, 1993). Due to space limitations, psychological violence is not considered here. Rather, this chapter focuses specifically on physical violence by men toward their intimate partners, also known as *battering* (Carden, 1994; Walker, 1979, 1984). The chapter discusses, in turn, the extent of the problem, typologies of batterers, and the process of male socialization and development. It puts the spotlight on certain facets of the male socialization process that potentiate battering.

MALE VIOLENCE AGAINST WOMEN: EXTENT OF THE PROBLEM

The victimization of women by their male partners is of towering dimensions. C. Everett Koop, the former U.S. Surgeon General, identified *domestic violence* as "the number one health problem for women in the United States, causing more injuries to women than automobile accidents, muggings, and rapes combined" (Hart, 1993, p. 18). Straus and colleagues, using national probability sampling, estimated that at least 2 to 3 million women are assaulted by their male partners each year in the United States (Straus & Gelles, 1990; Straus, Gelles, & Steinmetz, 1980). These investigators also found that one eighth of husbands had physically abused their wives in the preceding 12 months (Straus & Gelles, 1990). In these studies, most of the assaults involved "minor" violence (e.g., pushing, slapping, shoving, or throwing things). However, assaults took the form of severe beatings in 3 out of every 100 cases (Straus & Gelles, 1990). Other investigators have estimated that between one fifth and one third of American women will be assaulted by a male partner during their adult lives (Frieze, Knoble, Washburn, & Zomnir, 1980; Russell, 1982).

Browne (1993) pointed out that figures based on these types of national surveys represent marked underestimates of the problem. Such surveys typically do not include groups of women who are especially at risk, such as very poor women, those who do not speak English well, those in military families, and those who are hospitalized, homeless, or incarcerated. She suggested that a more accurate estimate "may be as high as 4 million women severely assaulted by male partners in an average twelve month period" (Browne, 1993, p. 1078).

These staggering statistics are the result of both power differentials between men and women—in which men have the greater physical, economic, and political power in this country—and the socialization of males according to a masculinity ideology that devalues women, glorifies violence, and restricts the expression of emotions. The power differentials and the public policy response (i.e., Senator Biden's Violence Against Women Act) have been addressed in recent publications (Biden, 1993; Browne, 1993; Goodman, Koss, Fitzgerald, Russo, & Keita, 1993; Jones, 1994). This chapter focuses on the male emotion socialization and developmental processes. But first, some recent literature on family violence is briefly discussed to get a clearer picture of the types of men who are violent toward their female partners.

TYPOLOGIES OF MALE BATTERERS

Holtzworth-Munroe and Stuart (1994) comprehensively reviewed both the "rational/deductive" and "empirical/inductive" literature on typologies of male batterers, and identified three dimensions that have been useful in distinguishing among subtypes of batterers: Severity of Marital Violence, Generality of the Violence (i.e., toward the wife or toward others), and Psychopathology/Personality Disorders. Using these dimensions, the authors constructed a typology consisting of three subtypes of batterers: family only, dysphoric/borderline, and generally violent/antisocial. They also offered a developmental model, based on attachment theory, that illustrates how each subtype differs on variables of theoretical interest.

The family-only group (which should have been named *wife-only*) is the least offensive of the lot. These men exhibit low severity of violence, inflicted only on their wives, and at worst show evidence of mild forms of psychopathology, such as passive-dependent personality disorder. These men are the most likely to express remorse over and seek treatment for their violence, and are probably the most treatable. The authors estimated that 50% of batterers are of this type.

The middle group, the dysphoric/borderline batterers, exhibits moderately severe violence in and out of the home, and tends to have a range of diagnoses, including depression and schizoid and borderline personality disorders. The authors estimated that 25% of batterers are of this type. This group appears to be less homogeneous than the other two. Some subtypes of batterers in this group may be more treatable than others.

At the other end of the spectrum, the generally violent/antisocial batterers exhibit severe marital violence, including psychological and sexual abuse. They are generally violent toward others outside of the home, and are involved in criminal behavior and alcohol and drug abuse. When assessed, they tend to be diagnosed as antisocial or sociopathic (i.e., in two studies they showed elevations on Scales 2 [psychopathy] and 4 [depression] on the Minnesota Multiphasic Personality Inventory [MMPI]). The authors estimated that 25% of batterers are of this type.

This last group has a lot in common with the Type 1 batterers, who seem to calm down when they are aggressive toward their wives, recently identified by Gottman et al. (1995) in a study that combined interactional, self-report, and physiological measures. The Gottman et al. Type 1 batterers are thought to enact passionless, methodical violence, judging from the slowing of their heart rates during arguments with their wives, in which they were more emotionally aggressive than other groups of batterers. These batterers are the least treatable. Ironically, as Jacobson (1993) observed, one of the most common treatment interventions for batterers—anger-management training—may in fact increase their pathology, rather than ameliorate it, by giving them even more control over their violence.

MALE EMOTION SOCIALIZATION AND DEVELOPMENT

A theoretical model for understanding the emotional development of men has been presented elsewhere (Levant, 1992, 1995; Levant & Kopecki, 1995). The model integrates social learning and modern psychoanalytic perspectives, and takes into account the gender role socialization process and certain normative developmental traumas for males, which are briefly summarized here. This theory is based on the Gender Role Strain Paradigm (Pleck, 1981), which proposes that, to the extent that parents and peers subscribe to gender role stereotypes, children will be socialized accordingly. Prior to the late 1960s, traditional masculinity ideology prevailed. Hence, male children brought up in the postwar era were reared to conform to traditional norms of masculinity, of which Levant et al. (1992) identified seven: (a) avoidance of all things feminine, (b) restrictive emotionality, (c) toughness and aggression, (d) self-reliance, (e) achievement and status, (f) nonrelational attitudes toward sexuality, and (g) homophobia.

Emotion Socialization

Boys start out more emotionally expressive than girls, and remain so until at least 1 year of age. The developmental influences of mothers, fathers, and peer groups combine to result in the suppression and channeling of male emotionality: (a) Mothers work harder to manage their more excitable and emotional male infants, going to special lengths to ensure their son's contentment. (b) Fathers take an active interest in their sons after the 13th month of life, and from that point on socialize them along the strictly defined lines of traditional masculinity. (c) Both parents participate in the gender-differentiated development of language for emotions, discouraging their son's expression of both vulnerable and caring emotions, and encouraging his expression of anger through aggression, including retaliation. (d) Gender-segregated peer groups complete the job, helping boys learn action skills rather than emotional skills, and ensuring compliance with traditional norms.

Gender-bifurcated socialization has three major results: (a) widespread alexithymia (the inability to put emotions into words), (b) overdevelopment of anger and development of the emotional funnel system (the tendency to funnel the expression of vulnerable emotions through the channel of anger), and (c) nonrelational sexuality (or unconnected lust) due to the suppression and channeling of tender feelings into sexuality.

Normative Developmental Traumas

Normative developmental traumas during the separation-individuation phase of early childhood, in which boys are required to give up their dependence on their mothers much earlier than are girls, has three major consequences: (a) Defensive autonomy: As boys grow up, yearnings for maternal closeness and attachment bring up fears of losing their sense of separateness and their masculine identity. Consequently, many adult men feel much safer being alone than being close to someone. (b) Unconscious dependence on women: The yearnings for maternal attachment never completely go away, but go underground and take the form of often unconscious, certainly unacknowledged dependence on women. (c) Destructive entitlement: This loss of the holding environment, which robs boys of the tranquility of childhood, is never acknowledged, much less mourned. It leaves men vulnerable to developing "destructive entitlement"—a feeling that people in their adult lives are required to make up for these losses.

CONTRIBUTIONS OF MALE SOCIALIZATION TO BATTERING

In this final section, certain facets of the male socialization process that potentiate battering are discussed. The intent here is not to imply that all men are batterers, or even that all men are capable of battering. Rather, it is to shed some light on those socialization processes that, in combination with the power differentials noted earlier, have made battering the problem that it is.

Avoid All Things Feminine

Battering is potentiated by the "avoid all things feminine" dictum of traditional masculinity ideology, which is strongly reinforced during the middle childhood years of gender-segregated play. This dictum fosters the devaluation of women, which in turn provides justification for the expression of aggression against females.

Emotion Socialization

The overdevelopment of anger. The male emotion socialization process potentiates battering by (a) overemphasizing the expression of anger through acts of aggression, and (b) underemphasizing the ability to identify and express vulnerable and caring emotions, some of which then come to be expressed aggressively. This complex aspect of the socialization process can be seen in some of the literature on language development, where it has been found that parents encourage their sons' expression of anger and aggression, and discourage their sons' learning to express vulnerable emotions (such as sadness and fear). Fivush (1989) found that mothers spoke more about sadness with daughters than sons, and only spoke about anger with sons. Greif, Alvarez, and Ulman (1981) had parents "read" stories to their children using wordless books; the authors videotaped and transcribed these conversations. Mothers talked about anger twice as frequently with sons as compared with daughters. Finally, Fuchs and Thelen (1988) found that school-age sons expected their parents to react negatively to the expression of sadness, whereas school-age daughters expected their mothers to react more positively to the expression of sadness than they would to anger. Thus, the expression of anger through aggression is fostered in boys—an aspect of emotion socialization that potentiates battering.

Vulnerability transformation. As a result of male emotion socialization, anger is one of the few emotions boys are encouraged to express. Consequently, the outlawed vulnerable emotions, such as hurt, disappointment, fear, and shame, get funneled into the anger channel. Long (1987) referred to this as "the male emotional funnel system," the final common pathway for all those shameful, vulnerable emotions, which it is too unmanly to express directly. This process, which I call vulnerability transformation, is seen in certain batterers who transform vulnerable feelings such as shame and hurt into rage, into which they ignite instantaneously, as when a match is struck to magnesium. Vulnerability transformation has been observed by other investigators, such as Faulk (1974), who described the "dependent-passive" batterer—a man who generally tries to please his wife, but explodes violently in response to some perceived slight on her part.

The Rubber Band Syndrome. Due to the general lack of sensitivity to emotional states that characterizes alexithymia, many men do not recognize anger in its mild forms, such as irritation or annoyance, but only detect it when they are very angry. Such men let minor irritations build and build until they explode. Such men may be victims of a process named the *Rubber Band Syndrome*. This process has also been described in the literature (see e.g., Caesar's [1986] "nonexposed altruist" and Hershorn & Rosenbaum's [1991] overcontrolled hostility group).

Are males more prone than females to express anger in words? Recent research using the State–Trait Anger Expression inventory (STAXI) State Anger (S-Anger) scale (Spielberger, 1994) indicates that males score higher on the S-Anger scale as well as two of its subscales: "Feel like expressing anger physically" and "Feel like expressing anger verbally." At first blush, the findings on the latter subscale are surprising and would seem to weaken support for the proposition that male emotion socialization encourages males to express anger through acts of aggression. On the contrary, this finding seems to suggest that men are even more prone than women to express their anger in words— a nonaggressive, emotionally skilled form of expression, as might be captured, for example, in the following hypothetical item: "Feel like telling my spouse that I am angry at her for what she did this morning." However, although the two items that comprise this subscale do reflect the expression of anger verbally as compared with its expression physically ("Feel like screaming" and "Feel like shouting at someone"), they do not reflect the emotionally skilled expression of anger in words, but rather reflect the venting of anger through vocalizations (including verbal and paralinguistic communication). Hence, these results do in fact support the proposition that males are socialized to express anger through physical and verbal acts of aggression.

Trauma

The normative developmental traumas of early childhood, which result in defensive autonomy, unconscious dependence on women, and destructive entitlement, at the very least potentiate a tendency toward exploitative relationships—in which a man assigns a considerable number of his needs to his partner, which he expects her to care for without any requirement for reciprocity on his part. In addition, any behavior of the wife that threatens to make the husband aware of his dependence on her can arouse feelings of shame, which might then get transformed into rage.

In cases where the traumatization is more severe than is normative, these dynamics can potentiate two related forms of battering. The first is one in which the man is *desperately dependent* on his partner. This type is similar to Faulk's (1974) "dependent-suspicious" batterer, who is irrationally jealous of his wife, very dependent on her, and controlling of her actions. It is also similar to Elbow's (1977) "defender," who is overly dependent on his wife and overprotects her, admixing love and hate. The second type is termed *narcissistic*. This type of man experiences an enormous sense of destructive entitlement, and relates to his wife as if she were part of himself (or a *self-object*, in Kohout's [1971] sense of the term). Unconsciously, in relating to his partner not as a separate being but as an extension of himself, he may expect her to do for him as his mother did before he was required to separate from her: to anticipate and satisfy his every physical, psychological, and emotional need. When his partner fails to do that—whether by forgetting to restock the refrigerator with beer or falling short in her ability to shore up his flagging sense of self-esteem— he gets angry. Sometimes he gets furious, and at times he turns violent. A batterer of this type attempts to justify his violent behavior as a "loss of control," by which he really means he fears losing control of his wife, whom he regards as an essential part of himself. This type is similar to Elbow's (1977) "incorporator," who sees his partner as part of himself and needs her to complete himself.

CONCLUSION

This chapter attempted to begin the enormous, but overdue task of examining the problem of male violence against female partners from the perspective of the new psychology of men. This problem has been studied for some time by family violence researchers. It is clear that it is of huge proportions and, further, that it has political, social, and economic roots, in addition to those more psychological in nature. It is also clear, from the psychological perspective, that the problem is very complex—batterers are not a homogeneous group. New work on developing systems to classify batterers is promising. Further work in this area, including attempts to validate the classification systems, may eventually offer reliable methods to determine which batterers can benefit from treatment and which cannot.

The new psychology of men may offer a fresh perspective for this endeavor. By recasting male socialization and development from a gender-aware perspective, the new psychology of men has offered insights into the roots of a wide range of contemporary male problems. This chapter highlighted that a preliminary application of this perspective to the phenomenon of battering has begun to yield some insights into its roots. Continued work in this area may result in the development of a gender-aware theoretical foundation for developing classification systems.

REFERENCES

Betz, N. E., & Fitzgerald, L. F. (1993). Individuality and diversity: Theory and research in counseling psychology. *Annual Review of Psychology, 44*, 343–381.

Biden, J. R., Jr. (1993). Violence against women: The Congressional response. *American Psychologist, 48*, 1059–1061.

Brannon, R. (1985). A scale for measuring attitudes about masculinity. In A. Sargent (Ed.), *Beyond sex roles* (pp. 110–116). St. Paul, MN: West.

Brooks, G. R., & Silverstein, L. B. (1995). Understanding the dark side of masculinity: An interactive systems model. In R. F. Levant & W. S. Pollack (Eds.), *A new psychology of men* (pp. 280–333). New York: Basic Books.

Browne, A. (1993). Violence against women by male partners. Prevalence, outcomes, and policy implications. *American Psychologist, 48*, 1077–1087.

Caesar, P. L. (1986). Men who batter: A heterogeneous group. In L. K. Hamburger (Chair), *The male batterer: Characteristics of a heterogeneous population*. Symposium presented at the annual meeting of the American Psychological Association, Washington, DC, August 23.

Carden, A.D. (1994). Wife abuse and the wife abuser: Review and recommendations. *The Counseling Psychologist, 22*(4), 539–582.

David, D., & Brannon, R. (Eds.). (1976). *The forty-nine percent majority: The male sex role*. Reading, MA: Addison-Wesley.

Elbow, M. (1977). Theoretical considerations of violent marriages. *Social Casework, 58*, 515–526.

Faulk, M. (1974, July). Men who assault their wives. *Medicine, Science and the Law*, pp. 180–183.

Fivush, R. (1989). Exploring sex differences in the emotional content of mother child conversations about the past. *Sex Roles, 20*, 675–691.

Frieze, I. H., Knoble, J., Washburn, C., & Zomnir, G. (1980, March). *Types of battered women*. Paper presented at the meeting of the Annual Research

Conference of the Association for Women in Psychology, Santa Monica, CA.

Fuchs, D., & Thelen, M. (1988). Children's expected interpersonal consequences of communicating their affective state and reported likelihood of expression. *Child Development, 59*, 1314–1322.

Goodman, L. A., Koss, M. P., Fitzgerald, L. F., Russo, N. F., & Keita, G. P. (1993). Male violence against women. Current research and future directions. *American Psychologist, 48*, 1054–1058.

Gottman, J. M., Jacobson, N. S., Rushe, R. H., Short, J. W., Babcock, J., La Taillade, J. J., & Waltz, J. (1995). The relationship between heart rate reactivity, emotionally aggressive behavior and general violence in batterers. *Journal of Family Psychology, 9*(3).

Greif, E. B., Alvarez, M., & Ulman, K. (1981, April). *Recognizing emotions in other people: Sex differences in socialization.* Paper presented at the meeting of the Society for Research in Child Development, Boston, MA.

Grusznski, R., & Bankovics, G. (1990). Treating men who batter: A group approach. In D. Moore & F. Leafgren (Eds.), *Problem solving strategies and interventions for men in conflict* (pp. 201–211). Alexandria, VA: American Association for Counseling and Development.

Hart, B. (1993). The legal road to freedom. In M. Hansen & M. Harway (Eds.), *Battering and family therapy. A feminist perspective* (pp. 13–28). Newbury Park, CA: Sage.

Hershorn, M., & Rosenbaum, A. (1991). Over- vs. undercontrolled hostility: Application of the construct to the classification of martially violent men. *Violence and Victims, 6*, 151–158.

Holtzworth-Munroe, A., & Stuart, G. L. (1994). Typologies of male batterers: Three subtypes and the differences among them. *Psychological Bulletin, 116*(3), 476–497.

Jacobson, N. (1993, August). *Domestic violence: What are the marriages like?* Paper presented at the annual convention of the American Psychological Association, Toronto, Ontario, Canada.

Jones, A. (1994). *Next time she'll be dead: Battering and how to stop it.* Boston: Beacon.

Kohout, H. (1971). *The analysis of the self: A systematic approach to the psychoanalytic treatment of narcissistic personality disorders.* New York: International Universities Press.

Levant, R. F. (1992). Toward the reconstruction of masculinity. *Journal of Family Psychology, 5*, 379–402.

Levant, R. F. (1995). Toward the reconstruction of masculinity. In R. F. Levant & W. S. Pollack (Eds.), *A new psychology of men* (pp. 229–251). New York: Basic Books.

Levant, R. F., Hirsch, L., Celentano, E., Cozza, T., Hill, S., MacEachern, M., Marty, N., & Schnedeker, J. (1992). The male role: An investigation of norms and stereotypes. *Journal of Mental Health Counseling, 14*(3), 325–337.

Levant, R., & Kopecki, G. (1995). *Masculinity reconstructed.* New York: Dutton.

Long, D. (1987). Working with men who batter. In M. Scher, M. Stevens, G. Good, & G. A. Eichenfield (Eds.), *Handbook of counseling and psychotherapy with men* (pp. 305–320). Newbury Park, CA: Sage.

Pleck, J. H. (1981). *The myth of masculinity.* Cambridge, MA: MIT Press.

Rotundo, E. A. (1993). *American manhood: Transformations in masculinity from the revolution to the modern era.* New York: Basic Books.

Russell, D. E. H. (1982). *Rape in marriage.* New York: Macmillan.

Spielberger, C. S. (1994, August). *Gender differences in the experience, expression, and control of anger.* Paper presented at the annual convention of the American Psychological Association, Los Angeles, CA.

Straus, M. A., & Gelles, R. J. (1990). *Physical violence in American families: Risk factors and adaptations to violence in 8145 families.* New Brunswick, NJ: Transaction.

Straus, M. A., Gelles, R. J., & Steinmetz, S. (1980). *Behind closed doors: Violence in the American family.* Garden City, NJ: Anchor Press.

Walker, L. E. (1979). *The battered woman.* New York: Harper & Row.

Walker, L. E. (1984). *The battered woman syndrome.* New York: Springer.

III

STRESS IN THE WORKPLACE

7

Job Stress in the Shifting Canadian Economy

Chok C. Hiew
University of New Brunswick, Canada

ABSTRACT

Increased stress in the workplace, produced by a persistent double-digit unemployment and downward shifts in the Canadian economy, was examined in two studies of employed and unemployed workers. In the first study, the Job Stress Survey (JSS) was given to 104 employees of a government department, in which salaries were frozen for the past few years. Mean stress scores for the JSS (including Stress Index and Job Pressure, and Lack of Support scales) were found to be similar to those reported by U.S. samples. The findings also demonstrate that the JSS is an effective tool for diagnosing specific sources of occupational stress. In the second study, unemployed adults participated in a 10-week job preparedness and anger/stress-management program. The results indicate the value of incorporating Spielberger's AHA! Syndrome (Spielberger, Krasner, & Solomon, 1988) in evaluating the effectiveness of job retraining programs for unemployed workers.

As with most Western industrialized nations, Canada is in a period of economic transition. It faces a new global economic order characterized by such realities as a protracted recession, the permanent loss of manufacturing jobs to newly industrialized nations in Asia, more competitive forces elsewhere, loss of traditional global markets, the negative fall in the gross domestic product (GDP), a spiralling national debt, and the loss of faith in the ability of government, political, and financial leaders to turn the country around. Undoubtedly, it is futile for Canadians to hope that tinkering with the current system and riding out the current recession will offer a quick return to the status quo of more affluent times.

The effects of these new realities on Canada are profound and range far beyond the economic domain. The social network of services and medical care that Canadians have taken for granted is fast eroding, as drastic cuts in federal spending take their toll. Taking the case of children, the percentage of children living in Canada at a subsistence level has climbed steadily. Canada is not alone in discovering that the earliest victims of hard economic times are helpless, poor children. Globally, in developing countries in Asia, coinciding with economic development, the commercial sexual exploitation of children—through child trafficking, pornography, and prostitution—has reached alarming proportions (Hiew, 1992a, 1995).

THE SHIFT IN THE CANADIAN ECONOMY

The Canadian national debt continues to soar, with no sign of abating. In the province of New Brunswick, for example, despite government claims to have exercised "strict expenditure control measures," the budget for the 1993–1994 fiscal year ended nearly "three times deeper in the red than expected" (Staff, *Daily Gleaner*, August 19, 1994, front page). In fact, despite increased revenues from higher personal income tax, general taxes, and increased federal government transfer payments, as well as restraint in fiscal policy, the province has experienced serious annual deficits every year from 1987 to 1993. Unquestionably, there will continue to be daunting social, employment, and health implications. As the rate of the national debt increases and taxation far outpaces its productivity, the Canadian economic and social orders may shift to a crisis level, with profound effects on its citizens.

In recent years, most changes in the workplace have been in a negative direction. Prospects for creating new jobs and reducing double-digit unemployment rates remain uncertain and doubtful, as both government and business fail to revive the economy and create new jobs. Many young Canadians are unable to find employment and decent paying jobs even after completing a college education. Traditional careers have almost disappeared from the job market, and many new jobs are on a contractual basis. Therefore, young employees expect that they will have to look for new jobs on a periodic basis.

Although job prospects for the well educated remain relatively bright in some areas (e.g., high-tech and service industries), prospects for youths with limited education and marketable skills are dim or nonexistent. Predictably, the rate of chronic unemployment for the less educated has led to an alarming expansion in government expenditures in the form of income assistance and unemployment insurance payouts. Many young and mid-career workers face sudden loss or reduction in employment or early mandatory retirement as employee downsizing continues in the manufacturing, commercial, and government agencies. Those who have jobs are appreciative, but encounter greater job pressure and uncertainty as employers demand that their reduced workforce do more, often with less or frozen pay. These increased demands have also infringed on family life, as evidenced by the global increase in the number of work-related parental absences from young families (Hiew, 1992b).

The new sources of economic stress demand an assessment of occupational stress so that social solidarity will prevail in avoiding and preventing threats on the deterioration of a healthful worklife. Major shifts in the understanding and means of dealing with economic stressors need to be conceptualized and enacted.

This chapter reports findings related to job stress in two employment situations. In the first study, the Job Stress Survey (JSS; Spielberger, 1994) was administered to a sample of employees in a large government department, following several years of downsizing. The JSS has been used to identify specific sources of stress, including both organizational demands and interpersonal stressors typically reported by employees in various occupations (Spielberger & Reheiser, 1994a). The present study reports on the stress level of employees from various occupational levels; it also explores the value of the JSS in diagnosing and developing interventions for workplace stress.

In the second study, the focus is on a program designated to help unemployed adults prepare for work. Retraining has been the routine national strategy to help the unemployed learn marketable skills required by the job market. However, many unemployed youths seem unable to cope well with psychosocial stressors that also impede their efforts in academic upgrading and learning (Hiew, 1992c). The purpose here is to report on the efficacy of a 10-week job preparedness and anger/stress-management program.

TOWARD A HEALTHFUL WORKLIFE

Although there is no denying that Canada is facing an unprecedented economic crisis, no solution can exclude having a healthy workforce. A *healthy worklife* can be defined as one that promotes health and well-being in the workplace. A broad definition can be drawn from the World Health Organization's (WHO) notion of *occupational health*, in which physical and psychosocial well-being are included, as well as protection from adverse working conditions and health hazards. In Canada, as in many other countries, there is much hesitation in accepting psychosocial distress as a work problem.

Despite evidence that workers suffer from stress-related illnesses that spring directly from the work environment (e.g., Hiew, 1989; Orlandi, 1986; Quick, Murphy, & Hurrell, 1992), job stress has yet to be recognized in Canadian occupational health policies. It has also been clearly established that prolonged work stress is detrimental to the quality of work (e.g., Cooper & Payne, 1988; Keita & Sauter, 1992). Management responsible for sustaining high productivity and facing greater competition in the current economic context cannot ignore the issue of occupational stress.

A conceptual model for promoting a healthy worklife in organizations can be based on Albee's (1979) formula for the prevention of psychopathology. Simply put, the lack of health is considered to be created by biopsychosocial stress factors and an absence of adequate coping skills, self-esteem, and social support. Elias (1987) modified this concept by extending it from individual to potential organizational change as well.

In worksite settings, a healthier worklife may mean reducing job pressure stressors (i.e., frequent work changes, excessive paperwork, meeting deadlines, and frequent interruptions) and eliminating health hazards (e.g., safety measures in handling equipment). In addition to reducing organizational stressors, measures meant to increase employee competencies and empowerment are just as important. Steps can be taken to improve socialization practices (e.g., training programs to motivate and improve supervisor–worker relations) and to provide greater availability of social support among co-workers and with management (i.e., instrumental, emotional, or informational support).

Also, greater opportunities for connectedness with others to reduce isolation and enhance personal efficacy can be encouraged (e.g., help in conflicting work–parenting roles, access to college training to increase knowledge, and upgrading of work skills).

Substantial literature also indicates that organizational and community level factors are related to psychological functioning (Jeger & Slotnick, 1982; Sarason, 1982). In the specific setting of work organizations, results of a national survey across Canada, conducted by the Canadian Mental Health Association (1984), have shown similar links between psychosocial health and well-being. Over 1,400 working Canadians were interviewed to determine: (a) attitudes and opinions about work, (b) job satisfaction, (c) stress on the job, and (d) various mental health concerns. The two major findings focused on the significance of the workplace as a social environment, and the importance of balancing work with other aspects of life.

These findings led to two proposals. One proposal was the establishment of "workplace education" to improve the quality of social interaction among management, subordinates, and co-workers. Specifically, programs were proposed to improve personal and interpersonal skills to reduce and manage job stress and conflicts in social relations, and to create social support networks between supervisors and co-workers to help troubled employees.

The second proposal came from the research finding that people want more choices in arranging their time. Specifically, programs were proposed so that employment complements, rather than dominates or inhibits, other fulfilling life endeavours, such as family and community involvement, as well as opportunities for further education and learning. The second goal was "worklife choices," aimed at creating more flexible work-time arrangements. Organizations were encouraged to consult with employees, unions, and government to assist individual workers in negotiating work arrangements and to build a new work policy consensus.

The issue of job stress—viewed as work demands and lack of organizational support, and their relationship to health promotion and enhancing job productivity—has become even more timely in the context of the shifting economy. There is a need to conceptualize job stress as an interaction between the emotional and social needs of the worker in an organizational context (Spielberger & Reheiser, 1994a). The first step is to comprehensively assess job stress prior to any planned intervention. The JSS is a recently developed generic psychometric measure for assessing job stress (Spielberger, 1994). It is designed to overcome some of the limitations of existing job stress measures. The JSS has been used to assess two stable job stress factors: Job Pressure and Lack of Support, both of which have adverse effects on white-collar corporate workers (Turnage & Spielberger, 1991), as well as large samples of university, corporate, and military personnel (Spielberger & Reheiser, 1994b).

THE JOB STRESS SURVEY

The JSS instrument consists of 30 items (Spielberger, 1994). Each JSS item is used to assess the perceived severity or amount of stress experienced (on a

Table 7.1 JSS job stress factors and stressor items

Job stressor	
Job pressure	Lack of support
1. Working overtime	1. Lack of advancement
2. Assignment of new duties	2. Fellow workers not doing their jobs
3. Dealing with crisis	3. Inadequate supervisor support
4. Not in job description	4. Lack of recognition
5. Increased responsibility	5. Poor equipment
6. On-the-spot decisions	6. Poor supervisor relations
7. Frequent changes in activities	7. Negative attitude toward organization
8. Excessive paperwork	8. Participation in policymaking
9. Meeting deadlines	9. Low salary
10. Insufficient personal time	10. Poorly motivated co-workers

9-point scale) and the frequency of occurrence of the stressor (the number of days that stressor occurred in the past 6 months, again on a 9-point scale), which are likely to adversely affect the psychological well-being of employees. Examples of the 30 JSS job stressors include: "assignment of disagreeable duties," "excessive paperwork," and "working overtime." Factor analyses of the JSS have consistently identified two major job stress factors: (a) *Job Pressure*, which assesses aspects of work stress such as: "assignment of increased responsibility" and "making critical on-the-spot decisions"; and (b) *Lack of Support* within the workplace, such as: "inadequate support by supervisor," "difficulty getting along with supervisor," and "lack of participation in policymaking decisions." The following nine JSS scores were computed:

1. *Job Stress Severity:* Based on the sum of the scores of the 30 items. A score of 50 indicates average (moderate) stress severity.
2. *Job Stress Frequency:* Based on the sum of the scores of the frequency ratings of the 30 individual items. It has been empirically determined that a score of 35–40 indicates moderate stress frequency.
3. *Job Stress Index:* Measures the general stress level; computed from the cross-products of the 30 severity and frequency ratings. A score of 20 indicates moderate stress index.
4. *Job Pressure Severity:* Based on 10 job pressure items (see Table 7.1 for specific stressors) on the Job Pressure subscale. A score of 42–50 indicates average severity.
5. *Lack of Support Severity:* Based on 10 stressors (see Table 7.1) from the Organizational Support subscale. A score of 55–60 indicates average support severity.
6. *Job Pressure Frequency:* Based on the frequency of occurrence of the 10 stressors from the Job Pressure subscale. A score of 40–48 indicates moderate job pressure frequency.
7. *Lack of Support Frequency:* Based on the frequency of the other set of 10 stressors from the Organizational Support subscale. Moderate stress is shown by scores between 26–36.

8. *Job Pressure Index:* Based on the cross-products of the severity and frequency ratings of the Job Pressure items (i.e., measuring information about the amount of stress coming from the job itself). A score of 20–25 indicates average job pressure index.
9. *Lack of Support Index:* Based on the cross-products of the severity and frequency items of the Lack of Support items (i.e., amount of stress from the organizational and interpersonal contexts in which the employee works). A score of 20 indicates average index.

STUDY I. JOB STRESS IN GOVERNMENT EMPLOYEES

In the present study, the JSS was administered to a Canadian sample of managerial, professional, and clerical employees of the New Brunswick Department of Transport, a provincial government agency. Four branches—Planning, Traffic Engineering, Motor Vehicle (registration, driver records, and accounting), and Human Resources—participated in the survey.

One hundred and four employees completed the JSS. The number of subjects for each branch were: Planning ($n = 41$), 87% of total employees in the branch; Traffic Engineering ($n = 29$), 71% of total; Human Resources ($n = 18$), 82% of the total; and Motor Vehicle ($n = 16$), from three sections of the branch. The percentage of females in each branch was: Planning (24%), Traffic Engineering (27%), Motor Vehicle (81%), and Human Resources (100%). The mean age of employees for all branches combined was 39.5 years. Only 7 (out of 104) of these government workers were age 50 or above.

Results and Discussion

Table 7.2 shows the mean ratings and standard deviations for each branch for the nine JSS scores. In general, the mean stress ratings suggested that they were comparable with the ratings obtained for other corporations tested in the United States (Spielberger & Reheiser, 1994b).

Mean scores for the combined data of all branches showed moderate stress levels for most of the nine JSS scales. The major difference when compared with previous studies was that the Job Stress Frequency, especially Job Pressure Frequency, appeared lower for the Canadian sample.

Although there were some variations among the four branches, for seven of nine scales mean stress ratings were similar across the four branches, showing nonsignificant differences (see Table 7.2). Among the four branches, the Human Resources employees stood out as having the highest mean stress ratings. Significant high stress levels were specifically indicated in Job Pressure Index and Job Pressure Frequency scores. Apparently the nature of the work (support and services to all branches of the department) generated higher stress for Human Resources employees, for whom the job stressors were predominantly associated with the job itself. These results are shown in Table 7.3.

In comparing the Planning and Traffic Engineering branches, there were noticeable differences in the sources of stress. Traffic Engineering ratings reflected perceived higher stress in Job Pressure Severity and Frequency items in comparison with the Planning employees, where higher stress was perceived in the Lack of Support stressors. Numerically, Motor Vehicle had the lowest stress ratings among all sections in terms of Job Stress Index and Frequency, as well as Job Pressure Index and Frequency.

Table 7.3 shows the specific job stressors that were ranked highest by at least 25% of employees for each branch. The Human Resources branch showed the greatest number of job stressors (6) that were ranked highest in comparison with the other branches. Stress categories included both stressors from Job Pressure (e.g., "noisy work area," "frequent interruptions," "meeting deadlines," and "excessive paperwork") as well as Lack of Support ("inadequate supervisor support" and "negative attitudes toward organization") categories.

The Planning branch had four job stressors, three of which were in the Lack of Support category (e.g., "low salary," "poor opportunity for advancement," and "poorly motivated co-workers"). In addition, "frequent interruptions" was another job stressor. Motor Vehicle had similar (but one less) highly ranked job stressors (e.g., "poor opportunity for advancement," "low salary," and "frequent interruptions"). Finally, for Traffic Engineering, of the three identified stressors, two were similar to those stated in the Human Resources branch (e.g., "excessive paperwork" and "noisy work area"). The third stressor was "fellow workers not doing their job."

"Noisy work area" was ranked as the most severe stressor by the Human Resources employees, and was given the second highest rank by the Traffic Engineering branch, but this stressor is not included among the 10-item sets that define the Job Pressure and Lack of Support subscales. In previous factor analyses of the severity ratings of the 30 JSS items, the loadings for "noisy work area" generally fall on the Job Pressure factor (e.g., Turnage & Spielberger, 1991). However, these loadings were not as strong or less stable across different work settings than those of the 10 items comprising the Job Pressure scale, listed in Table 7.1. These results suggest that a noisy environment may be quite stressful when frequently experienced, as in the Human Resources and Traffic Engineering branches of the present study, but this stressor is not ranked high in severity in departments where noise does not appear to be a problem.

The main findings and suggestions for programmed job stress management can be summarized as follows:

1. Results of the JSS of employees ($N = 104$) from four branches (Planning, Traffic Engineering, Motor Vehicle, and Human Resources) of the Department of Transport indicated that, as a group, the normative data were similar to other groups tested in various employment settings in the United States. For example, the median Job Stress Intensity score was 50 for both the Canadian and U.S. samples. Despite the negative shift in the Canadian economy and a bleak employment future, scores on the two major job stressors were at or below those of their American counterparts.

2. There were important differences found among the four branches in terms of types of job stressors (Job Pressure vs. Lack of Support), as well as the

Table 7.2 Mean stress ratings and standard deviations for the nine JSS stress scales for each branch of the Department of Transport

Stress scales		Planning (n = 41)	Branch of department Traffic Engineering (n = 29)	Motor Vehicle (n = 16)	Human Resources (n = 18)	Total mean (N = 104)	U.S. mean
1. Job Stress Severity	M	47.70	50.00	51.90	50.80	50.10	50
	SD	11.99	12.51	10.47	8.76	11.33	—
2. Job Stress Frequency	M	31.10	30.00	29.40	35.70	31.50	35–40
	SD	15.04	15.20	11.29	11.84	13.96	—
3. Job Stress Index	M	17.50	17.30	16.60	21.30	18.20	20
	SD	9.49	10.56	7.73	9.35	10.47	—
4. Job Pressure Severity	M	42.30	47.00	46.50	48.30	46.00	42–50
	SD	13.13	11.58	13.03	9.63	12.17	—
5. Lack of Support Severity	M	54.50	54.10	56.30	53.30	54.30	55–60
	SD	14.33	16.02	10.62	11.27	13.64	—

6. Job Pressure Frequency	*M*	32.46	34.40	28.70	41.30	34.00	40–48
	SD	17.86	17.72	15.19	14.66	17.03	—
7. Lack of Support Frequency	*M*	36.90	30.30	35.10	34.10	34.10	26–36
	SD	18.70	19.51	14.82	19.02	18.30	—
8. Job Pressure Index	*M*	14.20	17.80	13.60	22.70	17.10	20–25
	SD	10.40	9.90	7.74	10.33	10.22	—
9. Lack of Support Index	*M*	23.70	19.80	21.40	21.30	21.50	20
	SD	13.29	15.81	12.12	14.90	13.98	—

Table 7.3 Job stressors ranked highest by each branch of the Department of Transport

Branch	Job stressors*
Planning (*n* = 41)	1. Low salary 2. Advancement (lack of) 3. Frequent interruptions 4. Poorly motivated co-workers
Traffic Engineering (*n* = 29)	1. Excessive paperwork 2. Noisy work area 3. Fellow workers (not doing their job)
Motor Vehicle (*n* = 16)	1. Advancement (lack of) 2. Low salary 3. Frequent interruptions
Human Resources (*n* = 18)	1. Noisy work area 2. Frequent interruptions 3. Supervisor support (inadequate) 4. Meeting deadlines 5. Excessive paperwork 6. Negative attitudes (toward organization)

*Job stressors ranked highest by 25% or more of the employees in each branch.

intensity and frequency of specific job stress events. The highest ranked specific job stressors by branch were identified. Each branch provided information about stressors emanating from the job itself (Job Pressure) and from the organizational and interpersonal contexts (Lack of Support).

3. Further research is required to clarify the nature of each job stressor to understand the change strategies necessary to reduce work stress. For example, follow-up interviews with branch workers and Human Resources personnel are needed to develop steps to resolve each of the known organizational and interpersonal job stressors. Furthermore, given the mean age and gender proportion (below 40 years, 47% females, respectively) of the employees, the overlap between family life and worklife is especially salient. Such information can be provided to each branch administrator, and then can be used to mount efforts regarding job stress management. These stressors can be changed by improving the design and development of program, policy, or organizational change objectives. Programs on healthier worklife seminars and social support programs aimed at personal, interpersonal, and organizational change have been reported elsewhere (e.g., Hiew, 1987, 1989).

STUDY II.
ANGER MANAGEMENT IN UNEMPLOYED WORKERS

Youth programs aimed at promoting social competence as well as interconnectedness with employment organizations can improve the probability of finding employment (Hiew & MacDonald, 1990). However, greater problems are encountered with chronically unemployed workers and those with minimal educational backgrounds, especially in the current economic situation. Hiew (1992c) reported on an innovative job orientation and readiness program for unemployed youths (mean age 20 years). This "Foundations for Success" (FFS) program (developed by Christopher Collrin of Education for Success, Inc., and funded by the Canadian Employment and the New Brunswick Access Centre), which was conducted over 4 weeks, was completed by 52 participants (from an average of 10–12 participants per program). They showed significant changes in academic potential and motivation, classroom self-esteem, and self-efficacy to plan and implement career/life goals. In the 3-month follow-up, participants' self-efficacy to achieve career plans remained high, and over 75% enrolled in upgrading (high school equivalency) classes and community college-level trade courses.

Attempts to train/retrain and/or educate unemployed youths and adults who were formerly high school dropouts for entry into the workforce encounter a common problem: Many participants drop out before completing the job program. For example, Hiew (1992c) found that 25% dropped out of the community college-sponsored programs because of a variety of personal problems that impeded their desire to obtain remedial education for entry into the workforce. A major core problem was identified as inability to cope with stressors without resorting to some form of uncontrolled anger and violent behavior. The anger dimensions included feelings of hostility, as well as aggression that involved socially unacceptable behaviors.

Spielberger, Krasner, and Solomon (1988) described the anger–hostility–aggression triad as the "AHA! Syndrome." *Anger* refers to an emotional state consisting of angry feelings. *Hostility* involves angry feelings, but also has connotations of a complex set of attitudes that motivate aggressive behaviors directed at hurting or injuring others. *Aggression* concerns actual destructive or punitive behaviors directed toward other persons or objects. Coping with stressors may be more successful if all three components can be changed. From the experience of practitioners working with unemployed youths, the AHA! Syndrome matches the cluster of emotional, cognitive, and behavioral symptoms that triggered many of the surface problems that blocked these young adults from successfully completing job-training programs.

In assessing anger as an emotional state, it is important to distinguish between angry feelings in terms of intensity, and individual differences in anger proneness. Spielberger's (1979) State–Trait Personality Inventory (STPI) has been used to assess anger as a trait, as well as a state in which feelings of anger are experienced at a particular time. Also, Spielberger's (1988) Anger-Expression (AX) scale distinguishes between the expression of those feelings in terms of anger that is held in or suppressed, anger expressed in aggressive behaviors, and ways to control angry feelings. More generalized attitudes of hostility have been measured using the Cook–Medley (1954) Hostility (Ho) scale, derived from the Minnesota Multiphasic Personality Inventory (MMPI), which has been linked to psychosocial and health behaviors (Houston & Vavak, 1991).

THE PSSW PROGRAM

It was hypothesized that job preparedness programs aimed at unemployed youths could be more effective by reducing the three AHA! anger dimensions and replacing them with prosocial skills. In the Prosocial Skills for Success in the Workplace (PSSW) program described here (developed by Christopher Collrin in consultation with Chok Hiew, and funded by the New Brunswick branch of the Canadian Employment and Immigration Centre), anger/stress management and prosocial skills components were incorporated into the FFS programs (described earlier). The PSSW program focused on preparing youths for employment and pursuit of a career path. The program was a 10-week, 40-hour per week competency training program aimed at positive self-perception enhancement, anger/stress management, conflict resolution, and social skills. The program included physical recreation, employment preparation, job placement exposure, and reentry into the workforce. Two programs were conducted (n = 14 in each program).

The target group was unemployed adults who were interested in getting jobs, but had been unsuccessful in completing previous work orientation and job skills programs and/or in finding and keeping jobs. Twenty-three clients (82%) successfully completed the program (16 males, 7 females), with a mean age of 30.3 years (range 19–48 years). The average educational level was Grade 10. About half of the clients had some vocational training, and most had had sporadic employment.

Attendance over the duration of the program was high (mean attendance = 89%). As a whole, the clients improved significantly in classroom behaviors when evaluated by the Behavioral Academic Self-Esteem (BASE) questionnaire (Coopersmith & Gilberts, 1981). During a week of job shadow/job exposure at various job sites, employer ratings of the participants' work revealed above average assessments (mean rating of 4.1 on a 5-point scale, ranging from *poor* [1] to *outstanding* [5]).

The major intent here is to focus on the assessment of anger dimensions, the program effects on handling "hassles" (i.e., anger-provoking situations), and outcomes such as impulse control, coping strategies, and the reduction of anxiety and stress symptoms.

OVERCOMING THE AHA! SYNDROME

In the PSSW program, the training component on anger management/prosocial skills was based on a biopsychosocial stress model (e.g., Green & Shellenberger, 1991). The program was developed by selecting relevant components from a number of cognitive-behavioral anger/stress programs described in the literature (e.g., Davis, McKay, & Eshelman, 1982; Feindler & Fremouw, 1983; Goldstein, Glick, Irwin, Pask-McCartney, & Rubama, 1989; Meichenbaum, 1985; Novaco, 1978; Tubesing & Tubesing, 1988). It was hypothesized that the program had to take into account a number of social, psychological, and biological dimensions underlying the AHA! Syndrome. The emotional, cognitive-behavioral, and motivational problems of these adults were seen as the negative consequences of stressors (both internal and external), as well as a lack of environmental resources and community support.

The goal of the program was to replace these negative factors with social skills, self-efficacy, healthy self-perceptions, and social support related to work experience (Pransky, 1991). A broader aim of the PSSW program was to teach learned resourcefulness as described by Rosenbaum (1983; i.e., to become a healthy individual in control of one's emotions and behaviors, with the knowledge and skills needed to regulate cognitions, solve problems, delay immediate gratification, and develop a sense of self-efficacy). The ultimate goal was to empower participants to be resourceful and resilient people, with the abilities to cope adequately with life problems and pursue desirable personal and work aspirations.

The anger/stress-management component lasted 4 weeks in the 10-week PSSW program. Pilot research had indicated that this component, when conducted as a completely separate program, was too intense and intimidating for many participants, and failed to sustain participant interest and attendance. These limitations were overcome by rearranging the anger/stress component as part of the larger PSSW program.

The AHA! Syndrome objectives were interspersed with the other program components to enhance variety and interest, and to increase transfer of training to other life domains. The five program objectives were to help the participants: (a) become more aware of their styles of interacting with others; (b) learn to express their feelings in socially acceptable and nonaggressive ways; (c) develop skills in responding to others in more appropriate and effective ways; (d) experience stress management and physical fitness activities to improve coping—in relaxation—and lower stress; and (e) transfer these skills to real-life situations, thus enhancing their ability to successfully pursue a career/ life path to employability.

ASSESSING CHANGES IN THE EXPERIENCE, EXPRESSION, AND CONTROL OF ANGER

Pre- and postprogram measures of the AHA! Syndrome were assessed using Spielberger's (1988) Trait Anger (anger proneness), State Anger (anger intensity), and Anger Expression scales, and the Cook–Medley's Ho scale. It was predicted that changes in the AHA! Syndrome would also produce a variety of positive behavioral effects, as reflected in the following measures: (a) State and Trait Anxiety (Spielberger, 1979), (b) Impulse Control (Kendall & Wilcox, 1979), (c) Stress Symptoms (Shafer, 1987), and (d) Problem-Solving Coping Strategies (Folkman & Lazarus, 1985).

RESULTS AND DISCUSSION

Of a total enrollment of 28, 23 participants completed the PSSW program. The mean pre–post scores for the AHA! Syndrome and the anger-management

Table 7.4 Mean pre- and posttest scores for the AHA! Syndrome and anger-management measures

Factors	Mean scores		Correlated *t* tests
	Pre	Post	
AHA! Syndrome measures			
1. Trait Anger	23.7	19.2	2.66**
2. State Anger	13.2	12.1	n.s.
3. Anger Expression	31.5	23.8	3.92**
4. Hostility	25.8	22.1	1.94*
Anger-management measures			
1. Trait Anxiety	23.6	20.4	3.29**
2. State Anxiety	19.1	17.4	n.s.
3. Impulse Control	66.7	60.8	2.74*
4. Stress Symptoms	137.7	62.7	4.20***
5. Problem-Focused coping	18.4	15.5	2.01*
6. Emotion-Focused coping	22.0	16.6	2.52*

*$p < .05$. **$p < .01$. ***$p < .001$.

measures are reported in Table 7.4. The results of analyses of the three anger measures that assess the AHA! Syndrome reveal significant reductions in Trait Anger and Anger Expression. The reduction in scores on the Hostility measure was also marginally significant. Postprogram scores for Trait Anger were positively correlated with Anger Expression ($r = .73, p < .001$) and Hostility ($r = .58, p < .01$). Anger Expression also correlated significantly with Hostility ($r = .37, p < .05$).

As predicted, the impact of changes in the AHA! Syndrome were reflected by significant reduction in trait anxiety, improvement in impulse or self-control as rated by the trainers, and a reduction in physical, emotional, cognitive, and behavioral distress symptoms, as seen in Table 7.4. Postprogram reductions in stress symptoms were also associated with significant decreases in Trait Anger ($r = .38, p < .04$) and Anger Expression ($r = .43, p < .02$) scores. In addition, participants improved significantly in the increased use of both problem- and emotion-focused strategies to cope with stressors (see Table 7.4).

Trainer ratings indicated that 61% of the participants showed improvement in the anger-program component: controlling anger, managing stress, and improving interpersonal communication skills. In describing how they dealt with "hassles" at the beginning and end of the PSSW program, participants typically reported hassles involving friends, acquaintances, and family members during which something was said or done that created moderate to intense anger on the participants' part. Prior to participating in the program, about 30% reported they had used anger-control methods in hassle situations; after completing the program, 57% reported that they used the anger-control methods they had learned.

The participants also reported the type of anger-coping responses, both positive (e.g., "talk it out," "walk away calmly") and negative ("hit back," "broke something"), that they used. The results indicate that most participants used positive actions in coping with stressful situations in pre- and postprogram situations, but there was a reliable drop in the proportion of negative actions. The decrease when responding to previously anger-provoking social situations fell from 87% to 35% by the end of the program.

In conclusion, the findings suggest that unemployed adults with previous inability to obtain or secure unemployment on their own not only lack education and marketable skills, but also experience social–environmental stress and lack of anger-coping skills. Job readiness training programs, designed to prepare such adults for the workforce, can be made more effective by incorporating stress and emotional control as integral components. The AHA! Syndrome provides an important cluster of symptoms that describe this population, and is a promising tool for the assessment of emotional, cognitive, and behavioral dimensions of anger, hostility, and aggression.

Assessments of Trait Anger and Anger Expression (Spielberger, 1979, 1988) proved to be useful psychometric measures, whereas the Cook–Medley Ho scale needs further refinement to be useful for this group. The results also show that job preparedness programs for the unemployed can modify the triad of anger constructs and reduce their vulnerability to stress.

These findings, together with the results of Study I on the JSS reported earlier, further support the notion that employment issues are intimately related to the consequences of undesirable stress and emotions, whether experienced on the job (as job stress) or in seeking to join or rejoin the workforce. Most helpful to participants is the enhancement of emotional health brought about by a balance between greater use of anger-coping and impulse-control strategies, as well as acquiring new social skills and problem-solving behaviors. As the Canadian economy continues to shift and change in the new global economic order, it behooves all those concerned with preparing the workforce to deal with job stress to learn and know more about themselves, and to be more creative in meeting and coping with the challenges ahead.

REFERENCES

Albee, G. (1979). Primary prevention. *Canada's Mental Health*, 27, 5–9.

Canadian Mental Health Association. (1984). *Work and well-being: The changing realities of employment*. Toronto: Author.

Cook, W., & Medley, D. (1954). Proposed hostility and pharisaic-virtue scales for the MMPI. *Journal of Applied Psychology*, 38, 414–418.

Cooper, C. L., & Payne, R. (Eds.). (1988). *Causes, coping and consequences of stress at work*. Chichester, England: Wiley.

Coopersmith, S., & Gilberts, R. (1981). *Behavioral academic self-esteem: A rating scale*. Palo Alto, CA: Consulting Psychologists, Inc.

Davis, M., McKay, M., & Eshelman, E. R. (1982). *The relaxation and stress reduction workbook*. New York: New Harbinger Publications.

Elias, M. J. (1987). Establishing enduring prevention programs: Advancing the legacy of Swampscott. *American Journal of Community Psychology*, *15*, 539–553.

Feindler, E., & Fremouw, W. (1983). Stress inoculation training for adolescent anger problems. In D. Meichenbaum & M. Jaremko (Eds.), *Stress reduction and prevention* (pp. 451–485). New York: Plenum.

Folkman, S., & Lazarus, R. S. (1985). If it changes it must be a process: Study of emotion and coping during three stages of a college examination. *Journal of Personality and Social Psychology*, *48*, 150–170.

Green, J., & Shellenberger, R. (1991). *The dynamics of health and wellness: A biopsychosocial approach*. Fort Worth, TX: Holt, Rinehart & Winston.

Goldstein, A., Glick, B., Irwin, M., Pask-McCartney, C., & Rubama, I. (1989). *Reducing delinquency: Intervention in the community*. New York: Pergamon.

Hiew, C. C. (1987). *Occupational stress management in the workplace: A manual for the Canadian Mental Health Association*. Fredericton, Canada: University of New Brunswick Press.

Hiew, C. C. (1989). Stress management and prevention in health psychology. *Japanese Journal of Health Psychology*, *2*, 28–38.

Hiew, C. C. (1992a). Endangered children in Thailand: Third world families affected by socio-economic changes. In G. Albee, L. Bond, & T. Monsey (Eds.), *Improving children's lives: Global perspectives on prevention* (pp. 129–145). Newbury Park, CA: Sage.

Hiew, C. C. (1992b). Separated by their work: A cross-cultural study on families with fathers living apart. *Environment and Behavior*, *24*(2), 206–225.

Hiew, C. C. (1992c). *The foundations for success report: A career counselling program for youths in transition*. Fredericton, Canada: University of New Brunswick Press.

Hiew, C. C. (1995). Child resilience programs: Responding to sexually exploited children in Asia. In *Children worldwide* Geneva: International Child Catholic Bureau.

Hiew, C. C., & MacDonald, G. (1990). Promoting competence in adolescents through pre-employment skills training and the development of a support system. In J. F. Saucier & L. Houde (Eds.), *Prevention psychosociale dans l'enfance et l'adolescence*. Montreal: Presses de l'Universite de Montreal.

Houston, B. K., & Vavak, C. R. (1991). Cynical hostility: Developmental factors, psychosocial correlates and health behaviors. *Health Psychology*, *10*, 9–17.

Jeger, A. M., & Slotnick, R. S. (Eds.). (1982). *Community mental health and behavioral-ecology*. New York: Plenum.

Keita, G. P., & Sauter, S. L. (Eds.). (1992). *Work and well-being: An agenda for the 1990s*. Washington, DC: American Psychological Association.

Kendall, P. C., & Wilcox, L. (1979). Self-control in children: Development of a rating scale. *Journal of Consulting and Clinical Psychology*, *47*, 1020–1029.

Meichenbaum, D. (1985). *Stress inoculation training*. New York: Pergamon.

Novaco, R. W. (1978). Anger and coping with stress. In J. Forey & D. Rathzen (Eds.), *Cognitive behavior therapy* (pp. 135–173). New York: Plenum.

Orlandi, M. (1986). The diffusion and adoption of worksite health promotion innovations: An analysis of barriers. *Preventive Medicine*, *15*, 522–536.

Pransky, J. (1991). *Prevention: The critical need*. Springfield, MO: Burrell Foundation.

Quick, J. C., Murphy, L. R., & Hurrell, J. J., Jr. (Eds.). (1992). *Stress & well-being at work: Assessments and interventions for occupational mental health*. Washington, DC: American Psychological Association.

Rosenbaum, M. (1983). Learned resourcefulness as a behavioral repertoire for the self-regulation of internal events: Issues and speculations. In M. Rosenbaum, C. M. Franks, & Y. Jaffe (Eds.), *Perspectives on behavior therapy in the eighties* (pp. 54–73). New York: Springer.

Sarason, S. B. (1982). *The culture of the school and the problem of change* (2nd ed.). Boston: Allyn & Bacon.

Shafer, W. (1987). *Stress management for wellness*. New York: Holt, Rinehart & Winston.

Spielberger, C. D. (1979). *Preliminary manual for the State-Trait Personality Inventory (STPI)*. Tampa, FL: University of South Florida Press.

Spielberger, C. D. (1988). *Manual for the State-Trait Anger Expression Inventory (STAXI)*. Odessa, FL: Psychological Assessment Resources.

Spielberger, C. D. (1994). *Professional manual for the Job Stress Survey (JSS)*. Odessa, FL: Psychological Assessment Resources.

Spielberger, C. D., Krasner, S. S., & Solomon, E. P. (1988). The experience, expression and control of anger. In M. P. Janisse (Ed.), *Individual differences, stress and health psychology* (pp. 89–107). New York: Springer-Verlag.

Spielberger, C. D., & Reheiser, E. C. (1994a). The Job Stress Survey: Measuring gender differences in occupational stress. *Journal of Social Behavior and Personality*, *9*(2), 199–218.

Spielberger, C. D., & Reheiser, E. C. (1994b). Job stress in university, corporate and military personnel. *International Journal of Stress Management*, *1*(1), 19–31.

Staff (1994, August 19). *Daily Gleaner*, p. 1.

Tubesing, N., & Tubesing, D. (1988). *Structural exercises in stress management*. Duluth, MN: Wholeperson Press.

Turnage, J. T., & Spielberger, C. D. (1991). Job stress in managers, professionals, and clerical workers. *Work & Stress*, *5*(3), 165–176.

8

Occupational Stress and Informed Interventions

Ann M. O'Roark
Executive Consultant, St. Petersburg, Florida, USA

ABSTRACT

Occupational stress is now a well-established, pervasive problem in the workplace. However, overcoming persistent gaps between research-supported knowledge and at-risk worker behavior has received less rigorous attention. This chapter describes psychological consultation that guides organizational clients in using psychological tests to assess job stress, interpret results, and prepare action plans called informed interventions. *In this assessment-based consultation, which involved calibration of present conditions with optimal performance objectives, the Job Stress Survey (JSS) was used along with the Myers–Briggs Type Indicator (MBTI) and other personality measures. Three calibration applications are outlined, emphasizing the critical role of the psychologist as translator and transformer of assessment data into organizational information. Stress profiles collected from 209 managers indicated that all 16 MBTI types rated relations with or lack of support from supervisors either first or second among the 30 JSS stressors in perceived severity. Used with "calibration consultation," the JSS allows executives and work groups to prepare informed interventions for follow-up actions that impact cognitive and affective factors related to stress reduction and improved performance.*

Psychological data pertinent to effective performance become acutely critical in an era of rapid technological change, globalization of the industrial-business community, and escalation of workplace violence. Consequently, the accessibility of psychological information for those who can benefit most from it rises steadily higher on the professional agenda (Campbell, 1992). Cultural lag in social attitudes, documented early in this century by investigators such as Mead (1969) and Weber (see Parsons, 1967), is less prevalent at the end of the century. However, information gaps (e.g., that some U.S. adults still believe that no human has walked on the moon) emphasize the importance of sharpening transfer-of-knowledge techniques.

Unfortunately, bridging the gap between scientific research and the work-a-day world of the manager remains less compelling for psychologists than traditional attention to test validities, reliabilities, and correlation coefficients.

121

This order of priorities is not surprising given cautious, suspicious public attitudes reinforced by federal and legal sanctions against using invasive psychological questionnaires for selection and promotion. However, assessment of workplace stress addresses factors that influence effective performance, and can also be beneficial to employees.

Experiences of stress and strain in work settings are generally attributed to interactions between an individual and that person's occupational environment. French, Caplan, and Van Harrison (1982) theorized that work stress results primarily from incompatible person–environment fit, which generates psychological strain and, with increasing numbers, stress-related disorders. More recently, Lazarus (1991) recommended that job stress be addressed within a model that conceptualizes stress as a process involving transactions between a person and the environment. Lazarus' approach also calls for a detailed appraisal of individual coping skills and specific stressors associated with a particular job, and addresses a major limitation of research on sources of job stress (viz. ambiguity in the definition of *occupational stress*; Schuler, 1991).

In the past decade, some occupational stress researchers have focused on antecedent conditions, whereas others have studied the consequences of stressful circumstances. Confusion continues to arise from the range and scope of item content in measures of occupational stress. Taxonomies of job stress have included functional concepts such as *role ambiguity, role conflict,* and *work overload*, along with individual differences in attitudes, personality traits, and health characteristics. Although macrolevel concepts such as *general organizational climate* have highlighted employers' responsibilities for humane management practices and are consistent with theories in industrial-organizational psychology, there remains a wide gap between such concepts and empirical research on the assessment of occupational stress, which is needed to guide informed and effective workplace interventions.

ASSESSING JOB STRESS

The Job Stress Survey (JSS; Spielberger, 1994), along with other recently developed psychometric instruments (e.g., Barone, Caddy, Katell, & Hamilton, 1988; Osipow & Spokane, 1981), was constructed to assess stress in the workplace from a generic perspective. The JSS provides a sound foundation for consultation, and allows comparison across individuals, different occupational levels, and work environments. Consistent with Lazarus' (1991) conceptualization of occupational stress, the JSS was developed in accordance with its author's seminal definition of *stress*:

> . . . *a complex psychobiological process that consists of three major elements. The process is* initiated *by a situation or stimulus that is potentially harmful or dangerous* (stressor). *If a stressor is* interpreted *as dangerous or threatening, an* anxiety reaction *will be elicited. Thus, our working definition of stress refers to the following temporal sequence of events: Stressor → Perception of threat → Anxiety state. (Spielberger, 1979, p. 17)*

Empirically developed and technically refined, the JSS exemplifies increasing efforts to narrow the distance between what is known by researchers in applied psychological science and what is experienced by those holding jobs in the "real world" of work. In addition to conforming to scientific psychometric standards, the JSS meets gap-closing criteria of simplicity and face validity from the client's perspective.

This chapter discusses important barriers that psychologists need to overcome when applying assessment results to the development of informed interventions for work and business settings, and outlines methods used in conducting calibration consultations. Three types of calibration approaches are described: consultations with individuals, consultation workshops with management or work units, and longitudinal consultations that may involve employees from different departments and different levels of responsibility.

BARRIERS IN REAL-WORLD SETTINGS: SORTING FACT FROM FANTASY

Psychology's role in supporting decision making in business settings reduces typical central issues in assessment—test construction, validity, reliability—to a small band of attention in a broader spectrum of considerations. In their book *Assessment for Decision*, Peterson and Fishman (1987) provided an overview of special problems encountered when the assessment of human functions is used to guide practical choices in work settings. Fenn's (1991) "Bambi Meets Godzilla: Psychological Assessment in Real-World Settings" considers assessment in the workplace as part of a larger system; nothing occurs in isolation. As Fenn observed, numerous difficulties arise when there is too much reliance on behavioral observations, to the neglect of trait-based assessments. Arguments supported by cogent case studies provide strong support of the need for psychometrically sound assessment instruments, which combine personality trait data with situational frequency information.

Contributors to *Assessment for Decision*, credentialed and schooled in principles of "tests and measurement," wrote candidly about what it is like beyond the shelter of the clinic, at the worksite where the reception of psychologists and psychological tests is often lacking in warmth and viewed with skepticism. These consultants and authors lamented the isolation of the academic psychologist from workplace realities. They emphasized the survival value of nurturing the funny-bone while staying in daily contact with down-to-earth humility when taking psychology to work "in real-world zones of business combat" (Fenn, 1991, p. 515).

Demonstrating that their own humor is alive and well, the contributors to *Assessment for Decision* conveyed strong warnings about unsuspected complexities encountered in conducting assessments in work settings. The key to success is a dual specialization in assessment and industrial-organizational psychology. It is essential for a consultant to see how organizations sometimes house a host of conflicting operating models and competing outcome agendas—to the point that the assessment task becomes overwhelmed by other considerations.

With the Godzilla caveat in mind, a consultant can work with greater confidence when using assessment tools like the JSS. Quantified, yet understandable to executives, managers, and work groups, JSS results can have a positive impact on workplace decisions because clients can easily use them to: (a) sort fact from fantasy, pinpointing what is most frustrating to employees; and (b) generate informed interventions, thereby increasing the odds for developing successful action plans for reducing stress and improving productivity.

UPTIGHT, OUT-OF-TOUCH, IRRELEVANT, SPOOKY

Organizational clients, unfortunately, yet at times accurately, consider psychologists to be uptight, out-of-touch with the real world, and unapproachable. Furthermore, many executives, managers, and work-team members believe that psychologists' tests are irrelevant, spooky, and unintelligible. Evidence of these views can be seen almost daily in editorial cartoons and TV sitcoms. Such folk wisdom usually fails to recognize advances in scientific psychology, harking back to early psychoanalytic theories and Freudian couch techniques. Malingering suspicions also show up in court cases, where test items are scrutinized for violations of privacy or protected rights. The fantasy, a *folie-en-mass*, is that psychological tests are irrelevant exercises in compulsive obsessiveness or similar narcissistic psychobabble.

Unnamed varieties of fearful notions spring up in work groups when people learn that the consultation will include psychological assessment. Employees at all levels become uncomfortable and reluctant participants. It takes a down-to-earth, human-like-everyone-else consultant to deliver the psychological goods. However, as interpreter and adapter of psychological assessment data for guiding workplace decision making, the consulting psychologist must be knowledgeable.

Dual evaluation standards, professional and practical, must be met for a psychologist to be an effective consultant in assessing stress in the workplace. To achieve credibility in the eyes of both the professional and organizational communities, an effective consultant must use a double-specialized delivery system. *Double-specialized* implies both high professional standards and acceptance by a receiver, which entails the translation of psychometric information, considered essential in psychological circles, into a language that is acceptable and usable to the organizational client. The demanding role of the psychological consultant as a translator-interpreter is described in the next section.

CONSULTANT AS TRANSFORMER-TRANSLATOR-INTERPRETER

A no-frills overview of the consulting psychologist's role in using personality assessment in the workplace is outlined in the following list.

- Transformer
  A transformer of data into information
  A demystifier of "spooky" psychological tests (e.g., relevant, usable)
  A giver of feedback (e.g., from an experienced eye, a particular mind set)
- Translator
  An adapter of the information to the culture
  A quality assurance representative
  An interpreter of feedback (e.g., intention of the author, importance in client's culture)
  A problem solver of expected best and worst scenarios (e.g., gather facts first, build scenario next)

The first step in carrying out the transformer task is to demystify the spooky side of psychological testing. When relevant assessment data are presented as feedback from a consultant with an experienced eye and a specialized, trained mind set, consumers are likely to find tests more palatable.

The bigger challenge, requiring a "real-world" knowledge base, is the translator role, which takes the consultation a step beyond literal language translation in adapting relevant information to the organizational culture. Effectiveness in this role requires training in business, sociology and group dynamics, and conceptualizing skills. The extensive knowledge base of the professionally trained psychologist is also needed to ensure high-quality interpretation of assessment data.

Definitions of *organizational culture* vary somewhat from discipline to discipline and decade to decade, but Schein (cited in Schein & Bennis, 1965) suggested one persistent theme: a deeper level of understanding of the basic assumptions and beliefs shared by the members of an organization. These usually unconscious formulations are a learned product of group experience, which establishes an organization's taken-for-granted view of itself and its environment. The ideal situation is when there is an optimum alignment between the organizational culture and the belief systems and social background of members of the organization.

When the culture of an organization becomes stagnant or frozen, several types of problems are likely to arise: failure to integrate new technologies, management and intergroup conflicts, ineffective meetings, and reductions in productivity. Consultants can assist with unfreezing organizational culture by providing information about present beliefs, practices, and sources of stress. In providing relevant factual information, the intent in planning informed interventions is to shift management's responsibility for shaping flexible and healthy cultures in one or more of the following ways: (a) changing what managers pay attention to, measure, and control; (b) facilitating constructive reactions to critical incidents and crises; and (c) revising the criteria used for recruitment, selection, promotion, retirement, and termination.

Factual information regarding specific occupational stressors provides objective evidence of the inhibitions, constraints, and problems within the organization. Consultants with knowledge of options in diverse systems and cultures can transform, translate, and adapt assessment data into language that can be readily understood within a particular organizational culture. Following transformation and translation of assessment information, the consultant shifts to here-and-now organizational priorities. The consultant's goal is to move as unobtrusively as possible to problem solving and scenario building (Schwartz, 1991). This requires developing blueprints of what it might be like if things go well, if they go poorly, or if they stay about the same. What would be appropriate standards, actions, and objectives under each circumstance? The role of the consultant includes assessing the present state, as well as evaluating the path from the present to diverse goals under challenging conditions.

JSS: A GRASS-ROOTS GENERIC INSTRUMENT

Overcoming workplace attitudes that limit consultation effectiveness is not accomplished by polished consulting skills alone. Assessment instruments must be technically sound and substantive, while coming across as user-friendly and natural. The JSS fills that order. With a grass-roots beginning and an on-the-job developmental history, the JSS has consumer credibility advantages over assessment questionnaires built from abstract models of stressful versus ideal work settings.

Construction of the JSS began with a real-world request from leaders of the Florida Division of Criminal Law Enforcement for expert psychological assistance in complying with the mandates issued by the National Advisory Commission on Criminal Justice Standards and Goals (1973). The federal regulations stipulated that every police agency should establish a formal process to select qualified police applicants. These requirements were extended by the Florida legislature to include an effort "to retain well-qualified and experienced officers for the purpose of providing maximum protection and safety to the citizens of, and visitors to, this state" (Spielberger, Spaulding, & Vagg, 1981a, p. 9). Recognition of work stress as a leading contributor to turnover led to the construction of the Police Stress Survey (PSS)—a guide for the development of stress-management programs for law enforcement officers (Spielberger, Westberry, Grier, & Greenfield, 1981b).

Items from the PSS proved equally useful in a similarly developed Teacher Stress Survey (Grier, 1982), and subsequent research led to the construction and validation of the JSS for use across a range of occupations and work settings. Evidence accumulated (e.g., Spielberger & Reheiser, 1994a; Turnage & Spielberger, 1991) regarding the utility of the JSS across occupational level (management, professional, clerical) and user-acceptability in a variety of work settings (military, business and industry, health care). In a recent study, Spielberger and Reheiser (1994b) reported impressive evidence of gender differences, which supports consultant analysis of individual JSS items in preparation for informed interventions to reduce organizational stress.

In its construction and validation, the JSS was targeted for applied use, especially for workplace education and training. Attention was initially directed toward establishing and demonstrating that the JSS fulfilled rigorous testing standards and showed reliable psychometric qualities (Spielberger et al., 1981b). Research with the JSS revealed a two-factor structure underlying the 30-item questionnaire. The usefulness of the two JSS factors—Job Pressure and Organizational Support—can be seen in data reported by Hiew (see chap. 7, this volume), showing dramatic differences among departments of a Canadian government agency undergoing downsizing. Hiew's findings support the importance of tailoring informed interventions to address differences in the stress experiences of workers employed in a variety of work settings.

The accessibility and quality of the assessment data obtainable with the JSS stem from the down-to-earth simplicity of the information that can be obtained with this instrument. In addition, psychologists can provide clients with quick connections to popular reading materials (e.g., *Anger: The Misunderstood Emotion* [Tavris, 1982], *Ageless Body, Timeless Mind* [Chopra, 1993]), and can readily point out obvious links to management procedures (e.g., time management, project management). The JSS is also meaningfully connected to other personality assessment instruments (O'Roark, 1989).

USING THE JSS IN CALIBRATION CONSULTATION

This chapter provides consultants with examples of the use of assessment in calibration consultation designed to facilitate informed interventions. To prevent an organizational Godzilla from stepping on the implementation of an informed intervention, assessment data must be carefully adapted and aligned with unique workplace circumstances. This requires the psychological consultant to understand and tune-in to a particular organization's culture and dynamics, and to follow time-sequence patterns, such as those recommended by negotiation specialists (e.g., Ruben, 1988). It also requires doing extensive background homework, carefully setting the stage for the main event, and making sure that mind-set conditions are "ripe" for success.

Consultation with organizations can be effective only after: (a) correcting out-of-date client attitudes and emotions toward psychologists and psychological testing, (b) detailing the assessment procedure (administration, confidentiality, standards, time schedules) and disseminating results to participants, and (c) ensuring compatibility with the decision agendas of formal and informal leadership networks.

Calibration is the name given to utilizing assessment instruments, such as the JSS, in consultation with business and professional organizations. As defined in *Webster's Dictionary*, *calibration* involves a check or verification of measurement procedures associated with making adjustments within a desired range, or enhancing accuracy (e.g., as with thermostats and temperature). Based on an analysis and interpretation of test findings, several types of calibration consultation are possible, which can be applied in three organizational contexts: the individual, the department or work unit, and the organization as a whole. Individual employees' test scores can be compared with group averages, and group averages can be compared with other departments in the organization and with normative data. Group averages also contribute to mapping a corporate profile, which, in turn, can be used for comparison with other corporations.

As with all assessment procedures, the quality of the information collected with instruments such as the JSS depends on thorough preparation of data collection and thoughtful data analysis. Corporate clients must be briefed as to the assessment goals, methods, and intended outcomes. Lazarus' (1991) person–environment transactional theory of occupational stress and the empirical foundation underlying test instruments should also be described during the preparation phase.

The JSS is closely aligned with Lazarus' theory of stress as a transactional process. The transactional factors—Personality and Actual Pressures—can be presented in terms of: (a) Perceived Severity of the Stressor, determined in part by the personality of the individual and the experience he or she brings to the equation; and (b) Frequency of Stress Occurrences, which the activities and requirements of the business or organization adds to the equation. Two categories of individual differences are assessed by the JSS subscales: (a) Organizational Support, which involves relationships with executives and supervisors; and (b) Job Pressures (i.e., the task demands and general workload). When used in calibration consultation, the JSS gives a direct, easy-to-follow message: Job stress is a function of transactions between work and worker. These aspects of the transactional process can be traced to the way work is managed (e.g., the extent to which executives, managers, and supervisors are supporting the worker [or each other]) and how burdensome the employee's workload is and in what time frames.

Each JSS stressor item is rated for perceived severity as compared with "assignment of disagreeable duties," which serves as an anchor. For each item (e.g., "working overtime," "difficulty getting along with supervisor"), the amount of perceived stress associated with a particular stressor event can be determined. Whether that stressor has more or less impact than it has for other employees at a similar occupational level (e.g., managers, professionals, clerical personnel) can be evaluated. If a worker has a strong negative emotional reaction to something that goes on frequently in his or her workplace, it is likely that he or she will experience stressful overload more often than a co-worker who does not react strongly to that occurrence.

APPLICATIONS OF CALIBRATION CONSULTATION

The goal of calibration consultation is to assist managers in the preparation of plans for improving the quality of worklife, which includes enhancing individual health and increasing corporate productivity. As summarized in the following list, the three distinct phases of calibration consultation are: (a) administration and analysis of tests such as the JSS, (b) individual and/or collective feedback of test results, and (c) working with client(s) to prepare informed interventions.

• Phase 1: Administration—Describe calibration program, collect data, analyze data

- Phase 2: Feedback—Hand back test results, interpret guidelines
- Phase 3: Planning Informed Interventions—Prepare individual performance contract or career plan, suggest workshop solution, recommend matrix task team

Applications of calibration consultation in one-to-one individual sessions, workshop groups, and longitudinal contexts are described next.

One-to-One Calibration Consultation

One-to-one calibration consultation involves procedures with individuals. For such applications, there are two possible goals: (a) preparing a job performance-improvement contract, and (b) mapping a long-term career-development plan. Whenever possible, one-to-one calibration consultation gives attention to both short- and long-term considerations. Guidance for using "collaborative" methods in assessment sessions with individual clients is provided in Fischer's (1985) *Individualizing Psychological Assessment*.

One-to-one sessions, which demonstrate a corporate value for the development of human resources and the promotion of personal growth, are recommended in organizations that give priority to self-regulation and individual responsibility for stress management. When this feedback can be given privately, the primary emphasis should be on individual development. The individual calibration agenda follows.

1. Present test results sheets. When reviewing the JSS results:
   - Point out the following information: Severity Average—highest and lowest items, Frequency Average—highest and lowest items, Stress Index—"5" anchor, top three overstressors. (Follow manual guidelines for other tests.)
   - Present a written professional report when possible: Review contents with client, and respond to questions.
2. Collaborate to determine priority objectives and actions: Identify data highlights. Client provides specific critical incidents to illustrate those highlights.
3. Clarify expected outcomes and calibration goals (A and/or B): A. Job Performance Goals. Worksheet Two: Complete; B. Career Path Planning. Worksheet Three: Complete.

The preceding agenda is used in Phase 2 of calibration consultation, summarized previously. One-to-one feedback sessions generally begin with establishing rapport and reviewing goals and desired outcomes. The consultant then provides an explanation of scores on all tests that were administered in Phase 1, with as much background information as the client finds useful. Whenever possible, a brief, written professional summary of results is provided.

When focusing on the JSS in calibration consultation, the consultant guides the feedback discussion in a review of stressors that are experienced strongly and frequently. It is desirable to identify and give immediate attention to no more than two or three stressors. For these selected stressors, the consultant should request detailed examples relating to critical incidents and recent events. It is also important for the consultant to keep in mind that, when no stressor items are reported as at least average in perceived severity or frequency, boredom has set in. In such cases, the consultant should point out that it may be time for job enrichment or change. However, low JSS scores may also indicate that individuals are denying job pressures or reactions to them, or that some other factor is inhibiting their ability to discriminate between experiences.

The final part of the feedback session in one-to-one consultation concentrates on developing strategies, action plans, and directions for independent work. Worksheets are provided for recording the ideas and decisions that are made. Client follow-through is significantly improved when: (a) the consultant recommends and guides initial worksheet entries, and (b) there is at least one follow-up feedback session in which finished worksheets are reviewed and the consultant responds to client "afterthoughts." A follow-up session also provides an opportunity to consider how realistic the expectations are, and to examine how goals can be adjusted in best, worst, or unexpected organizational scenarios.

Group Calibration Workshops

Calibration consultation with groups involves more extensive and complex administrative work than one-to-one consultation. Two strategies for using JSS data in group applications, described later, follow essentially the same three-phase procedures outlined previously. It is important for senior executives to preview plans with those who will be asked to participate in group calibration consultations. Therefore, methods and possible outcomes are discussed with key leaders (i.e., amended as needed to meet organizational requirements), written out, and then reaffirmed.

The particulars of group consultation (e.g., agenda, dates, duration) impact each participant. Therefore, failure to review plans before beginning consultation can cause unintentional confusion and unnecessary imposition, thus defeating the important goal of reducing stress levels. Consequently, in introducing and implementing the calibration consultation process, consideration of the participants' needs pays long-term dividends. From the outset, participants in group consultation should be informed that they are not required or compelled to complete the assessment questionnaires. They should also be assured of the confidentiality of any personal information that they are asked to provide. Announcements and agendas should clearly indicate that sealed envelopes with confidential personal data will be delivered individually to each participant.

In group consultation workshop sessions, participants are informed of the average scores for the group, which are used by the consultant to explain JSS terminology and to provide guidelines for the interpretation of results. Using group averages in discussing results also sets the stage for a transition from concern with individual stress to work-group conditions. When possible, graphs showing each individual's scores are anonymously plotted to illustrate the wide range of stress experiences within the group. Figure 8.1 depicts mean JSS Severity and Frequency scores for each individual of a group of managers who participated in a calibration consultation workshop for public utility managers.

After reviewing the average ratings for the 30 JSS stressors in group calibrations, the items with the strongest average Severity and Frequency scores are either affirmed or rejected as important by group members, and the assumed impact of the affirmed stressors on group effectiveness and efficiency is discussed. Confirmed stressors are then assigned to separate task groups for the generation of stress-reduction ideas. Finally, the task groups report to the total group, where suggestions are collectively clarified and amended. After stress-reduction suggestions are reviewed and sanctioned by group consensus, priorities can be established using a weighted voting process. Some organizations continue the calibration process by convening annual reassessment workshops, which permit tracking the effectiveness of intervention activities.

Longitudinal Calibration Consultation

Longitudinal calibration consultation is the most complex application. A gantt, or pert-chart calendar, of time frames and activities (e.g., "milestones") keeps the calibration on track and provides information and incentive for subgroups that must complete their separate activities in time to meet the deadline for a collective report. To illustrate longitudinal consultation, the following information tracks a program consultation with executives of a regional medical center, who selected a cross-department, longitudinal approach in order to stimulate corporate-wide cohesiveness and enhance mid-level manager initiatives. The decision to use this approach was based on a JSS survey of management personnel, which indicated that "meeting deadlines," "frequent interruptions," "dealing with crisis situations," and "making on-the-spot decisions" were the top-ranked stressors.

In addition to reducing stress for those stressful events with strong ratings, the executives identified a need to strengthen mid-level managers' conceptual and leadership skills. Concurrent with cross-department task group work on plans for reducing stressful work processes, individual departments addressed stressors affecting their particular group. For five major departments, the two stressors rated by each department as most troublesome were:

Nursing: "frequent interruptions," "insufficient personnel"
Training and Education: "lack of opportunity for advancement," "insufficient personal time"
Professional Resources: "frequent interruptions," "excessive paperwork"
Finance: "excessive paperwork," "frequent interruptions"
Facilities/Food Services: "fellow workers not doing their jobs," "dealing with crisis situations"

Calibration consultation activities with the regional medical center were spread across a 12-month period, concluding with selection by the chief executive officer of five of the interventions submitted by task groups for imple-

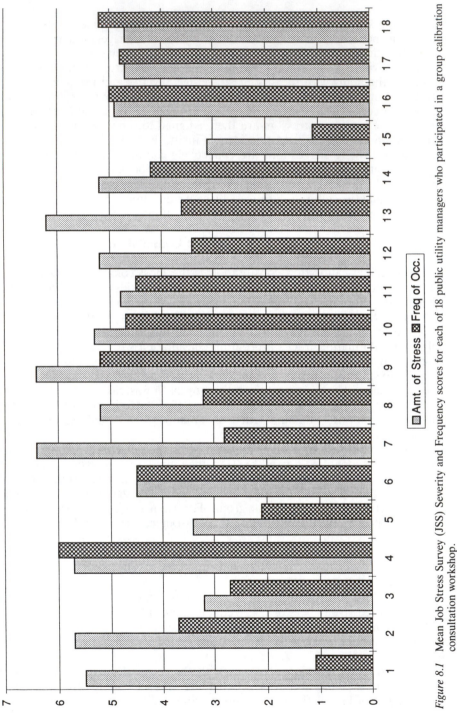

Figure 8.1 Mean Job Stress Survey (JSS) Severity and Frequency scores for each of 18 public utility managers who participated in a group calibration consultation workshop.

mentation. The specific intervention that was endorsed most enthusiastically was a plan to improve dissemination of management information, including daily schedules of major changes such as plans for facility renovations. That plan included the designation of a managers' lounge for informal gatherings and bulletin board notices, which was a highly visible outcome of the informed intervention activities initiated in the longitudinal calibration consultation program.

A reassessment of occupational stress at the regional medical center 2 years after the initial assessment showed some interesting changes in the leading stressors. Nearly all of the stressors that were targeted for reduction were rated lower in the follow-up assessment. However, as might be expected at a busy medical facility, "frequent interruptions" was once again rated as a major source of stress. The three leading stressors that were not previously highly ranked were: "insufficient personnel," "inadequate salary," and "inadequate equipment."

PROFILES IN STRESS

Traditional management theorists are divided in their preference for giving attention to aggregate phenomena (macrolevel analysis), as contrasted with attention given to personality and other individual differences. Greisinger (1990) advocated following in the footsteps of Chester Barnard (1939), who observed how cooperative human systems (businesses) can transcend their parochial interests in the production and exchange of goods in order to focus on underlying expectations of "personal betterment."

In the assessment of occupational stress, the JSS lends itself to both organizational goals and the needs of the individual employee. JSS Severity ratings reflect, to some extent, personality characteristics that vary from person to person, whereas JSS Frequency ratings assess aggregate occurrences in the environment. Calibration consultation is enriched when the assessment of both individual and organizational characteristics includes several types of psychological tests. As time and funds permit, additional instruments can be included to assess individual and collective variables pertinent to important organizational activities and assignments.

The MBTI, for example, provides easy-to-interpret information about individual differences in personality, which are especially pertinent to preferred problem-solving strategies and coping modes (Myers & McCaulley, 1989). The MBTI was developed to assess individual preferences in the use of perception and judgment in the context of Jung's (1921/1971) theory of psychological types. Jung's theory personalizes calibration by means of a developmental model and specific hypotheses about advantages and disadvantages associated with each type. When MBTI results are reported in standardized type tables, displaying all 16 MBTI psychological types it is easy to provide feedback that reflects each individual's MBTI type, along with the full complement of types for the entire work group. Combining MBTI and JSS feedback in calibration consultation with groups moves the consultation toward team building. In addition to suggesting what each type can contribute to improving group performance, type theory emphasizes the appreciation of diversity, and affirms that each type can be equally healthy and important.

JSS data obtained in numerous consultations were sorted by MBTI dominant type and analyzed to determine if specific stressors were more likely to be perceived as stressful by certain personality types. Rank ordering of item-severity ratings of the 30 JSS items given by executives with a particular MBTI dominant function indicated that "support from supervisor" was perceived as the most severely stressful source of stress by the Thinking (T) and Sensing (S) dominant types. This item placed second for the Intuitive (I) and third for the Feeling (F) dominants, who rated "relationship with supervisors" as more stressful. Working overtime ranked 30th for all dominants, except the thinking group, which placed it 29th. "Performing tasks not included in one's job description" and "inadequate personal time" were also of little concern for these busy managers, who do not worry about how much time they invest in their work. Indeed, most corporate cultures expect managers to do whatever it takes, as was found to be a key indicator of success in studies conducted by the Center for Creative Leadership (Lombardo & McCaulley, 1994).

MBTI specialist Lawrence (1993), a past-president of the Association for Psychological Type, considers stress overload to be a function of the emotional maturity and stability achieved by an individual, which results from the development of special competencies associated with each type. The importance of individual differences in determining reactions to stressful events can also be seen in the results of a study of numerous gender differences in the Perceived Severity and Frequency ratings of JSS items (Spielberger & Reheiser, 1994b). Research on possible interactive effects of gender and MBTI preferences on the Perceived Severity of JSS stressor events is needed to facilitate the implementation of informed interventions.

WHAT'S IMPORTANT!

Investigations into occupational stress, job stress, and work stress have increased more than fiftyfold over the past two decades (Spielberger & Reheiser, 1994b). In a recent major survey, one in three workers reported occupational stress as the single greatest source of stress in their lives (Northwestern National Life, 1991). Unfortunately, those who undergo stressful experiences and psychologists who undertake research about stress all too frequently fail to connect.

This failure appears to be due, in large measure, to significant differences in priorities. Workers want prescriptions that will provide relief from stress, today. Researchers want data about stress that are theoretically relevant, accurate, and replicable. Both intentions have merit. Both groups can learn from each other. Workers need to learn what leads to becoming overloaded and "stressed out," and what coping options are available, safe, and effective. Researchers must learn to listen to their customers' concerns, like businesses do when they are searching for excellence.

Corporate and business clients, who are psychology's customers, want assessments that do not take a lot of time and that provide realistic and unambiguous clues about what to do. They do not want to be talked down to or mystified by esoteric statistics and psychobabble. Only management gurus and slick-product pushers give sure-fire answers or advice. Professional psychologists can and must deliver messages that meet the two KISS criteria: "Keep it short and simple," without forgetting usable "Knowledge involves street smarts." The JSS assessment does just that, and also provides a wealth of credible information. When used in calibration consultation by a skilled psychological consultant, the JSS can make an important contribution to informed interventions for both individual workers and corporate decision makers.

REFERENCES

Barnard, C. I. (1939). *Dilemmas of leadership in the democratic process.* Princeton, NJ: Princeton University Press.

Barone, D. F., Caddy, G. R., Katell, A. D., Roselione, F. B., & Hamilton, R. A. (1988). The Work Stress Inventory: Organizational stress and job risk. *Educational and Psychological Measurement, 48*, 141–154.

Campbell, D. (1992). *Manual for the Campbell Interest and Skill Survey.* Minneapolis, MN: National Computer Systems, Inc.

Chopra, D. (1993). *Ageless body, timeless mind.* New York: Crown.

Fenn, D. S. (1991). Bambi meets Godzilla: Psychological assessment in real-world settings. *Contemporary Psychology, 36*, 515–516.

Fischer, C. (1985). *Individualizing psychological assessment.* Monterey, CA: Brooks-Cole.

French, J. R. P., Jr., Caplan, R. D., & Van Harrison, R. (1982). *The mechanisms of job stress and strain.* Chicester, England: Wiley.

Greisinger, D. W. (1990). The human side of economic organization. *Academy of Management Review, 15*, 478–499.

Grier, K. (1982). *A study of job stress in police officers and high school teachers.* Unpublished doctoral dissertation, University of South Florida, Tampa.

Jung, C. G. (1971). *Psychological types* (H. C. Baynes, Trans., rev. by R. F. C. Hull). In *The Collected works of C. G. Jung* (Vol. 6). Princeton, NJ: Princeton University Press. (Original work published in 1921)

Lawrence, G. D. (1993). *People types and tiger stripes.* Gainesville, FL: Center for Applications of Psychological Type.

Lazarus, R. S. (1991). Psychological stress in the workplace. In P. L. Perrewe (Ed.), *Handbook on job stress* (pp. 1–13). Corde Madera, CA: Select Press.

Lombardo, M. M., & McCauley, C. (1994). *Benchmarks: Developmental reference points for managers and executives.* Greensboro, NC: Center for Creative Leadership.

Mead, M. (1969). Research with human beings: A model derived from anthropological field practice. *Daedalus, 98*, 361–386.

Myers, I. B., & McCaulley, M. H. (1989). *Manual: A guide to the development and use of the Myers-Briggs Type Indicator.* Palo Alto, CA: Consulting Psychologists Press.

National Advisory Commission on Criminal Justice Standards and Goals. (1973). *Report on police.* Washington, DC: U.S. Government Printing Office.

Northwestern National Life. (1991). *Employee burnout: America's newest epidemic*. Minneapolis, MN: Author.

O'Roark, A. M. (1989). Using personality assessment as a development intervention with managerial populations. In B. J. Fallon, H. P. Pfister, & J. Brebner (Eds.), *Advances in industrial organizational psychology: 24th Congress of the International Union of Psychological Science* (pp. 355–363). Amsterdam: North-Holland, Elsevier Science Publishers.

Osipow, S. J., & Spokane, A. R. (1981). *Occupational Stress Inventory Manual research version*. Odessa, FL: Psychological Assessment Resources.

Parsons, T. (1967). Evaluation and objectivity in social science: An interpretation of Max Weber's contributions. In T. Parsons (Ed.), *Sociological theory and modern society* (pp. 79–101). New York: The Free Press.

Peterson, D. R., & Fishman, D. B. (1987). *Assessment for decision*. New Brunswick, NJ: Rutgers University Press.

Ruben, J. V. (1988, August). *Some wise and mistaken assumptions about conflict and negotiations*. Presidential address at the annual convention of the American Psychological Association, New York.

Schein, E. H., & Bennis, W. G. (1965). *Personal and organizational change through group methods*. New York: Wiley.

Schuler, R. S. (1991). Foreword. In P. L. Parrewe (Ed.), *Handbook on job stress* (pp. i–iv). Corde Madera, CA: Select Press.

Schwartz, P. (1991). *The art of the long view*. New York: Doubleday.

Spielberger, C. D. (1979). *Understanding stress & anxiety*. London, England: Harper & Row, Ltd.

Spielberger, C. D. (1994). *Professional Manual for the Job Stress Survey (JSS)*. Odessa, FL: Psychological Assessment Resources.

Spielberger, C. D., & Reheiser, E. C. (1994a). Job stress in university, corporate and military personnel. *International Journal of Stress Management, 1*, 19–30.

Spielberger, C. D., & Reheiser, E. C. (1994b). The Job Stress Survey: Measuring gender differences in occupational stress. *Journal of Social Behavior and Personality, 9*, 199–218.

Spielberger, C. D., Spaulding, H. C., & Vagg, P. R. (1986). *Professional manual for the Florida Police Standards Psychological Test Battery* (Human Resources Institute Monograph Series 3, No. 5). Tampa, FL: University of South Florida, College of Social and Behavioral Sciences.

Spielberger, C. D., Westberry, L. G., Grier, K. S., & Greenfield, G. (1981). *The Police Stress Survey: Sources of stress in law enforcement* (Human Resources Institute Monograph Series Three, No. 6). Tampa, FL: University of South Florida, College of Social and Behavioral Sciences.

Tavris, C. (1982). *Anger: The misunderstood emotion*. New York: Simon & Schuster.

Turnage, J. J., & Spielberger, C. D. (1991). Job stress in managers, professionals, and clerical workers. *Work & Stress, 5*, 165–176.

IV

STRESS AND HAPPINESS

9

Testing for Stress and Happiness: The Role of Personality Factors

John Brebner
University of Adelaide, South Australia

Maryanne Martin
University of Oxford, England

ABSTRACT

Six different theoretical conceptions of the relationship between happiness and personality—based on the work of Eysenck, Gray, Argyle, Strelau, Martin, and Brebner—are outlined in this chapter. Predictions derived from these theories of the relation of happiness to factors of Extraversion, Neuroticism, Sensitivity to Punishment, and the neo-Pavlovian factors of Mobility and Strength of Excitation were confirmed. However, including personality measures associated with different theoretical conceptions in the same multiple-regression equation did not substantially increase the explained variance in happiness, as measured by the Oxford Happiness Inventory or the Personal State Questionnaire. Thus, irrespective of the theoretical framework, the personality scales—in relation to happiness—appear to assess similar dimensions of the stress-related variance. Happier individuals tended to make relatively positive attributions when presented with ambiguous events. No linear relationship was found between happiness and the tendency to make positive generalizations from past events, but Brebner's results suggest that this relationship might be nonlinear, and that further research is required to evaluate this possibility.

This chapter is concerned with testing for happiness, and with the relationship between happiness and personality. Although psychological research on negative moods and depressive feelings has a long history, until recently there were relatively few studies of happiness and positive well-being. Some attention has been directed toward positive aspects of mental health (e.g., Jahoda, 1958) and gerontological aspects of well-being (e.g., Larson, 1978).

The precise nature of happiness can be discussed at length, and a convincing case can also be made for a variety of positive cognitive states (e.g., contentment, elation, amusement, and enjoyment), as observed by Furnham and

The support of the British Council and the Leverhulme Trust is gratefully acknowledged.

Brewin (1990). However, the concern here is with the overall, general state of happiness, which, like eustress (which is happiness or subjective well-being resulting from "stressful" activities, such as rock climbing, bungee jumping, etc.) is a negative indicator of stress reactions and other states producing unhappiness. The independence of positive and negative affective states is undeniable, as shown by Bradburn (1969); such states often occur together and can be equally strong, but one or the other tends to predominate at any time. The existence of mixed emotional states is acknowledged, but is not pursued in this chapter.

It is widely recognized that some people are typically happy, whereas others are less so. Psychologists have addressed the question of whether people can be characterized by their happiness (Diener, Sandvik, & Pavot, 1991). The research evidence suggests that people who lay claim to being extremely happy on some occasions are also those who are unhappiest at other times. Such findings implicate emotional lability as an important factor in "hitting the heights and plumbing the depths" of happiness, as can be seen most dramatically in manic–depressive reactions.

Despite the fact that positive and negative states have been regarded as independent since Bradburn (1969), intense affect occurs in both directions for the emotional person, and emotionality is mobile rather than stable. Moreover, emotionality appears to vary as a response to information, rather than being simply a spontaneous fluctuation in an individual's state. A significant implication is that Happiest–Unhappiest is a psychological dimension that refers to people who are usually happy or unhappy, but not necessarily intensely so. If emotional stability implies placidity, stable individuals should be characterized by remaining in or close to a neutral emotional state, and emotional instability should be related to strong positive and negative affective states.

In considering personality factors that affect happiness or unhappiness, a good starting point is to look at Diener et al. (1991) in relation to Bradburn's result that positive and negative affect are independent. Following Bradburn (1969), Positive and Negative Affect can be conceptualized as two orthogonal dimensions, as in Fig. 9.1. Diener et al. (1991) identified individuals who fall in the upper right quadrant as happy when their emotional state moves to the left, toward the vertical axis, and increasingly unhappy as it moves toward the horizontal. Weaker emotional effects would be obtained for the same degree of movement for people located in the bottom-left quadrant, who fall at the lower end of the postulated dimension of Emotionality, increasing diagonally from bottom left to top right in Fig. 9.1.

The Diener et al. view at first may seem to be at odds with Eysenck's well-established model of personality, which relates happiness to Extraversion and unhappiness to Neuroticism. Eysenck's Neuroticism dimension has been found to be negatively related to Happiness scores on the Oxford Happiness Inventory (OHI; e.g., Furnham & Brewin, 1990), rather than being related to strong feelings of both happiness and unhappiness. In this and other studies (e.g., Brebner, 1991), Extraversion correlated positively and significantly with happiness, as Eysenck predicted.

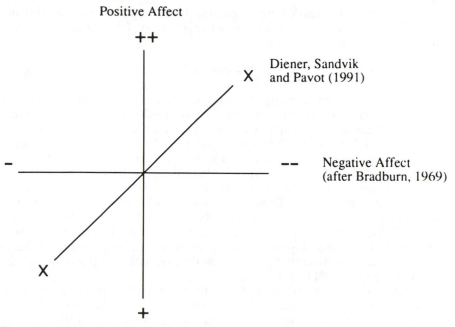

Figure 9.1 Diener, Sandvik, and Pavot (1991) results described in terms of Bradburn's (1969) model.

Eysenck's third factor, Psychoticism, shows a zero correlation with happiness in some studies (e.g., Furnham & Brewin, 1990), although a *prima facie* case might be entertained for the existence of a negative relationship with happiness. To retain Bradburn's independence of positive and negative affect and accommodate the Diener et al. findings within Eysenck's framework, it is only necessary to identify Extraversion with Positive Affect (+) on the vertical axis of Fig. 9.1., and Neuroticism with Negative Affect (−) along the horizontal axis.

Ryff (1989) suggested that the literature on happiness "is founded on conceptions of well-being that have little theoretical rationale" (p. 1069), but this is not always the case. Her selective view ignored the work of Eysenck and Eysenck (1985) and Gray (1972), who theorized that introverts and extraverts were differentially sensitive to punishment and reward, respectively, due to the central action of separate inhibitory and activating behavioral mechanisms within the limbic system. More recently, other possible explanations have been advanced; related to these, several questionnaires to measure happiness have been developed.

EXPLANATIONS FOR CHARACTERISTIC HAPPINESS AND RELATED TESTS

The various theoretical views of characteristic happiness are not mutually exclusive, and the degree to which tests of happiness are measuring the same thing is a matter for empirical investigation. A study that bears on these issues is described next, after first outlining six explanations for characteristic Happiness as a personality dimension.

1. Eysenck

According to Eysenck, being characteristically happy is a product of stable Extraversion (E), whereas unhappiness is due to the relatively strong emotional responsiveness of people who score high on the Neuroticism (N) scale of the Eysenck Personality Questionnaire (EPQ). In the manual for an earlier version of the EPQ (Eysenck & Eysenck, 1975), a person with a high Neuroticism score is described as "a worrier": He or she is easily affected by negative events, and takes a long time to return to a baseline of neutral emotionality after a negative experience. Thus, Neuroticism would be expected to correlate positively with measures of Unhappiness, but negatively with Happiness. Furnham and Brewin (1990) found a Pearson correlation of $-.43$ ($p < .001$) between N scores and Happiness scores, as measured by the OHI. E scores should correlate positively with happiness; the correlation of E scores with the OHI was .55 ($p < .001$).

In Eysenck's system, measures of Extraversion and Neuroticism are independent of one another, and can be represented in two dimensions, locating Extraversion on the vertical axis and Neuroticism on the horizontal axis. This representation raises this question: Where, precisely, does happiness lie in relation to the personality dimensions of Eysenck's system? Is happiness due equally to stability and extraversion? Are stable, introverted people more or less happy than their extraverted counterparts?

If Eysenck's Extraversion dimension is placed in Fig. 9.1 along the vertical axis, the Neuroticism dimension is on the horizontal axis, and both factors have equal effects on happiness–unhappiness, the Happiness–Unhappiness dimension can be represented by a diagonal, from top left (stable Extraversion) to bottom right (unstable Introversion). Thus, the Happiness–Unhappiness dimension would be at right angles to the dimension ascribed to Diener et al. (1991). This representation is consistent with Eysenck's prediction that measures of Happiness will correlate positively with Extraversion and negatively with Neuroticism, which, as we have already seen, has been borne out experimentally.

The Diener et al. (1991) findings imply that measures of Happiness should correlate positively with both Extraversion and Neuroticism, as should measures of Unhappiness. Both sets of findings are compatible if different aspects of happiness are examined; these aspects can be separately identified as Characteristic Happiness or Placidity on Eysenck's diagonal dimension, and Volatile Emotionality or Extremism on the Diener et al. diagonal at right angles to it. Thus, Extraversion attenuates Negative Affect, whereas Neuroticism accentuates it. People in the top-left and bottom-right quadrants are typically happy and unhappy, respectively, but less intensely so than those in the top-right quadrant.

In earlier studies, Costa and McCrae (1980), using different measures (Cattell's and Bradburn's tests), only found positive correlations. That is, Bradburn's Negative Affect scale correlated positively and significantly with Neuroticism, but the correlation between Neuroticism and Positive Affect was effectively zero; Positive Affect correlated positively with Extraversion, but Negative Affect produced a correlation close to zero. Although the negative correlations between Neuroticism and Happiness in the two studies by Furnham and Brewin (1990) and Brebner (1991) do not replicate Costa and McCrae's findings, those results could be accommodated in Fig. 9.1 if their measure of Positive Affect measured Extraversion but not Neuroticism, and their measure of Negative Affect assessed Neuroticism but not Extraversion. In view of the established relationships between these personality variables and Happiness, it seems unlikely that Eysenck's Extraversion and Neuroticism factors are not involved at all. It may be that Extraversion and Neuroticism are correlated in some samples, and this affects their relationships with other measures. In Furnham and Brewin's study, for example, the correlation between Extraversion and Neuroticism was − .36 for their student subjects.

2. Gray

Gray's model, which is also concerned with worrying and anxiety, is essentially an important modification of Eysenck's theory, and relies on some of the same evidence for support (Gray, 1981). However, there are also a number of studies testing the central tenet of Gray's model, which is that the dimension of Anxiety runs diagonally downward and across Eysenck's two-dimensional representation (see Fig. 9.2). In other words, Gray recognized that both Extraversion and Neuroticism are involved in Anxiety and Worry, so that the dimension properly lies between low Neuroticism in association with high Extraversion, and high Neuroticism in association with low Extraversion (see Diaz & Pickering, 1993). Based on this premise, it follows that Extraversion and Neuroticism will show inverse relationships with Unhappiness or Happiness measures, a result, as previously seen, that has been found with some tests but not others.

Gray's view is that there are separate brain processes operating that respectively inhibit responding in the presence of punishment or nonreinforcement, or activate responding under reward or reinforcement conditions. It is his behavioral inhibitory system that is represented by the dimension running from low Neuroticism and high Extraversion to high Neuroticism and low Extraversion. Gray's behavioral activating system runs at right angles to the inhibitory system (i.e., in terms of the Eysenckian personality dimensions), between low Neuroticism and low Extraversion to high Neuroticism and high Extraversion, and is characterised at the high end of the scale by impulsive behavior.

Gray's postulated dimensions fit along the diagonals in Fig. 9.2, with Anxiety being highest where Negative Affect (or Eysenckian Neuroticism) is high and Positive Affect (or Extraversion) is low. Impulsivity is at right angles to Anxiety, being high when both Positive and Negative Affect (or Neuroticism and Extraversion) are high (i.e., high in the top-right quadrant, and low in the bottom-left quadrant).

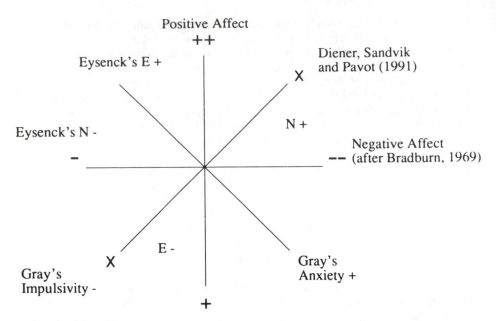

Positive Affect
++

Eysenck's E +

Diener, Sandvik
and Pavot (1991)
X

N +

Eysenck's N -

Negative Affect
-- (after Bradburn, 1969)

E -

X

Gray's
Impulsivity -

Gray's
Anxiety +

+

Figure 9.2   Combining Eysenck's (1985) and Gray's (1972) theory on Bradburn's (1969) model.

Although the reliance on Eysenck's personality factors Extraversion and Neuroticism is clear, it is less obvious what their relative contributions are. Is Neuroticism more influential than Extraversion within the inhibitory system, effectively pulling the Anxiety dimension toward Neuroticism? Similarly, is Extraversion more influential than Neuroticism for the activating system? Looking at conditions rather than people, is punishment more effective in inhibiting behavior than reward is in activating it? Work by learning theorists such as Miller and Dollard in the 1940s would suggest that punishment and reward situations produce escape and approach behaviors of unequal strengths, and that the effects are not symmetrical for approach and avoidance segments of behavior (Dollard & Miller, 1950).

Questionnaires developed to test Gray's model have met with mixed success in distinguishing the hypothesised systems from Eysenck's dimensions (MacAndrew & Steele, 1991; Wilson, Gray, & Barrett, 1990), but the original Sensitivity to Punishment (SP) scale (Torrubia & Tobeña, 1984) has been found (Diaz & Pickering, 1993) to correlate equally strongly, and opposite to the directions as expected, with Neuroticism ($r = .48$) and Extraversion ($r = -.48$). The sample tested was composed of 171 volunteers approximately balanced for gender. In this study, as would be expected from Gray's model, Impulsivity correlated significantly with the Eysenckian dimensions Extraversion ($r = .26$, $p < .001$) and Neuroticism ($r = .38$, $p < .001$), and Anxiety measured by the Trait scale from the State–Trait Anxiety Inventory (STAI; Spielberger, Gorusch, Lushene, Vagg, & Jacobs, 1983) correlated negatively with Extraversion ($r = -.27$, $p < .001$) and positively with Neuroticism ($r = .59$, $p < .001$).

More recently, separate scales to test sensitivity to both punishment and reward (Sensitivity to Punishment, Sensitivity to Reward [SPSR]) have been developed by Torrubia and his co-workers at the Autonomous University of Barcelona at the Jaume 1 University of Castellon, and are used in the studies reported later. Torrubia presents evidence in this section for individual differences in appraising threat and coping with stress, which are related to SPSR and Gray's behavioral inhibitory system.

3. Argyle

The question of how far a person's characteristic bias toward happiness is mediated by social factors, rather than being simply an expression of personality, is obviously an important one. Argyle's work in the area of happiness, which has looked at behaviour in social situations (Argyle & Martin, 1991; Argyle, Martin, & Crossland, 1989), has shown that, in dyadic interactions with strangers in a waiting room, extraverted individuals initiate conversations, talk more, smile more, and attempt more amusing behaviors, such as telling jokes, than their less extraverted counterparts. Ruch (1994) refined the difference in the smiling behavior of introverts and extraverts to the degree that only responses involving action of both the zygomatic major muscle and orbicularis oculi muscle, which are symmetric and last longer than ⅔ sec, distinguish between introverts and extraverts.

Using multiple regression, Argyle and Lu (1990a) identified the social skills of extraverts, rather than Extraversion itself, as mediating their high scores on the OHI because the standardised regression coefficient (Beta) for Extraversion decreased markedly when assertiveness was entered into the regression. Argyle's work emphasises the importance of socially mediated reinforcement in the maintenance of day-to-day happiness, and is a corrective to "pure" personality explanations, which ignore the fact that most everyday behavior occurs in social contexts, and that satisfaction with recent social interactions largely determines the individual's current status as happy or not (Cooper, Okamura, & Gurka, 1992).

It is not possible to review the role of social factors in happiness extensively in the present chapter, but some studies seem to link personality and happiness across different social contexts. Diener, Sandvik, Pavot, and Fujita (1992), for example, showed that extraverted individuals have higher levels of self-reported happiness, regardless of whether they live by themselves or with others, or work in nonsocial rather than social occupations. These results from more than 16,500 individuals held good across race, gender, and age. However, it was also shown that extraverts are significantly more likely to work in social occupations and to live in multiperson households. The study does not relate extraverts' happiness to their sociability outside their homes and work contexts, and it is still likely that interpersonal transactions are an important source of enjoyment for extraverts, as shown by Argyle and Lu (1990b).

The home environment is likely to be an important source of general happiness if it is satisfactory, but attempts to compare the happiness of people as a function of their living environments, such as Heineken and Spaeth's (1988) research on a group of over-sixties, are fraught with the possibility of confounding variables. Although their residents of family-type community housing were rated happiest, the comparison with nursing home residents inevitably raises the question of health status. Nevertheless, even in that study, personality factors were deemed more important than housing settings for expressed happiness. Other possible confounding factors also exist, and there is a risk of responses from some environments being affected by "socially correct" responding. However, Diener, Sandvik, Pavot, and Gallagher (1991) found that social desirability actually enhanced happiness, rather than being an artifact of response bias. The obvious likelihood is that social environments and interpersonal interactions play important roles for everyone's happiness, but the portable, social behaviour of extraverts may reduce the importance of particular environments for them.

The present research did not attempt to extend Argyle's work on social skills. However, one recent personality test, Rusalov's Structure of Temperament Questionnaire (Rusalov, 1989), has separate scales for behaviour in social and impersonal situations, and was included in the present study to compare the relationships of the two types of scales with the Happiness measures. The Structure of Temperament Questionnaire is based on neo-Pavlovian personality theorising, and is outlined after introducing Strelau's Pavlovian Temperament Survey.

4. Strelau

Strelau's (1983) book, *Temperament-Personality-Activity*, provided a systematic exposition of his theoretical position and the evidence supporting it, most of which is from studies carried out within the former Eastern Bloc of Socialist People's Republics. His position exemplifies neo-Pavlovian theorising in personality research, although other approaches (e.g., Rusalov, 1989) offer slightly different interpretations along the same broad lines. More recently, Strelau and Angleitner (1994) spearheaded the cross-cultural development of Strelau's Pavlovian Temperament Survey (PTS) in a number of countries including Australia, Germany, Hungary, and England, as well as Poland, where it originated, and Russia (Bodunov, 1993). Although neo-Pavlovian models regard temperament as biologically based and personality as the expression of the genetically determined structure of temperament in environmental and interpersonal transactions during an individual's life, individual differences is one of the main areas in which parallels and similarities among theories and findings have emerged in psychological research carried out independently in the Western and Eastern Blocs. It has also become evident that the main questionnaires that have been developed can survive translation and produce similar patterns of relationships and results in different countries (see Stough, Brebner, & Cooper, 1991).

In Strelau's PTS, there are three scales. Originally, there were four main types of nervous systems that Pavlov believed could reliably be distinguished from one another through their behavior. The distinctions were based on the strength of the nervous system in terms of its ability to withstand intense stimulation and remain in an excitatory state before switching into protective or transmarginal inhibition; the balance between excitation and inhibition, which, for Pavlov, were separate cortical states; and the mobility or speed of switching between excitation and inhibition. The three scales of the PTS measure Strength of Excitation (SEXC), Strength of Inhibition (SINH), and Mobility (MOBY). Presumably, the Pavlovian balance between excitation and inhibition is simply the ratio of SEXC/SINH. Strelau's own contribution to the present volume renders further explanation unnecessary here, except briefly insofar as happiness is concerned.

Strelau's approach suggests that *how* individuals deal with stress will reflect their temperamental makeup. This will be shown by those people high on SEXC and MOBY but low on SINH, continuing to perform effectively as the intensity of stimulation, or the degree of stress increases, because of their capacity to withstand negative stimulation, and their flexibility in selectively responding or withholding responses. A strong inhibitory tendency would be associated with greater reactivity to environmental pressures (Karwowska & Strelau, 1990) and the tendency to be unable to cope and the need to escape from the source of stress. This tendency would be greater for individuals high on SINH but low on the MOBY scale: Such people might be located near Gray's Anxiety pole in Fig. 9.2. Therefore, SEXC and MOBY are expected to correlate positively with happiness and SINH to correlate negatively.

Rusalov's (1989) revision and translation of his Structure of Temperament Questionnaire (STQ) into English has made another neo-Pavlovian test accessible to Western personality researchers. As stated earlier, it was included in the present study to compare the relationships his social and impersonal scales bore with happiness.

The STQ has eight scales: four recording behavior in social situations, and four referring to impersonal contexts. The scales are Social Ergonicity and Ergonicity (SER and ER), which measure endurance or strength of response; Social Emotionality and Emotionality (SEM and EM); Social Plasticity and Plasticity (SP and P), which refer to the ability to adapt behavior to current demands; and Social Tempo and Tempo (ST and T), which are concerned with the speed of responding in different contexts. Rusalov's own view of happiness is that it represents the degree of concordance between anticipated outcomes and actual outcomes, which is assessed through excitation of interneurons that have "copied" the activity of the pyramidal neurons of the cortex, which underlie decisions to behave/respond, along the collateral pyramidal tract (Rusalov, 1989). Including the STQ in this study is not a hypothesis-testing exercise, as far as his interpretation is concerned; interest is confined to whether the social scales show higher correlations with the PSQ and OHI than the impersonal scales, and how high the various correlation coefficients are in their own right.

5. Martin

Martin's cognitive propagational model of emotion (Martin, 1990; Martin & Williams, 1990) postulates intimate connections between emotion, personality, and cognition. This model proposes that cognitive processes that lead to and maintain a particular emotional state tend to be enhanced when that emotion is experienced. Similarly, cognitive processes that maintain a particular personality type are habitually used by individuals with that personality type (Martin, 1985). The origins of these links between emotion/personality and cognition may be either integral or inferred (Martin, Horder, & Jones, 1992; Martin & Jones, in press). The inferred bias hypothesis proposes that the links arise as empirically learned generalisations from specific episodes involving both particular thoughts and particular emotions or aspects of personality. The integral bias hypothesis proposes, in contrast, that the links with particular patterns of cognitive processing constitute fundamental characteristics of different emotions and personality types. Initial evidence concerning the development of anxiety favours the integral bias account.

Thus far, the predictions of the propagational model have generally been evaluated with respect to negative emotions, such as anxiety and depression, and the personality trait of Neuroticism. However, the model also predicts that cognitive processes that are likely to increase a person's happiness and well-being should be enhanced in appropriate cases. The cognitive factor focused on here is Attributional Valence. *Valence* refers to whether a cognitive appraisal is positive or negative (see Ortony, Clore, & Collins, 1988). Some individuals make consistently positive valence attributions, whereas others make consistently negative ones. Many of the situations encountered in everyday life are neither clearly positive or negative, but ambiguous. In these ambiguous situations, which pervade everyday life, the type of causal explanation that people give for them may be important in determining how they feel generally. In such situations, it is predicted that people who score highly on the OHI will select more positive and fewer negative explanations, whereas the opposite will be true for low OHI scorers.

To test this prediction, a number of ambiguous episodes were devised and three possible explanations were provided for each episode. The explanations were either positive, negative, or neutral in character. In a study carried out in collaboration with G. V. Jones and A. Renton, participants were required to select one of the three explanations for each of 20 ambiguous events, and their tendency to make positive or negative attributions was compared with a number of other state and trait measures.

EXPERIMENTAL STUDY TWO

Subjects in this study completed the OHI, the Beck Depression Inventory (BDI; Beck, Ward, Mendelson, Mock, & Erbaugh 1961), Visual Analogue Scales of Happiness (VASH), and the Attributional Valence Questionnaire (AVQ).

Visual Analogue Scales of Happiness (VASH)

Visual analogue scales have been used quite widely to assess general levels of happiness (see Martin, 1990). The state measures of Happiness asked how subjects felt at the moment. The trait measures of Happiness asked how subjects had felt in general over the last month. In both cases, a 100-point scale ranging from 0 (*not at all*) to 100 (*extremely*) was used. In both cases, four different measures were taken: Happy, Content, Exuberant, and Self-Confident.

Attributional Valence Questionnaire (AVQ)

This questionnaire was developed by Martin, Jones, and Renton. Twenty events were chosen that can occur in student life. Each event was relatively ambiguous in emotional tone, allowing for plausible explanations of the events to be positive, negative, or neutral. A panel of students confirmed that the events and explanations were reasonably commonplace and plausible, and that the assignment of explanations into the positive, negative, or neutral categories was appropriate. For each event, the subject had to choose one of three explanations. An example follows.

You stand for election to a committee. You win the post you stood for. Why did you win the election?

Positive: People have confidence in me.

Negative: People think I'll be a pushover in committee meetings.

Neutral: No one knew any of the candidates well, so the voting was fairly random.

METHOD

The subjects consisted of 91 students from the University of Oxford. Of these, 36 were female and 55 were male. The mean age was 20.3 years (SD = 1.6 years). The subjects were divided at the median into two groups: the High OHI group (OHI greater or equal to 38, n = 46) and the Low OHI group (OHI less than 38, n = 45).

RESULTS

Measures of Happiness

The mean levels of the OHI and the various state and trait measures of Happiness did not differ significantly between males and females, with the exception that males rated themselves as significantly more self-confident (see Table 9.1).

The OHI is highly correlated with the other trait measures of Happiness (see Table 9.2) and the state measures of Happiness (see Table 9.3). To discover which of the four state and four trait components of Happiness best predict OHI scores, a series of hierarchical, stepwise, multiple-regression analyses were performed. The trait measures were examined, followed by the state

Table 9.1 Mean levels of Happiness and Depression of males and females

	Females	Males	t test	sig
OHI	38.2	37.6		ns
Trait				
Happiness	62.4	63.8		ns
Contentment	60.0	61.3		ns
Exuberance	44.7	50.9		ns
Self-Confidence	47.1	63.6	3.15	**
State				
Happiness	62.8	70.3		ns
Contentment	66.1	72.5		ns
Exuberance	41.1	48.0		ns
Self-Confidence	56.4	68.7	2.19	*
BDI	6.3	4.5		ns

$*p < .05.$ $**p < .01.$

measures, and finally the significant factors from both analyses were compared. Gender was included as an independent variable, but was not significant in these analyses.

First, a stepwise, multiple regression was performed, with OHI as the dependent variable and the trait measures of Happiness, Contentment, Exuberance, and Self-Confidence as the independent variables. Exuberance ($t = 2.63$, $p < .05$), Happiness ($t = 2.54, p < .05$), and Self-Confidence ($t = 2.42, p < .05$) were significant contributors. The coefficient of determination was .41, indicating that 41% of the variance in OHI scores was accounted for. The best fitting equation was OHI $=$ .12 Exub $+$ .15 Hap $+$ .11 SC $+$ 16.31, where Exub, Hap, and SC are Exuberance, Happiness, and Self-Confidence scores, respectively. Second, a similar analysis was performed with the state measures of Happiness. Exuberance ($t = 4.30, p < .001$) and Self-Confidence ($t = 3.18$, $p < .01$) were significant contributors. The coefficient of determination was .42, and the best fitting equation was OHI $=$ .17 Exub $+$ .13 SC $+$ 21.81. Third, a final stepwise, multiple regression was performed, with the five significant predictors of OHI as the dependent variables. State Exuberance ($t = 3.99, p < .001$), trait Happiness ($t = 3.97, p < .001$), and state Self-Confidence

Table 9.2 Correlations between trait measures of Happiness and Depression

	OHI	Hap	Cont	Exub	SC	BDI
OHI		.53***	.45***	.54***	.50***	− .46***
Happiness			.76***	.55***	.49***	− .39***
Contentment				.54***	.44***	− .42***
Exuberance					.49***	− .23*
Self-Confidence						− .53***
BDI						

$*p < .05.$ $**p < .01.$ $***p < .001.$

Table 9.3 Correlations between OHI and state measures of Happiness

	OHI	Hap	Cont	Exub	SC
OHI		.52***	.53***	.59***	.54***
Happiness			.80***	.64***	.52***
Contentment				.64***	.57***
Exuberance					.53***
Self-Confidence					

*$p < .05$. **$p < .01$. ***$p < .001$.

($t = 2.28, p < .05$) were the best predictors. The coefficient of determination was .51, and the best fitting equation was OHI = .19 Tr Hap + .14 St Exub + .09 St SC + 13.55, where Tr and St indicate trait and state, respectively.

Attributional Valence

Analysis of variance (ANOVA) conducted on the number of positive and negative attributions revealed that females gave significantly fewer positive attributions than males. High OHI scorers gave more positive attributions than low OHI scorers (see Fig. 9.3). There was no significant three-way interaction between gender of subject, OHI group, and attributional valence.

A hierarchical, stepwise, multiple-regression analysis was performed to test whether any of the other measures of Happiness could account for a significant degree of variance in attributional valence (AV) beyond that accounted for by OHI scores. The attributional valence measure was the difference between the number of positive and negative attributions made by each subject. Three successive analyses were carried out. First, stepwise, multiple regression with OHI scores, trait measures of Happiness, and gender revealed that only OHI scores ($t = 4.05, p < .001$) and gender ($t = 2.49, p < .05$) were significant contributors. The coefficient of determination was .20. The best fitting equation was AV = .11 OHI + 1.67 Sex − 8.33. Second, a similar analysis with OHI scores, state measures of Happiness, and gender revealed again that only OHI scores ($t = 4.05, p < .001$) and gender ($t = 2.49, p < .05$) were significant contributors. Thus, the same equation as previously stated is the best fit. Third, to discover whether any additional variance in attributional valence can be accounted for by depression, the BDI, OHI, and gender were entered into a stepwise, multiple regression. This revealed significant contributions of OHI ($t = 2.63, p < .05$), BDI ($t = 2.31, p < .05$), and gender ($t = 1.97, p = .05$). The coefficient of determination was .25. The best fitting equation was AV = .08 OHI − .18 BDI + 1.33 Sex − 5.53.

DISCUSSION

The results of this study reveal something about the relationship between OHI scores and several different aspects of happiness, and also about the

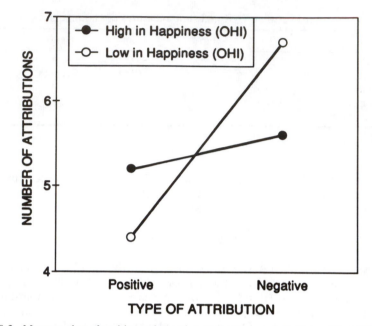

Figure 9.3   Mean number of positive and negative attributions made by high and low OHI scores.

relationship between OHI scores and attributional valence. A person's OHI score is related to his or her state and trait levels of Exuberance, Self-Confidence, Contentment, and General Happiness. These measures are also significantly correlated with each other. The three components that make the strongest contributions to OHI scores are the long-term level of General Happiness and the current levels of Exuberance and Self-Confidence.

High OHI scorers tended to make relatively positive attributions when presented with ambiguous events. Similarly and independent of a person's OHI score, high BDI scorers tended to make relatively negative attributions. These findings provide support for the propagational account of the interconnectedness of emotional and cognitive aspects of personality. A person who has a tendency toward happiness is also likely to have a tendency toward making a positive appraisal of ambiguous situations. A question for future research (cf. Martin & Jones, in press) is whether such relations are integral or inferred— innate or acquired.

6. Brebner

The view of Extraversion first put forward by Brebner and Cooper (1974) was an explicit attempt to amalgamate Eysenck's two separate theories in terms of reactive inhibition and cortical arousal, respectively, because both appeared to have considerable experimental support, although neither of the hypothesised central processes can be directly observed or measured. The amalgamation was effected by drawing a distinction between the central processes concerned with stimulus analysis and those concerned with response organisation. Although this is one of the oldest distinctions in psychology, it was and still is exceedingly difficult to point to any particular brain activity that can be related reliably to one process rather than the other, despite technological advances over the last 20 years. For this reason, like many predecessors facing the same problem, the model was operationalised in behavioural terms. It was suggested that central excitation from either process would appear as the tendency to continue in or augment behaviour associated with stimulus analysis or response organisation, whereas central inhibition would manifest as the opposite tendency to cease or attenuate that behaviour. Extraverts and introverts differ in that introverts derive excitation from stimulus analysis but inhibition from response organisation. For extraverts, the reverse is the case; they derive excitation from response organisation and inhibition from stimulus analysis.

Various studies have provided evidence supporting the essential distinction made by the model (e.g., Brebner & Cooper, 1978), but this is not surprising given its origins. The testability of the model has been criticised by Eysenck and Eysenck (1985) on the grounds that, to make accurate predictions, it is necessary to know the degree of excitation or inhibition from stimulus analysis, response organisation, perceptual responses, and response feedback. Although to show differences in the performance of introverts or extraverts deriving from the model, it is necessary to bias or unbalance any experimental task in the direction of stimulus analysis (e.g., Brebner & Cooper, 1974) or response organisation (e.g., Brebner & Flavel, 1978), or to allow subjects to choose between stimulus analysis or response organisation (e.g., Brebner & Cooper, 1978), the model is no more or less testable than any other invoking hypothetical constructs (e.g., Eysenck's cortical arousal theory). The criticism that, "In practice, we usually have extremely sketchy information about most of these factors" (Eysenck & Eysenck, 1985, p. 216), would simply mean that there is similarly sketchy information about the overall arousal levels of introverts and extraverts, postulated by Eysenck, because this is a function of these very factors that are never absent in any experimental context.

The further argument, "As a consequence, it would typically be possible to account for any set of data in a post hoc fashion" (Eysenck & Eysenck, 1985, p. 216), would again similarly apply to Eysenck's own theory. But, provided the necessary condition of biasing the experimental conditions appropriately is met, or the possibility exists for biases toward stimulus analysis or response organisation to show themselves, it is not the case that any set of data can be explained. For example, where a free-operant situation is employed (Brebner & Cooper, 1978), there would be no possible post hoc explanation if a greater tendency to respond had been shown by introverts, particularly to the least interesting/stimulating stimuli. As the data show, however, this was not found. Instead, in line with the prediction derived from the model in standard fashion before undertaking the experiment, it was extraverts who responded far more frequently. Even Eysenck's inverted-U model of extraversion is not capable of explaining any set of data, even though, by joining pairs of points at different parts of the U, one can demonstrate an increase, a decrease, or no change between the two points. But data are obtained in an experimental context where, however imperfectly, the degree of likely arousing effect is observed and recorded, and can be compared with data from other contexts predicted to have more or less arousing effects. Whatever the model, explanations are constrained by the need for consistency and coherence in their predictions across studies.

The relationship between measures of Happiness, as measured by the Personal State Questionnaire (PSQ; Brebner, 1983) and Extraversion in the Brebner–Cooper model is mediated by two related factors. First, there is the tendency for introverts to engage in greater analysis of available stimuli or information than do extraverts. Given that they perform less stimulus analysis than introverts, extraverts should be characterised by a greater tendency to generalise from past situations to current ones. Introverts, in contrast, will be more affected by present information. Second, extraverts' stronger responding tendency may give them greater control over impersonal situations, so that, as Tiggemann, Winefield, and Brebner (1982) found, when faced with the task of gaining control of an auditory stimulus, they show less learned helplessness than introverts. But, as Argyle's research indicates, extraverts' greater social assertiveness gives them more control in interpersonal contexts. So, from either impersonal or interpersonal contexts, extraverts are more likely to generalise from positive events in the past than from negative ones.

That extraverts have an "optimistic" view of the world is scarcely a matter of great controversy, but their tendency to use generalisation as a way to reduce stimulus analysis needs to be tested. To do so, Brebner (1991) employed a simulated "betting" task. Two similar experiments were carried out on the tendency by introverts and extraverts to generalise from either negative or positive past events (i.e., losses or wins). Briefly, subjects were introduced to a simple, computer-controlled "betting" game (involving only notional monetary gains or losses), in which a tone was sounded. Subjects listened to the tone and placed a "bet" on whether it heralded a win or a loss on the next spin of a computerised "fruit machine" or "one-armed bandit." The resulting win or loss then appeared on the screen, providing feedback to subjects. A cumulative record of wins and losses also appeared on the screen after every result.

In both experiments, the first phase was a discrimination phase, in which all subjects learned to discriminate between seven tones equally stepped between 150 and 1050 Hz. The discrimination phase was succeeded by a training phase, in which only two tones were sounded—the lowest frequency 150 Hz tone with a low probability of 0.15 of preceding a win, and the highest 1050 Hz tone with a high probability of 0.85 of being followed by a win. Subjects could only lay "bets" of 20 cents or $1.00 on the tones. During this training phase, subjects learned that the low-frequency tone was associated with losing, but the high-frequency tone with winning. The instructions they followed were to "Attempt to maximize your winnings," and the extent to which learning occurred and the instruction was followed was seen in the amounts bet on the two tones.

A final test phase, in which only the middle five tones varying in frequency from 300 to 900 Hz were presented, was then undertaken by all subjects. In this phase, subjects had greater control over the amount they could "bet," and they could place "bets" of 20, 40, 60, or 80 cents, or $1.00. In both experiments, all tones were intended to have the same probability of 0.50 of predicting a win on the fruit machine. But in one experiment, a computer-programming mistake made the probability of the 300 Hz tone preceding a win 0.65, rather than 0.50.

In the experiment that was programmed as intended, extraverts "bet" higher amounts on the tones as their frequency increased, showing the predicted gradient of generalisation, and indicating that extraverts' behavior was affected by the expectation that tones of higher frequency would be followed by a win on the fruit machine. In contrast, introverted subjects showed a much lower gradient for the amounts bet as the tone frequency increased, supporting the hypothesis that introverts would be more affected by the losses in the training phase.

In the other study, the programming error that raised the probability of the lowest frequency tone heralding a win from 0.50 to 0.65 in the test phase produced a serendipitous finding of considerable relevance and interest to the original experimental aim. Extraverts performed as in the previous experiment (i.e., they generalised from the probabilities of high frequencies winning and low frequencies losing, as occurred in the training session, and produced a generalisation gradient with amounts "bet" increasing across the five tones as their frequency increased). But introverted subjects behaved differently. Instead of a weaker generalisation gradient, they responded to the increased likelihood of the 300 Hz tone winning and matched their bets more accurately to that.

Brebner (1991) concluded,

introverts varied their behavior to match differences in the success probability of tones rather than generalising from previous training. Extraverts generalised rather than matching their behavior to the unintended differences in success probability. On the basis of this result, it is suggested that introverts update their estimates of population parameters more frequently than extraverts do and make more use of available information to do so. (p. 100)

These results suggest, as the Brebner–Cooper model states, that introverts and extraverts deal with information in different ways, with introverts processing more stimulus information than extraverts typically do. Is this the foundation of extraverts' relatively happier status? It is important to note that extraverts' generalisation reflected previous positive events, whereas introverts' behavior could be regarded as more "realistic." Alloy and Abramson (1979) strongly suggested that being realistic, rather than optimistic, is linked to depressive tendencies, and this might implicate neuroticism along the same lines as Eysenck suggested. However, following previous work by Cameron and Meichenbaum (1982), Roger and Jamieson (1988) showed that continued attention to emotionally distressing information, which is termed *rehearsal* or *rumination*, and measured by Roger's Emotional Control Scale, is negatively related to physiological indices of adaptation or recovery. Without anticipating the chapter by Roger in this section, it can be pointed out that both Roger's rumination, and the greater attention to available information shown by introverts in the "betting" experiments, show a bottom–up, more detailed, and specific investigation of current information, rather than a top–down treatment based on its general similarity to previous situations. A bottom–up approach requires the individual to assess more events, whether negative or positive, whereas a top–down approach allows a more selective treatment, which, for extraverts, apparently favours positive events. Naturally, in association with emotionality, these different approaches would produce stronger negative or positive effects. But the basic mechanism suggested here, for differences in introverts' and extraverts' happiness, is how information is dealt with, rather than the intensity of the effect produced. Extraversion provides the mechanism for dealing with detectable environmental changes, incoming stimuli, or information, either in a detailed and specific way, or as belonging to a more general class of events identified by the similarity of some feature(s). Neuroticism determines the intensity of the emotional states activated by that information and, on the Eysenck Personality Questionnaire-Revised (EPQ-R) or earlier versions, that Eysenckian dimension is associated with negative rather than positive states.

THE EXPERIMENTAL STUDY

From the six different theoretical standpoints outlined previously, at least seven personality factors for which questionnaires have been developed are related to characteristic happiness, with two other factors also being implicated. Eysenck sees Extraversion (E) and Neuroticism (N) as the relevant personality factors, with E and N having been shown to correlate positively and negatively with happiness in past researches. Gray's behavioral inhibitory or activating systems are sensitive to punishment and reward, respectively; Torrubia's SP and SR measures would be expected to show SP negatively related to happiness and SR positively related to it. Strelau's SEXC and MOBY measures are expected to correlate positively with happiness, but SINH is expected to correlate negatively.

Additionally, Argyle and Lu accepted a role for Eysenck's factors, but pointed to social assertiveness as mediating the relationship between E and happiness, as measured by the OHI. Brebner's suggestion that extraverts' positive generalisation explains their chronic happiness completes the present list. As stated, the STQ scales are included to see if the four social scales correlate more highly with the PSQ and OHI than the impersonal scales—a result that would support the relatively greater importance of social behaviour.

The predicted relationships between personality and happiness have the status of hypotheses because they are derived from theoretical positions. But two questions pose themselves. First, how different are the theories as far as predicting happiness is concerned? Gray's 45-degree rotation of Eysenck's dimensions still has Anxiety and Impulsivity related to E and N. Also, parallels between neo-Pavlovian personality dimensions and Eysenck's factors have often been considered, although an exact correspondence does not seem justified experimentally (e.g., Brebner, 1980). Strelau's PTS questionnaire has been used along with the EPQ to compare the relationship between temperamental properties of the nervous system and Eysenck's model of personality (Ruch, 1992). Moreover, both Argyle and Brebner brought extraversion into their explanations. This degree of communality means that, although the predictions can be easily tested, it is more difficult to test between the various explanations.

The correlations obtained between the various personality factors and measures of Happiness provide a starting point, and show whether the expected relationships emerge or not. Beyond that, multiple regression can be employed to discover whether the personality tests are really measuring different features of happiness. If entering different personality tests into the same regression to predict happiness markedly increases the multiple correlation, it can be concluded that they deal with different portions of the variance (i.e., they measure different aspects of happiness). However, if there is no increase in the multiple correlation beyond that obtained separately with the various tests, they will be seen to be tapping into the same overall, general state of happiness, despite their different theoretical backgrounds. The standardised regression coefficients (Beta weights) for individual tests can be used to show the unique contribution of specific tests, and in this way the relevance of particular personality factors for happiness can be assessed. The second question that arises concerns the nature of measures of Happiness. This is addressed in the following explanation of the two measures used—the OHI and the Personal State Questionnaire (PSQ).

THE HAPPINESS MEASURES

The Oxford Happiness Inventory (OHI)

The OHI is described in detail by Argyle (see chap. 10, this volume), therefore only brief mention of the major characteristics is made here. The OHI is basically an inverted form of the BDI (Beck, Weissman, Lester, & Trexler, 1974), with additional items to cover aspects of happiness not included in that inventory. There are 29 items forming a single scale for Happiness. Items include questions about being happy, being optimistic for the future, being in control, having a good influence on things, being attractive, and having fun with other people. Furnham and Brewin (1990) gave values of Cronbach's alpha between 0.64 and 0.87 for the OHI. They also stated it has a demonstrated test–retest reliability of 0.78, but provided no further details. (The actual r value given is -0.78, $p = 1094$, but this is surely a proofreading error.) In a recent unpublished study of 95 Adelaide student volunteer subjects, made up of 68 females and 27 males with a mean age of 22.58 years ($SD = 8.15$), the writer obtained a Cronbach's alpha of 0.90 for the OHI, showing the test to be internally consistent.

The Personal State Questionnaire (PSQ)

The PSQ was developed independently of the OHI (Brebner, 1983). It began as an attempt to evaluate the importance for people's current affective states of lasting effects, such as physical and mental health status, and recent events, which provide a record of reinforcement, such as enjoying novel experiences, finding people helpful, or being satisfied with recent celebrations. Both sorts of effects are considered likely to generalise to other aspects of life, but recent reinforcements are taken to have comparatively short-lived effects. Despite their different backgrounds, the correlation between the OHI and the PSQ in the previous study was +0.63 and was significant beyond the 0.01 level.

The PSQ has 37 items, with no subscales (see appendix). In addition to the 37 items, respondents are provided with four subsequent items in which they can describe recent events, whether positive or negative, that have affected them, and say how strong the effect was. Responses volunteered here may be used to identify effects outside of the 37 items acting to produce extreme scores.

The internal consistency of the PSQ is high (e.g., Cronbach's alpha was 0.93 in the group mentioned earlier). Test–retest measures of the PSQ reflect changes in the schedule of short-lived reinforcements, as expected, but generally produce correlation coefficients around 0.65, unless some broad effect can be seen on the group being tested. For student samples, there is a lowering of the group's mean score just prior to examinations. This is due partly to less social enjoyment as would be anticipated, but greater variability is also introduced into answers to some items (e.g., those about the person's mental health and state, his or her recent life or foreseeable future being stressful, or him or her coping with problems recently, which acts to reduce test–retest correlations at certain times of the academic year). This result, along with the positive correlation with the OHI, may serve to validate the PSQ as a Happiness measure. A cross-cultural study with V. M. Rusalov, which is currently incomplete, shows that the translated PSQ can be used in other societies. It produced a significant difference in the Happiness scores of Australian and Russian students in 1992—a result that again tends to validate the PSQ as a measure of Happiness.

As is the case for other measures of Happiness, the PSQ has been found to show statistically significant positive correlations with Extraversion and negative correlations with Introversion. In the study mentioned, for example, the Pearson correlation was $r = 0.31$ with E and $r = -0.52$ with N. The correlation between the PSQ and OHI, and their similar correlations with E and N, suggest both are testing similar aspects of happiness. If this is the case, similar relationships with other personality factors should be obtained for both tests.

METHOD

The present study involved the computer-controlled administration of five questionnaires to a group of 90 psychology students. As signaled, the tests used were the 1991 revised and extended EPQ, the EPQ-R, the SPSR, the PTS, the OHI, and the PSQ. A smaller group of 70 other psychology student volunteers completed the questionnaires, except that Rusalov's STQ was substituted for Strelau's PTS. All subjects in the larger group undertook the test of generalisation, or "betting" experiment, similar to that described earlier. After the seven tones—varying in frequency between 150 and 1050 Hz—had been presented for discrimination purposes, subjects entered a training phase of 100 trials. On 50 of the trials, a tone of 1050 Hz was presented, which had a probability of 0.80 of preceding a win on the next spin of the wheel of the computerised "fruit machine," as previously described. On the remainder of the trials, a tone of 150 Hz had a matching 0.80 probability of preceding a loss. Trials were randomly ordered. During this phase, subjects "bet" 20 cents or $1.00 on the likelihood of a win occurring, and learned to associate the high-frequency tone with winning and the low-frequency tone with losing.

The subsequent test phase of the experiment presented five tones with frequencies of 300, 450, 600, 750, and 900 Hz randomly ordered. Subjects again "bet" on the likelihood of a tone being associated with a win, but were now permitted to vary their bets between 20, 40, 60, 80, and 100 cents. Four blocks of 50 trials each were presented to subjects, with a running tally of wins and losses shown during each block. All subjects were instructed that the point of the task was to maximize their winnings. Unlike in the training phase, in the test phase all five tones had the same likelihood of 0.50 of preceding a win.

RESULTS

Questionnaire Data

Means and Reliabilities. Table 9.4 shows the mean and median scores, the standard deviations, and Cronbach's alphas obtained for each of the scales used. The high alpha values attest to the internal consistency of the scales.

Pearson Correlations. The Pearson correlations between the Happiness measures—the OHI and the PSQ—and the various personality scales, including the STQ, are shown in Table 9.5. It can be seen that the OHI and PSQ correlate very highly in this student sample. With that, the pattern of correlations with the personality scales is practically identical for the two Happiness measures, suggesting that both are dealing with individuals' overall, general happiness. The expected significant positive and negative correlations with E and N were obtained. Eysenck's Psychoticism produced small, but statistically significant negative correlations with the OHI and PSQ. Torrubia's SP scale correlated negatively with the Happiness tests, as predicted, but the SR scale showed R values very close to zero. Being sensitive to reward or reinforcement, therefore, does not appear to affect one's general happiness. This is discussed further later.

Strelau's PTS scales for Excitation (SEXC) and Mobility (MOBY) produced the anticipated significant positive correlations. SINH, measuring the Strength of Inhibition, showed correlations around zero with the OHI and PSQ. From

Table 9.4 Scale means, *SD*s, medians, and alphas

Test/scale	Mean	SD	Median	Alpha
PSQ	258.0	47.3	264.0	.946
OHI	67.2	12.3	68.0	.929
E	14.7	5.6	15.5	.878
N	13.6	6.0	13.0	.881
P	7.3	4.4	7.0	.782
SP	12.4	6.0	14.0	.838
SR	13.2	4.1	14.0	.738
SEXC	50.6	8.2	50.0	.864
SINH	57.8	6.7	59.0	.814
MOBY	58.9	8.3	60.0	.905
ER	6.5	2.4	7.0	.614
SER	8.6	2.6	9.0	.780
EM	5.1	3.5	5.0	.858
SEM	6.9	2.5	7.0	.703
PL	8.5	2.8	9.0	.789
SPL	6.6	3.0	6.0	.757
T	8.7	2.4	9.0	.660
ST	8.6	2.8	9.0	.697

Table 9.5 Pearson correlations for Happiness measures and the personality tests

	Measure	
Test	PSQ	OHI
OHI	.837***	—
E	.464***	.436***
N	−.438***	−.506***
P	−.230*	−.283**
SP	−.593***	−.561***
SR	.044	−.032
SEXC	.467***	.550***
SINH	−.002	.109
MOBY	.601***	.647***
ER	.358**	.283*
SER	.239*	.379**
EM	−.258*	−.246*
SEM	−.259*	−.294*
PL	.329**	.315**
SPL	.072	.018
T	.299*	.321**
ST	.227*	.299*

Note. $N = 90$.
*$p < .05$. **$p < .01$. ***$p < .001$.

Table 9.6 Pearson correlations between personality scales

Scale	Scale						
	N	P	SP	SR	SEXC	SINH	MOBY
E	−.129	.055	−.518***	.466***	.355**	−.186*	.438***
N		.125	.708***	.318***	−.469***	−.167	−.566***
P			−.038	.208	−.081	−.280**	−.158
SP				.032	−.514***	−.014	−.626***
SR					−.102	−.432**	−.164
SEXC						.241*	.741***
SINH							.252*

Note. N = 90.
*p < .05. **p < .01. ***p < .001.

this result, inhibitory strength appears to be independent of one's general happiness.

Table 9.5 shows the correlations obtained between the eight scales of Rusalov's STQ and the OHI and PSQ. There are no important differences between the social and impersonal scales for Ergonicity, Emotionality, or Tempo in the way they correlate with the Happiness measures. The correlations are in the same direction and are statistically significant, although not very large. Social Plasticity, however, correlates around zero with both the OHI and PSQ, whereas the comparable correlations for Plasticity are just over .30 and significant. It appears from these results that there is no clear difference in the relationships Rusalov's Social and Impersonal scales have with happiness, and the significant correlations that are obtained do not explain much of the variance.

The intercorrelations for the personality scales are shown in Table 9.6. It is evident that E and N are related to almost all the scales from the other two questionnaires. SR, which correlates near zero with the OHI and PSQ, correlates positively with both E and N and negatively with SINH. SINH correlates negatively with both E and N, but the *R* values are low. The correlations for SP, SEXC, and MOBY with E and N form a similar pattern: The positive scales SEXC and MOBY correlate positively with E and negatively with N, whereas SP does the opposite. The scales of the PTS are positively correlated, with an *R* value as high as .741 for SEXC and MOBY.

Multiple Regressions. Multiple regressions were performed using Statistical Package for the Social Sciences-Extended (SPSS-X; Norusis, 1993). The Enter procedure was used to obtain the Beta coefficients to show the contributions of particular scales. Table 9.7 shows the obtained values for R, R^2, and Beta when the scales from the EPQX-R, SPSR, and PTS were entered in two sets of three separate regressions: In one set, the OHI was the dependent variable; in the other, the PSQ. As Table 9.7 shows, the R values were around .60, or just under in the case of the SPSR. Looking at the R^2 values, roughly 30%–40% of the variance was explained by each test. If the OHI and PSQ are valid measures, the role of personality factors for general happiness can be seen to

Table 9.7 Multiple regression

Test	OHI			PSQ		
	R	R^2	Beta	R	R^2	Beta
EPQX-R (N = 90)	650	422	E = 340*** N = − 396*** P = − 256***	638	407	E = 362*** N = − 372*** P = − 239***
SPSR	549	302	SP = − 549*** SR = − 006	580	336	SP = − 579*** SR = 053
PTS	658	434	SEXC = 164 SINH = − 066 MOBY = 542***	623	388	SEXC = 069 SINH = − 167* MOBY = 591***

Note. Decimals have been omitted from table.

be an important one. The Betas that are significant show that E, N, P, SP, and MOBY are predictors of the OHI and PSQ. The relationship between SEXC and the OHI or PSQ disappears when MOBY enters the equation. A slight "suppressor" effect (Tabachnick & Fidell, 1989) of either SEXC or MOBY acting on the relationship between SINH and the PSQ may be present in the results. That is, SEXC or MOBY may take up variance that is irrelevant to SINH's relationship with the PSQ, thereby producing a small but significant Beta. However, the increase in Beta over the R value is small and its significance marginal, so that this effect will only be of interest if replicated in further studies.

It is interesting to find out what happens when the scales from different tests are combined and entered into the same multiple regression. The scales were developed from different theories, and the results of multiple regressions in which they are combined should be informative regardless of the outcome. Table 9.8 gives the values found for R, R^2, and the Beta coefficients. It is clear from the table that the increases in R and R^2 are small, and at most explain an additional 10% of the variance. Thus, regardless of the theoretical background, the scales from the three personality tests cover similar portions of the variance with the Happiness measures.

The Beta values in Table 9.8 show SP and MOBY predicting the PSQ and OHI. SEXC, SINH, and SR have negligible effects, whereas E, N, and P give smaller Beta values of variable significance. The effect of MOBY when scales from the different personality tests are "mixed" together as predictors, rather than pairs of tests being combined, can be seen in Table 9.9. The number of possible mixes of the personality scales is multifarious. Table 9.9 shows only a few examples of the highest acceptable R values obtained by mixing scales from different tests. It is included to demonstrate that, when mixing scales together, the best mixes do not produce any increase in multiple R values.

Data from the Generalisation Experiment

The generalisation experiment produced a generalisation gradient as expected. But the increases in mean amounts "bet" on the five test tones as their

Table 9.8 Multiple-regression combining scales

Tests (N = 90)	Dep. Var. PSQ			Dep. Var. OHI		
	R	R²	Beta	R	R²	Beta
EPQ-R & PTS	.692	.479	E = − .142	.734	.539	E = .230*
			N = − .179			N = − .226*
			P = − .200*			P = − .225*
			SEXC = .045			SEXC = .140
			SINH = − .142			SINH = − .056
			MOBY = .358*			MOBY = .292*
EPQ-R & SPSR	.674	.454	E = .197	.666	.444	E = .259*
			N = − .082			N = − .184
			P = − .290**			P = − .282**
			SP = − .419**			SP = − .279*
			SR = .041			SR = .024
PTS & SPSR	.675	.456	SEXC = .018	.685	.469	SEXC = .127
			SINH = − .075			SINH = − .004
			MOBY = .417**			MOBY = .412**
			SP = − .325**			SP = − .238*
			SR = − .092			SR = − .054

frequency increased (see Table 9.10) was smaller than in former studies. Moreover, the difference between the amounts "bet" on the two highest and two lowest tones (TN 5623), which serves as a measure of the gradient of generalisation, failed to correlate significantly with any of the personality scales. This result may reflect that the relationship between generalisation and personality factors, like Extraversion, is a nonlinear one. Previous research with the generalisation, "betting" task has used smaller groups of extreme scorers on Extraversion as subjects, and markedly different generalisation gradients have been found for different personality groups (Brebner, 1991). Moreover, when a median split is performed on the present data, significant Pearson correlations with the generalisation measure are obtained for some groups (e.g., $r = .391$ for high scorers on SP). To test this nonlinear possibility, it would be desirable to look at the results from a large sample of different subjects. By including other subjects for whom partial data were available, a larger group of 169 students who had completed the generalisation experiment, and the EPQ-R and the SPSR questionnaires, data for further analysis were provided.

Using data from this larger group, multiple regressions were carried out, with the generalisation gradient measure as the dependent variable and the personality scales as predictor variables. The relevant results for the present purpose are given in Table 9.11. They show that when a median split is performed on the SP scale, different results are obtained for high and low scorers. For the higher scorers, entering SP, P, and N into the equation gives a multiple correlation of .505. For the lower scorers, the comparable correlation is .202, and no other combination of variables produces a higher correlation, whereas

Table 9.9 Multiple regression: Mixed scale examples

	Dep. Var. PSQ			Dep. Var. OHI	
R	R²	Beta	R	R²	Beta
.707	.500	MOBY − .341** SP = − .370*** P = − .269** SR = .162**	.713	.508	MOBY = .417*** SP = − .309** P = − .229**
Positive Scales	"Forcing" Entry				
.626	.392	MOBY = .490*** E = .225* SEXC = .007	.668	.446	MOBY = .470*** E = .175* SEXC = .131
.641	.411	MOBY = .498** E = .239* SR = .014	.670	.449	MOBY = .544*** E = .218* SR = − .044
Without MOBY					
.574	.329	SEXC = .311** E = .406*** SR = − .113	.622	.387	SEXC = .402*** E = .369** SR = − .163

Note. $N = 90$.

the R values for higher scorers are around .400. No such difference is found when the SR scale is subjected to a median split.

Selective though they are, these data allow the possibility that the generalisation gradient is related to personality factors that affect happiness, but in a nonlinear fashion. Further investigation of this possibility requires a different experimental approach from that used in this study.

DISCUSSION

Eysenck's Extraversion and Neuroticism are the only positive and negative personality scales to produce sizeable positive and negative correlations with

Table 9.10 Means and standard deviations (*SDs*) for amounts "bet" on the five test tones

	Tone				
	300	450	600	750	900
Mean	48	51	55	56	62
SD	17	16	15	17	18

Table 9.11 Multiple regression

TN71 > 0	R	Dep. Var. TN5623 R²	Beta		
SP > 14	.207	.043	SR = − .251	E = .158	
	.505	.255	SP = − .340*	P = .277	N = − .357*
	.452	.204	SP = − .293	E = − .080	N = − .257
	.396	.157	SR = − .135	SP = − .363*	
	.408	.166	P = .181	E = .001	N = − .453**
SP < 14	.193	.037	SR = .006	E = .190	
	.202	.040	SP = − .095	P = − .009	N = − .134
	.282	.079	SP = .018	E = .218	N = − .215
	.202	.040	SR = .115	SP = − .184	
	.281	.079	P = .005	E = .212*	N = − .205*
SR > 14	.199	.039	SR = − .174	E = .217	
	.288	.083	SP = .051	P = − .149	N = − .254
	.271	.073	SP = .165	E = .126	N = − .321
	.153	.023	SR = − .094	SP = − .142	
	.295	.083	P = − .158	E = .076	N = − .196
SR < 14	.063	.004	SR = .007	E = .060	
	.172	.029	SP = .114	P = .077	N = − .218
	.167	.027	SP = .164	E = .076	N = − .236
	.061	.003	SR = .030	SP = − .056	
	.158	.025	P = .081	E = .037	N = − .120

the PSQ and OHI, although the same pattern is present less strongly for Rusalov's Ergonicity and Emotionality measures. Although Torrubia's SR is independent of SP, it does not correlate positively with the PSQ or OHI. Given its positive correlation with N, it may be wrong to regard SR as a positive aspect of personality. For example, it may be that high SR scorers are more sensitive to failure to achieve reinforcement than they are to success in achievement. Strelau's SEXC correlates positively with the PSQ and OHI, but SINH shows correlations around zero with them. If SINH had also correlated with happiness, it would have been possible to argue that SEXC and SINH contribute to happiness through controlling behavior in different ways, but the results do not support this. It is, of course, always arguable that better measures of Happiness would produce different results. But that line of argument needs to await the production of other Happiness tests.

Using E and N as positive and negative dimensions, the relationships between the main Personality and Happiness measures shown in Tables 9.5 and 9.6 can be shown by plotting their respective correlations, as shown in Fig. 9.4. Low N and high E characterises those scoring high on SEXC, MOBY, the PSQ, and the OHI. Torrubia's SP shows the opposite, and is related to high N and low E. It is possible that this represents Gray's Anxiety dimension, which would be in agreement with both Gray's and Eysenck's views on personality and happiness. Because they are from a different group, the results for the

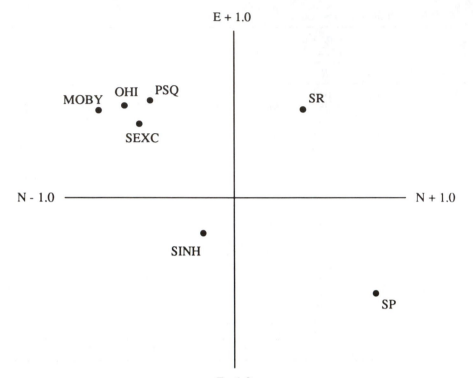

Figure 9.4   Locating Happiness and Personality measures on Eysenck's orthogonal model.

STQ scales are not included on Fig. 9.4. The positions of the SR and SINH scales may allow the further possibility of a dimension like Gray's Impulsivity, but, being based on only two scales from one sample, this interpretation could easily be challenged. It should be pointed out that dealing with the intensity and frequency of positive and negative states, as has been done in Figs. 9.2 and 9.4, offers a different approach than that previously taken by Diener, Larsen, Levine, and Emmons (1985), although the two may not be incompatible.

The multiple correlations in Table 9.7 are reasonably high and explain between 30%–40% of the variance. From the Beta values, it can be seen that all three of Eysenck's scales from the EPQX-R make a significant contribution. From the SPSR test, only SP is a predictor for the PSQ and OHI. MOBY from the PTS gives the only high Beta value from that test, although the small Beta for SINH is significant for the PSQ.

Combining the scales by pairing the personality tests (see Table 9.8) produces multiple *R*s, which are only slightly higher than those from the individual tests. The smaller Beta values still show similar patterns for the PSQ and OHI. The main feature of these results, however, is that the combinations of different scales fail to produce marked increases in R values. This shows that, whatever the theoretical background for the scales, as far as the Happiness measures are concerned, they are dealing with similar portions of the variance. As Table 9.9 shows, mixing scales, rather than combining tests, has no great effect on R values either, pointing to the same conclusion. MOBY can again be seen to predict the Happiness measures, although the Beta values for E and SEXC rise to almost comparable levels when MOBY is not in the equation. Too much should not be made of individual predictors from the present, single data set, and firm conclusions should await replication. Nevertheless, the present data provide a starting point, and are suggestive of a positive relationship between the capacity to switch between excitatory and inhibitory states and general happiness. The utilisation of such a capacity in defensive coping with negative information, and also in responding appropriately to valid positive information, can easily be raised as a mechanism helping to maintain a happy state, but more specific studies are needed to test this.

The generalisation experiment, carried out to test Brebner's proposal that positive generalisation promotes happiness, produced the expected gradient of generalisation, which is shown in Table 9.10. But using the difference between amounts "bet" on the two highest and lowest tones as a measure of generalisation, there appeared to be no relationship between generalisation and any of the personality measures from the lack of any significant Pearson correlations. The data in Table 9.11, however, keep alive the possibility that nonlinear relationships may be shown to exist in future research. In view of previously obtained differences in generalisation for different personalities (Brebner, 1991), and the multiple R values up to .50 obtained for high scorers when a median split was performed on the SP data in the present study, it does not seem unduly optimistic to suggest that future research may support the view that different personalities generalise differently, and that this affects their view of events and their characteristic happiness.

In summary, Eysenck and Gray receive support for their views, Strelau's personality factors can be fitted with Eysenck's and Gray's, as shown in Figure 9.4, and his MOBY scale produces high correlations with the Happiness measures. Rusalov's social scales were not more strongly related to the PSQ and OHI than his impersonal scales, but Social Ergonicity, Emotionality, and Tempo did produce significant correlations with them, although these were not large. Generalisation was not found to correlate significantly with any of the personality measures, but the possibility of a nonlinear relationship is retained and seems to warrant further study.

APPENDIX

The Personal State Questionnaire (PSQ)

1. How good has your health and physical state been lately?
2. How good has your mental health and state been lately?
3. How much of your recent life has been free of stress?
4. To what extent has life been exciting recently?
5. To what extent could you have managed without an occasional quiet day lately?
6. How contented are you with things lately?
7. How much have you enjoyed any novel experiences lately?
8. To what extent have you been able to do what you wanted to do recently?
9. How strongly would you have liked to maintain your recent day-to-day activities?
10. How lively, outgoing, and extraverted are you?
11. How easy have you found coping with problems lately?
12. How socially mature and sophisticated would you rate yourself?
13. What proportion of your recent decisions have you made quickly rather than deliberating for a long time?
14. How often have you found people to be helpful recently?
15. To what extent have you been able to control the things happening to you lately?
16. How much of your recent time has been spent in places that would be called attractive?
17. How much time have you spent enjoying yourself recently?
18. How much of your recent time have you spent in leisure or recreational pursuits?
19. How much have you enjoyed any time spent in the company of people other than close friends lately?
20. How satisfied are you with recreational facilities you have used recently?
21. How much of the next few weeks are you expecting to be enjoyable?
22. How much have you enjoyed the scenery you have seen recently?
23. What proportion of the food you have eaten recently would you rate as good or delicious?
24. How enjoyable have you found any recent tourist activities?
25. How much of your recent time has been spent enjoying peace, quiet, and tranquility?
26. To what degree have your recent hopes and expectations been satisfied?
27. How much have you enjoyed any radio or television you have heard/seen lately?
28. How much of the foreseeable future do you expect to be stressful?
29. How satisfactory have you found any activities recently that involved an element of risk-taking?
30. How satisfactory have you found your sporting activities recently?
31. How optimistic are you that you will be successful in the next few months?

32. How satisfying have you found listening to music at home lately?
33. How satisfying have you found going to films, concerts, or plays lately?
34. How contented have you been lately with your relationships with those very close to you?
35. How satisfied have you been with any recent celebrations (e.g., weddings, parties, birthdays) you have taken part in?
36. How highly would you rate your own self-esteem lately?
37. How good has your overall personal state been lately?

The PSQ © by John Brebner is published with permission of the author. Permission to use this test may be obtained directly from the author.

REFERENCES

Alloy, L. B., & Abramson, L. Y. (1979). Judgement of contingency in depressed and nondepressed students: Sadder but wiser? *Journal of Experimental Psychology: General, 108*, 441–485.

Argyle, M., & Lu, L. (1990a). Happiness and social skills. *Personality and Individual Differences, 11*, 1255–1261.

Argyle, M., & Lu, L. (1990b). The happiness of extraverts. *Personality and Individual Differences, 11*, 1011–1017.

Argyle, M. (1987). *Psychology of happiness*. London: Methuen.

Argyle, M., Martin, M., & Crossland, G. (1989). Happiness as a function of personality and social encounters. In J. Forgas & J. M. Innes (Eds.), *Advances in social psychology: An international perspective* (pp. 189–204). Amsterdam: Elsevier.

Beck, A. T., Ward, C. H., Mendelson, M., Mock, J., & Erbaugh, J. (1961). An inventory for measuring depression. *Archives of General Psychiatry, 4*, 561–571.

Beck, A. T., Weissmann, A., Lester, D., & Trexler, L. (1974). The measurement of pessimism: The Hopelessness Scale. *Journal of Consulting and Clinical Psychology, 42*, 861–865.

Bodunov, M. V. (1993). Factor structure of the Pavlovian Temperament Survey in a Russian population: Comparison and preliminary findings. *Personality and Individual Differences, 14*, 557–563.

Bradburn, N. M. (1969). *The structure of psychological well-being*. Chicago: Aldine.

Brebner, J. (1980). Reaction time in personality theory. In A. T. Welford (Ed.), *Reaction times* (pp. 309–320). London: Academic Press.

Brebner, J. (1983, September). *Personality factors in stress and anxiety*. Paper presented at the international conference on Stress and Anxiety, Rhynia, Poland.

Brebner, J. (1991). Personality and generalisation as a source of stress. In C. D. Spielberger, I. G. Sarason, J. Strelau, & J. Brebner (Eds.), *Stress and anxiety* (Vol. 13, pp. 93–101). Washington, DC: Hemisphere.

Brebner, J., & Cooper, C. J. (1974). The effect of a low rate of regular signals upon the reaction times of introverts and extraverts. *Journal of Research in Personality, 8,* 263–276.

Brebner, J., & Cooper, C. (1978). Stimulus or response induced excitation: A comparison of the behavior of introverts and extraverts. *Journal of Research in Personality, 12,* 306–311.

Brebner, J., & Flavel, R. (1978). The effect of catch-trials on speed and accuracy among introverts and extraverts in a simple RT task. *British Journal of Psychology, 69,* 9–15.

Cameron, R., & Meichenbaum, D. (1982). The nature of effective coping and the treatment of stress-related problems: A cognitive-behavioral perspective. In I. Goldberger & S. Bernitz (Eds.), *Handbook of stress* (pp. 183–209). New York: The Free Press.

Cooper, H., Okamura, L., & Gurka, V. (1992). Social activity and subjective well-being. *Personality and Individual Differences, 13,* 573–583.

Costa, P. T., & McCrae, R. R. (1980). The influence of extraversion and neuroticism on subjective well-being. *Journal of Personality and Social Psychology, 38,* 668–678.

Diaz, A., & Pickering, A. D. (1993). The relationship between Gray's and Eysenck's personality spaces. *Personality and Individual Differences, 15,* 297–305.

Diener, E., Larsen, R. J., Levine, S., & Emmons, R. A. (1985). Intensity and frequency: Dimensions underlying positive and negative affect. *Journal of Personality and Social Psychology, 48,* 1253–1265.

Diener, E., Sandvik, E., & Pavot, W. (1991). Happiness is the frequency, not the intensity, of positive versus negative affect. In F. Strack, M. Argyle, & N. Schwarz (Eds.), *Subjective well-being* (pp. 119–140). Oxford: Pergamon.

Diener, E., Sandvik, E., Pavot, W., & Fujita, F. (1992). Extraversion and subjective well-being in a U.S. national probability sample. *Journal of Research in Personality, 26,* 205–215.

Diener, E., Sandvik, E., Pavot, W., & Gallagher, D. (1991). Response artifacts in the measurement of subjective well-being. *Social Indicators Research, 24,* 35–56.

Dollard, J., & Miller, N. E. (1950). *Personality and psychotherapy.* New York: McGraw-Hill.

Eysenck, H. J., & Eysenck, S. B. G. (1975). *Manual of the Eysenck Personality Questionnaire.* London: Hodder & Stoughton.

Eysenck, H. J., & Eysenck, M. (1985). *Personality and individual differences: A natural science approach.* New York: Plenum.

Furnham, A., & Brewin, C. R. (1990). Personality and happiness. *Personality and Individual Differences, 11,* 1093–1096.

Gray, J. A. (1972). The psychophysiological nature of introversion-extraversion: A modification of Eysenck's theory. In V. D. Nebylitsin & J. A. Gray (Eds.), *Biological bases of individual behaviour* (pp. 182–205). London: Academic Press.

Gray, J. A. (1981). A critique of Eysenck's theory of personality. In H. J. Eysenck (Ed.), *A model of personality* (pp. 246–273). Berlin: Springer-Verlag.

Heineken, E., & Spaeth, G. (1988). Situational and differential psychological determinants of subjective well-being in later life. *Zeitschrift für Gerontologie, 21*, 289–294.

Jahoda, M. (1958). *Current concepts of positive mental health*. New York: Basic Books.

Karwowska, S. R., & Strelau, J. (1990). Reactivity and the stimulative value of managerial styles. *Polish Psychological Bulletin, 21*, 49–60.

Larson, R. (1978). Thirty years of research on the subjective well-being of older Americans. *Journal of Gerontology, 33*, 109–125.

MacAndrew, C., & Steele, T. (1991). Gray's behavioral inhibition system: A psychometric examination. *Personality and Individual Differences, 12*, 157–171.

Martin, M. (1985). Neuroticism as predisposition toward depression: A cognitive mechanism. *Personality and Individual Differences, 6*, 353–375.

Martin, M. (1990). On the induction of mood. *Clinical Psychology Review, 10*, 669–697.

Martin, M., Horder, P., & Jones, G. V. (1992). Integral bias in the naming of phobia-related words. *Cognition & Emotion, 6*, 479–486.

Martin, M., & Jones, G. V. (in press). Integral bias in the cognitive processing of emotionally linked pictures. *British Journal of Psychology*.

Martin, M., & Williams, R. (1990). Imagery and emotion: Clinical and experimental approaches. In P. J. Hampson, D. F. Marks, & J. T. E. Richardson (Eds.), *Imagery: Current developments* (pp. 268–306). London: Routledge.

Norusis, M. J. (1993). *SPSS for Windows, Release 6*. Chicago: SPSS Inc.

Ortony, A., Clore, G. L., & Collins, A. (1988). *The cognitive structure of emotions*. Cambridge: Cambridge University Press.

Roger, D., & Jamieson, J. (1988). Individual differences in delayed heart rate recovery following stress: The role of extraversion, neuroticism and emotional control. *Personality and Individual Differences, 9*, 721–726.

Ruch, W. (1992). Pavlov's types of nervous system, Eysenck's typology and the Hippocrates-Galen temperaments: An empirical examination of the asserted correspondence of three temperament typologies. *Personality and Individual Differences, 13*, 1259–1271.

Ruch, W. (1994). Extraversion, alcohol, and enjoyment. *Personality and Individual Differences, 16*, 89–102.

Rusalov, V. M. (1989). Object-related and communicative aspects of human temperament: A new questionnaire of the structure of human temperament. *Personality and Individual Differences, 10*, 817–827.

Ryff, C. D. (1989). Happiness is everything, or is it? Explorations on the meaning of psychological well-being. *Journal of Personality and Social Psychology, 57*, 1069–1081.

Spielberger, C. D., Gorusch, R. L., Lushene, R. E., Vagg, P. R., & Jacobs, G. A. (1983). *Manual for the State-Trait Anxiety Inventory: STAI (Form Y)*. Palo Alto, CA: Counseling Psychologists Press.

Stough, C., Brebner, J., & Cooper, C. J. (1991). The Rusalov Structure of Temperament Questionnaire (STQ): Results from an Australian sample. *Personality and Individual Differences, 12*, 1355–1357.

Strelau, J. (1983). *Temperament-Personality-Activity*. London: Academic Press.

Strelau, J., & Angleitner, A. (1994). Cross-cultural studies on temperament: Theoretical considerations and empirical studies based on the Pavlovian Temperament Survey. *Personality and Individual Differences, 16*, 331–342.

Tabachnick, B. G., & Fidell, L. S. (1989). *Using multivariate statistics.* New York: Harper & Row.

Tiggemann, M., Winefield, A. H., & Brebner, J. (1982). The role of extraversion in the development of learned helplessness. *Personality and Individual Differences, 3*, 27–34.

Torrubia, R., & Tobeña, A. (1984). A scale for the assessment of "susceptibility to punishment" as a measure of anxiety: Preliminary results. *Personality and Individual Differences, 5*, 371–375.

Wilson, G. D., Gray, J. A., & Barrett, P. T. (1990). A factor analysis of the Gray-Wilson Personality Questionnaire. *Personality and Individual Differences, 11*, 1037–1045.

10

Testing for Stress and Happiness: The Role of Social and Cognitive Factors

Michael Argyle and Maryanne Martin
University of Oxford, England

Luo Lu
Institute of Behavioral Sciences, Kaohsiung, Taiwan

ABSTRACT

This chapter reviews the development of the Oxford Happiness Inventory (OHI) and reports research findings with it. The OHI has been found to have high internal consistency, test–retest reliability, and validity in predicting friends' judgments. It correlates with the Beck Depression Inventory (−.47), Positive Mood (.50), Satisfaction (.60), and other personality dimensions, especially Extraversion (average .50) and Neuroticism (−.45), and with social skills measures (e.g., Assertiveness, Cooperativeness, Leadership, and Internal Locus of Control). The link with Extraversion was found to be related to the social skills of extraverts and enjoyable leisure activities. In studies of cognitive factors in happiness, happy people had a positive attributional style, ruminated about good things, were better able to imagine positive events, and were less able to imagine negative events. Several aspects of leisure that also correlated with happiness, as measured by the OHI, included commitment to serious leisure, social leisure, and watching certain kinds of television. In a longitudinal study, social support was predictive of happiness. It was concluded that the OHI provides a satisfactory measure of happiness as a stable personality trait, which is linked to Extraversion by virtue of the social skills and cognitive style of extraverts.

What is meant by *happiness*? If people are asked this question, they give two kinds of answers. They may report that they: (a) are experiencing a positive emotional state such as joy, or (b) are satisfied with life as a whole or parts of it. Therefore, it would seem that there may be at least two components to happiness. However, happiness is not the opposite of unhappiness or depression, although it is negatively related to both and has somewhat different causes (Argyle, 1987). If happiness were simply the opposite of depression, it would not be necessary to measure or study it at all because much is known about depression.

It would seem that there are three possible components of happiness: positive emotion, satisfaction, and absence of negative emotions such as depression or anxiety. There are several measures of each of these components that correlate with each other at about .50. In addition, a recently suggested fourth component is related to self-fulfillment and other "depth" elements, such as positive relations with others, purpose in life, and personal growth (Ryff, 1989). A similar dimension of emotional experience was previously found; it seemed to be produced by solving an important emotional problem, getting on well with loved ones, or feeling overwhelmed by the beauty of nature, as opposed to having a hot bath or watching a TV thriller (Argyle & Crossland, 1987).

A number of measures of Happiness have also been previously proposed, but none has been widely accepted or oriented to British subjects or culture. For these reasons, a new measure was constructed (Argyle, Martin, & Crossland, 1989; Martin, Argyle, & Crossland, 1988). This chapter reports research in which this measure was used. No attempt is made to review the general literature on happiness because this was previously reported by Argyle (1987) and Strack, Argyle, and Schwarz (1991).

THE OXFORD HAPPINESS INVENTORY: CONSTRUCTION AND PROPERTIES

Construction of the Oxford Happiness Inventory

The success of the Beck Depression Inventory (BDI) is impressive. It is widely used in Britain and elsewhere. After consultation with Beck, the 21 BDI items were redrafted using the same format, but reversing each item (e.g., Item 1):

0. I do not feel happy.
1. I feel fairly happy.
2. I am very happy.
3. I am incredibly happy.

Given that positive and negative emotions are not the opposite of one another, 11 items were added to cover several aspects of happiness that were not yet included. The preliminary 32-item Happiness scale was then presented to eight graduate students, who ranked the four choices for each item. The students were also asked to comment on the face validity of each item. This led to some redrafting and three items being dropped, leaving the final version at 29 items.

Internal Structure

Argyle et al. (1989) found an Alpha coefficient of .90 with 347 subjects. Furnham and Brewin (1990) found an Alpha of .87 with 101 subjects, and

Noor (1993), with a shorter version of the OHI, found an Alpha of .84 with 180 subjects.

With such high Alphas, it would not be expected that there would be a clear division into factors. However, Argyle et al. (1989) carried out factor analyses with several groups of subjects and found seven factors: Positive Cognition, Social Commitment, Positive Affect, Sense of Control, Physical Fitness, Satisfaction with Self, and Mental Alertness. Alpha scores varied from .64 to .84. However, this factor structure varied somewhat between samples, and therefore its stability is not assured. The subscales have been used in some later studies. Argyle and Lu (1990b) found somewhat different correlations with other measures. Noor (1993) used two of the scales—Positive Cognition and Positive Affect; factor analysis of these produced a single factor.

Furnham and Brewin (1990) also factor analysed the OHI with 101 subjects and obtained three factors: Satisfaction with Personal Achievement, Enjoyment and Fun in Life, and Vigour and Good Health, each of which had satisfactory Alpha scores.

Reliability

The test–retest reliability of the OHI is quite high. Different studies have found reliabilities of .81 over 4 months, .53 over 6 months, and .67 over 5 months; Noor's (1993) shorter version was .71 over 8 months. Valiant (1993) found a reliability of .83 over 3 weeks, and found that scores on the scale were little affected by events during that time. Noor found that the OHI was more stable than the General Health Questionnaire, which had a reliability of only .28 over an 8-month period. Valiant found that the BDI was less reliable than the OHI over 3 weeks, at .51, although with a small number of subjects. It looks as if the OHI is assessing a stable feature of personality, not a state or mood.

Validity

There have been two validity studies, each using judgments by friends. Argyle, Martin, and Crossland (1989) asked members of a psychology class to rate people they knew on a 10-point happiness scale, and to also try to include some people who were either low, medium, or high on this scale. With 147 individuals rated in this way, the correlation with the OHI was .43. Valiant (1993) obtained similar ratings from friends, and found a correlation of .64 with her initial measure, and .49 at Time 2, with 36 subjects.

CORRELATES OF THE OHI

Three basic research methods were used in the work to be reported: (a) cross-sectional studies in which correlations are reported with the OHI; (b) cross-sectional studies in which multiple regressions are calculated, with the OHI as the dependent variable and the others as predictors (although this gives weak evidence for causality, it shows which of the variables entered has the strongest relationship with the OHI, which cannot be explained by the other variables); and (c) longitudinal studies, in which the OHI and other variables are assessed at Time 1 and the OHI again at Time 2. Multiple regressions then show whether any of the other variables are predictors of OHI at Time 2 when OHI at Time 1 has been taken into account (i.e., whether they can predict changes over time in the OHI). This gives much stronger evidence for causality. In some cases, a series of such regressions has been done so that a path analysis can be shown of the pattern of causal linkage between two or more other variables.

Age and Sex

Two of the samples tested had a reasonable age spread. Lu and Argyle (1991), with 114 adult subjects, found that young people had higher OHI scores ($r = -.22$). In a number of multiple regressions, in which other variables such as Extraversion were controlled, this fell to $-.15$, $-.18$, and $-.19$. Noor (1993), in her study with 145 adult women, found a correlation of $-.28$, which fell to $-.16$ in multiple regressions. In her second study, it fell to less than this when further variables were controlled. The other studies used students and found no age differences.

Several of these studies found a nonsignificant tendency for females to have higher scores. However, Argyle and Lu (1990b), with 63 adults, found a biserial correlation of .26 with gender, with females scoring higher.

Other Happiness Measures

It was expected that the OHI would correlate positively with measures of Positive Mood and Satisfaction, and negatively with measures of Negative Mood.

Positive Mood. A correlation of .54 was found with a Current Mood scale for happy, and .32 with the Bradburn Positive Affect scale. Valiant (1993) asked subjects to keep diaries, which were then content analysed for mood. She found that the OHI correlated with percentage of time happy at .45 and .46 before and after measures, and $-.73$ and $-.40$ with percentage of time depressed.

Satisfaction. The OHI also correlated with measures of Satisfaction. A correlation of .57 was found with a Life Satisfaction Index, and .60 with a Positive Life Events Questionnaire (Argyle et al., 1989).

Negative states. For depression, the OHI correlated $-.52$ with the BDI, $-.40$ with the Current Mood scale for depressed, and $-.32$ with the Bradburn Negative Affect scale.

Other Personality Dimensions

The negative relation with the BDI has already been reported. A negative relation was also found with the Eysenck Neuroticism scale of $-.47$ (Argyle

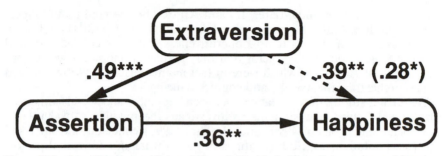

Figure 10.1 Assertion as a mediator of the relationship between Extraversion and happiness. The figure in the parentheses (.28) is the reduced coefficient when the mediator is taken into account.

et al., 1989). Argyle and Lu (1990b) found it to be − .45, and Furnham and Brewin (1990) found it to be − .42. Noor (1993) found a correlation of − .39 with Neuroticism and − .26 with the General Health Questionnaire (GHQ).

The strongest and most consistent correlate of happiness was found to be with Extraversion, as measured on the Eysenck Personality Questionnaire (EPQ) of Eysenck and Eysenck (1975). Argyle and Lu (1990a) found a correlation of .46 using 131 subjects, Furnham and Brewin (1990) found a correlation of .55 with 101 subjects, and Thomas (1993) found a correlation of .43 with 62 subjects. In several of the studies to be reported later, Extraversion remained a predictor of happiness in multiple regressions, where other personality variables, such as Cooperativeness, or situational ones, such as TV Watching, were included.

Noor (1993) found that Locus of Control correlated highly (i.e., .47) with the OHI, and that Locus of Control was a predictive factor in her longitudinal multiple regression. Locus of Control also interacted with other variables such as Social support, as reported later.

Valiant (1993) carried out a content analysis of diaries to score "pawn" and "origin"—the experience of being controlled and controlling, respectively. Origin had a nonsignificant relation with depression and none with happiness. Pawn correlated with depression and negatively with the OHI, − .32 at Time 2. However, in longitudinal multiple regression, pawn did not survive as a predictor of happiness, so not being controlled is only a correlate of happiness.

Social Competence

These studies treated Happiness as the dependent variable and Social Competence as a possible causal factor. Argyle and Lu (1990b) gave 63 adult subjects measures of social skills in a longitudinal design over 6 months. It was found that Assertiveness was a predictor of happiness and was itself predicted by Extraversion (Fig. 10.1). The relation with assertiveness was confirmed by Cooper (1993) with a correlation of .25, although this did not survive a multiple regression, and by Crook (1993) with a correlation of .31.

Several other measures of social skills correlate with the OHI. Negative relations were also found with various measures of Self-Consciousness and

Social Anxiety in this study. Later, Lu and Argyle (1991) found that Cooperativeness predicted later happiness in a longitudinal study with 114 subjects. A factor analysis of the 36-item Cooperativeness scale was carried out, and four factors were found. The factor that best predicted happiness was Cooperation in Joint Activities, which were in fact mainly leisure activities such as "choirs, orchestras, theatricals, and country dancing."

Five further studies of the relations between happiness and social skills were carried out by third-year students to investigate the possible causal role of other social skills. Sleep (1990) and Graham (1990) collected and analysed data from 51 students, including ratings of their verbal and nonverbal performance and their social skills in natural situations. The OHI correlated with overall verbal skills at .45, especially with initiating conversation and expressing interest in others. It correlated with total nonverbal communication at .54, especially with ratings of amounts of gaze, bodily contact, and facial expressiveness. The OHI correlated with two measures of general social skills: Social Awareness and Evidence of Social Success. Sleep found that low scores on the OHI were related to withdrawal from social situations and engagement in solitary activities.

Cooper (1993) used 70 subjects, mostly Oxford medical students. He developed a heterosexual skills questionnaire, which was found to have four factors. The factor Confidence in Ability to Communicate (i.e., with the opposite sex) correlated with the OHI at Time 1 at .31 and predicted OHI scores at Time 2, whereas Extraversion did not.

Crook (1993) used 156 Oxford students in a cross-sectional design to investigate the correlation between happiness and leadership skills. He constructed a 21-item scale of leadership skills, which was found to have two main factors: Informal Social Influence and Occupying Formal Leadership Positions. The total scale correlated .52 with the OHI, but only the second factor was predictive in a multiple regression. Social Competence, as assessed by the Social Competence Questionnaire (Com. Q), correlated .38 with the OHI.

Thomas (1993) used a sample of 63 students in a cross-sectional study of friendship skills. She constructed a 20-item friendship skills questionnaire, which was found to have two main factors: General Gregariousness and Intimacy Skills. The whole scale correlated .37 with the OHI; the first factor correlated .39, but the second was not significant. She used the measures of social skills of Riggio (1986); the Social Expressivity scale correlated .30 with the OHI and Body Language correlated .29.

To summarise, the following social skills have been found to be associated with happiness, and in most cases there is evidence that this is a causal relationship:

Assertiveness
Cooperativeness
Verbal Skills
Nonverbal Skills
Friendship Skills

Relationship Skills
Leadership Skills
Lack of Social Anxiety or Self-Consciousness

TESTING THEORIES ABOUT ORIGINS OF HAPPINESS

Explaining the Link with Exraversion

This correlation is consistent and striking. It has been found before, but it has not yet been explained. Various possibilities have been investigated.

Hoorens (1994) measured Social Desirability Response Set, as well as Unrealistic Optimism and Illusory Superiority, to see if these might be common factors that could explain the OHI/Extraversion relation; they could not. The same was found by Pavot, Diener, and Fujita (1990) with another measure of Subjective Well-Being. V. Hoorens (personal communication, 1993) gave a Dutch version of the OHI to 92 Dutch high school children, and found that it correlated with optimism for positive events (e.g., "living beyond 80") at .28 and expectation of negative ones (e.g., "getting AIDS") at − .36, and also with self-ratings on positive traits (e.g., "trustworthy") at .36, but there was no relation with negative ones (e.g., "jealous"). The positive events were interpreted as "unrealistic" optimism, which some were (e.g., "winning a high artistic or national award"), but others were not. The positive traits were seen as "illusory superiority," although this would not apply to "friendly" or "good-humoured."

If the OHI/Extraversion relation is a genuine one, not due to response sets, it might be because extraverts engage in more enjoyable leisure activities. Argyle and Lu (1990a) gave 131 student subjects a list of 37 leisure activities, and asked them to report how often they did them. The list was factor analysed, and yielded five factors. Two of them, Factor 3 (teams and clubs) and Factor 4 (parties and dances), correlated with Extraversion and were also predictive of happiness in a multiple regression, especially Factor 4, which contained items about going to parties, dances, and debates. Factor 3 contained items about belonging to teams and clubs. Hence, part of the explanation of the OHI/Extraversion relation is that extraverts engage in more enjoyable leisure activities than do introverts.

The reason that extraverts do these things more may be because they have better social skills—the skills needed to go to dances and debates, meet new people, and so on. This relationship was reported previously, and is pursued in more detail later. The reason that extraverts are able to enjoy all these social events is at least partly due to their social skills.

Previous work on nonverbal communication has shown that extraverts smile more; stand or sit closer; gaze more; speak more, faster, and with a higher pitched voice; and are more expressive than introverts. This positive nonverbal style has been found to lead to popularity and social effectiveness in many situations (Argyle, 1988). Sleep (1990) and Graham (1990) found that extraverts had higher scores for rated verbal and nonverbal skills, and for more general aspects of social skills, which might be described as "rewardingness."

One of the most chararacteristic differences between extraverts and others is in liking to meet strangers, and hence liking parties. Thorne (1987) put pairs of extraverts together in a room, with minimal instructions, and found that they tried very hard to get to know one another—by asking questions, finding things they had in common, agreeing, and paying compliments. In contrast, pairs of introverts often sat in total silence. This situation was used as a class experiment for several years, and these results were replicated. Some pairs of introverts sat in silence for 5 minutes. Thorne suggested that extraverts have a confident expectation that they will like and get on well with strangers.

Gray (1972) proposed that because of differences in brain structure extraverts magnify rewards, whereas introverts magnify punishments. He also stated that the greatest source of rewards and punishments is other people (J. A. Gray, personal communication, 1992). There is support for this theory from physiological research, and also from the finding by Pavot et al. (1990) that extraverts are happier than others in nonsocial as well as social situations. It offers a quite different explanation for the happiness of extraverts.

Our research suggests that extraverts are happier than others because they have better social skills—they are more assertive and cooperative, and use positive nonverbal and verbal styles. This leads them to expect that social encounters will go well, and enables them to take part in and enjoy a range of social situations, such as clubs and teams, parties, and dances.

Cognitive Factors in Happiness

It is possible that particular ways of perceiving and thinking about events are conducive to the formation and maintenance of happiness. There is evidence that happy people have particular attributional styles, and that they exhibit particular patterns of mental imagery.

Earlier research has demonstrated, in general terms, that happy people show the "Pollyanna effect"—that is, they have a positive bias to see things in a positive light, they remember good things, and they are optimistic about the future. It has often been found that depressives interpret bad events as internal (i.e., due to themselves), global (i.e., will happen in other spheres), and stable (i.e., will continue to occur; e.g., Martin & Clarke, 1985). Martin, Argyle, and Crossland (1988) gave the OHI and the Attributional Style Questionnaire to subjects. They found that unhappy people blame themselves for unhappy events, and happy people do the same for happy ones; hence they show the internal, stable, and global attributional style in reverse. In the same study, the relationship between happiness and rumination was investigated. It was found that happy people ruminate about good events in the past, and they cannot stop thinking about them. If they think a bad thing, it is to see how it might be put right. In contrast, unhappy people ruminate about bad things. If they think about good things, it is to wonder how they might go wrong.

However, Valiant (1993) found that the overall rating of events on diary days for being positive rather than negative had a high correlation with depression

($r = -.69$ and $-.30$ for the before and after measures), but no significant relation with happiness. There was no relation between the OHI and giving a positive evaluation to events, so evidently the "Pollyanna effect" did not work here.

The cognitive propagational theory of emotion (Martin, 1990a; Martin & Williams, 1990) proposes that thoughts and emotions are reciprocally related. Particular patterns of thought lead to associated emotions, which in turn reinforce the original patterns of thought. The manipulation of mental imagery constitutes a major component of several different methods of mood induction in the laboratory (see Martin, 1990b). Further, an individual's level of mental imagery for emotional material has been shown in a longitudinal study (Martin, 1990a; Martin & Williams, 1990) to be a good predictor of subsequent emotional well-being. In further work, Martin examined imagery and happiness across two sets of participants.

In the first part of the study, participants were asked to generate typical thoughts that come to mind when in each of the following mood states: elated (e.g., "I am glad to be alive"), depressed (e.g., "Nobody really cares about me"), or anxious (e.g., "There are too many pressures on me"). In the second part, new participants judged the ease of imageability of these different types of thought, and their happiness was assessed using the OHI. It was found that enduring happiness, as indicated by higher OHI scores, was accompanied by increased imagery for elated thoughts and decreased imagery for depressed thoughts, but by unchanged level of imagery for anxious thoughts. That is, happiness was associated not with a general change in imagery, but rather with a spectrum of changes. The nature of any individual change was dependent on the content of the relevant cognitive representation. These results are consistent with the propagational theory of emotion. They suggest that happy people experience relatively high levels of imagery when considering an elated thought and relatively low levels of imagery when considering a depressed thought. The bias toward imagery for elated thought should lead to such thoughts being better remembered (e.g., Paivio, 1991) and, via the availability heuristic (Kahneman, Slovic, & Tversky, 1982), to a more optimistic view of the world, which in turn contributes to happiness.

SOME CAUSES OF HAPPINESS

Social Support

In her second study, Noor (1993) used 180 employed women, who were Oxford graduates or senior Oxford secretaries, in a longitudinal design with an 8-month interval. She found in regression analysis that OHI scores at Time 2 were predicted by "partner quality," which was assessed by a 14-item scale about partner support and companionship. Happiness was more weakly predicted by "appraisal support"—that is, the perceived availability of someone to talk to about one's problems. However, Social Support did not emerge as a factor in her first study of 145 employed women, who were mainly nurses, social workers, and secretaries. The main difference between the two samples was that the second sample consisted of women of higher occupational status.

Lu and Argyle (1992) studied 65 adults who were asked about social support received in the previous 6 months. In a multiple regression, happiness was predicted by satisfaction with relationships with people from whom support had been received. As usual, extraversion also predicted happiness. But the effects of social support were independent of extraversion, and therefore were evidently not due to involvement in social activities or networks.

Work

Only one study investigated the effect of work on happiness using the OHI. In Noor's (1993) first study of nurses, social workers, and others, the initial cross-sectional regression analysis found that happiness was predicted by Employment and reported Job Challenge. The second variable stayed in when more variables had been controlled. There was also an interaction between Job Challenge, Work Support, and Locus of Control: High Job Challenge reduced happiness when work support was low for those with internal control. However, in Noor's second study with the Oxford graduates, there were no significant effects of the work-role variables studied on happiness; these were Overload, Tedium, and Autonomy.

Leisure

Other research has shown that leisure is an important source of happiness. Argyle and Lu (1990a) investigated the possible effect of leisure on happiness with 131 student subjects. A list of 37 common leisure activities was created; subjects indicated on 5-point scales how often they participated in each and how much they enjoyed them. Factors 3, 4, and 5 correlated with the OHI at .26, .43, and .20. Factor 3 (teams and clubs) and Factor 4 (parties and dances) survived a multiple regression, but Factor 5 (games, jokes, and cinema) did not; the regression included both sets of factors, together with sex and extraversion. Two of the enjoyment factors correlated with the OHI, but disappeared in the multiple regression.

Lu and Argyle (1994) investigated whether serious leisure made a special contribution to happiness. This was a cross-sectional study with 114 adult subjects, who were asked whether they had a seriously committed leisure activity; 79 said they did (e.g., voluntary work, music, hobbies, or education). Those with the serious leisure had higher OHI scores than the others; they rated their leisure as more satisfying psychologically, socially, and physically, but in multiple regression only the social satisfaction component predicted OHI scores. Extraversion was also predictive of happiness independently of the effects of Social Satisfaction (see Fig. 10.2).

The study of cooperativeness in connection with social skills was reported earlier. The Cooperation factor that best predicted happiness was Cooperation in Joint Leisure Activities (Lu & Argyle, 1994).

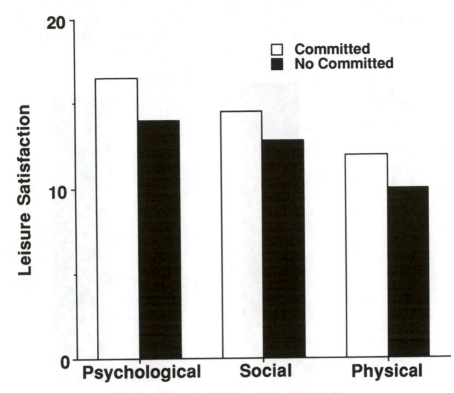

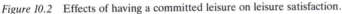

Figure 10.2 Effects of having a committed leisure on leisure satisfaction.

Watching TV

Because people spend so many hours watching TV, it must be a source of satisfaction. Does it make them any happier? Lu and Argyle (1993) studied 114 adult subjects and asked them to report their TV watching. On average, they watched for 2 hours a day, 3 programmes. Happiness was predicted as usual by Extraversion, but negatively with total TV watching. Subjects were also asked how many times per week they watched soap operas. This had a positive relation with happiness. The mean scores based on medium splits on amount of watching are shown in Fig. 10.3.

Discriminant function analyses found the characteristics of different groups. High soap watchers were more often female, older, and extroverted, as well as being happier. The high TV and irregular soap watchers were the least happy. The reason for the link between unhappiness and high TV watching is probably that the highest watchers tend to include the old, ill, socially isolated, and so on and may be unhappy for other reasons. The explanation for the link between happiness and enthusiasm for soap operas is probably that this provides a circle of imaginary friends, whom viewers feel they almost know—a set of "parasocial" relationships (see Argyle, in press).

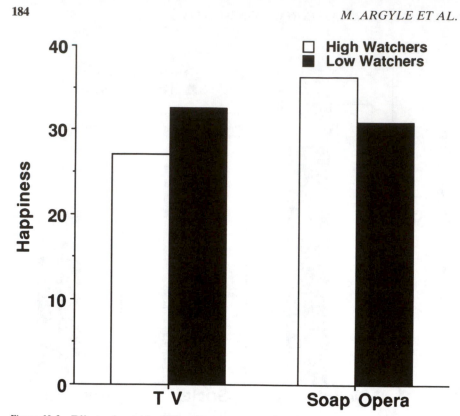

Figure 10.3 Effects of watching TV and soap operas on happiness.

DISCUSSION

Is the OHI a Satisfactory Measure of Happiness?

The issue brought up by Ryff (1989)—that there may be further "depth" components of happiness not included in past scales—was raised earlier. It was questioned whether the OHI was too strong in the social and enjoyment sphere, after the Argyle and Lu (1990a) study on Extraversion. However, these doubts were partly allayed by the finding that serious and committed leisure was a strong source of happiness measured in this way; the kinds of serious leisure mentioned had nothing to do with parties.

Is the OHI a State or Trait Measure?

It was hoped it would be a trait measure; however, happiness is partly the tendency to have positive moods. It was found that the OHI does correlate with positive moods at about .50 and, similarly, in reverse, with depressed ones. However, it was also found that the OHI is very stable over time—more so than measures of negative states like the BDI and the GHQ, and is less sensitive to temporary situations.

Why Are Some Individuals Happy?

Happy people tend to be extraverted, not neurotic, and high on internal control, and to have certain social skills and cognitive styles. Which of these is the most fundamental? The strongest correlation is with extraversion, at .4 or .5 or more, and this survived several multiple regressions. The most likely explanation of this is in terms of extraverts' greater social skills. However, extraverts have other properties, and their tendency to magnify rewards may be important. Extraversion was still a predictor independently of social skills or other social factors, so there may be nonsocial processes operating too. This could be linked with the cognitive styles of happy people, which enable them to look on the bright side, or Gray's magnification of rewards.

The Relation with Social Skills

Correlations have been found between happiness and a wide range of social skills, including relationship skills and leadership. This points to the great importance of social relationships to happiness, and the need to have the skills to conduct them successfully.

REFERENCES

Argyle, M. (1987). *The psychology of happiness*. London: Methuen.

Argyle, M. (1988). *Bodily communication* (2nd ed.). London: Methuen.

Argyle, M. (in press). *The social psychology of leisure*. London: Routledge.

Argyle, M., & Crossland, J. (1987). The dimensions of positive emotions. *British Journal of Social Psychology, 26*, 127–137.

Argyle, M., & Lu, L. (1990a). The happiness of extraverts. *Personality and Individual Differences, 11*, 1011–1017.

Argyle, M., & Lu, L. (1990b). Happiness and social skills. *Personality and Individual Differences, 11*, 1255–1261.

Argyle, M., Martin, M., & Crossland, J. (1989). Happiness as a function of personality and social encounters. In J. P. Forgas & J. M. Innes (Eds.), *Recent advances in social psychology: An international perspective* (pp. 189–203). North Holland: Elsevier.

Cooper, M. (1993). *Social competence and subjective well-being: The relationship between happiness and heterosexual skills*. Unpublished manuscript, Oxford University, Oxford, England.

Crook, P. (1993). *Leadership and happiness*. Unpublished manuscript. Oxford University, Oxford, England.

Eysenck, H. J., & Eysenck, S. B. G. (1975). *Manual for the Eysenck Personality Questionnaire*. London: Hodder & Stoughton.

Furnham, A., & Brewin, C. R. (1990). Personality and happiness. *Personality and Individual Differences, 11*, 1093–1096.

Graham, M. (1990). *The social psychology of extraversion*. Unpublished manuscript, Oxford University, Oxford, England.

Gray, J. A. (1972). The psychophysiological nature of introversion-extraversion: A modification of Eysenck's theory. In V. B. Neblitsyn & J. A. Gray (Eds.), *Biological bases of individual behavior* (pp. 182–205). New York: Academic Press.

Hoorens, V. (1994). *Is the happiness-extraversion relation due to response sets?* Unpublished manuscript, University of Groningen, The Netherlands.

Kahneman, D., Slovic, P., & Tversky, A. (Eds.). (1982). *Judgment under uncertainty: Heuristics and biases*. Cambridge, England: Cambridge University Press.

Lu, L., & Argyle, M. (1991). Happiness and cooperation. *Personality and Individual Differences, 12*, 1019–1030.

Lu, L., & Argyle, M. (1992). Receiving and giving support: Effects on relationships and well-being. *Counselling Psychology Quarterly, 5*, 123–133.

Lu, L., & Argyle, M. (1993). TV watching, soap opera and happiness. *Kaohsiung Journal of Medical Sciences, 9*, 501–507.

Lu, L., & Argyle, M. (1994). Leisure satisfaction and happiness as a function of leisure activity. *Kaohsiung Journal of Medical Sciences, 10*, 89–96.

Martin, M. (1990a). Cognitive basis of anxiety. In P. J. D. Drenth, J. A. Sergent, & R. J. Takens (Eds.), *European perspectives in psychology* (Vol. 2, pp. 269–283). New York: Wiley.

Martin, M. (1990b). On the induction of mood. *Clinical Psychology Review, 10*, 669–697.

Martin, M., Argyle, M., & Crossland, J. (1988). On the measurement of happiness. *Proceedings of the Annual Conference of the British Psychological Society*, p. 33.

Martin, M., & Clark, D. M. (1985). Cognitive mediation of depressed mood and neuroticism. *IRCS Medical Science, 13*, 352–353.

Martin, M., & Williams, R. (1990). Imagery and emotion: Clinical and experimental approaches. In P. J. Hampson, D. F. Marks, & J. T. E. Richardson (Eds.), *Imagery: Current developments* (pp. 268–306). London: Routledge.

Noor, N. M. (1993). *Work and family roles in relation to women's well-being*. Unpublished thesis, Oxford University, Oxford, England.

Paivio, A. (1991). *Images in mind: The evolution of a theory*. London: Harvester Wheatsheaf.

Pavot, W., Diener, E., & Fujita, F. (1990). Extraversion and happiness. *Personality and Individual Differences, 11*, 1299–1306.

Riggio, R. F. (1986). Assessment of basic social skills. *Journal of Personality and Social Psychology, 51*, 649–660.

Ryff, C. D. (1989). Happiness is everything, or is it? Explorations on the meaning of psychological well-being. *Journal of Personality and Social Psychology, 57*, 1069–1081.

Sleep, T. (1990). *Positive mood induction in introverts and extraverts*. Unpublished manuscript, Oxford University, Oxford, England.

Strack, F., Argyle, M., & Schwarz, N. (Eds.). (1991). *Subjective well-being.* Oxford: Pergamon.

Thomas, R. (1993). *Social competence and subjective well-being.* Unpublished manuscript, Oxford University, Oxford, England.

Thorne, A. (1987). The press of personality: A study of conversation between introverts and extraverts. *Journal of Personality and Social Psychology, 53,* 718–726.

Valiant, G. (1993). Life events, happiness and depression: The half empty cup. *Personality and Individual Differences, 15,* 447–453.

11

Testing for Stress and Happiness: The Role of the Behavioral Inhibition System

Rafael Torrubia
Autonomous University of Barcelona, Spain

César Avila and Javier Moltó
Jaume I University, Castelló, Spain

Immaculada Grande
Autonomous University of Barcelona, Spain

ABSTRACT

This chapter presents a brief, selective review of findings from investigations of stress and happiness that tested hypotheses derived from Gray's (1982) neuropsychological model of emotion and personality. Research results relating to the following topics are presented: (a) construction of the Sensitivity to Punishment: Sensitivity to Reward (SPSR) questionnaire; (b) effects of individual differences in behavioral inhibition on approach–avoidance conflicts, such as multiple-choice exams, and on extinction procedures in a laboratory task; and (c) cognitive mechanisms that affect sensitivity to punishment. Based on the findings in these studies, it was concluded that individual differences in the functioning of the behavioral inhibition system, as defined by Gray, can significantly contribute to the expression of different emotions, including stress reactions and happiness.

The emotions elicited by an objective event may be very different depending on how one appraises the situation. According to Lazarus and Folkman (1984), emotions can be positive (e.g., joy or love) or negative, such as the emotional reactions that are evoked by stress (i.e., anger, guilt, depression, or anxiety). The appraisal of a particular event as positive means that it is perceived as having good implications, whereas the appraisal of an event as dangerous or threatening is likely to generate a state of anxiety or fear.

Preparation of this chapter was supported by DGICYT Grant PB91-0519-CO2 from the Spanish Ministry of Science and Education. We wish to thank Dr. John Brebner for his valuable comments on the text.

Stress and happiness can be considered, in some respects, to be incompatible conditions. As defined by Lazarus and Folkman (1984), *stress* is: "a particular relationship between the person and the environment that is appraised by the person as taxing or exceeding his or her resources and endangering his or her well-being" (p. 19). *Happiness* is related to the ability to both minimize levels of stress and anxiety, and to maximize coping skills (Endler, 1988). Argyle and Lu (1990) identified three main components of happiness: Positive Affect, Satisfaction, and Absence of Distress.

In keeping with the definitions of *stress* and *happiness* proposed by Lazarus and Argyle, state anxiety would be expected to be elevated as a consequence of stress, and for the absence of this emotion to be one of the central features in the experience of happiness. Because these expectations have been confirmed in several recent personality studies (see Brebner, chap. 9, this volume), it would seem important to take individual differences in vulnerability to anxiety into account in research on both stress and happiness. Gray (1982, 1987a) has made important contributions to understanding the neuropsychology of anxiety, based on his pharmacological, behavioral, and physiological research with animals. Gray's model for emotion and personality involves an important modification and extension of Eysenck's (1967) personality theory, in which a significant role is given to individual differences in anxiety.

Since the beginning of the 1980s, the research program of our group has included a number of studies with human subjects designed to test hypotheses derived from Gray's (1982) theoretical model. An early development in this empirical work was the construction of the Sensitivity to Punishment (SP) scale (Torrubia & Tobeña, 1984), which was designed to assess individual differences in the functioning of the behavioral inhibition system (BIS). In Gray's model, the BIS is responsible for individual differences in anxiety. In recent years, psychometric and behavioral research has examined the effects of such differences on psychophysiology and behavior.

This chapter presents a brief, selective review of our research group's work. Emphasis is given to those investigations that were most directly related to the study of stress and happiness. Three particular aspects of the program are addressed: (a) the construction of the Sensitivity to Punishment: Sensitivity to Reward (SPSR) questionnaire; (b) the effects of individual differences in behavioral inhibition on approach–avoidance conflicts, such as multiple-choice exams, and on extinction procedures in a laboratory task; and (c) cognitive mechanisms responsible for mediating sensitivity to punishment.

THE BEHAVIORAL INHIBITION SYSTEM AS A BIOLOGICAL SUBSTRATE FOR ANXIETY

Anxiety as an emotional state is a universal experience that can be observed not only in humans, but also in lower mammals such as the rat (Gray, 1987a). Within normal limits, state anxiety is an adaptive response in the emotional repertoire that stimulates and facilitates behavioral adjustments when a person is faced with potential dangers. However, when the anxiety intensity is disproportionate to the potential danger, or when highly intense anxiety is frequently manifested, it can interfere with normal functioning and may have distressing consequences. The frequency and intensity of anxiety states experienced over time provide the basis for defining Individual Differences in trait anxiety as a personality dimension (Spielberger, Gorsuch, & Lushene, 1970).

As the starting point for his theoretical model, Gray postulated the existence of three separate, interacting systems for the control of emotional behavior. These emotional systems and the types of stimuli that activate each system are: (a) the behavioral inhibition system (BIS), which is activated by signals that threaten potential punishment or frustrating nonreward, or by novel stimuli; (b) the behavioral activation system (BAS), which is responsible for behavior in response to signals indicative of reward or nonpunishment; and (c) the fight–flight system, responsible for behavior in response to actual unconditioned punishment or unconditioned nonreward. Anxiety and frustration would correspond with activity of the BIS, elation or relief would be emotions produced by the activity of the BAS, and anger and/or terror would be the emotions produced by the activity of the fight–flight system.

The BIS has been identified with some of the septo-hippocampal system's functions (Gray, 1982). At a psychological level, the BIS has two different modes of functioning: checking and control. In the checking mode, the BIS acts as a comparator. According to Gray (1988), "its chief function is to monitor ongoing behavior, checking continuously that outcomes coincide with expectations. In this role, it scans incoming sensory information for threatening or unexpected events and, if they occur, brings all other behavior to a halt, so as to evaluate the nature of the threat" (p. 29). Functioning in this checking mode could be mainly related to the cognitive processes preceding activation of the control mode.

The stimuli producing a change from checking to control mode are cues of punishment, cues of nonreward, and novel stimuli. In the control mode, the outputs of the BIS when confronting these stimuli are: (a) an inhibition of ongoing behavior; (b) an increase of attention to the environment; and (c) an increase of arousal. Individual differences between high- and low-anxious subjects would be related to the threshold of activation of the BIS in the checking mode, and with the strength with which outputs (i.e., behaving actively or in an inhibited way) would be produced in the control mode. Thus, subjects high on trait anxiety would have a lower activation threshold and/or would be more responsive to cues of punishment than subjects low on trait anxiety.

MEASURING INDIVIDUAL DIFFERENCES IN THE BIS AND THE BAS: THE CONSTRUCTION OF THE SPSR QUESTIONNAIRE

According to Gray, individual differences in the operation of the three emotional systems would give rise to three major dimensions of personality. Anxiety and Impulsivity would be the personality dimensions related to the functioning of the BIS and the BAS, respectively. Trait anxious subjects should be those having a high reactive BIS and high impulsive subjects should be those with a high reactive BAS. More tentatively, Gray (1987b) proposed that the dimension of Psychoticism could be related to the fight–flight system.

Gray's approach is a special case in the study of personality. The majority of authors have gone from psychometrics to biology, first describing the most relevant traits and dimensions and then, in some cases, proposing models for the biological bases of these traits. However, Gray first investigated the neuropsychology of emotions in animals, and then extended the model to humans (Zuckerman, 1983). For this reason, Gray's approach to the study of emotions has implied neuropsychological hypotheses that have been mainly tested in animals, but not so widely at the human level. The lack of specific self-report measures for the constructs of Anxiety and Impulsivity, as dimensions based on the concepts of BIS and BAS, has also tended to inhibit the application of the model to humans. The majority of empirical work conducted to test the model has been done using the combination of Eysenck's Extraversion and Neuroticism scales (Eysenck & Eysenck, 1964, 1975) as psychometric tools to measure individual differences in the functioning of the BIS and the BAS (Gupta & Shukla, 1989; Nichols & Newman, 1986).

Stable individual differences in the BIS and the BAS are the biological basis for Anxiety and Impulsivity traits, respectively. Nevertheless, few attempts have been made to test Gray's theoretical formulations using psychometric methods. The publication of the Susceptibility to Punishment scale (Torrubia & Tobeña, 1984) showed the possibility of measuring individual differences in the functioning of the BIS at a self-report level. In the development of the scale, it was expected that a homogeneous construct would be found based on: (a) behavior inhibition (passive avoidance) in situations involving the possibility of aversive consequences (punishment or frustrative nonreward) or novelty, (b) worry or cognitive processes produced by the possibility of punishment or failure, and (c) emotional states such as fearfulness about such aversive stimuli. The items were based on these constructs and developed in a rational way. The obtained results showed adequate internal consistency and good construct validity. The Susceptibility to Punishment scale was positively correlated with the Manifest Anxiety Scale (Taylor, 1953) and the Neuroticism (N) scale (Eysenck & Eysenck, 1975), negatively correlated with Eysenck's Extraversion (E) scale, and orthogonal to the Impulsiveness (Imp) scale of the Impulsiveness, Venturesomeness, and Empathy Questionnaire (IVE; Eysenck & Eysenck, 1978). Later on, new empirical data gave support to the scale's usefulness and validity (de Flores & Valdés, 1986; Díaz & Pickering, 1993; Moltó, 1988; Torrubia, Gomà, Martí, Muntaner, & Tobeña, 1985).

More recently, using a similar procedure, a new effort has been made to develop the SPSR questionnaire. It includes both a revised version of the Susceptibility to Punishment scale (the Sensitivity to Punishment [SP] scale) and a new scale aimed at measuring individual differences in the activity of the BAS (Sensitivity to Reward [SR] scale; Torrubia, Avila, Moltó, & Segarra, 1993). Each scale of the SPSR questionnaire is comprised of 24 items with a yes/no format (see appendix).

Similar to what was done for SP, in the development of the SR scale it was hypothesized that a homogeneous construct should appear based on: (a) a

Table 11.1 Intercorrelations of Sensitivity to Reward, Sensitivity to Punishment, EPQ
scales, and Impulsiveness for males ($n \geq 776$; above diagonal) and females
($n \geq 1274$; below diagonal)

	SR	SP	E	N	P	L	Imp
SR		12**	33**	33**	18**	−36**	44**
SP	01		−47	58**	−07	−05	10*
E	34**	−50**		−17**	11**	−13**	24**
N	27**	54**	−18**		14**	−18**	40**
P	19**	−10**	09**	12**		−37**	51**
L	−27**	03	−15**	−15**	−32**		−35**
Imp	43**	−01	28**	32**	46**	−35**	

Note. Decimals have been omitted from table.
*$p < .01$. **$p < .001$.

tendency to approach behavior when faced with cues of reward or nonpunishment, (b) a tendency to orient attention toward positive signals, and (c) a
heightened conditionability to rewarding events. It was expected that SP should
be related positively with measures of Anxiety and Neuroticism and negatively
with Extraversion. It was also hypothesized that the SR scale should correlate
positively with Impulsivity, Extraversion, and Neuroticism, and should not be
correlated with Trait Anxiety measures. SP and SR should be orthogonal, as
predicted by the model.

The SPSR questionnaire was constructed as a research instrument, using
mainly undergraduate samples in its psychometric development. The results
obtained with these samples show that internal consistency (Cronbach's alpha
coefficient) of the SP was 0.84 in both sexes, and that of SR was 0.77 in males
and 0.76 in females. Test–retest correlations obtained ranged from 0.89 within
a 3-month period to 0.57 over a 3-year period. As an illustration of the content
validity of the scales, the highest loadings for SP are obtained for items 47, 5,
and 37; the highest ones for SR are obtained for items 46, 38, and 30 (see
appendix) after principal component analysis.

As regards construct validity, the obtained correlations with Eysenckian
dimensions, and with some Impulsivity and Anxiety scales, match largely with
predictions derived from Gray's personality theory (Table 11.1). SP and SR are
almost orthogonal; SR is positively related to both E and N, whereas SP is
positively related to N and negatively to E; SR is positively related to Imp,
whereas correlations between SP and Imp are close to zero; neither of the two
scales is highly related to P. The lower correlation obtained between SR and
P, in comparison with the ones obtained by Imp, can be taken as evidence that
SR and Imp are probably not measuring the same construct. Correlations
between SP and Trait Anxiety from the State–Trait Anxiety Inventory (STAI;
Spielberger, Gorsuch, & Lushene, 1970), calculated in a small student sample,
were 0.56 in males ($n = 45$) and 0.62 in females ($n = 122$).

Data recently collected in Australia by Brebner (chap. 9, this volume) show
a similar pattern of results to those obtained in Spanish samples. The English
version of the SPSR questionnaire was administered to a sample of male and

Table 11.2 Intercorrelations of Sensitivity to Punishment, Sensitivity to Reward, and
EPQ scales in Brebner's study

	SP	ASP	SR	ASR	E	N
ASP	.89***					
SR	.20	.21				
ASR	.33*	.20	.90***			
E	−.28*	−.33**	.47***	.42***		
N	.72***	.71***	.29*	.35**	−.09	
P	.04	.07	.06	.18	.04	.13

Note. ASP = Australian version of SP; ASR = Australian version of SR. *N* = 72, except in
correlations with SP or SR (*N* = 57). Decimals have been omitted from table.
*p < .05. **p < .01. ***p < .001.

female Australian students. Alpha reliabilities were 0.82 for SP and 0.78 for
SR. As additional proof of the constructs' robustness, correlations with E, N,
and P were also similar when a slightly different version of the SPSR questionnaire, adapted by Brebner for an Australian group, was administered (Table
11.2).

Most Trait Anxiety scales focus more on cognitive and somatic components
than behavioral ones. Otherwise, the content of Impulsivity scales usually
places more emphasis on acting on the spur of the moment, in an unreflective
way, than acting purposefully to obtain reward. However, the SP and SR scale
items are more oriented toward measuring individual differences in sensitivity
to punishment or reinforcement and the resulting behavior patterns (behavioral
inhibition or approach). The results obtained provide preliminary evidence
that consistent patterns of behavioral inhibition and approach, supposedly
related to the functioning of the BIS and the BAS, respectively, can be detected
and measured at a self-report level.

The next step should be to determine the degree to which SP and SR scales
can predict behavior both in real-life and laboratory contexts (some of this
work is presented later). Evidence indicating a relationship between SP and
selection of activities containing threatening stimuli or novelty is described in
Gomà (1991), where a difference was found in SP scores between high-risk
sports participants and a control group. Recent studies have also shown that
SP is positively related to a measure of Pessimism and negatively to both self-
esteem (Sarmany, Pérez, & Torrubia, 1994) and happiness (Brebner, chap. 9,
this volume). In addition, research is needed to study the relationships between
the SP and SR scales and other scales constructed with similar purposes
(MacAndrew & Steele, 1991; Wilson, Gray, & Barrett, 1990).

INDIVIDUAL DIFFERENCES IN BEHAVIORAL INHIBITION: APPROACH–AVOIDANCE CONFLICTS AND RESISTANCE TO EXTINCTION

Behavioral inhibition is a behavior pattern that can be observed from the
earliest periods of life. Many studies support the notion that children can be

distinguished by the degree to which inhibition of action is evoked by unfamiliarity and challenge. Some of the more clear-cut manifestations of behavioral inhibition in children are the tendencies to withdraw, seek a parent, and inhibit play and vocalization in the presence of unfamiliar people or events (Kagan, Snidman, & Reznick, 1989). Similar individual differences in inhibition have also been observed in many animal species ranging from rats to monkeys (Suomi, 1985). Although this pattern of behavior may not necessarily be due only to biological or inherited factors, research indicates that behavioral inhibition, timidity, and fearfulness tendencies are some of the most inheritable behavior characteristics in children (Matheny, 1989). In addition, Social Introversion scores on the Minnesota Multiphasic Personality Inventory (MMPI) have also proved this to be the most inheritable scale in adolescents (Kagan et al., 1989). Some studies have shown that behavioral inhibition persists over the childhood years (Asendorpf, 1989; Kagan, Reznick, & Snidman, 1988), and that this trait is a risk factor for multiple anxiety, overanxiousness, and phobic disorders in children (Biederman et al., 1990).

According to Gray's model, stable individual differences in the BIS can give rise to different behavior patterns at a social level (Gray, 1982). Highly reactive BIS subjects may have a tendency to show a passive coping style, characterized by a tendency to avoid environments containing threat and novelty situations to avoid punishment or nonreward. Potential aversive consequences of active behavior in humans can include physical damage, social failure, and rejection, as well as their subjective consequences, such as anxiety (Leary, 1990). The main manifestations of this style would be "shyness, social withdrawal, sensitivity to punishment and failure, a tendency to be easily discouraged, and a failure to develop active means of coping with situations" (Fowles, 1987, p. 422).

It could be argued that the inhibited behaviors mentioned previously, which are observed in children, adults, and nonhuman species, are mediated by the BIS. Two studies are presented next on the relationship between individual differences in the functioning of the BIS and inhibited patterns of behavior. The first, carried out in a real-life situation, investigated coping styles to uncertainty in approach–avoidance conflicts; the second, conducted in the laboratory, was designed to study individual differences in resistance to extinction.

Behavioral Inhibition in Approach–Avoidance Conflicts: Type of Errors in Multiple-Choice Exams

A high degree of ambiguity or uncertainty is one of the main sources of stress (Krohne, 1993). This type of uncertainty is present in conflict situations, in which responding and inhibition are equally possible alternatives (i.e., approach–avoidance or avoidance–avoidance conflicts). In these situations, experimental research using go/no go discrimination tasks has shown that an overactivity of the BIS is associated with a heightened avoidance motivation, manifested as a tendency toward behavioral inhibition (Avila, Moltó, Segarra, & Torrubia, in press; Hagopian & Ollendick, 1994; Newman, Widom, & Nathan, 1985). Assume that experimental results in the laboratory should serve to predict behavior in real-life situations. The current interest in this study was to investigate behavior inhibition in multiple-choice examinations.

Multiple-choice exams, when correction-for-guessing is applied, provide a real-life context in which a particular type of uncertainty can be experienced by subjects: The conflict is between responding or not responding to a given question when response can lead either to reward or punishment. It was expected that this would be a good procedure to test for a behavioral tendency to respond or not (disinhibition–inhibition) in real-life situations. The exams consisted of questions with several wrong-answer choices and only one correct answer. Points are deducted for incorrect responses. Every question in these exams has some characteristics of an approach–avoidance conflict, as subjects must choose between either responding (approach) or not responding (avoidance). If they decide to make a response, this can be correct or incorrect. For each question correctly completed, one point is gained. For each question incorrectly completed, a fraction of a point (depending on the number of items) is marked off. Finally, if subjects decide not to respond (omit), no point is gained or lost.

Multiple-choice exams have two interesting characteristics. First, each question can be considered a go/no go discrimination, in which the final response of the subject will depend on different factors. The most important, of course, is knowing the correct response. If subjects are sure of the correct answer choice, their most probable decision will be to respond. If subjects are uncertain about which is the correct answer, the final decision will depend on different factors that modulate their approach–avoidance tendencies. If a subject finally makes a response (correct or incorrect), the approach tendencies will have been stronger than the avoidance one; but if he or she omits a response, avoidance tendencies will have been stronger.

The second characteristic is that subjects who take multiple-choice exams are highly motivated to obtain their best performance. Students must pass these exams to advance in their curricular development. Thus, multiple-choice exams can be of interest to study Gray's model in humans. As Gray (1987c) indicated, "only with animal subjects is it possible (with rare exceptions, and those generally in the clinical domain) to study the anxiety that is provoked by the threat of punishment that truly matters to the subject" (p. 497). However, exams give reinforcement that is extremely relevant to students, and reinforcements involved on exams are more powerful than those usually employed in laboratory tasks.

Two types of errors can be considered in a multiple-choice exam. On the one hand, incorrect responses may be considered commission errors because they are provoked by a failure to inhibit a response that results in punishment. On the other hand, blanks may be considered omission errors because there is a failure to respond for reward.

A study was conducted to investigate response styles in multiple-choice exams (Avila, Moltó, Segarra, & Torrubia, 1991). It was expected that differences between subjects in type of errors should emerge on the basis of their personality characteristics. It was assumed that maximum probability of conflict or uncertainty should be found among students with medium levels of knowledge (medium marks), and that students with either high or low marks should not experience as high a level of conflict during an exam. The hypothesis was that, in partialing out the level of knowledge in exams, individual differences in the BIS should be related to the type of errors. Predictions were that there should be more omissions and less incorrect responses in SP + subjects than in SP − ones.

Results from four groups of undergraduate students, each responding to a different subject matter, were considered. Two groups (taking histology and medical psychology) were from the second-year medicine class at the Autonomous University of Barcelona; the other two groups (general psychology and statistics) were first-year psychology students at the Jaume I University of Castelló. Only people in the middle level of the score distribution (mean ± 1 SD) were included in the analysis. The gender distribution for the groups studied consisted of 42 males and 68 females in the histology group, 48 males and 61 females in the medical psychology group, 35 females in the general psychology group, and 41 females in the statistics group. Results of only one exam were taken into account for each subject. In all cases, the exams were of the multiple-choice type, with either four or five options.

Statistical analyses were performed separately for each sex within each group. Analyses of covariance (ANCOVA), considering the number of correct responses as covariate, were carried out to control for the effects of achievement. Two-level factors of the SP, based on scores in the SP, were considered; subjects were classified as SP + (scores above or equal to the median) or SP − (scores below the median). The dependent variables were incorrect responses and omissions. The results show that both SP + male groups and three of four SP + female groups made significantly less incorrect responses (Fig. 11.1), and had more omissions (Fig. 11.2) than their SP − counterparts. No differences in correct responses were obtained between these groups.

The results show that differences in behavior inhibition can be found in approach–avoidance conflicts in real-life contexts. The results also parallel findings obtained by Geen (1987) in a testing procedure involving repeated failure that permitted quitting as an acceptable option; high test anxiety subjects were more likely to quit than those low on this trait. In conflict situations, when the possibility exists of obtaining reward or punishment after a response is made, high trait anxious subjects have a tendency to inhibit behavior. Nevertheless (as was found in Geen's study), when passive avoidance is not possible, high trait anxiety subjects tend to show a different pattern of inhibited behavior by responding slowly and more cautiously than those low in trait anxiety.

Following Gray's description of the BIS, the tendency to make or inhibit responses in multiple-choice exams could depend on two different mechanisms: (a) differences in the appraisal of threat, and (b) differences in the response threshold for interruption of goal-directed behavior. In the first case, subjects perceiving the situation as more threatening (high SPs) would have a lower threshold for activating the control mode of the BIS because of a predisposition to detect a higher number of mismatches; and anxious subjects would have a tendency toward inhibition because of their higher sensitivity to

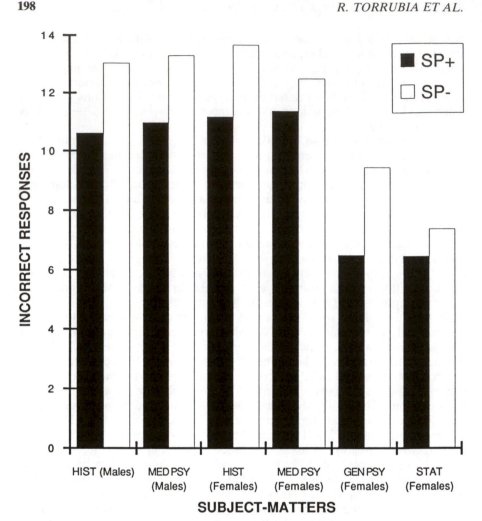

Figure 11.1   Adjusted mean incorrect response scores after partialing out the number of correct responses, of SP+ and SP− male and female subjects, for each subject matter.

punishment cues. In the second case, personality differences would affect response tendencies after an appraisal of threat. As a consequence, anxious and nonanxious subjects would differ in their response threshold to a given threatening situation once the BIS functions in control mode: Anxious subjects would have a higher response threshold than nonanxious subjects. Differences in the tendencies to actively respond or inhibit when subjects were uncertain could be indicating differences in their outcome expectations or confidence: Anxious subjects would have a higher expectation of punishment (see Carver & Scheier, 1992; Zinbarg & Revelle, 1989, for similar suggestions). The present results do not allow for a clear choice between the two possible mechanisms.

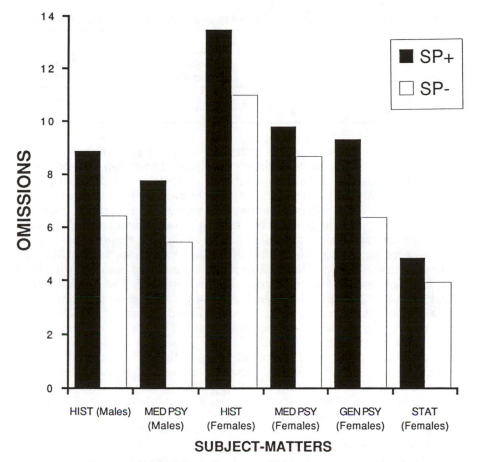

Figure 11.2 Adjusted mean omission scores after partialing out the number of correct responses, of SP+ and SP− male and female subjects, for each subject matter.

Moreover, they are not mutually exclusive, and could both contribute to the explanation of the inhibited behavior in approach–avoidance conflicts.

Sensitivity to Punishment and Resistance to Extinction

According to Gray's model, the BIS mediates the behavioral manifestations of passive avoidance (reducing risk of punishment by not responding) and extinction (suppression of responses that are not rewarded). Whereas some empirical research has shown that nonanxious subjects are less prone to passive-avoidance behavior than anxious ones, little evidence exists for BIS-mediated differences in resistance to extinction. A study was conducted to investigate individual differences in resistance to extinction (Avila, 1994). According to Gray's model, it should be expected that SP− subjects would have more resistance to extinction than SP+ subjects.

Table 11.3 Percentage of rewarded (% Rew) responses to each button in each phase

Responses	Phase I	Phase II	
		70% extinction group	30% extinction group
Button 1 %Rew	70%	0%	70%
Button 2 %Rew	30%	30%	0%

Ninety-two undergraduates (14 males and 78 females) who participated in the study were classified as SP+ or SP− according to whether their SP scores were above or below the median. Subjects completed two different phases (Phase I and Phase II), with three identical blocks of 100 trials each (a total of 600 trials), without interruption between phases. They were instructed to attain as many points as possible by choosing between two response alternatives in the form of two buttons in each trial. In Phase I, responses to the two buttons were partially rewarded for all the subjects: Responses to Button 1 were rewarded 70% of the time with a random amount of points ranging from 2 to 10, whereas responses to Button 2 were rewarded 30% of the time with a range from 8 to 20 points. In Phase II, one of the two responses remained as in Phase I, but the other was never rewarded in order to attain extinction. The computer randomly selected the extinction button for each subject. A summary of the procedure can be seen in Table 11.3.

Consistent with Gray's conceptualization of the BIS, statistical analyses revealed that SP− subjects were slower to extinguish previously rewarded behavior than SP+ subjects (Fig. 11.3). Although the obtained effect was general, the main differences were obtained for the first block of Phase II. These results are consistent with previous ones, indicating a better conditioning of high-anxious subjects (i.e., neurotic introverts) when punishment cues are used (Gupta & Shukla, 1989).

The results indicate that low-anxious subjects show a reduced tendency for the processing of stimuli signaling potential negative consequences, and are thus less likely to associate their responses with the negative consequences produced. Similar mechanisms have been proposed for explaining observed differences in sensitivity to punishment cues (Avila, Moltó, Segarra, & Torrubia, in press; Avila & Torrubia, 1994; Newman & Wallace, 1993). These findings suggest that individual differences in behavioral inhibition depend on how subjects cognitively process cues of punishment and nonreward.

THE BEHAVIORAL INHIBITION SYSTEM AND COGNITIVE PROCESSES

The translation of Gray's theory to the study of human anxiety has received a number of criticisms, especially concerning the involvement of the cognitive system (Howard, 1986). According to Eysenck (1992), the BIS has been well described at the neuropsychological level and is useful to explain anxiety in

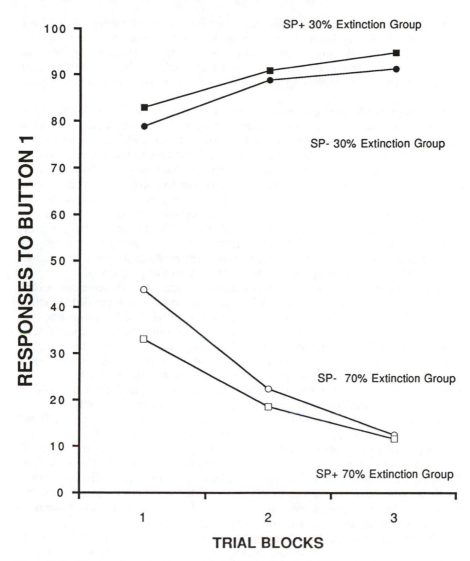

Figure 11.3 Mean responses to Button 1 during Phase II in both 70% extinction group and 30% extinction group for SP + and SP − subjects.

animals, but it has some limitations in explaining cognitive aspects of human anxiety. One of the problems is related to the description of individual differences in cognitive processes preceding activation of the BIS.

Cognitive functioning in anxiety has been widely studied during the last few years (see Eysenck, 1992; Williams, Watts, MacLeod, & Mathews, 1988). These studies have reported an automatic tendency to selectively encode emotionally threatening information in both trait anxious subjects (under stress or arousal) and clinically anxious patients (MacLeod, 1991; Mathews, May, Mogg, & Eysenck, 1990). In both groups of individuals, this selective encoding bias may be very general, serving to facilitate processing all threatening information. An opposite tendency is shown by low trait anxiety subjects, who respond in such situations by decreasing the degree of selective encoding of threatening information.

This cognitive framework could serve to clarify the mechanism underlying observed differences in associating punishment and nonreward cues with their negative consequences. If threatening stimuli automatically attract the attention of trait anxious subjects, these stimuli will produce in these subjects more interference effects on a central task after having received instructions to ignore them. Hence, a study was conducted to test this hypothesis (Grande, Avila, Moltó, & Torrubia, 1993). The experimental task consisted of associating a neutral stimulus (i.e., a red circle) with an aversive stimulus (a loud noise) while performing a point-scoring reaction time (PSRT) task, where correct responding was rewarded with points that could be exchanged for money. It was expected that trait anxious subjects should make a stronger association between this neutral stimulus and its acquired aversive properties.

A computerized task was developed to study individual differences in inhibition of goal-directed behavior. Inhibition, as shown by increased reaction time (RT), should be produced by the presence of the cue for punishment (a red circle) while subjects were performing a continuous instrumental task (cued-choice RT) with monetary incentives. Subjects completed three successive experimental conditions with the same set of stimuli, but with different instructions: Prepunishment, punishment, and postpunishment. Each condition had 200 trials. A colored circle (6-cm diameter) and then a two-digit number (3 × 3 cm) were visually presented for 2 seconds in each trial. The interval between the circle and digits was varied randomly between 100 and 300 msec. The number and color of the circle changed from trial to trial. Subjects had to perform a continuous odd–even number discrimination RT task: pressing button "E" (for even numbers) and button "O" (for odd numbers) on a response panel. Subjects were rewarded for correct discriminations (with an amount of money inversely proportional to their RT) and punished for wrong discriminations (with a deduction of 5 cents). The total amount of money earned appeared in the screen throughout the task.

The instructions for the Prepunishment condition told subjects to ignore colored circles during performance of the task. Before starting the Punishment condition, subjects were instructed that they would receive punishment (a loud noise via headphones) if they responded to the two-digit number in the presence of a red circle (the colors of the circles were easily distinguishable). Before the beginning of the Postpunishment condition, specific instructions emphasized the absence of punishment after any response and told subjects to ignore the colored circles. The three conditions presented the same sequence of two-digit numbers and colors. There were 20 "red trials" (trials with the red circle) and 180 "non-red trials" in each condition. The "red trials" appeared mixed in with 180 "non-red trials." The interval between the appearance of the circle and the digits in the "red trials" was always 100 msec.

The task was administered to 26 male undergraduates selected on the basis of their extreme scores (mean $\pm$ 1 SD) on the SP (14 classified as SP + and 12 as SP −). All the subjects also had medium scores on the SR scale (between 1 SD below or above the mean). The punishments received in the Punishment condition for both SP groups did not differ significantly (0.85 for SP − and 0.66 for SP +). The introduction of the punishment contingencies in the Punishment condition produced a significant general slowing in the response speed of the PSRT task. However, there were no differences between the SP groups in this slowing of response times in this condition.

Trait anxiety differences (SP + vs. SP −) were related to response times in the "red trials" in the Postpunishment condition. Figure 11.4 shows the times in the PSRT task of high- and low-anxious groups for "red" and "non-red trials." The Anxiety $\times$ Condition $\times$ Type of Trial interaction approached significance ($p < .07$), indicating that SP + subjects had a larger difference in RT between "red" and "non-red trials" in the Postpunishment condition than SP − subjects. As a consequence, the high-anxiety group showed a higher level of behavior interference in the presence of a punishment cue than SP − subjects.

Because a previous study showed that subjects' reaction to motivationally significant stimuli habituated rather quickly with repeated trials (Newman et al., 1993), response times to the "red trials" were also analyzed by dividing the "red trials" of the Postpunishment condition into four blocks of 50 trials. Figure 11.5 shows large differences between SP − and SP + subjects found in the first block ($p < .05$). These results show how a cue previously associated with punishment automatically interfered with goal-directed behavior, although the instructions had explicitly emphasized that this cue did not have any motivational significance, and told subjects to ignore it.

The present results are similar to those obtained in several other studies that show that the presence of threatening words interferes with normal cognitive functioning (Eysenck, 1992). In these studies, anxious subjects had a greater tendency to selectively encode threatening stimuli. This type of bias seems to operate at a pre-attentive, nonconscious level. Similar processes could be hypothesized to explain the observed differences (i.e., the punishment cue would produce a greater level of interference on the PSRT task in anxious subjects because they would have acquired a selective attentional bias toward this stimulus). The automatic effect of interference seems to be an indicator of an emotional response elicited by the punishment cue, which is similar to that found by Öhman and co-workers (Öhman, Dimberg, & Esteves, 1989) in their research studies in Pavlovian conditioning to fear-relevant stimuli, such as pictures of snakes or angry faces. Öhman indicated that once a fear-evoking stimulus is detected, ongoing behavior is interrupted, emotions are activated, and control is relinquished from an automatic perceptual level to a conscious controlled level, which stimulates further analyses of the situation before action is taken.

Nevertheless, the procedure goes beyond this attentional bias in showing differences between anxious and nonanxious subjects in the ability to extinguish the association between a secondary (red circle) and a primary (loud

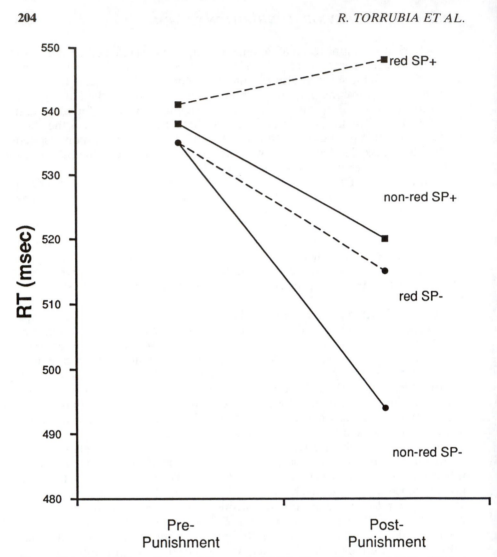

Figure 11.4 Mean RTs on "red" and "non-red trials" in Prepunishment and Postpunishment
conditions for each personality group.

noise) aversive reinforcer: Anxious subjects are slower to cancel or unlearn
this association. These differences could be produced in two different ways:
(a) in the strength of the association at the stage of learning the relationship
between a neutral stimulus and the aversive stimulus in the Punishment condition, and/or (b) in a different speed of suppression of this association in the
Postpunishment condition.

Although the experimental procedure did not allow for determining which
of these processes was operating, previous research seems to show that differences are produced at the acquisition stage. There are two kinds of evidence

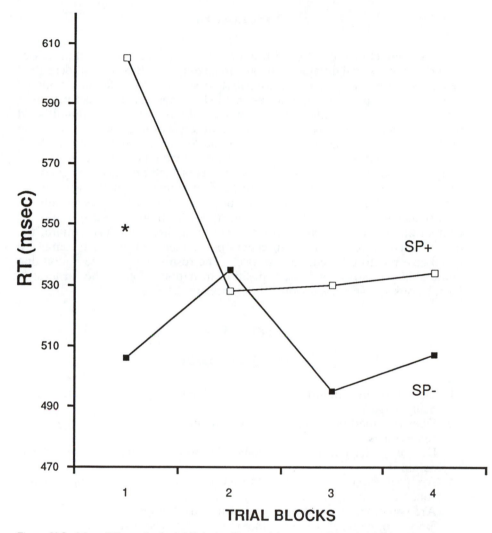

Figure 11.5 Mean RTs on "red trials" during Postpunishment condition divided into four blocks (*p < .05).

of differences at this stage. First, attentional studies suggest that anxious subjects have an automatic tendency to selectively recognize threat-related stimuli (Eysenck, 1992), whereas nonanxious subjects show a tendency to shift their attention away from these stimuli (Derryberry & Reed, 1994; MacLeod & Mathews, 1988). Second, research also suggests that low-anxious subjects show a tendency to reduced processing of punishment cues in mixed-incentive learning tasks (Avila et al., in press; Avila & Torrubia, 1994). These cognitive processes could lead to differences in both frequency and aversive conditioning.

CONCLUSION

Gray's model provides a good framework to study psychological processes underlying individual differences in human anxiety. The BIS is a well-described neuropsychological system that contributes basically to different emotional expressions. A plausible interpretation of the empirical data, derived from Gray's model, is that differences in conditionability to aversive stimuli could be at least one of the causal factors for the differences in selective recognition of threatening information between high and low trait anxiety subjects. Such differences could be partially responsible for individual differences in the primary appraisal of threat. The attentional bias of high-anxious subjects could act as an amplifier of aversive properties of threatening stimuli, whereas the contrary would happen in low-anxious subjects. Thus, differences in information processing could predetermine the type of stimuli processed and the content of the information to which attention is directed. Furthermore, the differences observed in processing cues of punishment or frustrative nonreward could give rise to different coping styles. The results support the notion that vulnerability to stress or a predisposition to happiness could be, at least in part, a consequence of individual differences in the BIS.

APPENDIX

SPSR Questionnaire

1. Do you often refrain from doing something because you are afraid of it being illegal?
2. Does the good prospect of obtaining money motivate you strongly to do some things?
3. Do you prefer not to ask for something when you are not sure you will obtain it?
4. Are you frequently encouraged to act by the possibility of being valued in your work, in your studies, with your friends, or with your family?
5. Are you often afraid of new or unexpected situations?
6. Do you often meet people of the opposite sex whom you like?
7. Is it difficult for you to telephone someone you do not know?
8. Do you like to take some drugs because of the pleasure you get from them?
9. Do you often renounce your rights when you know you can avoid a quarrel with a person or an organization?
10. Do you often do things to be praised?
11. As a child, were you troubled by punishments at home or in school?
12. Do you like being the center of attention at a party or a social meeting?
13. In tasks that you are not prepared for, do you attach great importance to the possibility of failure?
14. Do you spend a lot of your time on obtaining a good image?

15. Are you easily discouraged in difficult situations?
16. Do you need people to show their affection for you all the time?
17. Are you a shy person?
18. When you are in a group, do you try to make your opinions the most intelligent or the funniest?
19. Whenever possible, do you avoid demonstrating your skills for fear of being embarrassed?
20. Do you often take the opportunity to pick up people of the opposite sex?
21. When you are with a group, do you have difficulties selecting a good topic to talk about?
22. As a child, did you do a lot of things to get people's approval?
23. Is it often difficult for you to fall asleep when you think about things you have done or must do?
24. Does the possibility of social advancement move you to action, even if this involves not playing fair?
25. Do you think a lot before complaining in a restaurant if your meal is not well prepared?
26. Do you generally give preference to those activities that imply an immediate gain?
27. Would you be bothered if you had to return to a store when you noticed you were given the wrong change?
28. Do you often have trouble resisting the temptation of doing forbidden things?
29. Whenever you can, do you avoid going to unknown places?
30. Do you like to compete and do everything you can to win?
31. Are you often worried by things that you said or did?
32. Is it easy for you to associate tastes and smells to very pleasant events?
33. Would it be difficult for you to ask your boss for a raise (salary increase)?
34. Are there a large number of objects or sensations that remind you of pleasant events?
35. Do you generally try to avoid speaking in public?
36. When you start to play with a slot machine, is it often difficult for you to stop?
37. Do you, on a regular basis, think that you could do more things if it was not for your insecurity or fear?
38. Do you sometimes do things for quick gains?
39. Comparing yourself to people you know, are you afraid of many things?
40. Does your attention easily stray from your work in the presence of an attractive stranger?
41. Do you often find yourself worrying about things to the extent that performance in intellectual abilities is impaired?
42. Are you interested in money to the point of being able to do risky jobs?
43. Do you often refrain from doing something you like in order not to be rejected or disapproved of by others?
44. Do you like to put competitive ingredients in all of your activities?
45. Generally, do you pay more attention to threats than to pleasant events?
46. Would you like to be a socially powerful person?

47. Do you often refrain from doing something because of your fear of being embarrassed?
48. Do you like displaying your physical abilities even though this may involve danger?

The SPSR questionnaire remains the property of the authors. Permission to use this test may be obtained directly from the author.

REFERENCES

Argyle, M., & Lu, L. (1990). The happiness of extraverts. *Personality and Individual Differences, 11,* 1011–1017.

Asendorpf, J. N. (1989). Shyness as a final common pathway for two different kinds of inhibition. *Journal of Personality and Social Psychology, 57,* 481–492.

Avila, C. (1994). Sensitivity to punishment and resistance to extinction: A test of Gray's behavioral inhibition system. *Personality and Individual Differences, 17,* 845–848.

Avila, C., Moltó, J., Segarra, P., & Torrubia, R. (1991, July). *Personality and response to multiple choice question examinations in university students: A test of Gray's hypotheses.* Poster presented at the 5th conference of the International Society for the Study of Individual Differences, Oxford, England.

Avila, C., Moltó, J., Segarra, P., & Torrubia, R. (in press). Sensitivity to conditioned or unconditioned stimuli, what is the mechanism underlying passive avoidance deficits in extraverts? *Journal of Research in Personality.*

Avila, C., & Torrubia, R. (1994). *Personality differences in suppression of behavior as a function of the probability of punishment.* Manuscript in preparation.

Biederman, J., Rosenbaum, J. F., Hirshfeld, D. R., Faraone, S. V., Bolduc, E. A., Gersten, M., Meminger, S. R., Kagan, J., Snidman, N., & Reznick, J. S. (1990). Psychiatric correlates of behavioral inhibition in young children of parents with and without psychiatric disorders. *Archives of General Psychiatry, 47,* 21–26.

Carver, C. S., & Scheier, M. F. (1992). Confidence, doubt, and coping with anxiety. In D. G. Forgays, T. Sosnowsky, & K. Wrzesniewski (Eds.), *Anxiety: Recent developments in cognitive, psychophysiological and health research* (pp. 13–22). Washington, DC: Hemisphere.

de Flores, T., & Valdés, M. (1986). Behaviour pattern A: Reward, fight or punishment. *Personality and Individual Differences, 7,* 319–326.

Derryberry, D., & Reed, M. (1994). Temperament and attention: Orienting toward and away from positive and negative signals. *Journal of Personality and Social Psychology, 66,* 1128–1139.

Díaz, A., & Pickering, A. D. (1993). The relationships between Gray's and Eysenck's personality spaces. *Personality and Individual Differences, 15,* 297–305.

Endler, N. S. (1988). Hassles, health, and happiness. In M. P. Janisse (Ed.), *Individual differences, stress, and health psychology* (pp. 24–56). New York: Springer-Verlag.

Eysenck, H. J. (1967). *The biological bases of personality.* Springfield, IL: Thomas.

Eysenck, H. J., & Eysenck, S. B. G. (1964). *Manual of the Eysenck Personality Inventory.* London: University of London Press.

Eysenck, H. J., & Eysenck, S. B. G. (1975). *Manual of the Eysenck Personality Questionnaire.* London: Hodder & Stoughton.

Eysenck, M. V. (1992). *Anxiety: The cognitive perspective.* Hove, England: Lawrence Erlbaum.

Eysenck, S. B. G., & Eysenck, H. J. (1978). Impulsiveness and venturesomeness: Their position in a dimensional system of personality description. *Psychological Reports, 43,* 1247–1255.

Fowles, D. C. (1987). Application of a behavioral theory of motivation to the concepts of anxiety and impulsivity. *Journal of Research in Personality, 21,* 417–435.

Geen, R. G. (1987). Test anxiety and behavioral avoidance. *Journal of Research in Personality, 21,* 481–488.

Gomà, M. (1991). Personality profile of subjects engaged in high physical risk sports. *Personality and Individual Differences, 12,* 1087–1093.

Grande, I., Avila, C., Moltó, J., & Torrubia, R. (1993, July). *Personality and effects of cues of punishment on a choice reaction time task with monetary incentives.* Poster presented at the sixth meeting of the International Society for the Study of Individual Differences, Baltimore, MD.

Gray, J. A. (1982). *The neuropsychology of anxiety: An enquiry into the functions of the septo-hippocampal system.* Oxford: Oxford University Press.

Gray, J. A. (1987a). *The psychology of fear and stress* (2nd ed.). Cambridge, England: Cambridge University Press.

Gray, J. A. (1987b). The neuropsychology of emotion and personality. In S. M. Stahl, S. D. Iversen, & E. C. Goodman (Eds.), *Cognitive neurochemistry* (pp. 171–190). Oxford: Oxford University Press.

Gray, J. A. (1987c). Perspectives on anxiety and impulsivity: A commentary. *Journal of Research in Personality, 21,* 493–509.

Gray, J. A. (1988). The neuropsychological basis of anxiety. In C. G. Last & M. Hersen (Eds.), *Handbook of anxiety disorders* (pp. 10–37). New York: Pergamon.

Gupta, S., & Shukla, A. P. (1989). Verbal operant conditioning as a function of extraversion and reinforcement. *British Journal of Psychology, 80,* 39–44.

Hagopian, L. P., & Ollendick, T. H. (1994). Behavioral inhibition and test anxiety: An empirical investigation of Gray's theory. *Personality and Individual Differences, 16,* 597–604.

Howard, R. C. (1986). Anxiety: Not the BIS alone. *Bulletin of the British Psychological Society, 39,* 16–17.

Kagan, J., Reznick, J. S., & Snidman, N. (1988). Biological bases of childhood shyness. *Science, 240,* 167–171.

Kagan, J., Snidman, N., & Reznick, S. (1989). The constructs of inhibition and lack of inhibition to unfamiliarity. In D. S. Palermo (Ed.), *Coping with uncertainty: Behavioral and developmental perspectives* (pp. 131–149). Hillsdale, NJ: Lawrence Erlbaum.

Krohne, H. W. (1993). Vigilance and cognitive avoidance as concepts in coping research. In H. W. Krone (Ed.), *Attention and avoidance* (pp. 19–50). Seattle, WA: Hogrefe & Huber.

Lazarus, R. S., & Folkman, S. (1984). Stress, appraisal and coping. New York: Springer.

Leary, M. R. (1990). Anxiety, cognition and behavior: In search of a broader perspective. *Journal of Social Behavior and Personality, 5,* 39–44.

MacAndrew, C., & Steele, T. (1991). Gray's behavioral inhibition system: A psychometric examination. *Personality and Individual Differences, 12,* 157–171.

MacLeod, C. (1991). Clinical anxiety and the selective encoding of threatening information. *International Review of Psychiatry, 3,* 279–292.

MacLeod, C., & Mathews, A. (1988). Anxiety and the allocation of attention to threat. *Quarterly Journal of Experimental Psychology, 38A,* 659–670.

Matheny, A. P. (1989). Children's behavioral inhibition over age and across situations: Genetic similarity for a trait during change. *Journal of Personality, 57,* 215–235.

Mathews, A., May, J., Mogg, K., & Eysenck, M. (1990). Attentional bias in anxiety: Selective search or defective filtering? *Journal of Abnormal Psychology, 99,* 166–173.

Moltó, J. (1988). Investigación psicométrica sobre la escala de Susceptibilidad al Castigo de Torrubia y Tobeña. [Psychometric research on Torrubia and Tobeña's Sensitivity to Punishment Scale]. *Análisis y Modificación de Conducta, 14,* 643–674.

Newman, J. P., & Wallace, J. F. (1993). Diverse pathways to deficient self-regulation: Implications for disinhibitory psychopathology in children. *Clinical Psychology Review, 13,* 699–720.

Newman, J. P., Wallace, J. F., Strauman, T. J., Skolaski, R. L., Oreland, K. M., Mattek, P. W., Elder, K. A., & McNeely, J. (1993). Effects of motivationally significant stimuli on the regulation of dominant responses. *Journal of Personality and Social Psychology, 65,* 165–175.

Newman, J. P., Widom, C. S., & Nathan, S. (1985). Passive avoidance in syndromes of disinhibition: Psychopathy and extraversion. *Journal of Personality and Social Psychology, 48,* 1316–1327.

Nichols, S., & Newman, J. P. (1986). Effects of punishment on response latency in extraverts. *Journal of Personality and Social Psychology, 50,* 624–630.

Ohman, A., Dimberg, U., & Esteves, F. (1989). Preattentive activation of aversive emotions. In T. Archer & L. G. Nilsson (Eds.), *Aversion, avoidance, and anxiety. Perspective on aversively motivated behavior* (pp. 169–193). Hillsdale, NJ: Lawrence Erlbaum.

Sarmany, I., Pérez, J., & Torrubia, R. (1994). *Personality and coping styles.* Manuscript in preparation.

Spielberger, C. D., Gorsuch, R. C., & Lushene, R. E. (1970). *Manual for the State-Trait Anxiety Inventory.* Palo Alto, CA: Consulting Psychologists Press.

Suomi, S. J. (1985). Response styles in monkeys: Experiential effects. In H. Klar & L. J. Siever (Eds.), *Biologic response styles: Clinical implications* (pp. 2–17). Washington, DC: American Psychiatric Press.

Taylor, J. A. (1953). A personality scale of manifest anxiety. *Journal of Abnormal and Social Psychology, 48,* 285–290.

Torrubia, R., Avila, C., Moltó, J., & Segarra, P. (1993, July). *The Sensitivity to Punishment and Sensitivity to Reward scales: Norms, reliability and construct validity.* Poster presented at the sixth meeting of the International Society for the Study of Individual Differences, Baltimore, MD.

Torrubia, R., Gomà, M., Martí, A., Muntaner, C., & Tobeña, A. (1985, June). *The assessment of the anxiety trait by means of the Susceptibility to punishment scale: Some results about reliability and validity.* Poster presented at 2nd conference of the International Society for the Study of Individual Differences, Sant Feliu de Guíxols, Spain.

Torrubia, R., & Tobeña, A. (1984). A scale for the assessment of "susceptibility to punishment" as a measure of anxiety: Preliminary results. *Personality and Individual Differences, 5,* 371–375.

Williams, J. M. G., Watts, F. N., MacLeod, C., & Mathews, A. (1988). *Cognitive psychology and emotional disorders.* Chichester: Wiley.

Wilson, G. D., Gray, J. A., & Barrett, P. T. (1990). A factor analysis of the Gray-Wilson Personality Questionnaire. *Personality and Individual Differences, 11,* 1037–1045.

Zinbarg, R., & Revelle, W. (1989). Personality and conditioning: A test of four models. *Journal of Personality and Social Psychology, 57,* 301–314.

Zuckerman, M. (1983). Comments on chapter 6. In M. Zuckerman (Ed.), *Biological bases of sensation seeking, impulsivity, and anxiety* (pp. 219–227). Hillsdale, NJ: Lawrence Erlbaum.

V

STRESS, EMOTION, AND COPING

12

Temperament and Stress: Temperament as a Moderator of Stressors, Emotional States, Coping, and Costs

Jan Strelau
*University of Warsaw and Silesian University,
Warsaw and Katowice, Poland*

ABSTRACT

This chapter focuses on individual differences in temperament as a major factor in stress phenomena. Primarily biologically determined, temperament is one of the most basic foundations of personality. In stress research, temperament has been ascribed the status of a moderator that modifies stressors, emotional states, ways of coping, and consequences (costs) of stress. In examining the effects of individual differences in temperament on stress reactions, all constructs relating to stress have been defined and located among broader conceptualizations. Theoretical conceptions of stress–temperament relations are supported by empirical findings reported in the literature, as well as by data collected in our laboratory. Age-specific (children and adults) relations between temperament and stress have been demonstrated. Particular attention has been given to how temperament traits, alone and in interaction with other factors, increase the risk of developing behavior disorders and pathology. Taking Kendler and Eaves' (1986) model for the joint effect of genotype and environment on psychiatric illness as a starting point, several models of temperament–environment interaction were developed to show the role that temperament plays as a moderator of behavior, and as a determinant of health consequences resulting from chronic or excessive states of stress.

For many decades in research on stress, not much attention was paid to individual differences. This was due to the specific understanding of stress. Selye (1950, 1956), one of the pioneers in research on stress, considered stress to be a physiological reaction that is entirely determined by stimuli intensity. Such an understanding of stress has not given place at all to the individual

This chapter is a thoroughly extended version of a paper presented at the NATO Advanced Research Workshop "Stress and Communities," June 14–18, 1994, Chateau de Bonas, France. I thank Stevan E. Hobfoll for his help in preparing this manuscript. Part of this research was supported by Grant 11108-91-02 from the Committee for Scientific Research.

differences approach. In his later publications, in which more attention was paid to psychological phenomena, stimuli intensity was, for him, the determinant of stress.

As Selye (1975) wrote, "it is immaterial whether the agent or situation we face is pleasant or unpleasant; all that counts is the intensity of the demand for readjustment or adaptation" (p. 15). The individual differences approach was not present at all in studies where stress was limited to stressors (e.g., Elliot & Eisdorfer, 1982; Weick, 1970). As underlined by McGrath (1970), there is no place for individual differences if stress would be regarded as an external factor—as a stress-inducing situation.

One of the pioneers of the individual differences approach to stress was Haggard (1949), who wrote almost 50 years ago that "some of the factors which influence an individual's ability to tolerate and master stress include: the nature of his early identifications and his present character structure, and their relation to the demands and gratifications of the present stress-producing situation" (p. 458).

The appropriate understanding of the role of individual differences as co-determinants of the phenomenon of stress was possible due to approaches to stress developed in the 1960–1970s. Of most significance was Lazarus' (1966; Opton & Lazarus, 1967) contribution. After discovering that stressful conditions did not produce dependable effects in stress intensity and level of performance as a consequence of stress, Lazarus, Deese, and Osler (1952; cited in Lazarus, 1993) "concluded that to understand what was happening we had to take into account individual differences in motivational and cognitive variables, which intervened between the stressor and the reaction" (p. 3). His transactional theory of stress, in which appraisal of a given situation as threatening is one of the most crucial postulates, classifies stress as an individual-specific phenomenon. The process of appraisal that takes place in the individual is always a subjective one. This means, among other things, that it runs differently in different people.

A 14-volume series, entitled *Stress and Emotion,* edited by Spielberger, Sarason, and co-editors since 1975, has been in existence for almost two decades. The series, of which this volume is a part, presents dozens of chapters in which the role of individual differences in determining stress, especially in respect to trait anxiety, became evident. The group of researchers who consider the individual differences approach as one of the most important paradigms in the study of stress has increased since the 1960s (e.g., Appley & Trumbull, 1967; Chan, 1977; Kagan, 1983; Krohne & Laux, 1982; Lazarus, 1991; Magnusson, 1982; Strelau 1988).

The stress literature is composed of such phenomena as stressors, the state of stress, coping with stress, and consequences of stress, as expressed in physiological and/or psychological costs. The individual differences approach may be applied to each of them. Some authors underline the fact that stressors and stress can hardly be separated from each other. Such a view makes operationalizations of these constructs difficult. For example, Kagan (1983) defined the *stressor* conjunctively as a class of events and a specific reaction to exemplars of that class. Thus, the stressor has been regarded by him as a construct composed of the stress-inducing event and the undesirable affective reaction to this event. There exists an enormous number of factors that, in interaction with each other, determine the individual-specific components of stress. A list of some of them has been presented elsewhere (Strelau, 1989a).

Among the many determinants of individual differences, considerable attention was devoted to personality characteristics. The latter have been mostly considered as moderators of stress (i.e., as antecedent conditions that interact with other conditions in producing stress or in coping with stress; Folkman & Lazarus, 1988). Among the many personality traits, considerable research was devoted to such stable characteristics as: hardiness (e.g., Kobasa, 1979; Kobasa & Puccetti, 1983), repression sensitization (e.g., Krohne, 1986), self-esteem (e.g., Chan, 1977; Ormel & Schaufeli, 1991), locus of control (e.g., Ormel & Schaufeli, 1991; Parkes, 1984), self-confidence (e.g., Holohan & Moos, 1986), sense of coherence (Antonovsky, 1987), and so on.

Before entering the subject of this chapter, which concentrates on different issues of the temperament–stress relationship, it is necessary to define the main constructs under discussion. This allows avoiding misunderstandings and confusions.

TEMPERAMENT AS A MODERATOR OF STRESS

Among personality attributes, a special place in research on stress should be given to temperament. For the purpose of this chapter, *temperament* is defined as referring to basic, relatively stable personality traits that are present from early childhood on and occur in man and animals. Being primarily determined by biological factors, temperament undergoes slow changes caused by maturation and individual-specific genotype-environment interactions.

In several temperament theories, the assumption that temperament plays an important role in moderating stress is incorporated as one of the most important postulates. For example, Kagan (1983) considered the two types of temperament distinguished by him—inhibited and uninhibited temperaments—as representing different vulnerability to experience stress under situations of unexpected or unpredictable events. At the beginning of his research on sensation seeking, Zuckerman (1964) concluded that some individuals are resistant to sensory deprivation, whereas others react under such conditions in a way that suggests perceptual isolation is stressful. His definition of *sensation seeking* underlines the willingness of sensation seekers to take physical and social risks (Zuckerman, 1979, 1991a). According to Nebylitsyn (1972) and Strelau (1983), the functional significance of temperament is evident when individuals are confronted with extreme situations or demands.

In arousal-oriented theories of temperament, which refer to the concepts of *optimal level of arousal* or *stimulation,* temperament characteristics are regarded as moderators in experiencing the state of stress under extreme levels of stimulation, as exemplified in the domain of Extraversion (Eysenck, 1970; Eysenck & Eysenck, 1985), stimulus screening (Mehrabian, 1977), reactivity

(Strelau, 1983, 1988), sensation seeking (Zuckerman, 1991a, 1994) or approach–withdrawal tendencies (McGuire & Turkewitz, 1979).

The following question arises: Why should temperament traits be considered
as important variables moderating stress phenomena? Being more or less un-
specific, rather formal characteristics, they penetrate all kinds of behavior,
whatever the content or direction of this behavior. In so doing, they contribute
to a variety of stress phenomena. Connected mainly with energetic and temporal characteristics of behavior, they take part as moderators in all stress
phenomena that may be characterized by means of energy and time. Many
temperament characteristics are related to emotions, as expressed in a tendency to generate emotional processes (Strelau, 1987). As commonly accepted
(see e.g., Lazarus, 1991, 1993) emotions are one of the core constructs for
understanding stress.

The statements drawn previously may be illustrated by referring to temperament in respect to four stress-related events: (a) the impact of temperament
in determining the intensity of stressors, (b) the role of temperament as a
codeterminant of the state of stress, (c) the moderating effect of temperament
in coping with stress, and (d) the contribution of temperamental traits to the
psychophysiological and/or psychological costs of the state of stress.

THE UNDERSTANDING OF STRESS PHENOMENA

There is no agreement regarding the understanding of stress and related
phenomena. Thus, before entering the main object of this chapter, some explanations are needed regarding the position taken here among the different
conceptualizations in the domain of stress.

First of all, a trait approach to stress is not advocated here, as suggested by
Schonpflug (1993)—that is, that individual differences in tendencies to react
in a given way are the main determinants of stress. However, personality traits,
and among them first of all temperament, play an essential role in moderating
stress.

Stressors and Psychological Stress

Psychological stress is defined here as a state characterized by strong negative emotions, such as fear, anxiety, anger, hostility, or other emotional states
evoking distress, accompanied by physiological and biochemical changes that
evidently exceed the baseline level of arousal. Neuroendocrine changes are
inherent attributes of emotions, thus they cannot be ignored as components of
psychological stress. This statement is based on strong empirical evidence. The
most representative studies are those conducted by Frankenhaeuser (1979,
1986; see also Magnusson, Klinteberg, & Stattin, 1991) with respect to adrenal-
medullary and adrenal-cortical changes as a reaction to stressors.

It seems that such an understanding of the state of stress—underlying the
importance of both emotions and arousal as unseparable components of the
state of stress, with more or less expressed modifications regarding both the

concept of *arousal* and the nature of emotions—can be met among many researchers in the domain of stress. However, this view differs from Lazarus' (1993). His definition of *stress* does not recognize arousal as a component. In fact, he reduced the state of stress to emotions.

However, most researchers on stress differ regarding the causes determining the state of stress. According to Strelau (1988), the state of stress is caused by a lack of equilibrium (occurrence of discrepancy) between demands and the individual's capability (capacity) to cope with them. Such a conceptualization of stress can also be found in the literature (see Krohne & Laux, 1982; McGrath, 1970; Ratajczak & Adamiec, 1989; Schulz & Schonpflug, 1982). The magnitude of the state of stress is a function of the size of discrepancy between the demands and capacities, assuming the individual is motivated to cope with the demands with which he or she is confronted.

The demands are regarded as *stressors* or *stress-inducing situations*. The following may be considered as demands: unpredictable and uncontrollable life events, hassles, significant life changes, situations of extreme high or extreme low stimulative value, internalized values, and standards of behavior. Demands exist in two forms: objective and subjective, the latter as a result of individual-specific appraisal. Appraisal of threat, harm, and challenge, whether running consciously or unconsciously—the cause of stress according to Lazarus (1966, 1991)—is typical for humans, but not animals (i.e., only in man may it be subject to studies). Humans also differ from animals in that objectively existing stressors may be modified by the process of appraisal, which elevates or reduces the effect of objective stressors.

Demands that exist objectively act independently of the individual's perception. This refers to traumatic or extreme life changes, such as death, bereavement, disaster, and war. As shown by Holmes and Rahe (1967), there is a high degree of consensus between groups and among individuals about the significance of life events. The fact that correlations of about .9 exist across age, sex, marital status, and education—in the intensity and time necessary to accommodate to specific life events—speaks in favor of the existence of objective, universal stressors (see Aldwin, Levenson, Spiro, & Bosse, 1989; Freedy, Kilpatrick, & Resnick, 1993; Pellegrini, 1990). *Universal stressors* implies if such a stress-inducing situation occurs, it develops the state of stress in all normal individuals. Stressors like disasters or war may serve as examples here. In this case, individual-specific appraisal plays a rather mediating role by elevating or declining the stress-inducing effect.

Stressors are not objective because of the fact that environmental factors considered as life events exist outside the individual, but because they develop the state of stress when in interaction with the individual. This is valid for all individuals within a normal human population, and probably can be extended to all mammals at least. The reaction of animals to disasters, such as fire or flood, or to the loss of their partner or offspring cannot be explained by the process of individual-specific appraisal, but by the fact that population-specific features of animals in interaction with environmental events develop the state of stress. Population-specific, genetically determined characteristics of the organism—such as kind and sensitivity or reactivity of receptors, which are features of neurobiochemical mechanisms—interact with the environmental factors in such a way that threat and harm are experienced by all normal individuals. As argued by Corson and O'Leary Corson (1979) in a study conducted on dogs, it is not the stimulus per se that evokes the state of stress to noxious stimuli, but the constitutionally determined, species-specific vulnerability to given stressors.

An individual's capability to cope with demands depends on the following characteristics: intelligence, special abilities, skills, knowledge, personality and temperamental traits, features of the physical makeup, experience with stress-inducing situations, coping strategies, and actual (physical and psychic) state of the individual.

Depending on the specificity of the demands, different individual characteristics influence individuals' capabilities. Capabilities, too, may occur in two forms. They exist objectively, and as such they may be subject to measurement. But they also may be subjectively experienced, the latter being a result of individual-specific appraisal. In both forms (objective and subjective), the imbalance between them may be considered a source of psychological stress. What is underlined here is that the state of stress is a result of interaction between real or perceived demands and individuals' response capability as it exists in reality or as it is perceived by them.

The interactional approach to the causes of the state of stress is present in different conceptualizations. However, views differ in specific aspects of the interactional processes. For example, McGrath (1970) underlined that the imbalance between demands and capacities must be substantial. The notion of *substantial* may be operationalized in different ways (e.g., in terms of costs paid or intensity of emotions generated by the causes of stress). Lazarus (1991; Lazarus & Folkman, 1984) emphasized that the relationship between the person and the environment must be appraised as taxing or exceeding his or her capabilities, thus giving priority to the subjective (perceived) relationship.

If *stress* is defined in terms of resources, which has become a popular view more recently (see Hobfoll, 1988, 1991; Schonpflug, 1993; Schonpflug & Battmann, 1987), potential or actual loss of valued resources—regarded here as the causes of the state of stress—can be understood only if the interaction between invested and gained resources is taken into account. "*Resources* are defined as those objects, personal characteristics, conditions, or energies that are valued by the individual or that serve as a means for attainment of these objects, personal characteristics, conditions, or energies" (Hobfoll, 1989).

When defining *stress* in terms of resources, it is important to realize that, in addition to perceived loss, actual (objectively existing) loss or lack of gain is regarded as a source of stress. This is especially evident in the theory of conservation of resources developed by Hobfoll (1989). The extension of causes of stress to objectively existing factors does not violate the interactional approach to stress, in which the individual plays an important role in regulating the balance between demands and capacities, or, regarding stress from another perspective, in regulating the balance between resources allocated and resources gained.

In summary, in the case of objective stressors, threat and harm (in other terms, *loss* or *threat of loss of resources*) are incorporated into the population-specific interaction between the individual and life events. Here appraisal plays the role of mediator of the stress-inducing situation. In reference to subjective stressors, threat, harm, and challenge are the result of individual-specific appraisal, thus appraisal of threat, harm, and challenge (or appraisal of loss of resources) are the causes of stress. In many situations, both objective and subjective stressors interact with each other. For both stressors, temperament may be considered, along with other factors, as a moderator of the relationship between demands and capabilities.

Coping with Stress

The state of stress is inseparable from coping. *Coping* with stress is understood in this chapter as a regulatory function that consists of maintaining the adequate balance between demands and capacities or of reducing the discrepancy between demands and capacities. Efficient coping, which results in match or goodness of fit between demands and capacities, reduces the state of stress, whereas inefficient coping leads to the increase of the state of stress (see Vitaliano, DeWolfe, Maiuro, Russo, & Katon, 1990). As underlined by Lazarus (1993; Lazarus & Folkman, 1984), with respect to subjectively experienced stressors, coping consists of managing specific demands appraised as overwhelming or taxing. "Coping is highly *contextual,* since to be effective it must change over time and across different stressful conditions" (Lazarus, 1993, p. 8).

Coping, which leads to resolving the state of stress, may also be considered from the point of view of a resource management process in terms of gains and loss (Schonpflug & Battmann, 1987). The benefits of coping consist of gains in or savings of resources, whereas the costs of coping incorporate allocation, loss, and consumption of resources. An individual copes with stress by means of replacement, substitution, or investment of resources (Hobfoll, 1989). The intensity, extent, and persistence with which coping attempts are applied refer to *effort expenditure*—a construct broadly discussed by Schonpflug (1993), taking into account the individual differences approach.

Consequences of Stress

A low discrepancy between demands and capacities, assuming it is not a chronic state, may result in positive changes as measured by means of efficiency of performance or developmental shifts. According to Chess and Thomas (1986), absence of stress may constitute a poorness of fit. "New demands and stresses, when consonant with developmental potentials, are constructive in their consequences" (p. 158; see also Chess & Thomas, 1991). As these authors emphasized, excessive stress, resulting from a demand the individual is unable to cope with, leads to maladaptive functioning.

Maladaptive functioning and behavior disorders, including pathology resulting from excessive or chronic stress, are regarded in this chapter as consequences or costs of stress. *Excessive stress* consists of extremely strong negative affects accompanied by unusually high elevation of the level of arousal.
Chronic stress is regarded as a state of stress not necessarily excessive, but
experienced permanently or frequently. As a consequence of both excessive
and chronic stress, changes in the organism occur that may result in psychological functioning, such as increased levels of anxiety and depression, or in
physiological or biochemical disturbances, expressed in psychosomatic diseases
or other health problems.

The consequences of excessive and chronic stress explain why the phenomenon of stress became one of the main subjects of interest in health psychology.
Rahe (1987), taking as a point of departure the concept of *arousal,* put forward
the following hypothesis that contributes to the understanding of the relationship between stress and health:

> *The brain, with its rich interconnections and multiple influences on all organ systems
> of the body, appears to respond to psychosocial stresses primarily through neurotrans-
> mitter and hormonal pathways. . . . These brain effects are thereby transmitted to
> most of the organ systems of the body; which of these many alterations are singled
> out for study depends on the physiological interests of the investigators. (p. 229)*

Not all excessive or chronic states of stress lead to the negative consequences
described here. Stress should be regarded as one of the many risk factors
(external and internal) contributing to maladaptive functioning and disorders.
When the state of stress is in interaction with other factors that decrease or
damper the consequences of stress, maladjustment or behavioral disturbances
may not occur.

TEMPERAMENT AND STRESS: HYPOTHESIZED RELATIONSHIPS AND EMPIRICAL EVIDENCE

Having defined the major constructs, this chapter concentrates on the relationship between temperament and stress by referring to such aspects of the
latter as stressors, the state of stress, coping with stress, and consequences of
stress. The considerations presented herein should be regarded not as arguments based on conclusive evidence, but rather as a starting point for formu-
lating hypotheses regarding the temperament–stress relationship.

THE IMPACT OF TEMPERAMENT IN THE REGULATION OF THE DEMAND–CAPABILITY INTERACTION

Showing the role of temperament as a moderator of stress here is not meant
to diminish the significance of other external and internal factors in determining
the state of stress. It is not suggested that temperament plays an important

role in all stress-inducing situations. Rather, temperament may contribute significantly in determining the state of stress at least from the three following perspectives: (a) from the point of view of intensity characteristics (stimulative value) of demands, (b) taking into account the optimal level of arousal as a standard for normal functioning, and (c) by considering emotion-oriented temperamental traits as expressed in tendencies to elicit emotions, especially negative ones.

Temperament Traits as Moderators of the Intensity Characteristics of the Demand–Capability Relationship

As postulated by Selye (1975), "deprivation of stimuli and excessive stimulation are both accompanied by an increase in stress, sometimes to the point of distress" (p. 21). Among others, Lundberg (1982), McGrath (1970), Strelau (1988), and Weick (1970) also considered intensity of demands as a stressor.

All life events that can be interpreted in terms of intensity of stimulation and, consequently, in terms of arousal effects, as assumed by Rahe (1987), may be regarded as factors possible to be moderated by different temperamental traits. Which of the specific temperament characteristics plays the role of moderator, by elevating or reducing the stimulative value of life events, depends on the kind of events.

As underlined by Ursin (1980), under high-level arousal, the tolerability to high-intensity life events is lowered. This is caused by the process of augmentation of acting stimuli. Under low-level arousal, there occurs a decrease in tolerability to life events of low stimulative value (e.g., deprivation, isolation), this being the result of suppression processes with respect to acting stimuli.

In several publications (Strelau, 1983, 1988, 1994), the following idea was developed: that arousal-oriented temperament dimensions are based on the assumption that there exist more or less stable individual differences in the level of arousal. Some individuals are permanently rather highly aroused, whereas others have a chronically low level of arousal. To underline the fact that there exist relatively stable individual differences in the level of arousal, Gray (1964) introduced the concept of *arousability* when discussing the relationship between arousal and strength of the nervous system. Extending this concept to other arousal-oriented temperament traits, one may say that, in individuals characterized by high arousability, stimuli of given intensity (S_n) develop a high level of arousal $(A_{n + x})$, whereas in individuals having low arousability, the level of arousal to the same stimuli is lower $(A_{n - x})$. This might be expressed as follows:

$$S_n \rightarrow A_{n + x} = \text{high arousability}$$
$$S_n \rightarrow A_{n - x} = \text{low arousability}$$

There exists at least a dozen temperament traits for which the construct of arousal has been used when referring to their biological background. The difference between these traits is that they refer to different understandings or aspects of arousal; they also differ in identifying physiological or biochemical

Table 12.1 Arousability and temperament traits

High arousability	Low arousability
Introverts	Extraverts
Neurotics	Emotionally stable
High emotionality	Low emotionality
Sensation avoiders	Sensation seekers
Weak type of CNS	Strong type of central nervous system (CNS)
High reactives	Low reactives
High-anxiety individuals	Low-anxiety individuals
Low impulsives	High impulsives
Augmenters (Petri)	Reducers (Petri)
Reducers (Buchsbaum)	Augmenters (Buchsbaum)
Inhibited temperament	Uninhibited temperament
Withdrawal tendency	Approach tendency

mechanisms of arousal (Strelau, 1994). A list of the arousal-centered temperament traits that refer to different characteristics of behavior is given in Table 12.1. These are the traits referred to here when discussing the demand–capability interaction.

Without going into the specificity of the different arousal-oriented temperament traits, one may predict that temperament traits that refer to low arousability (e.g., extraversion, high sensation seeking, or strong type of nervous system), when in interaction with life events characterized as demands of low stimulative value (e.g., deprivation or isolation), act as moderators that increase the state of stress, leading in extreme cases to excessive stress. In turn, temperament traits characterized by high arousability (e.g., introversion, low sensation seeking, or weak type of nervous system), when in interaction with life events characterized as demands of high stimulation value (e.g., death, disaster, or traumatic stressors), act as moderators increasing the state of stress, again leading in extreme cases to excessive stress (see Fig. 12.1).

As can be seen from Fig. 12.1, the same temperament trait, depending on the kind of environment (demand), operates as a moderator of stress or not. Furthermore, opposite poles of the same trait may be considered as moderators of stress, depending on the specificity of demands with which they interact. For example, when highly reactive individuals or introverts (both characterized by high arousability) are confronted with high stimulation, they experience the state of stress differently than low reactive individuals or extraverts. In turn, for individuals characterized by low arousability (e.g., extraverts or low reactives), low stimulation (e.g., deprivation, isolation) leads to the state of stress.

Neuroticism is one of the most representative temperament traits based on the construct of *activation*. Eysenck (1983) hypothesized "that *ceteris paribus* high N individuals live a more stressful life, not in the sense that they necessarily encounter more stressful stimuli (although that may be so) but because identical stressful stimuli produce a greater amount of strain in them" (p. 126). According to Eysenck, strain is equal to the understanding of the state of

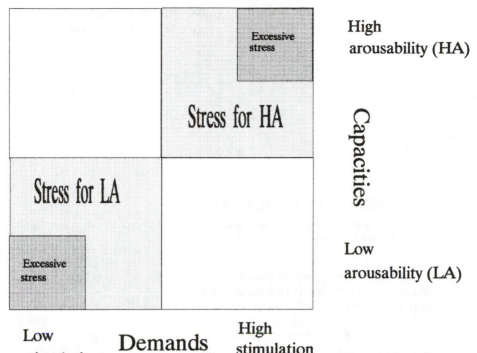

Figure 12.1 Arousability and the state of stress.

stress. Figure 12.2, taken from Eysenck (1983) in a modified form, illustrates the relationships between the intensity of stressors and state of stress as moderated by temperament traits, such as Neuroticism or Emotionality.

Figure 12.2 shows that a life event that develops a low-intensity state of stress may be moderated by Emotionality or other temperament traits in such a way as to increase the state of stress and reverse. The same state of stress, in terms of intensity, may result from low-intensity life events being in interaction with high emotionality, as well as from high-intensity life events interacting with low emotionality.

The Deviation from Optimal Level of Arousal, Moderated by Temperament, as a Source of Stress

As was shown by Wundt (1911), the sign of emotion depends on the strength of sensory stimuli; this relationship has an inverted U shape (see also Schneirla, 1959). The fact that stimuli intensity is a source of positive or negative hedonic tones has been applied to the concept of *optimal level of arousal* (Berlyne, 1960), where the hedonic tone plays the role of the affective-motivational process regulating the need for stimulation. Low-level arousal, a result of weak stimulation, as well as high-level arousal, resulting from stim-

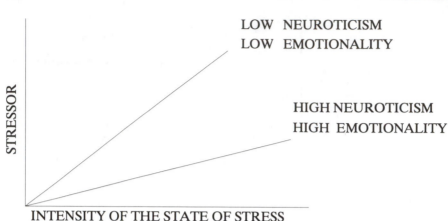

Figure 12.2   The relationship between intensity of stressors and the state of stress moderated by temperament traits.

ulation of high intensity, are regarded as sources of a negative hedonic tone, the increase of which results in a state of stress.

An intermediate level of arousal, evoked by stimuli of average intensity, is a source of positive hedonic tone. Life events, objectively of the same intensity, may be a source of a positive or negative hedonic tone, thus nonstressing or stressors, depending on the position an individual occupies on a given temperament dimension. This relationship can be attributed without much simplification to such dimensions as Extraversion (Eysenck, 1970; Eysenck & Eysenck, 1985), Sensation Seeking (Zuckerman, 1979, 1991a, 1994), and Reactivity (Strelau, 1983, 1988).

Referring to Table 12.1, composed of the arousal-oriented temperament traits, it can be generalized that, under high-intensity stressors, individuals characterized by high arousability experience a negative hedonic tone (state of stress). In response to the same stressors, low-arousability individuals may not experience distress; they may even experience a positive hedonic tone, as exemplified by sensation seekers.

Temperamentally Determined Tendency to Express Negative Emotions Under Stress-Inducing Situations

Temperament traits moderate the state of stress not only by regulating the intensity (arousal) component of stress, but also by taking part in the regulation of the optimal level of arousal regarded as a source of hedonic tone. Some of the temperament dimensions, such as Neuroticism, Emotionality, and Emotional Reactivity—which, independently of their specificity, are defined in terms of a tendency (disposition) to generate given emotions—operate as moderators of the state of stress by increasing or decreasing the emotional response to stressors, depending on the position an individual occupies on the emotion-oriented temperament dimension (see Strelau, 1987). This is especially evident with respect to temperament traits that refer to negative emotions. As vividly expressed by Buss and Plomin (1984), "Emotionality equals distress, the tendency to become upset easily and intensely" (p. 54).

Selected Evidence Illustrating the Moderating Effect of Temperament on the State of Stress

The possible interactions between demands and capacities, in which temperament plays a moderating role in determining the state of stress, may be exemplified by selected studies. Aldwin et al. (1989) conducted a study on thousands of men ages 40–88. The results show that emotionality, as measured by items from the Neuroticism scale of the Eysenck Personality Inventory (EPI) contributed to the reported number of stress events. High-emotional individuals (neurotics) reported more life events and more hassles as compared with low-emotional (emotionally stable) individuals.

Bolger and Schilling (in press) conducted a study on 166 married couples, who judged for 6 weeks the experience of daily distress to daily stressors by means of a diary method. The results show that neuroticism is strongly related to experienced distress to daily stressors. When interpreting their data, these authors suggested that the results support Watson and Clark's (1984) statement that neuroticism should be regarded as a tendency to experience distress even in the absence of stressors, due to the disposition to experience negative emotional states.

Kohn, Lafreniere, and Gurevich (1991) showed that trait anxiety and hassles contributed to perceived stress, accounting for over 50% of the variance in stress reactions. Anxiety in this study was measured in over 200 undergraduate students by means of Spielberger's (1983) State–Trait Anxiety Inventory (STAI).

As already mentioned, sensation seeking is a trait in the definition of which risky behavior is incorporated as a need of high sensation seekers (Zuckerman, 1979). In other words, one may say that sensation seekers function in such a way as to raise the stimulative value of the situation or behavior to increase the level of arousal, which ensures optimal functioning. Interpreting this statement in terms of stress, one may say that situations and behaviors that are already stressors for a low sensation seeker (risk avoider) do not occur as such for high sensation seekers. Empirical findings support the sensation seeking–risk relationship (for a review, see Zuckerman, 1994). For example, in Horvath and Zuckerman's (1993) study on 500 undergraduate students, sensation seeking as measured by means of the Sensation Seeking Scale (SSS–Form V) was shown to be a good predictor of risky behaviors as assessed by the General Risk Appraisal Scale (GRAS), which allows measuring risk appraisal and risky activities separately. In a study conducted on 139 students, Duckitt and Broll (1982) showed that, among six factors derived from Cattell's 16 PF, Extraversion moderated the impact of recent life changes on psychological strain (state of stress), as measured by the Langner Inventory.

A decrease in performance, resulting from a deviation from the optimal level of arousal, is an indicator of a state of stress. In relation to this, dozens

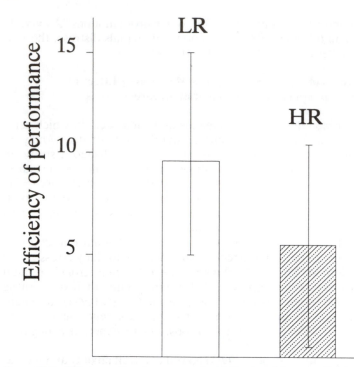

Figure 12.3 Efficiency of performance under highly stressful competition in high- (HR) and low-reactive (LR) weight lifters expressed in average scores and in standard deviations (Strelau, 1988).

of studies have shown that temperament characteristics, especially extraversion and neuroticism (Eysenck, 1970; Eysenck & Eysenck, 1985; Goh & Farley, 1977), strength of the nervous system, or reactivity (Klonowicz, 1987a, 1987b, 1992; Strelau, 1983, 1988; Zawadzki, 1991), play an important role as performance moderators.

For example, Zmudzki (1986; see also Strelau, 1988) showed that the efficiency of performance during starts in national and international competitions of weight lifters representing the Polish national team was different depending on the level of reactivity. These competitions were regarded as highly stressful demands. Reactivity was measured by means of the Strelau Temperament Inventory (Strelau, 1983). Taking the quartile deviation as a criterion for separating subjects differing in reactivity level, the author separated 19 low-reactive (LR) and 18 high-reactive (HR) individuals from 75 weight lifters. The efficiency of performance during 10 different national and international competitions was estimated by means of a 7-point scale. As can be seen in Fig. 12.3, efficiency of performance under the stressful situation was significantly higher in LR individuals as compared with HR weight lifters. This study is of special interest because it expresses aggregated data collected in natural settings. The efficiency of performance was measured in real competitions, and the result—expressed in Fig. 12.3 in a single number—is an outcome of studies conducted in 10 different situations, all of them being of the same kind and characterized as highly demanding.

It is highly probable that temperament dimensions—which differ not only in terms of arousal components and emotion-oriented tendencies, but represent a whole spectrum of qualitatively different behavior characteristics—play a different role in regulating the demand–capability balance, depending on the kind of stress taken into account. It might be assumed that the moderatory role of temperament may be specific, depending on whether one takes into account stress at work, community stress, natural or technical disasters, acculturative stress, or stress resulting from everyday life events. In studies on stress, it is not the state of stress itself, but coping with stress and the consequences of this state, on which researchers have mostly focused.

THE ROLE OF TEMPERAMENT IN COPING WITH STRESS

Despite the many studies conducted with respect to coping since Lazarus (1966) published his fundamental monograph, *Psychological Stress and the Coping Process,* not much attention has been paid to the role of personality, and especially to its specific component, temperament, as a moderator of coping. To show the role that temperament plays in coping with stress, two different approaches to coping are highlighted: (a) Lazarus' (1991; Folkman & Lazarus, 1988) view, according to which coping is a process that shapes emotions; and (b) the resource-oriented approach, which treats coping in terms of resource management processes (Hobfoll, 1989; Schonpflug 1993; Schonpflug & Battmann, 1987).

Temperament and Coping as a Process That Shapes Emotions

The individual differences approach incorporated in Lazarus' coping theory was mainly expressed in the assumption that the process of appraisal is individual specific, and that there exist situation-specific (contextual) coping processes, apart from individual differences in coping styles (Folkman & Lazarus, 1988; Lazarus, 1993). If coping is considered a process that shapes emotions (Lazarus, 1991), temperament characteristics may be considered as moderators taking part in the regulation of emotional processes. Looking at temperament in terms of a tendency to experience negative emotions, one may assume that such temperament traits as Neuroticism, Emotionality, or Emotional Reactivity cannot be neutral for the ongoing effort to manage specific demands appraised as taxing or overwhelming (Lazarus, 1993). For instance, Kagan (1983) has shown the role that inhibited temperament in children plays in moderating coping as a reaction to negative emotions.

As Folkman and Lazarus (1985) suggested, some strategies of coping, distinguished among the two basic coping styles (action and emotion oriented), depend on personality, and here the authors refer to the tendency to experience positive or negative mood. But also, if coping is considered in terms of styles the individual applies to change the unfavorable person–environment relationship (Folkman & Lazarus, 1985, 1988), it can be hypothesized that whether problem-focused coping or emotion-focused coping develops depends, to some extent, on the moderating role of temperament characteristics.

One may assume that so-called "action-oriented traits," such as Extraversion, Sensation Seeking, Strength of the Nervous System, or Activity, should facilitate the problem-focused coping style, which consists of undertaking effort to change the unfavorable person–environment relationship by means of coping actions. In turn, the emotion-oriented temperament traits (e.g., Withdrawal Tendency, Inhibited Temperament, Neuroticism, Emotionality, or Emotional Reactivity) may be considered variables that contribute to the development of the emotion-focused coping style.

A study that supports these two hypotheses was conducted by Parkes (1986). The author applied an interactional paradigm to study how 135 first-year female student nurses coped with stressful episodes. She took into account such variables as environmental factors, situational characteristics, temperament traits, and coping styles. Parkes found that Extraversion and Neuroticism, together with environmental and situational factors, predicted coping styles. Direct coping was rather typical for extraversion, whereas suppression occurred together with Neuroticism. These relationships were further modified by the environment and situation.

Other studies, not necessarily following the Lazarus paradigm, also support the hypothesis relating action-oriented coping styles to action-oriented temperament traits. Similarly, emotion-centered temperament characteristics appear to be related to emotion-centered coping styles. A few examples follow.

Bolger (1990), who defined *coping* as personality in action under stress, conducted a study on medical college students. He showed that neuroticism influences the coping strategies people select, and that it increases daily anxiety under examination stress. Baum, Calesnick, Davis, and Gatchel (1982) have taken a temperament characteristic—in this case screening as measured by Mehrabian's (1977) Stimulus Screening scale—as part of a coping style. In their study, conducted on over 200 residents of long- and short-corridor dormitories, *coping* referred to students' response to high-density dormitory settings. Residents who displayed the stimulus-screening coping style were more successful in adapting to the crowded environment. According to Mehrabian, screeners are able to screen irrelevant stimuli. In so doing, they reduce the stimuli's random character, which, in turn, leads to a lower level of arousal and more rapid decrease of arousal in comparison with nonscreeners.

In a study in which, apart from personality variables, the Pavlovian temperament traits were under control, Vingerhoets, Van den Berg, Kortekaas, Van Heck, and Croon (1993) showed that weeping in women, considered as emotion-focused coping, was negatively related to strength of excitation and strength of inhibition. Women occupying a high position on the Weeping dimension were characterized by both weak excitation and weak inhibition of the nervous system. The Pavlovian properties were measured by using the Revised Strelau Temperament Inventory (STI). Strelau and Szczepaniak (1994) have shown that task-oriented coping style correlates with action-oriented temperament characteristics (e.g., briskness), whereas emotion-oriented coping style was related to emotion-centered temperament characteristics (e.g., emotional reactivity). Coping style was measured by means of the Coping Inventory for Stressful Situations (CISS; Endler & Parker, 1990); the Formal Characteristics of Behavior–Temperament Inventory (FCB–TI; Strelau & Zawadzki, 1993) was used to assess temperament traits.

The Place of Temperament in a Resource-Oriented Approach to Coping

The view of coping as a resource management process proposes to move from coping as a regulator that shapes emotions to coping that consists of replacement, substitution, and investment of resources (Hobfoll, 1989; Schonpflug & Battmann, 1987). The degree to which an individual is engaged in coping with stress can be characterized by means of extent, intensity, and persistence with which resources are allocated and consumed. This approach, which offers a different view on coping, also allows one to look at temperament as a moderator of coping from a different perspective.

In his effort regulation theory, Schonpflug (1993) has shown how temperament traits, as understood by Strelau (1983), may contribute to effort expenditure. This core concept in Schonpflug's regulation theory has been considered by him as a quantitative dimension of coping involvement. Effort expenditure comprises all three formal characteristics of allocation and consumption of resources—intensity, extent, and persistence. Schonpflug has shown the place of temperament in effort regulation in the following two contexts:

1. Temperament traits as codeterminant of the amount of effort allocated in task performance. Here effort may be expressed in terms of subjective ratings, behavioral involvement, and level of arousal or biochemical changes. For example, high-anxiety individuals invest a greater amount of effort as compared with low-anxiety persons to obtain a comparable level of performance under highly demanding conditions.
2. Temperament as a regulator of the stimulative value of the conditions or activity under which coping occurs moderates the conservation of resources. To exemplify this statement, Schonpflug referred to the concept of *style of action,* which has been developed by Strelau (1983) on the basis of Tomaszewski's (1978) distinction between basic and auxiliary actions. Auxiliary actions, by means of preventive acts and checking operations, constitute supplementary portions of behavior and consume extra resources; but "under conditions of high risks and possibility of failure, the involvement in auxiliary activities may help in maintaining a high level of productivity and thus conserve resources" (Schonpflug, 1993, p. 16).

Strelau (1988) considered "styles of action" as strategies for coping with stress. The style of action, understood as the typical manner in which an action is performed by the individual, develops under environmental influences on the basis of the temperament endowment, especially reactivity. According to the regulative theory of temperament (Strelau, 1983), the style of action is considered one of the regulators of stimulation need. If auxiliary actions are divided into orienting, preparatory, corrective, controlling, and protective activities, as proposed by Tomaszewski (1978), it becomes clear that auxiliary actions lower the risk of failure in task performance under stressors.

Using Hobfoll's (1989) and Schonpflug's (1993) terminology, one may say that auxiliary actions contribute to the conservation of resources. Activities that lead directly to the attainment of a certain goal should be regarded as basic.

Considering the relation between auxiliary and basic actions from the point of view of intensity of stimulation means that auxiliary actions, by safeguarding, facilitating, or simplifying the basic ones, lower the stimulative value of activity or the situation in which the activity is performed. (Strelau, 1988, p. 157)

It has been hypothesized by Strelau (1983) that, in high-reactive individuals who are characterized by high levels of arousability, auxiliary actions (AA) will dominate over basic actions (BA). This style of action is thus labeled as the *adjunctive style*. In low-reactive individuals, for whom a low level of arousability is typical, there will be more of a balance between both basic and auxiliary actions, or a predominance of the former. This style of action is termed *straightforward style*. The relationship between reactivity and style of action may be expressed as follows:

High reactives: adjunctive style (BA < AA)
Low reactives: straightforward style (BA > AA)

Thus, coping strategies defined in terms of style of action, and strongly related to temperament, may be considered as moderators of conservation of resources aimed at avoiding or reducing the state of stress.

Selected Data Illustrating the Role of Temperament in Coping Viewed as a Resource Management Process

A series of experiments have been conducted to examine the important role that temperament plays in human functioning under stress. Most of them refer to effort undertaken when coping with demands, as measured by psychological and psychophysiological changes, and to the style of action as a coping strategy (see Strelau, 1983, 1988). Several studies on effort expenditure during coping with demands of different kinds have been conducted by Klonowicz (1974, 1985, 1987a, 1987b). In her experiments, measures of Reactivity and Mobility, as proposed by the regulative theory of temperament (Strelau, 1983) and measured by means of the Strelau Temperament Inventory, were considered moderators of effort expenditure. Depending on the specific experiment, the psychological indicators of effort expenditure were expressed in changes in anxiety and fatigue levels, the latter measured by number of mistakes during performance or by reaction time. The psychophysiological indicators comprised electrodermal activity (EDA) changes, and self-reported level of activation as measured by means of Thayer's Activation-Deactivation Adjective Checklist.

The most general finding from data obtained in these studies suggests that high-reactive individuals, when coping with demands characterized by stressors of high stimulative value (difficult task, stimuli of high intensity), allocate more effort in terms of psychological and psychophysiological changes as compared with low-reactive subjects. Under situations of lower stimulative value, there is no evident difference between high- and low-reactive individuals. When the demand–capability balance is threatened because of a low stimulative value of demands, effort expenditure may be higher in low-reactive individuals. In most of Klonowicz's experiments, an interactional effect was obtained, illustrating the contribution of mobility operating as an elevator of reactivity effects.

In her most recent experiments, Klonowicz (1990, 1992) studied effort expenditure as measured by heart rate (HR) changes while coping under different degrees of task difficulty in highly skilled simultaneous interpreters. The tasks consisted of listening, listening combined with simultaneous speech reproduction, and listening *cum* simultaneous transformation *cum* speech production— the first task being the easiest one and the last task being the most difficult. Individual characteristics comprised Reactivity as measured by Strelau's STI, and Anxiety, Anger, and Curiosity traits assessed by means of Spielberger's STPI. Limiting the presentation to individual characteristics, the data "indicate that reactivity temperament, trait-anxiety, and trait-curiosity influence cardiac activity during the anticipatory periods, task periods, and after-task recovery" (Klonowicz, 1990, p. 46). However, this finding holds true only for the more difficult tasks—shadowing and interpreting. The changes in resource demands monitored by HR were, among other variables, positively correlated with Reactivity, thus showing the moderator effect of this temperament trait on coping.

The role of temperament-determined style of action in coping with stress was shown in several studies in which Reactivity (in Pavlovian terminology, the reverse of Strength of Excitation) was the temperament variable (Strelau, 1983, 1988). It has never been viewed, however, from the perspective of effort regulation, as proposed by Schonpflug (1993). Using constructs belonging to this approach, one may say that high-reactive individuals by means of the auxiliary style perform more actions as compared with low-reactive subjects; thus, they allocate more resources to cope with stress. However, by allocating more resources in auxiliary actions, they avoid failures and maintain adequate levels of efficiency in task performance under highly stimulative situations. This, in turn, may be considered a gain of resources.

Thus, temperament-determined style of action, when viewed from the perspective of resource management process, can be characterized in terms of gains and losses—where the benefits of auxiliary actions, which are dominant in high-reactive individuals, exceed their costs when coping with stress.

In most of the cited studies, independent of the population (e.g., children, adolescents, adults) and type of task under investigation (e.g., mental load, motor performance), the results show that, under demands of high stimulative value for high-reactive individuals, the dominance of the adjunctive style ensures efficient functioning. For low-reactive individuals, in contrast, the prevalence of the straightforward style results in better functioning under stress (Strelau, 1983).

A study illustrating the role of auxiliary actions in high- and low-reactive individuals coping with stress under long-lasting and demanding mental load was conducted. Mundelein (1982) arranged seminatural experimental settings, in which adult subjects were instructed to work for 3 hours as an insurance agent operating within a computer system. The task was to calculate the amount of compensation for clients suffering loss. During this demanding work performance, signals of possible computer overloadings and disturbances were monitored. To avoid them, subjects were allowed to press special buttons, which in fact did not have influence on the computer system and were purely auxiliary actions. The function of pressing them consisted of protecting the basic actions (collecting and processing information and decision making) against possible disturbances. Results obtained in this study show that, with respect to the number and time of pressing protection buttons, high-reactive subjects obtained significantly higher scores as compared with low-reactive subjects. In this study, reactivity was measured by means of two procedures—Strelau's STI and the slope of reaction time (for description, see Strelau, 1983).

TEMPERAMENT AS A MODERATOR OF CONSEQUENCES OF STRESS: THE TEMPERAMENT RISK FACTOR

As already mentioned, excessive or chronic stress leads to behavior disorders, maladaptive functioning, and pathology regarded here as consequences (costs) of stress. Thomas and Chess (1977; Chess & Thomas, 1984, 1986; Thomas, Chess, & Birch, 1968) were pioneers who showed that behavior disorders in children cannot be explained by unfavourable environmental factors (stressors) only, and that an essential part of the variance in behavior disorders refers to a given configuration of temperament traits, termed by them as *difficult child* or *difficult temperament*. The pattern of difficult temperament is composed of such categories as irregularity (in biological functions), slow adaptability to changes in the environment, intense negative mood, and withdrawal responses to new situations or strange persons.

The number and quality of temperament traits (categories) that constitute the pattern of a difficult temperament has changed from study to study, and from author to author (e.g., Bates, 1980; Carey, 1986; Kyrios & Prior, 1990; Martin, 1989; Maziade, 1988). Essential for most of the conceptualizations with respect to the difficult temperament is that a given configuration of temperament characteristics (difficult temperament) does not lead to development of behavior disorders by itself. If the difficult temperament is in interaction with an inappropriate environment (e.g., family conflicts, divorce, parent–child dissonance), which is experienced by the child as a chronic or excessive state of stress, then there is a risk that behavior disorders or maladaptive functioning may develop.

Taking into account the match or mismatch between environmental demands and the individual's capacity, mainly defined in terms of temperament
categories, to cope with these demands, Chess and Thomas (1991) referred to
the concept of *goodness of fit* taken from biologists (Dubos, 1965). This also
has been applied in studies on job stress, where the person–environment fit
approach gained widespread acceptance (Edwards & Cooper, 1990; French,
Caplan, & Harrison, 1982).

> *There is goodness of fit when the person's temperament and other characteristics . . .*
> *are adequate to master the successive demands, expectations, and opportunities of*
> *the environment. If, on the other hand, the individual cannot cope successfully with*
> *the environmental demands, then there is poorness of fit. . . . With a poorness of fit,*
> *the individual experiences excessive stress and failures of adaptation, and his or her*
> *development takes an unfavourable course (p. 16) . . . A temperamental trait becomes*
> *a factor in pathological behavior, not by itself alone, but when it is combined with a*
> *poorness of fit. (Chess & Thomas, 1991, p. 18)*

Despite Chess and Thomas' intention to give the concepts of *difficult child*
or *difficult temperament* meaning only when considered in interaction with the
environment, these concepts have been criticized, among other things, for their
personological and evaluative context (e.g., Bates, 1980; Plomin, 1982; Rothbart, 1982; Strelau & Eliasz, 1994). The term *difficult* suggests that it is the
individual's temperament that causes difficulties; it also implies a negative
meaning attributed to the individual.

To underline that disturbances of behavior and pathology in children occur
only when temperament characteristics predisposing a child to poor fit interact
with an unfavorable environment, Carey (1986, 1989) introduced the concept
of *temperament risk factor* (TRF). However, he limited this concept to excessive
interactional stress experienced by children. To give the TRF a more universal
meaning, allowing one to extend this concept to the whole human population,
the definition of TRF has been modified (Strelau 1989b; Strelau & Eliasz,
1994). *Temperament risk factor* means any temperament trait or configuration
of traits that, in interaction with other factors acting excessively, persistently,
or recurrently (e.g., physical and social environment, educational treatment,
situations, the individual's characteristics), increases the risk of developing
behavior disorders or pathology or favors the molding of a maladjusted personality.

Assessing temperament traits as risky or not risky is meaningful only under
conditions that, given temperament traits or configurations of traits, are considered within the context of other variables with which they interact. Among
other things, this means that a particular configuration of temperament traits
considered as a TRF in one situation, or for a given environment, may not be
a TRF in other situations or other environments.

Using the concepts of *absolute* and *relative risk behaviors,* as understood by
Jeffery (1989), one may say that TRF belongs to the category of *relative risk.*
TRF may be assessed by the ratio of the chance of behavior disorders as
consequences of exposure to stressors in individuals with given temperament

traits, compared with the risk of behavior disorders in response to the same stressors in individuals who do not have these temperament traits. By studying the contribution of temperament to unfavorable consequences of the state of stress, it is important to consider that risk factors contribute to behavior disorders and psychopathology.

The epidemiological aspects of behavior disorders and pathology, taking into account temperament as one of the many risk factors, have been broadly discussed from theoretical and methodological perspectives by Carey and McDevitt (1989, 1994), Chess and Thomas (1984), Garrison and Earls (1987), Maziade (1988), Pellegrini (1990), and Rutter (1991). Kyrios and Prior (1990) postulated a theoretical model for the development of early childhood behavioral disturbances, in which, among other risk factors, the place of temperament in codetermining behavioral disorders has been shown.

Maziade (1988) postulated that when children with an adverse temperament (an equivalent to difficult temperament) interact with adverse environmental factors, they present special vulnerability (liability) to clinical disorders. Developing an additive and synergistic model of adverse temperament–adverse environment interaction, Maziade referred to Kendler and Eaves' (1986) models for the joint effect of genotype and environment on liability to psychiatric illness. The authors postulated that etiology of psychiatric disorders consists of the international effect between genes and environment. The joint effect of genes and environment on liability to psychiatric disorders may be composed of three basic models: (a) additive effects of genotype and environment, (b) genetic control of sensitivity to the environment, and (c) genetic control of exposure to the environment.

Taking these three basic models, as introduced by Kendler and Eaves (1986) and Maziade (1988), as a starting point, these models were adapted to the construct of *temperament risk factor.* Instead of limiting the consequences of stress to liability to illness, they have been extended to behavior disorders that can be met in a normal population when exposed to stress-inducing environments. Genotype has been replaced in the models by temperament. As postulated by many temperament researchers (see Buss & Plomin, 1984; Eysenck, 1970; Strelau, 1994; Zuckerman, 1991b), the genetic endowment plays an essential role in determining the variance of temperament traits. Also, when exemplifying the contribution of genes to liability to psychiatric disorders, Kendler and Eaves (1986) referred to traits such as Impassivity and Emotional Instability as influenced by genes, thus contributing—in interaction with a predisposing environment—to illness.

Without specifying the temperament traits or composition of traits that constitute the TRF, and that can be different for different environments, a distinction should be made between present and absent temperament risk factors. *TRF present* means that, given the presence of temperament traits or configuration of traits, vulnerability to behavior disorders will be evidenced. *TRF absent* implies that temperament traits or configurations of traits are different from those typical for TRF present, and that they do not constitute a risk factor for behavior disorders.

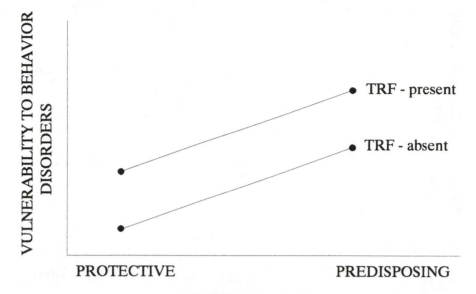

Figure 12.4   Vulnerability to behavior disorders as a function of temperament and environment with additive effects of both.

Regarding environment, a distinction has been made between protective and predisposing environments (Kendler & Eaves, 1986). In this context, *protective environment* means a lack of excessive or chronic stressors, which diminishes the probability of behavior disorders and pathology. In turn, *predisposing environment,* which can be characterized in terms of chronic or excessive stress-inducing environments, increases the probability of behavior disorders and pathology. Further, when using the term *behavior disorders,* pathology is possible, although this would imply extreme consequence of poorness of fit between temperament and environmental demands.

In line with Kendler and Eaves' (1986) considerations, five models for joint temperament and environment effect on vulnerability to behavior disorders or pathology are presented to show the different ways in which temperament and environment may interact with each other in producing the risk of behavior disorders.

1. Temperament and environmental control of behavior disorders. This model, depicted in Fig. 12.4, postulates that vulnerability to behavior disorders is a function of temperament and environment, with additive effects of both temperament and environment. Individuals in whom the TRF is present show, in comparison with individuals in whom the TRF is absent, higher vulnerability to behavior disorders and pathology. This tendency occurs independent of the kind of environment, whether protective or predisposing to vulnerability. In turn, the effect of exposure to protective or predisposing environment is the

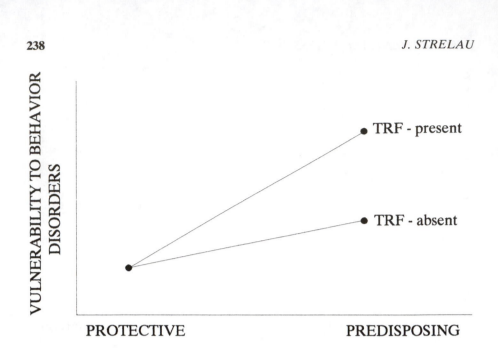

VULNERABILITY TO BEHAVIOR DISORDERS

PROTECTIVE   PREDISPOSING

ENVIRONMENT

Figure 12.5   Vulnerability to behavior disorders as a function of temperament and environment
with temperament control of sensitivity to the environment.

same, regardless of the individual's temperament characteristics. This model
underlines the significance of temperament as predisposing the individual to
poor fit, thus as a predisposition for developing behavioral disorders. As may
be exemplified by Eysenck's (1992) understanding, Psychoticism as a temperament trait is directly related to pathology and behavior disorders.

   2. *Temperament control of sensitivity to the environment.* It is hypothesized by this model (see Fig. 12.5) that vulnerability to behavior disorders is a
function of temperament and environment, with temperament influencing sensitivity to the environment. Particular temperament traits or configuration of
traits, regarded here as TRF, moderate the intensity of stressors by elevating
sensitivity to stress-inducing situations. As a consequence of increased sensitivity to the predisposing environment, vulnerability to behavior disorders is
higher in individuals in whom the TRF is present. As already exemplified,
temperament traits such as High Anxiety, Neuroticism, and Emotionality raise
the tendency to experience negative affects in terms of their frequency and
intensity.

   3. *Temperament control of exposure to the environment.* Temperament may
influence the vulnerability to behavior disorders by means of the individual's
behavior, which consists of selecting, creating, or approaching environments
that are predisposing or protecting with respect to vulnerability to behavior
disorders (see Fig. 12.6). TRF is composed of such temperament traits that
expose the individual to excessive or chronic stressors predisposing to behavior
disorders. Sensation seeking, characterized by undertaking risky activities and

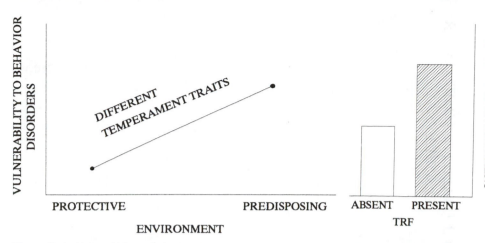

Figure 12.6   Vulnerability to behavior disorders as a function of temperament and environment with temperament control of exposure to the environment.

approaching risky environments (Stacy, Newcomb, & Bentler, 1993; Zucker-man, 1994), exemplifies the temperament-determined exposure to predisposing environment.

The two remaining models are secondary to the three described previously. They are probably closer to real-life situations, in which the interactions between temperament and environment are more complex in producing the risk of behavior disorders or pathology as a consequence of chronic or excessive stress.

4. Temperament control of behavior disorders and sensitivity to the environment. This model consists of a combination of Models 1 and 2. As depicted in Fig. 12.7, it postulates a synergistic effect of temperament with environment. TRF makes the individual more vulnerable to behavior disorders in a predisposing environment, whereas the absence of TRF protects the individual from negative consequences of the predisposing environment. In other words, TRF increases the risk of behavior disorders when in interaction with predisposing environment.

5. Temperament control of behavior disorders and exposure to the environment. This model (see Fig. 12.8) consists of a combination of Models 1 and 3. On the one hand, temperament by itself predisposes to vulnerability to behavior disorders. On the other hand, temperament controls the exposure to a predisposing environment. Thus, there exists a cumulative effect of the temperament risk factor on vulnerability to behavior disorders. First, the effect results from temperament traits that contribute to the risk of behavior disorders. Second, due to these temperament traits, the risk of exposure to predisposing environment increases, thus elevating the vulnerability to behavior disorders and pathology.

The models presented herein reflect the ways studies have been conducted, or can be conducted, to show the significance of temperament in producing

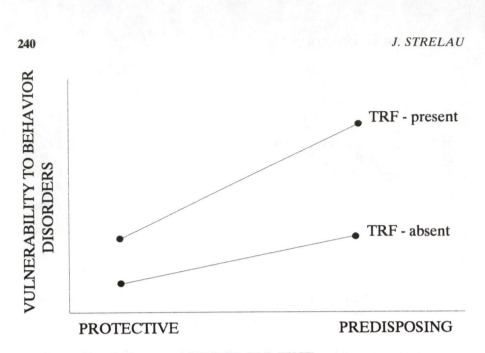

Figure 12.7   Vulnerability of behavior disorders as a function of temperament and environment with temperament control of vulnerability to behavior disorders and sensitivity to the environment.

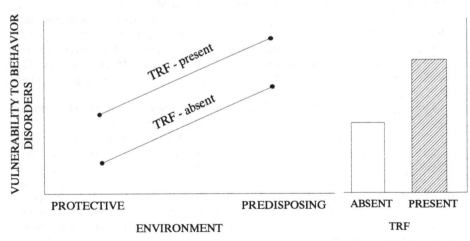

Figure 12.8   Vulnerability to behavior disorders as a function of temperament and environment with temperament control of vulnerability to disorders and exposure to the environment.

the consequences of stress. They also may serve as a starting point for putting forward hypotheses regarding the role that temperament plays as a moderator of behavior and health consequences of chronic or excessive stress.

THE TEMPERAMENT RISK FACTOR: SELECTED FINDINGS

Several books (e.g., Chess & Thomas, 1984, 1986; Garrison & Earls, 1987; Thomas, Chess, & Birch, 1968) and many articles have shown the role that temperament traits play in interaction with adverse environments in producing maladjusted personality, behavior disorders, and pathology. Many studies have been conducted in children, mainly under the influence of the two senior investigators in child temperament research—Thomas and Chess. Studies of adults stem mostly from different theories of temperament, not necessarily related to the New York psychiatrists. A selective review is given next.

Evidence from Studies on Children

The New York Longitudinal Study (NYLS) conducted by Thomas and Chess (1977), from early infancy until adulthood, gives ample evidence that when there is a poorness of fit between family environment and the child's temperament, behavior disorders occur. After reducing the Thomas–Chess nine temperament characteristics to four factors (Persistence, Withdrawal, Adaptability, and Mood) and reanalyzing the NYLS data, Cameron (1977, 1978) concluded that, from the age of 4 years, temperament risk factors, in interaction with family stressors, significantly predict future clinical cases. Barron and Earls (1984) have shown that temperament inflexibility in 3-year-old children and negative parent–child interaction have direct effect on behavior problems. Findings from Graham, Rutter, and George's (1973) study indicate that such temperament characteristics as low habit regularity and low fastidiousness, when in interaction with disturbed mothers, predicted the development of pathology in 3- to 7-year-old children.

A longitudinal study with a 2-year interval (Earls & Jung, 1987) demonstrated that, at the age of 3 years, poor adaptability and high intensity of emotional reactions were more powerful predictors of behavior disorders than family stressors, such as marital discord, maternal depression, and family life events. Studying 5- to 10-year-old children who attended a child guidance clinic, Malhorta, Varma, and Verma (1986) stated that Emotionality, when in interaction with lack of parental control and low intelligence, was the best predictor of occurrence of emotional disorders.

Evidence from Studies on Adolescents and Adults

Windle (1989) has shown that, for five temperament factors (Extraversion, Emotional Stability, Activity, Adaptability, and Task Orientation) in late adolescents and early adults, Emotional Instability and Introversion were the strongest predictors of mental health (e.g., factors such as anxiety, depression, loss of control, emotional ties). Kohn, Lafreniere, and Gurevich (1991) demonstrated the moderator effect of temperament on stress and consequences of stress in undergraduate students. Hassles and trait anxiety both contributed to perceived stress, hassles and temperament reactivity both had significant impact on minor ailments, and hassles and trait anxiety had a significant effect on psychiatric symptomatology.

A study conducted by Mehrabian and Ross (1977), also on university students, has shown that high arousability (the opposite pole of stimulus screening), when in interaction with long-lasting arousal states caused by life changes, may be regarded as a TRF for incidence of illness as judged by means of subjective ratings. The Type A behavior pattern in adolescents, regarded as an activity of high stimulative value when in interaction with high reactivity in comparison with low reactivity, increases the probability of developing a high level of anxiety (Strelau & Eliasz, 1994).

Complex Studies Focused on the TRF

In some of the studies listed earlier, multivariate analysis was applied to show causal relationships between variables being under control. Causal modeling became the most fruitful approach in studying the contribution of temperament, in interaction with other risk factors, to behavior disorders and pathology. Several more detailed examples are given to show the diversity as well as the complexity of approaches to the issue of temperament risk factor.

A longitudinal study conducted by Kyrios and Prior (1990) on 3- to 4-year-old children, and based on a "stress resilience" model of temperament, has shown the moderator role of high reactivity–low manageability and low self-regulation in behavioral adjustment under family stressors. These two temperament characteristics have influenced behavioral disturbances directly, as well as indirectly, by moderating the parental maladjustment, a family stressor, which was causally related to children's behavioral disturbances. This study exemplifies, to a large extent, Model 5.

One hundred and twenty children and their mothers were studied over a 1-year interval. The mean age of the children in the first phase of the study was 3.8 years; gender was equally represented in the sample. Most of the measures were taken in Phase 1; behavioral adjustment was assessed in both phases. The child variables were: behavioral adjustment, development history, fine and gross motor coordination, health history, facility attendance, word knowledge, stress, and temperament. Environmental variables consisted of marital adjustment, parental psychological functioning, childrearing practices, parental employment, and social status. Because the focus of this discussion is on the relationship of temperament–stress–behavioral adjustment, only information about measures of these variables is given. Temperament was measured by the Short Temperament Scale for Toddlers developed by Prior, Sanson, and Oberklaid (1989); stress was measured by the Coddington Life Events Record, which is a child-oriented adaptation of the Holmes and Rahe (1967) scale. Behavioral adjustment was assessed in the first phase by means of the Behavior Screening Questionnaire, constructed by Richman and Graham

(1971), and in the second phase by the Preschool Behavior Questionnaire developed by Behar and Stringfield (1974).

Using a broad statistical approach composed of factor analysis, correlational procedures, multiple regression, and path analysis of the obtained data, the authors concluded that temperament characteristics are the most predictive variables of child behavioral adjustment. Low self-regulation and high reactivity–low manageability contributed most to the variance of behavioral disturbances at the age of 3–4 years, and high reactivity–low manageability was the strongest predictor of behavioral maladjustment at the age of 4–5 years. According to Kyrios and Prior (1990),

> Generally, temperamental characteristics (particularly, low reactivity-high manageability) appeared to curtail the influence of adverse family factors on children's adjustment. In addition, the strength of relationships between temperament and children's behavioural adjustment differed as a function of time, of the specific temperamental characteristic examined, and of the source of behavioural ratings.

The Kyrios–Prior study has shown that, among several temperament characteristics being measured, high reactivity–low manageability and low temperament self-regulation became TRFs. The former temperament variable was composed of such characteristics as unmanageable, irritable, highly active, and intense. The latter one was composed of high distractability, low rhythmicity, and low persistence.

Studies conducted by Maziade et al. (1990) in the domain of psychiatric disorders have shown that extreme temperaments, in terms of easy and difficult temperament when taken alone, are bad predictors of clinical outcome. However, when these temperament constellations are considered in interaction with stressors, consisting in these studies of family dysfunctional behavior control, they became essential predictors of psychiatric disorders. This finding was replicated in several longitudinal studies at different ages: for example, when temperament was measured at the age of 4–8 months and psychiatric disorders judged at the age of 4.7 years (Maziade, Cote, Bernier, Boutin, & Thivierge, 1989), or when temperament was assessed at the age of 7 years and psychiatric status measured in preadolescence and adolescence (Maziade et al., 1990).

The latter study consisted of selecting, from a sample of almost 1,000 seven-year-olds, two subsamples: children with extremely easy temperaments (15 subjects) and children with extremely difficult temperaments (23 subjects). Temperament was assessed by means of the Thomas and Chess (1977) Parent Temperament Questionnaire. The clinical status of these children was assessed at the age of 16 years by means of structured and standardized psychiatric interviews, which allowed for DSM–III diagnoses. These diagnoses were done blind with respect to temperament data. Also the Youth Self-Report and Profile, developed by Achenbach and Edelbrock (1987) and aimed to distinguish between internalized and externalized symptoms, was administered. Family behavior control was measured by means of the McMaster Model of Family Functioning. Many other variables (e.g., socioeconomic status, cognitive functioning, etc.) were under control.

The data reported by Maziade et al. (1990) show that there was no statistically significant differences between extreme temperament at age 7 and the presence of definite psychiatric diagnoses at age 16. However, statistically significant relationships were found between temperament and internalized and externalized symptoms. Children with difficult temperament had significantly more reported symptoms. The results analyzed by means of stepwise logistic regression show that all children with extremely difficult temperaments who lived in dysfunctional families, an environment that might be considered a chronically acting stressor (predisposing environment), were diagnosed as having psychiatric disorders. For children in families with superior behavior control functioning (an example of a protective environment), there was no difference in psychiatric outcome between easy and difficult temperaments. This study exemplifies the powerful role of interaction between temperament and environment in determining consequences of experienced stress.

A study that shows the role of one temperament trait, Emotionality, in moderating the effect of stressors on the vulnerability to behavior disorders has been conducted by Aldwin et al. (1989). As already mentioned, this study showed that individuals characterized by high emotionality reported more stressors as compared with low-emotional persons. Most important, however, a high position on the temperament dimension allowed the prediction of mental health symptoms. Thus, High Emotionality, under conditions as studied by Aldwin et al. (1989), may be regarded as a temperament risk factor.

The study was conducted on over 1,000 men ages 40–88. Emotionality was assessed 10 years prior to measures of stress by means of items from the EPI. The authors distinguished between objective and subjective stressors. As a measure of objective stressors, Life Events were assessed by using a scale constructed by the senior author. For measuring subjective stressors, the Hassles scale developed by DeLongis, Folkman, and Lazarus (1988) was used. Mental health was assessed by means of the Hopkins Symptom Checklist (SCL–90; Derogatis, 1983).

Using multivariate analysis of data, the authors have shown that Emotionality had a stronger effect on mental health than Hassles and Life Events, but together Emotionality, Life Events, and Hassles accounted for almost 40% of the variance of the Global Severity Index. The interactional effect between Emotionality and Hassles on psychological symptoms is illustrated in Fig. 12.9. The results depicted in this figure have much in common with Model 4, which shows the synergistic effect of temperament and environment on psychological consequences of stress.

SUMMARY AND CONCLUSIONS

The aim of this chapter was to show the place of temperament in studies on stress phenomena, including stressors, state of stress, coping with stress, and consequences of stress. After reading it, a misleading impression might have developed that temperament is the only or the most important individual characteristic that moderates different aspects of stress. However, the intention

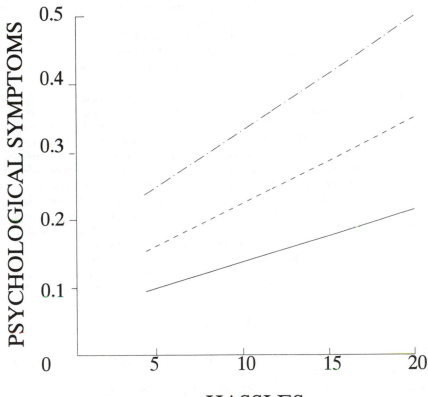

Figure 12.9 Effect of the interaction between emotionality and hassles on psychological symptoms.

was to demonstrate that temperament, as one of the many personal variables, cannot be ignored for a proper understanding of human functioning under stress. In other words, stress has been viewed in this chapter from a temperament perspective.

When studying the temperament–stress relationship, one has to keep in mind the specific aspects of stress, as well as the specific temperament characteristics and their configurations. Any conclusion regarding the role of temperament in moderating stress always refers to a particular temperament variable that interacts with a specific configuration of other variables contributing to the variance of stress phenomena.

A special position has to be given to the temperament risk factor in studies centered on the stress–temperament relationship because of the far-reaching consequences individuals pay as a result of excessive and/or chronic stress, to which temperament may contribute in different ways. Among the many risk factors regarded as causes of behavior disorders and pathology, temperament plays a specific role because of its low susceptibility to modification. Whereas some risk factors acting as stressors can be avoided or diminished by the individual (e.g., noise, crowd, job overload, parent–child conflict, etc.), others are hardly prone for modification or cannot be avoided at all. As Pelligrini (1990) emphasized, "some risk factors are more likely to be preventable or modifiable once they occur (e.g., marital discord), others simply are not (e.g., gender) or are less likely to be so (e.g., difficult temperament)" (pp. 206–207).

One of the senior researchers of child temperament, Rutter (1979), who studied protective factors in children's responses to stress, has shown the powerful influence of increasing number of risk factors for the epidemiology of behavior disorders. The probability of behavior disorders increases with the number of risk factors taken into account. The rate of behavior disorders was about the same for an individual with only one risk factor as compared with an individual being free from this risk factor. But when the number of risk factors acting jointly extended to four or more, the rate of behavior disorders increased to 20%. This finding is a strong argument for taking into account temperament as one of the many possible risk factors contributing to psychological, psychophysiological, and pathological consequences of stress.

The manifold temperament–stress issues presented in this chapter should be regarded as one of the possible ways that individual differences can be fruitfully applied to studies on stress.

REFERENCES

Achenbach, T. M., & Edelbrock, C. (Eds.). (1987). *Manual for the youth self-report and profile.* Burlington, VT: University of Vermont Press.

Aldwin, C. M., Levenson, M. R., Spiro III, A., & Bosse, R. (1989). Does emotionality predict stress? Findings from the normative aging study. *Journal of Personality and Social Psychology, 56,* 618–624.

Antonovsky, A. (1987). *Unraveling the mystery of health: How people manage stress and stay well.* San Francisco: Jossey-Bass.

Appley, M. H., & Trumbull, R. (1967). On the concept of psychological stress. In M. H. Appley & R. Trumbull (Eds.), *Psychological stress: Issues in research.* New York: Appleton-Century-Crofts.

Barron, A. P., & Earls, F. (1984). The relation of temperament and social factors to behavior problems in three-year old children. *Journal of Child Psychology and Psychiatry and Allied Disciplines, 25,* 23–33.

Bates, J. E. (1980). The concept of difficult temperament. *Merrill-Palmer Quarterly, 29,* 89–97.

Baum, A., Calesnick, L. E., Davis, G. E., & Gatchel, R. J. (1982). Individual differences in coping with crowding: Stimulus screening and social overload. *Journal of Personality and Social Psychology, 43,* 821–830.

Behar, L., & Stringfield, S. (1974). A behavior rating scale for the preschool child. *Developmental Psychology, 10,* 601–610.

Berlyne, D. E. (1960). *Conflict, arousal, and curiosity.* New York: McGraw-Hill.

Bolger, N. (1990). Coping as a personality process: A prospective study. *Journal of Personality and Social Psychology, 59,* 525–537.

Bolger, N., & Schilling, E. A. (in press). Personality and the problems of everyday life: The role of neuroticism in exposure and reactivity to daily stressors. *Journal of Personality.*

Buss, A. H., & Plomin, R. (1984). *Temperament: Early developing personality traits.* Hillsdale, NJ: Erlbaum.

Cameron, J. R. (1977). Parental treatment, children's temperament, and the risk of childhood behavioral problems: I. Relationships between parental characteristics and changes in children's temperament over time. *American Journal of Orthopsychiatry, 47,* 568–576.

Cameron, J. R. (1978). Parental treatment, children's temperament and the risk of childhood behavioral problems: 2. Initial temperament, parental attitudes, and the incidence and form of behavioral problems. *American Journal of Orthopsychiatry, 48,* 140–147.

Carey, W. B. (1986). The difficult child. *Pediatrics in Review, 8,* 39–45.

Carey, W. B. (1989). Introduction: Basic issues. In W. B. Carey & S. C. McDevitt (Eds.), *Clinical and educational applications of temperament research* (pp. 11–20). Lisse: Swets & Zeitlinger.

Carey, W. B., & McDevitt, S. C. (Eds.). (1989). *Clinical and educational applications of temperament research.* Lisse: Swets & Zeitlinger.

Carey, W. B., & McDevitt, S. C. (Eds.). (1994). *Prevention and early intervention: Individual differences as risk factors for the mental health of children.* New York: Brunner/Mazel.

Chan, K. B. (1977). Individual differences in reactions to stress and their personality and situational determinants: Some implications for community mental health. *Social Science and Medicine, 11,* 89–103.

Chess, S., & Thomas, A. (1984). *Origins and evolution of behavior disorders: From infancy to early adult life.* New York: Brunner/Mazel.

Chess, S., & Thomas, A. (1986). *Temperament in clinical practice.* New York: Guilford.

Chess, S., & Thomas, A. (1991). Temperament and the concept of goodness of fit. In J. Strelau & A. Angleitner (Eds.), *Explorations in temperament: International perspectives on theory and measurement* (pp. 15–28). New York: Plenum.

Corson, S. A., & O'Leary Corson, E. (1979). Interaction of genetic and psychosocial factors in stress-reaction patterns: A systems approach to the investigation of stress-coping mechanisms. *Psychotherapy and Psychosomatics, 31,* 161–171.

DeLongis, A., Folkman, S., & Lazarus, R. S. (1988). The impact of daily stressors on health and mood: Psychological and social measures as mediators. *Journal of Personality and Social Psychology, 54,* 486–495.

Derogatis, L. R. (1983). *SCL–90–R revised manual.* Baltimore, MD: Johns Hopkins University School of Medicine.

Dubos, R. (1965). *Man adapting.* New Haven, CT: Yale University Press.

Duckitt, J., & Broll, T. (1982). Personality factors as moderators of the psychological impact of life stress. *South African Journal of Psychology, 12,* 76–80.

Earls, F., & Jung, K. G. (1987). Temperament and home environment characteristics as causal factors in the early development of childhood psychopathology. *Journal of American Academy of Child and Adolescent Psychiatry, 26,* 491–498.

Edwards, J. R., & Cooper, C. L. (1990). The person-environment fit approach to stress: Recurring problems and some suggested solutions. *Journal of Organizational Behavior, 11,* 293–307.

Elliot, G. R., & Eisdorfer, C. (1982). *Stress and human health.* New York: Springer.

Endler, N. S., & Parker, J. D. A. (1990). *Coping Inventory for Stressful Situations (CISS): Manual.* Toronto: Multi-Health Systems.

Eysenck, H. J. (1970). *The structure of human personality* (3rd ed.). London: Methuen.

Eysenck, H. J. (1983). Stress, disease, and personality: The "inoculation effect." In C. L. Cooper (Ed.), *Stress research* (pp. 121–131). London: Wiley.

Eysenck, H. J. (1992). The definition and measurement of psychoticism. *Personality and Individual Differences, 13,* 757–785.

Eysenck, H. J., & Eysenck, M. W. (1985). *Personality and individual differences: A natural science approach.* New York: Plenum.

Folkman, S., & Lazarus, R. S. (1985). If it changes it must be a process: Study of emotion and coping during three stages of a college examination. *Journal of Personality and Social Psychology, 48,* 150–170.

Folkman, S., & Lazarus, R. S. (1988). Coping as a mediator of emotion. *Journal of Personality and Social Psychology, 54,* 466–475.

Frankenhaeuser, M. (1979). Psychoneuroendocrine approaches to the study of emotion as related to stress and coping. In H. E. Howe & R. A. Dienstbier (Eds.), *Nebraska Symposium on Motivation, 1978* (pp. 123–161). Lincoln: University of Nebraska Press.

Frankenhaeuser, M. (1986). A psychobiological framework for research on human stress and coping. In M. H. Appley & R. Trumbull (Eds.), *Dynamics of stress: Physiological, psychological, and social perspectives* (pp. 101–116). New York: Plenum.

Freedy, J. R., Kilpatrick, D. G., & Resnick, H. S. (1993). Natural disasters and mental health: Theory, assessment, and intervention. *Journal of Social Behavior and Personality, 8,* 49–103.

French, J. R. P., Jr., Caplan, R. D., & Harrison, R. V. (1982). *The mechanisms of job stress and strain.* London: Wiley.

Garrison, W. T., & Earls, F. J. (1987). *Temperament and child psychopathology.* Newbury Park, CA: Sage.

Goh, D. S., & Farley, F. H. (1977). Personality effects on cognitive test performance. *The Journal of Psychology, 96*, 111–122.

Graham, P., Rutter, M., & George, S. (1973). Temperamental characteristics as predictors of behavior disorders in children. *American Journal of Orthopsychiatry, 43*, 328–339.

Gray, J. A. (1964). Strength of the nervous system and levels of arousal: A reinterpretation. In J. A. Gray (Ed.), *Pavlov's typology: Recent theoretical and experimental developments from the Laboratory of B. M. Teplov* (pp. 289–364). Oxford: Pergamon.

Haggard, E. A. (1949). Psychological causes and results of stress. In D. B. Lindsley et al. (Eds.), *Human factors in undersea warfare*. Washington, DC: National Research Council.

Hobfoll, S. E. (1988). *The ecology of stress*. Washington, DC: Hemisphere.

Hobfoll, S. E. (1989). Conservation of resources: A new attempt at conceptualizing stress. *American Psychologist, 44*, 513–524.

Hobfoll, S. E. (1991). Conservation of resources in community intervention. *American Journal of Community Psychology, 19*, 111–121.

Holmes, T. H., & Rahe, R. H. (1967). The Social Readjustment Rating Scale. *Journal of Psychosomatic Research, 11*, 213–218.

Holohan, C. J., & Moos, R. H. (1986). Personality, coping, and family resources in stress resistance: A longitudinal analysis. *Journal of Personality and Social Psychology, 51*, 389–395.

Horvath, P., & Zuckerman, M. (1993). Sensation seeking, risk appraisal, and risky behavior. *Personality and Individual Differences, 14*, 41–52.

Jeffery, R. W. (1989). Risk behaviors and health: Contrasting individual and population perspectives. *American Psychologist, 44*, 1194–1202.

Kagan, J. (1983). Stress and coping in early development. In N. Garmezy & M. Rutter (Eds.), *Stress, coping and development in children* (pp. 191–216). New York: McGraw-Hill.

Kendler, K. S., & Eaves, L. J. (1986). Model for the joint effect of genotype and environment on liability to psychiatric illness. *The American Journal of Psychiatry, 143*, 279–289.

Klonowicz, T. (1974). Reactivity and fitness for the occupation of operator. *Polish Psychological Bulletin, 5*, 129–136.

Klonowicz, T. (1985). Temperament and performance. In J. Strelau (Ed.), *Temperamental bases of behavior: Warsaw studies on individual differences* (pp. 79–115). Warsaw, Poland: University of Warsaw Press.

Klonowicz, T. (1987a). Reactivity and the control of arousal. In J. Strelau & H. J. Eysenck (Eds.), *Personality dimensions and arousal* (pp. 183–196). New York: Plenum.

Klonowicz, T. (1987b). Reactivity, level of activation and anticipation: A scary world? *Polish Psychological Bulletin, 17*, 15–26.

Klonowicz, T. (1990). A psychophysiological assessment of simultaneous interpreting: The interaction of individual differences and mental workload. *Polish Psychological Bulletin, 21*, 37–48.

Klonowicz, T. (1992). *Stress w Wiezy Babel: Roznice indywidualne a wysilek inwestowany w trudna prace umyslowa* [Stress in the Babel Tower: Individual differences and allocation of effort]. Wroclaw: Ossolineum.

Kobasa, S. C. (1979). Stressful life events, personality and health: An inquiry into hardiness. *Journal of Personality and Social Psychology, 37,* 1–11.

Kobasa, S. C., & Puccetti, M. C. (1983). Personality and social resources in stress resistance. *Journal of Personality and Social Psychology, 45,* 839–850.

Kohn, P. M., Lafreniere, K., & Gurevich, M. (1991). Hassles, health, and personality. *Journal of Personality and Social Psychology, 61,* 478–482.

Krohne, H. W. (1986). Coping with stress: Dispositions, strategies, and the problem of measurement. In M. H. Appley & R. Trumbull (Eds.), *Dynamics of stress: Physiological, psychological, and social perspectives* (pp. 209–234). New York: Plenum.

Krohne, H. W., & Laux, L. (Eds.). (1982). *Achievement, stress, and anxiety.* New York: Hemisphere/McGraw-Hill.

Kyrios, M., & Prior, M. (1990). Temperament, stress and family factors in behavioural adjustment of 3–5-year-old children. *International Journal of Behavioral Development, 13,* 67–93.

Lazarus, R. S. (1966). *Psychological stress and the coping process.* New York: McGraw-Hill.

Lazarus, R. S. (1991). *Emotion and adaptation.* New York: Oxford University Press.

Lazarus, R. S. (1993). From psychological stress to the emotions: A history of changing outlooks. *Annual Review of Psychology, 44,* 1–21.

Lazarus, R. S., & Folkman, S. (1984). *Stress, appraisal, and coping.* New York: Springer.

Lundberg, U. (1982). Psychophysiological aspects of performance and adjustment to stress. In H. W. Krohne & L. Laux (Eds.), *Achievement, stress, and anxiety* (pp. 75–91). Washington, DC: Hemisphere.

Magnusson, D. (1982). Situational determinants of stress: An interactional perspective. In L. Goldberger & S. Breznitz (Eds.), *Handbook of stress* (pp. 231–253). New York: The Free Press.

Magnusson, D., Klinteberg, B., & Stattin, H. (1991). *Autonomic activity/reactivity, behavior and crime in a longitudinal perspective.* Reports from the Department of Psychology, No. 738. Stockholm, Stockholm University.

Malhorta, S., Varma, V. K., & Verma, S. G. (1986). Temperament as determinant of phenomenology of childhood psychiatric disorders. *Indian Journal of Psychiatry, 28,* 263–276.

Martin, R. P. (1989). Activity level, distractability and persistence: Critical characteristics in early schooling. In G. A. Kohnstamm, J. E. Bates, & M. K. Rothbart (Eds.), *Temperament in childhood* (pp. 451–461). Chichester: Wiley.

Maziade, M. (1988). Child temperament as a developmental or an epidemiological concept: A methodological point of view. *Psychiatric Developments, 3,* 195–211.

Maziade, M., Caron, C., Cote, R., Merette, C., Bernier, H., Laplante, B., Boutin, P., & Thivierge, J. (1990). Psychiatric status of adolescents who had extreme temperaments at age 7. *American Journal of Psychiatry, 147,* 1531–1536.

Maziade, M., Cote, R., Bernier, H., Boutin, P., & Thivierge, J. (1989). Significance of extreme temperament in infancy for clinical status in pre-school years: 1. Value of extreme temperament at 4–8 months for predicting diagnosis at 4.7 years. *British Journal of Psychiatry, 154,* 535–543.

McGrath, J. E. (Ed.). (1970). *Social and psychological factors in stress.* New York: Holt, Rinehart & Winston.

McGuire, I., & Turkewitz, G. (1979). Approach-withdrawal theory and the study of infant development. In M. Bortner (Ed.), *Cognitive growth and development: Essays in memory of Herbert G. Birch* (pp. 57–84). New York: Brunner/Mazel.

Mehrabian, A. (1977). Individual differences in stimulus screening and arousability. *Journal of Personality, 45,* 237–250.

Mehrabian, A., & Ross, M. (1977). Quality of life change and individual differences in stimulus screening in relation to incidence of illness. *Psychological Reports, 41,* 267–278.

Mundelein, H. (1982). *Simulierte Arbeitssituation an Bildschirmterminals: Ein Beitrag zu einer okologisch orientierten Psychologie* [Simulated job situation at computer terminals: A contribution to ecological-oriented psychology]. Frankfurt/Main: Fischer Verlag.

Nebylitsyn, V. D. (1972). *Fundamental properties of the human nervous system.* New York: Plenum.

Opton, E. M., & Lazarus, R. S. (1967). Personality determinants of psychophysiological response to stress: A theoretical analysis and an experiment. *Journal of Personality and Social Psychology, 6,* 291–303.

Ormel, J., & Schaufeli, W. B. (1991). Stability and change in psychological distress and their relationship with self-esteem and locus of control: A dynamic equilibrium model. *Personality and Social Psychology, 60,* 288–299.

Parkes, K. R. (1984). Locus of control, cognitive appraisal, and coping in stressful episodes. *Journal of Personality and Social Psychology, 46,* 655–668.

Parkes, K. R. (1986). Coping in stressful episodes: The role of individual differences, environmental factors, and situational characteristics. *Journal of Personality and Social Psychology, 51,* 1277–1292.

Pellegrini, D. S. (1990). Psychosocial risk and protective factors in childhood. *Journal of Developmental and Behavioral Pediatrics, 11,* 201–209.

Plomin, R. (1982). The difficult concept of temperament: A response to Thomas, Chess, and Korn. *Merrill-Palmer Quarterly, 28,* 25–33.

Prior, M. R., Sanson, A. V., & Oberklaid, F. (1989). The Australian Temperament Project. In G. A. Kohnstamm, J. E. Bates, & M. K. Rothbart (Eds.), *Temperament in childhood* (pp. 537–554). Chichester: Wiley.

Rahe, R. H. (1987). Recent life changes, emotions, and behaviors in coronary heart disease. In A. Baum & J. E. Singer (Eds.), *Handbook of psychology and health* (Vol. 5, pp. 229–254). Hillsdale, NJ: Erlbaum.

Ratajczak, Z., & Adamiec, M. (1989). Some dimensions in the perception of occupational hazards by coal miners. *Polish Psychological Bulletin, 20,* 171–182.

Richman, N., & Graham, P. J. (1971). A behavioural screening questionnaire for use with three year old children: Preliminary findings. *Journal of Child Psychology & Psychiatry, 12,* 5–33.

Rothbart, M. (1982). The concept of difficult temperament: A critical analysis of Thomas, Chess and Korn. *Merrill-Palmer Quarterly, 28,* 35–40.

Rutter, M. (1979). Protective factors in children's responses to stress and disadvantage. In M. W. Kent & J. E. Rolf (Eds.), *Primary prevention of psychopathology* (Vol. 3, pp. 49–74). Hannover, NH: University Press of New England.

Rutter, M. (1991). Nature, nurture, and psychopathology: A new look at an old topic. *Development and Psychopathology, 3,* 125–136.

Schonpflug, W. (1993). Effort regulation and individual differences in effort expenditure. In G. R. J. Hockery, A. W. K. Galillard, & M. G. H. Coles (Eds.), *Energetics and human information processing.* Dordrecht: Nijhoff.

Schonpflug, W., & Battmann, W. (1987). *Self-generated stress: Costs and benefits of coping.* Unpublished manuscript, Freie Universitat Berlin, Berlin.

Schneirla, T. C. (1959). An evolutionary and developmental theory of biphasic processes underlying approach and withdrawal. In M. J. Jones (Ed.), *Nebraska Symposium on Motivation* (Vol. 7). Lincoln: University of Nebraska Press.

Schulz, P., & Schonpflug, W. (1982). Regulatory activity during states of stress. In H. W. Krohne & L. Laux (Eds.), *Achievement, stress, and anxiety* (pp. 51–73). Washington, DC: Hemisphere.

Selye, H. (1950). *Stress.* Montreal: Acta.

Selye, H. (1956). *The stress of life.* New York: McGraw-Hill.

Selye, H. (1975). *Stress without distress.* New York: New American Library.

Spielberger, C. D. (1983). *Manual for the Strait-Trait Anxiety Inventory: STAI (Form Y).* Palo Alto, CA: Consulting Psychologists Press.

Strelau, J. (1983). *Temperament, personality, activity.* London: Academic Press.

Strelau, J. (1987). Emotion as a key concept in temperament research. *Journal of Research in Personality, 21,* 510–528.

Strelau, J. (1988). Temperamental dimensions as co-determinants of resistance to stress. In M. P. Janisse (Ed.), *Individual differences, stress, and health psychology* (pp. 146–169). New York: Springer.

Strelau, J. (1989a). Individual differences in tolerance to stress: The role of reactivity. In C. D. Spielberger, I. G. Sarason, & J. Strelau (Eds.), *Stress and anxiety* (Vol. 12, pp. 155–166). Washington, DC: Hemisphere.

Strelau, J. (1989b). Temperament risk factors in children and adolescents as studied in Eastern Europe. In W. B. Carey & S. C. McDevitt (Eds.), *Clinical and educational applications of temperament research* (pp. 65–77). Lisse: Swets & Zeitlinger.

Strelau, J. (1994). The concepts of arousal and arousability as used in temperament studies. In J. E. Bates & T. D. Wachs (Eds.), *Temperament:*

Individual differences at the interface of biology and behavior (pp. 117–141). Washington, DC: APA Books.

Strelau, J., & Eliasz, A. (1994). Temperament risk factors for Type A behavior patterns in adolescents. In W. B. Carey & S. C. McDevitt (Eds.), *Prevention and early intervention: Individual differences as risk factors for the mental health of children* (pp. 42–49). New York: Brunner/Mazel.

Strelau, J., & Szczepaniak, P. (1994, July). *Coping styles and temperament characteristics: A psychometric approach*. Paper presented at the XXIII International Congress of Applied Psychology, Madrid, Spain.

Strelau, J., & Zawadzki, B. (1993). The Formal Characteristics of Behaviour– Temperament Inventory (FCB–TI): Theoretical assumptions and scale construction. *European Journal of Personality, 7,* 313–336.

Thomas, A., & Chess, S. (1977). *Temperament and development.* New York: Brunner/Mazel.

Thomas, A., Chess, S., & Birch, H. G. (1968). *Temperament and behavior disorders in children.* New York: New York University Press.

Tomaszewski, T. (1978). Tatigkeit und Bewusstsein: Beitrage zur Einfuhrung in die polnische Tatigkeit Psychologie. Weinheim & Basel, Switzerland: Beltz Verlag.

Ursin, H. (1980). Personality, activation and somatic health: A new psychosomatic theory. In S. Levine & H. Ursin (Eds.), *Coping and health* (pp. 259–279). New York: Plenum.

Vingerhoets, A. J. J. M., Van den Berg, M. P., Kortekaas, R. T. J., Van Heck, G. L., & Croon, M. A. (1993). Weeping: Associations with personality, coping, and subjective health status. *Personality and Individual Differences, 14,* 185–190.

Vitaliano, P. P., DeWolfe, D. J., Maiuro, R. D., Russo, J., & Katon, W. (1990). Appraised changeability of a stressor as a modifier of the relationship between coping and depression: A test of the hypothesis of fit. *Journal of Personality and Social Psychology, 59,* 582–592.

Watson, D., & Clark, L. A. (1984). Negative affectivity: The disposition to experience negative emotional states. *Psychological Bulletin, 96,* 465–490.

Weick, K. E. (1970). The "ess" in stress. Some conceptual and methodological problems. In J. E. McGrath (Ed.), *Social and psychological factors in stress.* New York: Holt, Rinehart & Winston.

Windle, M. (1989). Predicting temperament-mental health relationships: A covariance structure latent variable analysis. *Journal of Research in Personality, 23,* 118–144.

Wundt, W. (1911). *Grundzuge der physiologischen Psychologie* (Vol. 3, 6th ed.). Leipzig: Engelmann.

Zawadzki, B. (1991). Temperament: Selekcja czy kompensacjz? [Temperament: Selection or compensation?]. In T. Tyszka (Ed.), *Psychologia i sport* (pp. 85–112). Warszawa: Academy of Sports Education Publisher.

Zmudzki, A. (1986). *Poziom reaktywnosci a powodzenie w trakcie startu u zawodnikow w podnoszeniu ciezarow* [Level of reactivity and success during competition in weight lifters]. Warszawa: Institute of Sports Publisher.

Zuckerman, M. (1964). Perceptual isolation as a stress situation: A review. *Archives of General Psychiatry, 11,* 225–276.

Zuckerman, M. (1979). *Sensation seeking: Beyond the optimal level of arousal.* Hillsdale, NJ: Erlbaum.

Zuckerman, M. (1991a). One person's stress is another person's pleasure. In C. D. Spielberger, I. G. Sarason, Z. Kulcsar, & G. L. Van Heck (Eds.), *Stress and emotion: Anxiety, anger, and curiosity* (Vol. 14, pp. 31–45). Washington, DC: Hemisphere.

Zuckerman, M. (1991b). *Psychobiology of personality.* Cambridge, England: Cambridge University Press.

Zuckerman, M. (1994). *Behavioral expressions and biosocial bases of sensation seeking.* New York: Cambridge University Press.

13

Emotion Control, Coping Strategies, and Adaptive Behavior

Derek Roger
University of York, England

ABSTRACT

Responding to shortcomings in earlier research on the moderating effects of personality on stress, Roger and his colleagues have proposed a new model based on emotion control. It has been suggested that continued rumination over emotional distress might contribute to delayed recovery. Scores from the Rehearsal subscale of the Emotion Control Questionnaire (ECQ; Roger & Najarian, 1989) proved to be strongly related to physiological indices such as heart-rate recovery (Roger & Jamieson, 1988) and cortisol secretion (Roger, 1988). More recently, the research has included a new coping inventory, the Coping Styles Questionnaire (CSQ; Roger, Jarvis, & Najarian, 1993). The results of a study of 320 undergraduates utilizing the CSQ during the first 6 months of adaptation at university demonstrated that the variance in health status and psychosocial adaptation was best explained by the interactive effects of life events, emotion control, and coping. These findings were confirmed by a second study, which also demonstrated event- and personality-related variability in coping styles.

It is widely assumed that *stress* causes *illness,* but there is little agreement over the way in which either of these constructs should be defined. For example, stress is frequently measured by scores on Life Event scales, despite widespread evidence showing that life events can seldom be recalled accurately (Jenkins, Hurst, & Rose, 1979) and are in any case confounded by illness (Schroeder & Costa, 1984). The measurement of illness would appear to be more reliable because it is based on relatively objective diagnostic criteria. But if indices such as medical records are used, they may be confounded by individual differences in thresholds for reporting illness.

Assuming that stress causes illness raises additional problems over the mechanism that might be involved in "translating" a cognitive process such as perceived threat into physical symptomatology. Recent advances in psychoimmunology have suggested that the most plausible candidate mechanism involves the sustained activation of the hypothalamic–pituitary–adrenal axis (Jemmott & Locke, 1984), and there is certainly good evidence for the role of corticosteroids in compromising immune function (Asterita, 1985). However, in view of the wide individual differences in both cognitive and physiological responses to stress, knowledge about physiological mechanisms can provide only a partial answer.

One explanation is that personality may be involved as a moderator variable. Early research indeed indicated that aspects of perceived control, such as locus of control and learned helplessness, might play a significant role, but the findings have been equivocal (Steptoe, 1983). For example, using Life Event scales to provide an index of stress, Kobasa's (1979) research on hardiness suggested that having an internal locus of control may serve as a buffer against stress. Denney and Frisch (1981) reported a trend in the same direction, but their results were not statistically significant. Although their study showed evidence for statistical main effects, neither Neuroticism nor any of the other personality factors included in the Denney and Frisch study acted interactively as moderators. In fact, when situational control is taken into account, having an internal locus of control has been shown to be associated with a greater susceptibility to stress among subjects who experienced high levels of uncontrollable life events (Meadows, 1989).

ROLE OF PERSONALITY IN STRESS

The role of personality in stress has also been explained in terms of stimulus intensity control—an explanatory model that includes Neuroticism and Extraversion, as well as a range of other constructs like Sensation Seeking and Augmenting–Reducing (Roger & Raine, 1984). The model argues that individual differences in these indices reflect underlying differences in basal cognitive or emotional arousal and arousability. In view of the role of physiological arousal in moderating immune function (Asterita, 1985), it might be expected that subjects who are low on basal arousal (i.e., extraverts or sensation seekers) would be less susceptible to stress-induced illness. Totman, Kiff, Reed, and Craig (1980) did not explicitly invoke this model in his study of experimentally induced colds. Nonetheless, he did report higher levels of infection among introverts compared with extraverts—a finding confirmed by Broadbent, Broadbent, Phillpotts, and Wallace (1984). However, subsequent research has indicated that, although rates of experimental infection increase with greater stress, the findings could not be explained by the personality differences proposed earlier (Smith, 1992). There are also issues over the precise definition of constructs like Extraversion and Neuroticism, which are in fact multidimensional. Neuroticism, for example, is composed of empirically discriminable components of hypochondriasis and social sensitivity (Roger & Morris, 1991; Roger & Nesshoever, 1987), but their differential contribution to outcomes has not been adequately explored.

More recently, Eysenck (1985, 1988) used the two orthogonal dimensions of Extraversion and Neuroticism to develop a model for explaining differential susceptibility to cancer and heart disease. Drawing on collaborative work with Grossarth-Maticek (e.g., Grossarth-Maticek, Eysenck, Vetter, & Schmidt, 1986), Eysenck proposed a model that relies, in part, on a distinction between *chronic stress,* which serves to inoculate or protect individuals against illness, and *acute stress,* which results in immunosuppression and increased suscepti- bility. The supportive evidence for this acute–chronic distinction is based on earlier work by Sklar and Anisman (1981), who concluded from their review of the literature that acute and chronic stress have different adaptational out- comes. However, they go on to say that this applies to physical but not social stressors. Most of the work reviewed by these authors was carried out on animals; the kinds of physical stressors involved were inescapable shock and noxious fumes. Social stressors, which might be seen as much more consistent with the psychosocial stressors of interest to research on stress in humans, produced no inoculation. As Sklar and Anisman pointed out, unlike physical stressors, "immunosuppression induced by social stress is not altered under chronic conditions" (p. 388).

Commenting on these and other inconclusive findings from research on the role of personality in stress and illness, Roger (1988, 1992) and Roger and Nash (1994) argued that the personality constructs used in earlier studies were inappropriate because they had not been developed specifically in the context of stress research. Roger and his colleagues proposed an alternative model based on emotion control, which developed from a programme of experimental work on the role of emotion control in moderating stress responses, using scales from the Emotion Control Questionnaire (ECQ; Roger & Najarian, 1989; Roger & Nesshoever, 1987) as independent variables. A number of au- thors have suggested that continued rumination over emotional distress might contribute to delayed recovery (e.g., Cameron & Meichenbaum, 1982), but existing scales that claim to measure emotional expressive style have proved inadequate. For example, a factor analysis of Byrne's Repression–Sensitization (R–S) Scale (Byrne, Barry, & Nelson, 1963) by Roger and Schapals (in press) uncovered primary factors concerned with depression and sociability, with fewer than 10 items from the 127-item scale addressed to expressive style.

The shortcomings in available measures of emotional style led to the con- struction and validation of the ECQ, which is composed of four empirically discriminable scales: Rehearsal, Emotional Inhibition, Aggression Control, and Benign Control. Rehearsal measures the tendency to be preoccupied with emotional upset, whereas Emotional Inhibition refers to "bottling up" or in- hibiting the expression of experienced emotion (and is thus distinct from the hypothesised emotional arousal or arousability encompassed by Neuroticism). The last two scales, Aggression Control and Benign Control, are moderately correlated, and have been shown to form part of the Extraversion constellation. Benign Control, for example, correlates substantially with established mea- sures of Impulsiveness (Roger & Nesshoever, 1987). Factor loadings for sample items from the scale are shown in Table 13.1.

RECENT STUDIES

Subsequent validation studies of the ECQ have shown that Rehearsal is particularly strongly related to physiological indices of adaptation. In the first

Table 13.1 Sample items (with factor loadings) from the ECQ

| | Factors | | | |
Items	F1	F2	F3	F4
40. I find it hard to get thoughts about things that have upset me out of my mind.	.62	.16	.02	.03
7. People find it difficult to tell whether or not I'm excited about something.	.09	.56	− .00	− .08
33. Even when I'm angry I seldom use bad language.	.02	.06	.50	− .00
9. Almost everything I do is carefully thought out.	.19	.01	− .01	.61

Note. F1 = Rehearsal, F2 = Emotional Inhibition, F3 = Aggression Control, F4 = Benign Control.

of these studies, heart-rate recovery following exposure to a moderate laboratory stressor was used as the dependent variable, with the effects of initial values controlled by statistical partialing (Roger & Jamieson, 1988). The stress manipulation consisted of performance on the Stroop task, where emotional involvement in the task can reliably be produced by provoking time pressure and evaluation apprehension in the subjects (Jamieson & Kaszor, 1986). Rehearsal was expected to maintain arousal by a continued preoccupation with the emotional upset of the task, and it was predicted that subjects who scored high on Rehearsal would take significantly longer to recover than low scorers.

Subjects were 22 male (mean age 20.41 years) and 23 female (mean age 19.56 years) students from the University of York. Heart rate was recorded via gel-filled silver-silver chloride electrodes. In addition to the ECQ, the Eysenck Personality Inventory (EPI; Eysenck & Eysenck, 1964) was also administered; scores for the separate components of Extraversion (impulsivity and sociability; Revelle, Humphreys, Simon, & Gilliland, 1980) and Neuroticism (hypochondriasis and social sensitivity; Roger & Nesshoever, 1987) were derived. Controlling for initial heart rate, the results showed that only the Rehearsal scale from the ECQ correlated significantly with heart-rate recovery [$r (43) = 0.39, p < .01$], a finding subsequently replicated in a number of studies using both correlational and analysis of variance (ANOVA) designs. All other coefficients between personality measures used in the study and heart rate recovery were nonsignificant.

The first validation study of the ECQ showed that Rehearsal in particular was significantly related to delayed heart-rate recovery, which is mediated, in part, by adrenaline secretion. Of equal importance, however, is the sustained activation of adrenocortical hormones, particularly cortisol. Because cortisol secretion increases significantly in response to psychosocial stressors, and has been shown to compromise immune function (Asterita, 1985), the action of this hormone constitutes an important mechanism linking psychological stress and illness. For the second study, 34 female student nurses (mean age 24.30

years) provided urine samples on two occasions: immediately after completing a nursing examination known to provoke considerable apprehension, and again 2 weeks later. Intervening stressors, subclinical infections during the intertest interval, and menstrual cycle effects were partialed out of the analyses.

The urine samples were assayed for urinary-free cortisol, and an index was derived from the difference in cortisol levels from the first to the second sample, expressed as a proportion of the "base rate" (Sample 2). Data on a variety of personality scales, including the EPI and the ECQ, were obtained. The results echo the findings obtained in the first study. Like heart-rate recovery, the cortisol-secretion difference ratio was significantly correlated only with the Rehearsal scale from the ECQ [r (32) = .526, p < .01], and there were no significant correlations for either of the separate components of the Extraversion (impulsivity and sociability) and Neuroticism (hypochondriasis and social sensitivity) scales.

Other studies by Roger and his colleagues have shown that the ECQ, and particularly Rehearsal, is significantly associated with a variety of other measures of Social and Psychological Adjustment among samples as diverse as prison inmates (McDougall, Venables, & Roger, 1991) and perinatal women (Nieland & Roger, 1993). The experimental findings have subsequently been incorporated into a training programme based on emotion control and attention control. The programme is aimed at facilitating adaptation to change. Controlled intervention studies have shown that the programme is effective in enhancing job satisfaction and reducing absenteeism (Nash & Roger, 1994; Roger, 1992).

More recently, stress research at York has included measures of coping style. As Monat and Lazarus (1991) pointed out, there is some confusion in the literature over the precise definition of *coping,* but coping inventories have typically isolated three coping "domains" involving Rational, Emotional, and Avoidance strategies (e.g., Endler & Parker, 1990). However, using a "scenario" technique, Roger, Jarvis, and Najarian (1993) generated a new item pool that resulted in the extraction of an additional domain labeled *Detachment.* The scenarios were composed of descriptions of emotional situations; the subjects were asked to respond by listing ways in which they would cope with these predicaments. Sample items for the four extracted factors are shown in Table 13.2 (loadings below the criterion value of .35 have been omitted).

A validation study of the four-factor Coping Styles Questionnaire (CSQ; Roger et al., 1993) showed that Rational and Detached Coping correlated to form an Adaptive Coping Styles domain. Emotional and Avoidance Coping also correlated positively (though less strongly) to form a Maladaptive Coping Styles dimension, and these adaptive and maladaptive clusters were in turn inversely correlated with one another. Inclusion of the ECQ in the study showed that these adaptive and maladaptive domains were also related in predictable ways to the ECQ subscales, with Adaptive and Maladaptive Coping Styles correlating negatively and positively, respectively, with Rehearsal. The correlations between the ECQ and CSQ factors are shown in Table 13.3.

The ECQ and CSQ have subsequently been used to investigate the interactive effects of coping styles and emotion control on adaptation (Roger, Na-

Table 13.2 Sample items (with factor loadings) from the CSQ

| | | Factors | | |
Items	F1	F2	F3	F4
16. Try to find out more information to help make a decision about things.	.67			
45. Just take nothing personally.		.64		
5. Become miserable or depressed.			.57	
43. Trust in fate—that things have a way of working out for the best.				.56

Note. Only relevant loadings are shown; all other loadings in the matrix were > .35. F1 = Rational Coping, F2 = Detached Coping, F3 = Emotional Coping, F4 = Avoidance Coping.

jarian, & Jarvis, 1994). The subjects in this study were 142 male (mean age 21.23) and 178 female (mean age 19.77) undergraduates who completed a series of Personality, Life Event, and Social Support scales, as well as a health and social adjustment checklist immediately after entering university. They were then followed up over two 3-month intervals and reassessed on their health and adjustment status, using scales that distinguished between categories for *worse, better,* and *unchanged* status.

The data for the study were initially subjected to regression analyses, with the health status and adjustment scores used as the dependent variables. Results showed that social adjustment was significantly predicted by Social Support, Academic Adjustment, and Rehearsal. Of more interest, however, was the change in health status toward worse health. These findings show that deteriorated health was accounted for by Emotional Coping, Rehearsal, and Negative Life Events. Rehearsal and Emotional Coping are known to correlate significantly, hence their co-occurrence in the regression analysis is not surprising. Because *stress* is defined in terms of Rehearsal in the emotion control model, further analyses were carried out on the interactive effects of Negative Life Events and Personality by omitting Emotional Coping and casting the data

Table 13.3 Correlations between CSQ and ECQ factors

| | CSQ | | | |
ECQ	F1	F2	F3	F4
F1	−.355**	−.486**	+.511**	+.236*
F2	−.141	+.171	+.121	+.385**
F3	+.067	+.022	+.010	+.054
F4	+.210*	+.258*	−.301**	−.148

Note. ECQ: F1 = Rehearsal, F2 = Emotional Inhibition, F3 = Aggresion Control, F4 = Benign Control. CSQ: F1 = Rational Coping, F2 = Detached Coping, F3 = Emotional Coping, F4 = Avoidance Coping.
$*p < .05.$ $**p < .01.$

Table 13.4 Mean scores for worse health status

Rehearsal	Negative Life Events	
	Low	High
Low	2.08	2.65
High	2.35	4.93

in the form of a two-way ANOVA. Subjects were selected for high and low scores on Rehearsal and Negative Life Events, and the mean scores for worse health status are shown in Table 13.4.

Results of the two-way ANOVA yielded significant main effects for Rehearsal ($F = 5.12$, $p < .02$) and Negative Life Events ($F = 10.37$, $p < .01$), as well as a significant interaction ($F = 3.63$, $p < .05$). Simple main effects for the interaction showed that the mean score in the high Rehearsal/high Negative Life Events cell was significantly higher than in the remaining cells. The results suggest that the deterioration in health status could be attributed to the triggering by negative events of a predisposing tendency to ruminate, which in turn results in sustained provocation of pituitary–hypothalamic–adrenal activation and heightened susceptibility.

A second longitudinal study of adaptational behavior among undergraduate students has extended the previous work by suggesting that coping styles are only relatively stable. The results of this unpublished study have shown that subjects who score high on Rehearsal tend to use more maladaptive strategies during the adaptational period as a function of Negative Life Events. As Negative Life Events increase, these subjects show a significant change toward engaging in more emotional and (to a lesser extent) avoidance coping.

The final study also included a measure of Self-Esteem, which also contributes toward the moderation of stress responses (Rector, Roger, & Nussbaum, 1993). This work has led, in turn, to the formulation of a multifactorial model that accords a primary role to self-perception. In the model, which is the focus of current research at York, *self-concept* is defined as a hypothetical construct that has no direct empirical referent. Self-concept is operationalised when a valence or attitude is held toward it—the esteem, either positively or negatively, with which it is regarded. Self-esteem may have either state or trait characteristics, but an underlying tendency toward negative self-esteem will lead to rehearsal of the emotional upset occasioned by situations, past or forthcoming, which results from the focusing of attention on perceived inadequacy.

Finally, the current research programme has also been extended to include a reformulation of so-called "Type A behavior," which is seen not as a typology, but rather as a dimension of achievement orientation. This approach is consistent with recent proposals for distinguishing between toxic and nontoxic Type A behavior (Burns & Bluen, 1992; Dembrowski & Costa, 1987). The alternative formulation proposes that Type As (toxic) are highly achievement-motivated individuals who behave as they do because of negative self-esteem and rehearsal, whereas Type Bs (nontoxic) are equally motivated, but have high self-esteem and consequently tend not to engage in rehearsal. This maladaptive process is construed, in the emotion control model, as a failure to exercise control over attention, allowing it to be distracted from a detached, present-oriented perspective to one governed by preoccupations with past or anticipated failures.

REFERENCES

Asterita, M. F. (1985). *The physiology of stress.* New York: Human Sciences Press.

Broadbent, D. E., Broadbent, M. H. P., Phillpotts, R. J., & Wallace, J. (1984). Some further studies on the prediction of experimental colds in volunteers by psychological factors. *Journal of Psychosomatic Research, 28,* 511–523.

Burns, W., & Bluen, S. D. (1992). Assessing a multidimensional Type A behaviour scale. *Personality and Individual Differences, 13,* 977–986.

Byrne, D., Barry, J., & Nelson, D. (1963). Relationship of the revised Repression–Sensitization Scale to measures of self description. *Psychological Reports, 13,* 323–334.

Cameron, R., & Meichenbaum, D. (1982). The nature of effective coping and the treatment of stress related problems: A cognitive-behavioral perspective. In L. Goldberger & S. Bernitz (Eds.), *Handbook of stress.* New York: The Free Press.

Dembroski, T. M., & Costa, P. T. (1987). Coronary prone behavior: Components of the Type-A pattern and hostility. *Journal of Personality, 55,* 211–235.

Denney, D. R., & Frisch, M. B. (1981). The role of neuroticism in relation to life stress and illness. *Journal of Psychosomatic Research, 25,* 303–307.

Endler, N. S., & Parker, J. D. A. (1990). Multidimensional assessment of coping. *Journal of Personality and Social Psychology, 58,* 844–854.

Eysenck, H. J. (1985). Personality, cancer and cardiovascular disease. *Personality and Individual Differences, 6,* 535–556.

Eysenck, H. J. (1988). Personality, stress and cancer. *British Journal of Medical Psychology, 61,* 57–75.

Eysenck, H. J., & Eysenck, S. B. G. (1964). *Manual of the Eysenck Personality Inventory.* London: University of London Press.

Grossarth-Maticek, R., Eysenck, H. J., Vetter, H., & Schmidt, P. (1986, July). *Results of the Heidelberg prospective psychosomatic intervention study.* Paper presented at the International Conference on Health Psychology, Tilburg University, The Netherlands.

Jamieson, J. L., & Kaszor, N. D. (1986). Social comparison and recovery from stress. *Canadian Journal of Behavioral Science, 18,* 140–145.

Jemmott, J. B., & Locke, S. E. (1984). Psychosocial factors, immunologic mediation, and human susceptibility to infectious diseases: How much do we know? *Psychological Bulletin, 95,* 78–108.

Jenkins, C. D., Hurst, M. W., & Rose, R. M. (1979). Life changes: Do people really remember? *Archives of General Psychiatry, 36,* 379–384.

Kobasa, S. (1979). Stressful life events, personality, and health: An inquiry into hardiness. *Journal of Personality and Social Psychology, 37,* 1–11.

McDougall, C., Venables, P., & Roger, D. (1991). Aggression, anger control and emotion control. *Personality and Individual Differences, 12,* 625–629.

Meadows, M. (1989). *Personality, stress and health.* Unpublished doctoral dissertation, University of York, England.

Monat, A., & Lazarus, R. S. (1991). *Stress & coping* (3rd ed.). New York: Columbia University Press.

Nash, P., & Roger, D. (1994, April). *Evaluating the effectiveness of a "challenge of change" training programme.* Paper presented at the British Psychological Society annual conference, Brighton, England.

Nieland, M., & Roger, D. (1993). Emotion control and analgesia in labour. *Personality and Individual Differences, 14,* 841–843.

Rector, N., Roger, D., & Nussbaum, D. (1993, July). *The moderating role of self-esteem in emotion control and health.* Paper presented at the 3rd European Congress of Psychology, Tampere, Finland.

Revelle, W., Humphreys, M. S., Simon, L., & Gilliland, K. (1980). The interactive effects of personality, time of day, and caffeine: A test of the arousal model. *Journal of Experimental Psychology, 109,* 1–31.

Roger, D. (1988, April). *The role of emotion control in human stress responses.* Paper presented at the annual conference of the British Psychological Society, University of Leeds, England.

Roger, D. (1992, April). *The development and evaluation of a work skills and stress management training programme.* Paper presented at the annual conference of the British Psychological Society, Scarborough, England.

Roger, D., & Jamieson, J. (1988). Individual differences in delayed heart-rate recovery following stress: The role of extraversion, neuroticism and emotional control. *Personality and Individual Differences, 9,* 721–726.

Roger, D., Jarvis, G., & Najarian, B. (1993). Detachment and coping: The construction and validation of a new scale for measuring coping strategies. *Personality and Individual Differences, 15,* 619–626.

Roger, D., & Morris, J. (1991). The internal structure of the EPQ scales. *Personality and Individual Differences, 12,* 759–764.

Roger, D., & Najarian, B. (1989). The construction and validation of a new scale for measuring emotional control. *Personality and Individual Differences, 10,* 845–853.

Roger, D., Najarian, B., & Jarvis, G. (1994, March). *The interactive effects of emotion control and coping strategies on adaptive behaviour.* Paper presented at the British Psychological Society annual conference, Brighton, England.

Roger, D., & Nash, P. (1994, September). *Effects of stress management training on health.* Paper presented at the British Psychological Society Health Psychology conference, Sheffield, England.

Roger, D., & Nesshoever, W. (1987). The construction and preliminary validation of a scale for measuring emotional control. *Personality and Individual Differences, 8,* 527–534.

Roger, D., & Raine, A. (1984). Stimulus intensity control and personality. *Current Psychological Research & Reviews, 3,* 43–47.

Roger, D., & Schapals, T. (in press). Repression-sensitization and emotion control. *Current Psychology.*

Schroeder, D. H., & Costa, P. T. (1984). Influence of life event stress on physical illness. *Journal of Personality & Social Behaviour, 46,* 853–863.

Sklar, L., & Anisman, H. (1981). Stress and cancer. *Psychological Bulletin, 89,* 369–406.

Smith, A. (1992, December). *Stress, health-related behaviour and susceptibility to experimentally-induced colds.* Paper presented at the British Psychological Society conference, London, England.

Steptoe, A. (1983). Stress, helplessness and control: The implications of laboratory studies. *Journal of Psychosomatic Research, 27,* 361–367.

Totman, R., Kiff, J., Reed, S. E., & Craig, J. W. (1980). Predicting experimental colds in volunteers. *Journal of Psychosomatic Research, 24,* 155–163.

14

Stress in Eastern and Western Cultures

Pittu Laungani
South Bank University, London

ABSTRACT

Stress is a common human experience that varies across cultures because of variations in physical, climatic, ecological, social, and political environments. Level of economic development and affluence contribute further to such variations. As a consequence of such differences, each culture acquires its own fundamental values and ideology, reflected in shared beliefs, attitudes, and social customs, and its own identifiable sets of stressors, many of which are culture-specific. This chapter argues that Western cultures (English culture in particular) may be distinguished from Eastern cultures (Indian culture in particular) in terms of the following four theoretical dimensions: individualism versus collectivism, cognitivism versus emotionalism, free will versus determinism, and materialism versus spiritualism. The nature of each of these dimensions—the beliefs, attitudes, values, and behaviours subsumed within it—and its relevance to understanding the problem of stress are articulated. The dimensions to the left are more applicable to people in Western cultures; those to the right are more relevant to people in Eastern cultures. The chapter highlights practical uses of the proposed model in designing culture-specific training strategies for the management of stress.

Some observations are so obvious that they do not need the pronouncements of experts to ensure their validation. For instance, it is a truism to suggest that each culture produces its own unique sources of stress. The level of stress experienced by those living in the rain forest regions of Northeast India, Cheerapunji being the prime example, is likely to be markedly different from that of people living in the Arctic Circle, say in the Baffin Islands. Clearly, cultures vary in terms of their political, social, economic, and physical environments, each exerting its own set of stressors on the people of those countries. Given wide individual variation in the perception of, and response to, stressful circumstances, it follows that there are differences both within and between cultures in terms of the experience of stress.

Cultures also vary with respect to their value systems, which have a significant bearing on the religious beliefs, kinship patterns, and social arrangements of the people of a particular culture. Values are best defined as the currently held, normative expectations that underlie individual and social conduct. Salient belief systems concerning right and wrong, good and bad, normal and abnormal, appropriate and inappropriate, proper and improper, and the like are, to a large measure, influenced by the values operative in the culture. When pressed as to why people hold particular beliefs and why certain beliefs are important and others less so, it is generally impossible to offer plausible explanations unless one experiences the historical evolution of cultural values and beliefs.

Values, like air, pervade the cultural atmosphere; people imbibe them, often without conscious awareness of their origins. Because certain values and behaviours are culture-specific, it follows that many stressors are also culture-specific. Consequently, one would expect to find differences within and between cultures in levels of stress, and in the coping mechanisms employed by persons from different cultures.

In this chapter, two cultures are singled out for a closer scrutiny: India as an example of Eastern culture, and England as a prototype Western culture. The focus is on the major parameters or factors that distinguish Eastern cultures from Western cultures, or, more specifically, English culture from Indian culture. Such a distinction becomes possible so long as the dominant values in a given culture remain static over time. From a heuristic point of view, an investigator can deduce a variety of testable hypotheses concerning the salient behaviour patterns of people within that culture.

It is only when the dominant value systems change or are in a state of flux, giving rise to a multiplicity of incongruent and incompatible belief systems, that deducing broad testable hypotheses becomes questionable. Given this caveat, it is suggested that the dominant values in both the contemporary Eastern (India) and Western (England) cultures, although diverse, are reasonably static, which allows the construction of a theoretical model from which a series of hypotheses can be meaningfully deduced and tested. To distinguish English culture from Indian culture, the following four interrelated factors are hypothesized:

Individualism——————Collectivism
Cognitivism——————Emotionalism
Free Will——————Determinism
Materialism——————Spiritualism

Each of the hypothesized factors needs to be understood as extending along a continuum, and not in dichotomous terms. The salient values and behaviours of groups of people may be described as more individualism-oriented and less collectivism-oriented and vice versa. In fact, these values can be described at any measurable point along the continuum, and, over time, may even move along the dimension from one end to the other. The theoretical bases of these factors have been described at length elsewhere (see Laungani, 1990a, 1990b, 1991a, 1991b, 1991c, 1992). In her research study, Sachdev (1992) provided a robust empirical validation of the four factors by means of specifically designed questionnaires that compared the beliefs and values of British-born Indian school children with those of Caucasian school children in West London.

Although both groups of children were born and socialised in a predominantly Western culture, each showed marked preferences in terms of their favoured value systems. Her research also enabled her to predict the sets of conditions under which an individual's position is likely to shift—in either direction—along each continuum. Several sets of related hypotheses have also been subjected to rigorous empirical tests in India (Sachdev, 1992). The analyses of the data lend further support to the previous model. Each concept is examined briefly, and its relationship to stress is traced.

INDIVIDUALISM VERSUS COMMUNALISM (COLLECTIVISM)

Although American psychologists prefer to use the term *collectivism* because of its neutrality, *communalism* is used here. The arguments for the retention of the word *communalism* have been discussed elsewhere (Laungani, in press). One of the distinguishing features of Western society is its increasing emphasis on individualism. At an abstract level, the concept has come to acquire several different meanings: an ability to exercise a degree of control over one's life, the ability to cope with one's problems, an ability to change for the better, reliance on oneself, being responsible for one's actions, self-fulfillment, and self-realization of one's internal resources. Individualism has also been the subject of considerable debate among Western thinkers (Bellah, 1985; Lukes, 1973; Riesman, 1954; Spence, 1985; Waterman, 1981). Some writers have argued that the notion of *individualism* is incompatible—even antithetical—with communal and collective interests. The "dog-eat-dog" philosophy is seen as divisive or inimical in terms of the promotion of communal goals, and in the long run it alienates fellow beings from one another. Archard (1987) argued that, even within a Marxist framework, it is difficult to reconcile the interests of individualism with those of the community. However, there are others—among them Sampson (1977) being the more outspoken of the defenders of individualism—who extol its virtues, which are in keeping with the spirit of capitalism and free enterprise. Sampson saw no reason why the philosophy of individualism should not also nurture a spirit of cooperation and coexistence.

How does the notion of *individualism* enable one to understand stress? First, individualism tends to create conditions that do not permit an easy sharing of one's problems and worries with others. Individualism, as Camus (1955) pointed out in his famous book, *The Myth of Sisyphus*, creates an existential loneliness in people that is compounded by a sense of the absurd, which is an integral part of the human condition. Camus warned that there is no easy escape from this human predicament. The emphasis on self-reliance—the expectation of being responsible for one's success or failure, which is integral to the notion of individualism—imposes severe stress on the individual.

Second, the philosophy of individualism has a strong bearing on the notion of *identity*. In Western society, psychologists and psychiatrists of virtually all theoretical persuasions construct identity in developmental terms, which starts from infancy. In the process of development, one's identity—according to received wisdom—passes through several critical stages from adolescence into adulthood. To acquire an appropriate identity, which asserts one's strengths, is located in reality, reflects one's true inner being, and leads to the fulfillment or realization of one's potential, is by no means easy. It often results in conflict, which, if unresolved, can lead to severe stress or, in extreme cases, an identity crisis (Erikson, 1963; Maslow, 1970, 1971; Rogers, 1961, 1980).

Third, individualism ensures that each individual is held responsible for his or her own problems. Consequently, any failures with attendant feelings of guilt are explained in individualistic terms.

One of the dominant features of individualism is its recognition of, and respect for, an individual's physical and "psychological" space. Vine (1982) reviewed the major studies in the area related to crowding—the invasion of physical and psychological space—and found that violating another person's physical and psychological space gives rise to stress. A separate study (Webb, 1978) has shown that, in extreme cases, it leads to neuroses and other psychosomatic disturbances. Closely related to the notion of physical and psychological space is the concept of *privacy*. Privacy implies a recognition of, and respect for, another person's individuality. It is concerned with defining boundaries that separate the self from others, both physically and psychologically. It is an idea of immense value in the West, respected and adhered to in all social relationships. The need for defining one's psychological and physical boundaries begins virtually at infancy. Several studies have demonstrated that the invasion of privacy also leads to severe stress (Greenberg & Firestone, 1977; Rohner, 1974).

In contrast, Indian society has been and continues to be community oriented (Kakar, 1981; Koller, 1982; Lannoy, 1976; Laungani, 1981; Mandelbaum, 1972; Sinari, 1984). Most Indians grow up and live in extended family networks. The structural and functional aspects of the extended family and the social and psychological consequences of living within it have been discussed elsewhere (Laungani, 1989). Suffice it to say that Indian society cannot be seen other than in familial and communal terms. It is, and has been for centuries, a family-oriented and community-based society. In Asian family life, one's individuality is subordinated to collective solidarity, and one's ego is suppressed into the collective ego of the family and the community. Consequently, when a problem (e.g., financial, medical, psychiatric, etc.) affects an individual, it affects the entire family. The problem becomes one of concern for the whole family. Seldom does one see personalised, private problems.

Indians often use the collective term *we* in their everyday speech. The use of the term *we*, or *hum*, signifies the suppression of one's personal ego into the collective ego of one's family and community. One speaks with the collective voice of others, and in so doing gains their approval.

A community in India is not just a collection of individuals gathered together for a common purpose. In the sense in which it is understood in India, a community has several common features. People within a group are united by a common caste rank, religious grouping, and linguistic and geographical boundaries. The members within a community generally operate on a ranking or hierarchical system. Elders are accorded special status, and their important

Table 14.1 Major features of individualism and communalism

Individualism	Communalism
Emphasis on high degree of self-control	Such emphasis unnecessary
Emphasis on personal responsibility	Emphasis on collective responsibility
Emphasis on self-achievement	Emphasis on collective achievement
Emphasis on nuclear families	Emphasis on extended families

role is clearly recognized. Elders, whether they come from rural areas or large metropolitan cities, are generally deferred to. On important issues, the members of a community may meet and confer with one another, and any decisions taken are often binding on the rest of the members within the community.

However, for an individual to remain part of the family and the community, he or she must submit to communal norms and not deviate to an extent where it becomes necessary for them to be ostracised. The pressure to conform to family norms and expectations can cause acute stress in individual family members, leading, in some instances, to psychotic disorders and hysteria (Channabasavanna & Bhatti, 1982; Sethi & Manchanda, 1978). The authors pointed out that the very act of living together in crowded physical environments, with little room for physical privacy, creates its own sets of stressors. On the whole, however, it would appear that extended family networks provide built-in safety measures against stress and mental disturbances. The emotional and physical intimacy shared by all members within a family group acts as a buffer against the stressors from which the European counterpart is not protected.

Although personal choice is central to an individualistic society, it is virtually nonexistent in a communalistic society. Occupations are largely caste-dependent, and caste, of course, is determined at birth. One is born into a given caste and is destined to remain in it until death. One's friends, too, are an integral part of one's extended family network; pressures from elders and threats of ostracism ensure that one stays within the confines of one's caste and community. One has little choice even in terms of one's marriage partner. Although the "style" of arranged marriages has undergone a change within Indian society, particularly in the urban sectors of the country, they are still the norm. One's life, to a large extent, centers around the extended family.

The major features of individualism and communalism are summarized in Table 14.1.

COGNITIVISM VERSUS EMOTIONALISM

This section is concerned with the way in which the British (the English in particular) construe their private and social worlds, and the ways in which they form and sustain social relationships. In broad terms, Pande (1968) suggested that British society is a work- and activity-centered society; in contradistinction, Indian society is relationship-centered. It should be emphasised that these different constructions of their social worlds are not accidental cultural developments. They stem from the inheritance of their different philosophical legacies.

In a work- and activity-centered society, people are more likely to operate on a cognitive mode, where the emphasis is on rationality, logic, and control. Public expression of feelings and emotions, particularly among the middle classes in England, is often frowned upon. The expression of negative feelings causes mutual embarrassment, and is often construed as being vulgar. In such a society, relationships are formed on the basis of shared commonalities. One is expected to "work at a relationship"—in a marriage, in a family situation, with friends, with colleagues at work, and even with one's children. In a work- and activity-oriented society, one's identity, self-image, and self-esteem grow out of one's work and attitude toward work. Work defines one's sense of worth.

However, work and its relationship to self-esteem acquire meaning only when seen against the background of time. The conception of time is both objective and subjective. At an objective level, time is seen in terms of an Einsteinian dimension, where each hour is divided into fixed moments of minutes, seconds, and milliseconds. Each moment (at least on earth) expires at the same speed—an hour passes not a moment sooner, not a moment later. At a subjective level, however, there are variations in perceptions of time. In a work- and activity-centered society, one's working life, including one's private life, is organized around time. To ensure the judicious use of time, one resorts to keeping appointment books, calendars, and computer-assisted diaries; one works to fixed time schedules; one sets deadlines; and one tries to keep within one's time limits. One is constantly aware of the swift passage of time, and to fritter it away is often construed as an act of criminality. Time, therefore, comes to acquire a significant meaning in a work- and activity-centered society. McClelland (1961) has shown that people in general, and high achievers in particular, use metaphors such as *a dashing waterfall, a speeding train,* and so on to describe time. The fear of running out of time—the fear of not being able to accomplish one's short- and long-term goals on time—is seen as one of the greatest stressors in Western society. Even casual encounters between friends or colleagues at work operate on covert agendas. Meeting people is seldom construed as an end in itself; it is a means to an end, with time playing a significant role.

This is not the case in non-Western societies in general, and in Indian society in particular. Although at an objective level time is construed in virtually the same way as it is in the West, at a subjective level time in India is seen in more flexible and even relaxed terms. Time, in Indian metaphysics, is not conceptualised in linear terms. A linear model of time signifies a beginning, a middle, and an end, or a past, a present, and a future. Time, in Indian philosophy, is conceptualised in circular terms, which means that time has no beginning, no middle, and no end. These differential conceptualisations have serious implications for understanding stress in both cultures.

For instance, at a day-to-day observational level, one does not notice the same sense of urgency among Indians that appears to have become the hallmark of Western society. Time in India is often viewed as "a quiet, motionless ocean" or "a vast expanse of sky." It therefore comes as no surprise to learn that in Hindi the word *kal* stands for both yesterday and tomorrow. One gleans the meaning of the word from its context. The only exceptions to this flexible construction of time are to be found in those situations that are considered auspicious: undertaking an important journey, christenings, betrothals, weddings, funerals, and so on. In these situations, one is expected to consult the family Brahmin priest, who then consults an almanac and calculates the most auspicious time for the commencement of that particular activity. Because of their religious significance, such events are seldom left to chance; one seeks divine guidance in their planning and execution.

The close physical proximity in which people continuously live and share their lives with one another forces a relationship-centered society to operate on an emotional mode. In such a society, feelings and emotions are not easily repressed, and their expression in general is not frowned upon. Crying, dependence on others, excessive emotionality, volatility, and verbal hostility—in both males and females—are not in any way considered signs of weakness or ill-breeding. Because feelings and emotions—both positive and negative—are expressed easily, there is little danger of treading on others' sensibilities and vulnerabilities, such as might be the case in work- and activity-centered societies. Given the extended-family structure of relationships, emotional outbursts are, as it were, "taken on board" by the family members. Quite often the emotional outbursts are of a symbolic nature—even highly stylised and ritualistic. To fully appreciate the ritualistic component of emotional outbursts among Indians, be they Hindus or Muslims, one must visualise it against the backdrop of the living conditions in India. In the urban areas, for those who are fortunate enough to live in a "pukka" house (a house built with bricks, cement, and mortar), it is common for a family of 8–10 persons to be living together in one small room. Given the extreme closeness of life, the paucity of amenities, the absence of privacy, the inertia evoked by the overpowering heat and dust, and the awesome feeling of claustrophobia, it is not surprising that families often quarrel, fight, and swear at one another (and assault one another from time to time as well). But their quarrels and outbursts are often of a symbolic nature, otherwise such quarrels would lead to a permanent rift, the consequences of which would be far more traumatic than those of living together. There is a surrealistic quality in such outbursts. At one level, they are frighteningly real, the words and abuses hurled at one another being callous and hurtful. Yet at another level, these outbursts are bewilderingly unreal. They serve no function other than the relief that such "cathartic" outbursts bring. However, in a hierarchical family structure, each member within the family soon becomes aware of his or her own position within the hierarchy, and in the process of familial adjustment learns the normative expressions of emotionality permissible to the person concerned.

However, in a relationship-centered society, one is forced into relationships; one cannot opt out of these relationships without severe sanctions being imposed. Several studies have shown that one's inability to sever enforced relationships based on birth and caste often leads to severe stress and neurosis

Table 14.2 Major features of cognitivism and emotionalism

Cognitivism	Emotionalism
Emphasis on rationality and logic	Emphasis on feelings and intuition
Feelings and emotions kept in check	Feelings and emotions expressed freely
Emphasis on work and activity	Emphasis on relationships
Relations based on shared interests	Relations based on caste and family

(Channabasavanna & Bhatti, 1982). The major features of cognitivism and emotionalism, and the relative differences, are summarized in Table 14.2.

FREE WILL VERSUS DETERMINISM

There does not appear to be a satisfactory end in sight to the philosophical and scientific wrangles concerning the nature of free will, predestination, determinism, and indeterminism. Although the Aristotelian legacy has undergone several transformations, it has remained with us for over 2,000 years (Flew, 1989). Prior to Newton's spectacular achievements, determinism was entangled in its theistic and metaphysical connotations. But after the publication of Newton's *Principia* in 1687, the concept of *determinism* was partially freed from its theistic connotations, and a nontheistic and mechanistic view of determinism in science, and indeed in the universe, gained prominence. A scientific notion of determinism, with its emphasis on causality or, conversely, its denial of noncausal events, found favour among the rationalist philosophers who embraced it with great fervour (Popper, 1972). However, it was not until the emergence of quantum mechanics in the early twentieth century that determinism in science, if not in human affairs, once again came to be seriously questioned. In keeping with his own views on the subject, Popper (1988) avoided the terms *determinism* and *free will* altogether. Instead, he proposed the term *indeterminism,* which, he argued is neither the opposite of determinism nor the same as free will.

Notwithstanding the unresolved debates in philosophy on the subject, there is a peculiar dualism in Western thinking concerning free will and determinism. Scientific research in medicine, psychiatry, biology, and other related disciplines, including psychology, is based on the acceptance of a deterministic framework, hence the concern with seeking causal explanations, and with predictability in accordance with rational scientific procedures of prediction. Yet at social, psychological, and commonsense levels, there is a strong belief in the notion of *free will.*

What is meant by free will? *Free will* might be defined as a noncausal, voluntary action. However, at a commonsense level, it is defined as exercising voluntary control over one's actions. Thus, free will allows an individual to do what he or she wills, and in so doing take credit for his or her successes, while also accepting blame for his or her failures and mishaps. Thus, one is forever locked into the consequences of one's own actions. This feature of Western society entraps a person into his or her own existential predicament, from which there appears to be no easy way out.

Rotter (1966) offered a neat solution to the dilemma of determinism and free will. The concept of *control* is central to Rotter's ideas. He argued that some individuals explain their actions in terms of internal control (free will) and some in terms of external control (determinism). On the basis of a self-administered questionnaire, The Locus of Control Scale, he found that perceived control exists in individually varying degrees. He regarded it as an enduring personality characteristic, and it seems that those who possess it to a high degree are able to moderate the impact of whatever stresses they encounter. Rotter defined *perceived control* as the principal coping mechanism for stress and other health-related problems. Studies suggest that those persons motivated by internal control—cognitive, informational, emotional, and behavioural control—are better able to cope with stress and other health hazards, including mental illness (Glass, Reim, & Singer, 1971; Mills & Krantz, 1979; Seligman, 1975; Thompson, 1981).

Indians, by virtue of subscribing to a deterministic view of life, in a teleological sense at least, are prevented from taking final responsibility for their own actions. The notion of *determinism* plays an extremely crucial role in Indian thinking. The law of karma, which involves determinism and fatalism, has shaped the Indian view of life over centuries (O'Flaherty, 1976; Sinari, 1984; Weber, 1963). In its simplest form, the law of karma states that happiness and sorrow are the predetermined effects of actions committed by a person either in his or her present life or in one of his or her numerous past lives. Things do not happen because people make them happen. Things happen because they were *destined* to happen. If one's present life is determined by one's actions in one's previous life, it follows that any problem that affects one was destined to happen.

The belief in the law of karma does not, as is mistakenly assumed by many, negate the notion of *free will*. As von-Furer-Haimendorf (1974) pointed out, in an important sense karma is based on the assumption of free will. The theory of karma rests on the idea that an individual has the moral responsibility for each of his or her actions, and hence the freedom of moral choice.

In a study of informants of psychiatric patients in India, Pandey, Srinivas, and Muralidhar (1980) found that the most commonly stated causes of psychotic disorders were attributed to sins and wrong deeds in previous and present life. These findings have been corroborated by Srinivas and Trivedi (1982). These authors studied 266 respondents selected from three villages in South India, and attributed, among other factors, "God's curse" as one of the most common causes of stress leading to mental disorders. Such a belief has its advantages: It takes away the blame that might otherwise be apportioned to the individual concerned.

Determinism engenders a spirit of passive, if not resigned, acceptance of the vicissitudes of life in the Indian psyche. This prevents a person from experiencing feelings of guilt, a state from which the Westerners, because of their fundamental belief in the doctrine of free will, cannot be protected. The main disadvantage of determinism, and there are many, lies in the fact that it often leads to a state of existential and, in certain instances, moral resignation,

Table 14.3 Major features of free will and determinism

Free will	Determinism
Emphasis on freedom of choice	Freedom of choice limited
Proactive	Reactive
Success or failure due largely to effort	Although effort is important, success or failure is related to one's karma
Self-blame or guilt is a residual consequence of failure	No guilt is attached to failure
Failure may lead to victim-blaming	No blame is attached to victim

compounded by a profound sense of inertia. One does not take immediate proactive measures; one merely accepts the vicissitudes of life without qualm. Although this may prevent one from experiencing stress, it does not allow one to make individual attempts to alleviate one's unbearable condition. The major features of free will and determinism are summarized in Table 14.3.

MATERIALISM VERSUS SPIRITUALISM

Materialism refers to a belief in the existence of a material world, or a world composed of matter. What constitutes *matter* is debatable; the question has never been satisfactorily answered (Trefil, 1980). If matter consists of atoms, it appears that atoms are made of nuclei and electrons. Nuclei, in turn, are made up of protons and neutrons. What are protons and neutrons made of? Gell-Mann (cited in Davies, 1990) coined the word *quarks*. But quarks, it appears, have their own quirks. In other words, the assumed solidity of matter may indeed turn out to be a myth (Davies, 1990).

The notion of the *solidity of matter* was robustly debated by Heisenberg in his now-famous research article on indeterminacy in quantum theory in 1927 (Heisenberg, 1930). Such debates are confined to journals of philosophy and science. At a practical, day-to-day level, however, aided by empiricism, one accepts the assumed solidity of the world that one inhabits, but not without paying a heavy price. Such an acceptance gives rise to the popular myth that all explanations of phenomena, ranging from lunar cycles to lunacy, need to be sought within the (assumed) materialist framework. This is evidenced by the profound reluctance among psychiatrists, medical practitioners, and psychologists in general to entertain any explanations that are of a nonmaterial or supernatural nature. Nonmaterial explanations are treated at best with scepticism, and at worst with scorn.

A materialistic philosophy also tends to engender in its subscribers the belief that one's knowledge of the world is external to oneself; reality is, as it were, "out there," and it is only through objective scientific enterprise that one will acquire an understanding of the external world and, with it, an understanding of "reality."

The few psychiatrists and psychologists who have steered away from materialistic explanations, or have shown the willingness to consider alternative, nonmaterial explanations, comprise a very small minority. Most of them are only too aware that anyone offering such explanations of phenomena is in danger of incurring the wrath of the scientific community. Nonmaterial explanations fall within the purview of the prescientific communities, or *superstitious* and *backward* societies, to be found mainly in underdeveloped, Third World countries.

Consider an example to illustrate such forms of thinking in Western society. For over 2,000 years, yogis in India have made claims about their abilities to alter their states of consciousness at will, thereby bringing their autonomic nervous states under voluntary control (Radhakrishnan, 1923/1989). In hatha yoga, yogic exercises—or *asanas* as they are called—were claimed to have therapeutic effects for a variety of physical and psychological disorders. Such claims were seldom taken seriously by Western scientists. They were dismissed as unsubstantiated exaggerations. It was not until Miller (1969) successfully trained his laboratory rats to lower and raise their blood pressure by selective reinforcement that the Western mind began to believe that there might be some substance in the claims made by yoga after all. Using a similar selective reinforcement strategy, Miller found that he could train his students to exercise voluntary control over their autonomic responses. Suddenly the yogis' claims began to acquire credibility. Miller's performing rats did the trick. Miller's findings opened the doors to yoga in American universities; research into altered states of consciousness, followed by its applications into techniques of biofeedback, became respectable. Therefore, it is hardly an accident when one realizes the importance given to yogic *asanas* in a variety of stress-management exercises designed by Western experts.

In Indian thinking, the notion of *materialism* is a relatively unimportant concept. The external world to Indians is not composed of matter—it is seen as illusory, it is *maya*. The concept of *maya,* as Zimmer (1951/1989) pointed out, "holds a key position in Vedantic thought and teaching" (p. 19). Because the external world is illusory, reality—or its perception—lies within the individual and not, as Westerners believe, outside the individual. According to Zimmer, this tends to make Indians more inward-looking and Westerners more outward-looking. Also, given the illusory nature of the external world, the Indian mind remains unfettered by materialistic boundaries. It resorts to explanations where material and spiritual, physical and metaphysical, and natural and supernatural explanations of phenomena coexist with one another. What might seem an irreconcilable contradiction to a Western mind, weaned on Aristotelian logic, nourished on a scientific diet, and socialised on materialism, empiricism, and positivism, leaves an Indian mind relatively unperturbed. To a Westerner, if A is A, A cannot then be not-A. If dysentery is caused by certain forms of bacteria, it cannot then be due to the influence of the "evil-eye." The two are logically and empirically incompatible. But to Indians, contradictions are a way of life. A is not only A but, under certain conditions, A may be not-A. One of the most interesting differences between Indian thinking and Western thinking is this: Indians intuitively believe the external

Table 14.4 Major features of materialism and spiritualism

Materialism	Spiritualism
The world is "real," physical	The world is illusory
Rejection of contradictory explanations of phenomena	Coexistence of contradictory explanations of phenomena
Reality is external to the individual	Reality is internal to the individual
Reality perceived through scientific enterprise	Reality perceived through contemplation and inner reflection

world to be illusory without actually "knowing" it; Westerners "know" it to be illusory, without actually believing it. This differential construction of one's physical world has an important bearing on the perception of stress and the methods employed for coping with it.

Indian beliefs and values revolve around the notion of *spiritualism*. The ultimate purpose of human existence is to transcend one's illusory physical existence, renounce the world of material aspirations, and attain a heightened state of spiritual awareness. Any activity—particularly yoga—that is likely to promote such a state is to be encouraged. Table 14.4 summarizes the major features of materialism and spiritualism.

CONCLUSION

Stress is a common human and animal experience. It occurs when coping resources are overstrained. It is the body's unhealthy or nonspecific response to external and internal stimuli; if unchecked, it can lead to severe psychological, physiological, and psychosomatic disturbances. There are obvious personality differences in people regarding their reaction to stressors and their consequent susceptibility to cancer and coronary heart disease (Eysenck, chap. 1, this volume). As shown in this chapter, there are vast cultural differences in terms of what constitutes stressors.

As a result, there are fundamental differences in the management of stress between the two cultures described herein. The methods of stress management in Western societies are too well known to merit a detailed discussion. They range from a variety of conventional individual and group psychotherapies, which include behaviour modification, relaxation techniques, time management, cognitive restructuring, rational-emotive therapy, and confrontational techniques, to nondirective, client-centered therapies and Freudian and neo-Freudian psychotherapies. There are also the less conventional techniques of stress management such as dance therapy, Alexander technique, art therapy, physical exercises, aerobics, sex therapy, and so on.

In India, however, stress is not seen as a major problem that would require the attention of experts. For a problem to be construed as a serious medical or psychiatric problem, there must be a set of accompanying somatic and/or psychological symptoms. As Rao (1986) pointed out, India does not have the trained psychiatric and psychological personnel to offer Western-type therapies to its people, with an estimated population of 923 million.

What, then, are the therapeutic alternatives available in India? First, there is a greater reliance on indigenous therapeutic treatments. The World Health Organization (WHO; 1978) reported that there are over 108 colleges of indigenous medicine in India, with over 500,000 practitioners of one of the following indigenous forms of healing: ayurveds, unani, and yoga.

Second, yoga, in all its variants, appears to be the most popular form of treatment for stress and other psychological disorders all over the country. Evidence of the efficacy of yoga therapy is quite convincing (Satyavathi, 1988). Encouraged by the results of yoga therapy, Vahia (1982) even suggested that yoga represents a new conceptual model of health and disease. Although several studies have pointed to the effectiveness of yoga therapy (Bhole, 1981; Dharmakeerti, 1982; Neki, 1979; Nespor, 1982), it is not seen as a panacea for all types of disorders.

Third, stress (with its accompanying somatic symptoms) in India is also explained in terms of sorcery, bewitchment, and spirits (Kakar, 1982). The belief in magical explanations is widespread, and persons specially qualified to remove spells and exorcise evil spirits, such as *bhoots, balas,* and *shaitans,* are summoned by family members of the afflicted person (Kakar, 1982).

Fourth, all over India, one may find an army of faith healers, mystics, shamans, pirs (holy men), bhagats, gurus, and practitioners of ayrvedic and homeopathic medicine. They are accorded the same respect and veneration as the medically trained psychiatrists in India. It would not be uncommon to find the concerned relatives of a distressed person consulting some, if not all, of these specialists for effective treatment.

Fifth, one must take into account the influence of religion in the management of stress. A token offering to one of the many deities, a visit to the local priest, a pilgrimage to a well-known shrine or *darga,* or a meeting with a Guru, in whose curative powers the family has unshakable faith, are some of the familiar therapeutic routes taken by the family members of an afflicted person. Occasionally, the family may consult with an astrologer, or undertake a visit to a shaman or a well-known *pir.* Psychotherapists in India do not have the specialised and important role in the treatment of stress and other mental disorders that they do in the West. A Western-trained psychiatrist or psychologist is one of many in the long queue of consultants, and by no means resides at the head of the queue.

Clearly, no culture or society has all the answers concerning the problems related to stress and its variants. It is only when cultures meet on equal terms and as equal partners and express a genuine willingness to learn from each other that tentative answers to universal questions may be found.

REFERENCES

Archard, D. (1987). The Marxist ethic of self-realization: Individuality and community. In J. D. G. Evans (Ed.), *Moral philosophy and contemporary problems.* Cambridge, England: Cambridge University Press.

Bellah, R. N. (1985). *Habits of the heart: Individuation and commitment in American life.* Berkeley, CA: University of California Press.

Bhole, M. V. (1981). Concept of relaxation in shavasana. *Yoga Mimamsa, 20,* 50–56.

Camus, A. (1955). *The myth of Sisyphus.* London: Hamish Hamilton.

Channabasavanna, S. M., & Bhatti, R. S. (1982). A study on interactional patterns and family typologies in families of mental patients. In A. Kiev & A. V. Rao (Eds.), *Readings in transcultural psychiatry* (pp. 149–161). Madras: Higginbothams.

Davies, P. (1990). *God and the new physics.* London: Penguin Books:

Dharmakeerti, U. S. (1982). Review of "Yoga and cardiovascular management." *Yoga, 20,* 15–16.

Erikson, E. (1963). *Childhood and society.* London: Penguin Books.

Flew, A. (1989). *An introduction to Western philosophy* (rev. ed.). London: Thames & Hudson.

Glass, D. C., Reim, B., & Singer, J. E. (1971). Behavioural consequences of adaptation to an environmental stressor. *Journal of Personality and Social Psychology, 7,* 244–257.

Greenberg, C. I., & Firestone, I. J. (1977). Compensatory response to crowding: Effects of personal space and privacy reduction. *Journal of Personality and Social Psychology, 35,* 637–644.

Heisenberg, W. (1930). *The physical principles of the Quantum Theory.* Berkeley, CA: California University Press.

Kakar, S. (1981). *The inner world: A psychoanalytic study of children and society in India.* Delhi: Oxford University Press.

Kakar, S. (1982). *Shamans, mystics and doctors.* London: Mandala Books, Unwin Paperbacks.

Koller, J. M. (1982). *The Indian way: Perspectives.* London: Collier Macmillan.

Lannoy, R. (1976). *The speaking tree.* London: Oxford University Press.

Laungani, P. (1981, December). *Investigating personality cross-culturally.* Paper presented at the National Conference of Applied Psychology, Bombay, India.

Laungani, P. (1989, October 28). Cultural influences on mental illness. *Political & Economic Weekly,* pp. 2427–2430.

Laungani, P. (1990a). Turning eastward: An Asian view on child abuse. *Health & Hygiene, 11,* 26–29.

Laungani, P. (1990b, March). *Family life and child abuse: Learning from Asian culture.* Paper presented at the 3rd International Child Health Congress, London, England.

Laungani, P. (1991a, June). *Child abuse and promoting child health across cultures.* Paper presented at the United Nations Conference on Action for Public Health, Sundsvall, Sweden.

Laungani, P. (1991b, July). *The nature and experience of learning: Cross-cultural perspectives.* Paper presented at a conference on Experiential Learning, Guildford, England.

Laungani, P. (1991c, July). *Stress across cultures: A theoretical analysis.* Paper presented at the conference of The Society of Public Health on

Stress and The Health Services at the Royal Society of Medicine, London, England.

Laungani, P. (1992). Assessing child abuse through interviews of children and parents of children at risk. *Children and Society, 6,* 3–11.

Laungani, P. (in press). *India and England: A psycho-cultural analysis.* London: Whiting & Birch Ltd.

Lukes, S. (1973). *Individualism.* Oxford: Basil Blackwell.

Mandelbaum, D. G. (1972). *Society in India* (Vol. 2). Berkeley, CA: University of California Press.

Maslow, A. (1970). *Motivation and personality* (2nd ed.). New York: Harper & Row.

Maslow, A. (1971). *The farther reaches of human nature.* New York: McGraw-Hill.

McClelland, D. C. (1961). *The achieving society.* Princeton: Van Nostrand.

Miller, N. E. (1969). Learning of visceral and glandular responses. *Science, 163,* 434–435.

Mills, R. T., & Krantz, D. S. (1979). Information, choice, and reactions to stress: A field experiment in a blood bank with laboratory analogue. *Journal of Personality and Social Psychology, 37,* 608–620.

Neki, J. S. (1979). Psychotherapy in India: Traditions and trends. In M. Kapur, V. N. Murthy, K. Satyavathi, & R. L. Kapur (Eds.), *Psychotherapeutic processes* (pp. 113–134). Bangalore, India: National Institute of Mental Health and Neurosciences.

Nespor, K. (1982). Yogic practices in world medical literature. *Yoga, 20,* 29–35.

O'Flaherty, W. D. (1976). *The origins of evil in Hindu mythology.* Berkeley, CA: University of California Press.

Pande, S. (1968). The mystique of "Western" psychotherapy: An Eastern interpretation. *The Journal of Nervous and Mental Disease, 146,* 425–432.

Pandey, R. S., Srinivas, K. N., & Muralidhar, D. (1980). Socio-cultural beliefs and treatment acceptance. *Indian Journal of Psychiatry, 22,* 161–166.

Popper, K. (1972). *Objective knowledge: An evolutionary approach.* Oxford, England: Clarendon.

Popper, K. (1988). *The open universe: An argument for indeterminism.* London: Hutchinson.

Radhakrishnan, S. (1989). *Indian philosophy* (Vol. 2). Delhi: Oxford University Press. (Original work published 1923)

Rao, V. (1986). Indian and Western psychiatry: A comparison. In J. L. Cox (Ed.), *Transcultural psychiatry* (pp. 291–305). Backenham, England: Croom Helm.

Riesman, D. (1954). *Individualism reconsidered.* New York: Doubleday Anchor Books.

Rohner, R. P. (1974). Proxemics and stress: An empirical study of the relationship between space and roommate turnover. *Human Relations, 27,* 697–702.

Rogers, C. (1961). *On becoming a person.* Boston: Houghton Mifflin.

Rogers, C. (1980). *A way of being.* Boston: Houghton Mifflin.

Rotter, J. B. (1966). Generalized expectancies for internal versus external control of reinforcement. *Psychological Monographs, 80,* 1–27.

Sachdev, D. (1992). *Effects of psychocultural factors on the socialisation of British born Indian children and indigenous British children living in England.* Unpublished doctoral dissertation , South Bank University, London.

Sampson, E. E. (1977). Psychology and the American ideal. *Journal of Personality and Social Psychology, 15,* 189–194.

Satyavathi, K. (1988). Mental health. In J. Pandey (Ed.), *Psychology in India: The state-of-the-art: Vol. III. Organizational behaviour and mental health* (pp. 217–288). New Delhi: Sage.

Seligman, M. E. P. (1975). *Helplessness: On depression, development and death.* San Francisco: Freeman.

Sethi, B. B., & Manchanda, R. (1978). Family structure and psychiatric disorders. *Indian Journal of Psychiatry, 20,* 283–288.

Sinari, R. A. (1984). *The structure of Indian thought.* Delhi: Oxford University Press.

Spence, J. T. (1985). Achievement American style: The rewards and costs of individualism. *American Psychologist, 40,* 1285–1295.

Srinivasa, D. K., & Trivedi, S. (1982). Knowledge and attitude of mental diseases in a rural community in South India. *Social Science Medicine, 16,* 1635–1639.

Thompson, S. C. (1981). Will it hurt if I can control it? A complex answer to a simple question. *Psychological Bulletin, 90,* 89–101.

Trefil, J. (1980). *From atoms to quarks: An introduction to the strange world of particle physics.* London: Athlone.

Vahia, N. S. (1982). Yoga in psychiatry. In A. Kiev & A. V. Rao (Eds.), *Readings in transcultural psychiatry* (pp. 11–19). Madras: Higginbothams.

Vine, I. (1982). Crowding and stress: A personal space approach. *Psychological Review, 2,* 1–18.

von-Furer-Haimendorf, C. (1974). The sense of sin in cross-cultural perspective. *Man, 9,* 539–556.

Waterman, A. A. (1981). Individualism and interdependence. *American Psychologist, 36,* 762–773.

Webb, S. D. (1978). Privacy and psychosomatic stress: An empirical analysis. *Social Behaviour and Personality, 6,* 227–234.

Weber, M. (1963). *The sociology of religion* (4th ed.). London: Methuen.

World Health Organization. (1978). *The promotion and development of traditional medicine.* (WHO Technical Report Series No. 622). Geneva, Switzerland: Author.

Zimmer, H. (1989). *Philosophies of India* (Bollingen Series XXVI). Princeton, NJ: Princeton University Press. (Original work published 1951)

Author Index

Subject Index

ACTH (adrenocorticotrophic hormone), 25
Activation, neuroticism and, 224–225
Adolescents:
  anger precipitation and, 62
  temperament risk factor in, 241–242
Adrenaline, 24, 28
Adrenocorticotrophic hormone (ACTH), 25
Adults, temperament risk factor in, 241–242
Age, Oxford Happiness Inventory scores and, 176
Aggression:
  defined, 113
  expression, gender differences in, 58, 95–96
  (*See also* AHA! Syndrome)
Agreeableness, in diabetes, 41–44
AHA! Syndrome, 113
  overcoming, 114–115
  PSSW program for, 114–117
Anger:
  definition of, 113
  discussions, gender differences in, 57–58
  of divorced mothers, 76
  expression, 62–64
    gender differences in, 95–97
    verbal, 96–97
    in women, 68
  expression scales, 113, 115, 116

management, in unemployed workers, 112–113
maternal, children's gender and, 85–87
overdevelopment of, 95–96
suppression, 62–64, 68
of women (*See* Mothers, custodial, anger of; Women; Women's Anger Study)
(*See also* AHA! Syndrome)
Antigen personality profile, 23
Antisocial personality disorder, batterers and, 93
Anxiety:
  biological substrate, behavioral inhibition system as, 190–191
  cognitive functioning in, 201–202
  happiness and, 143–144
  individual differences in, 190, 206
  scales, 193
  social, happiness and, 177–178
  state, 190
  vulnerability to, 190
Appraisals, event, 189
Approach–avoidance conflicts, behavioral inhibition in, 195–199
Arousal, 223
  optimal level, 217, 226
  temperament and, 223–226

UNDERSTANDING EATING DISORDERS:
Anorexia Nervosa, Bulimia Nervosa, and Obesity

Edited by LeeAnn Alexander-Mott and D. Barry Lumsden,
both of the University of North Texas, Denton

As the incidence of eating disorders such as anorexia nervosa, bulimia nervosa, and obesity (sometimes caused by compulsive eating) has risen, so has research and literature in the field. Presenting current knowledge of these eating disorder—the most common types found in adolescents and adults—this resource addresses issues relevant to all.

Examining the pertinent history, etiology, psychopathology, and sociology, the contributors—all acknowledged authorities in their particular areas—define these eating disorders and discuss issues of recovery and methods of treatment. They also consider the problem as it exists in both males and females in this multicultural society. The resulting volume is divided into four parts: the first gives an overview in general, and the next three focus individually on anorexia nervosa, bulimia nervosa, and obesity respectively.

This will be of interest to those working directly with eating disorders patients— doctors, psychologists, psychiatrists, counselors, nurses, and those working in eating disorder clinics and programs. Teachers and social workers will also find vital information for understanding and dealing with victims of eating disorders.

Contents: 1. General Issues. The Eating Disorders: An Historical Perspective. Critical Issues in the Developmental Psychopathology of Eating Disorders. Parenting and Family Factors in Eating Problems. Sexual Abuse and the Eating Disorders. 2. Anorexia Nervosa: Definition, Diagnostic Criteria, and Associated Psychological Problems; Theories of Etiology; Methods of Treatment. 3. Bulimia Nervosa: Definition, Diagnostic Criteria, and Associated Psychological Problems; Medical Complications; Methods of Treatment. 4. Obesity: Definition, Diagnostic Criteria, and Associated Health Problems; Socio-Cultural Perspectives; Methods of Treatment. Afterword. Index.

Readership: Educators, researchers, students, and other professionals in the field of health care, i.e. psychologists, psychiatrists, doctors, counselors, and social workers; families of eating disorders victims.

Taylor & Francis • August 1994 • 275pp
1-56032-294-2 CL $59.50x • 1-56032-295-0 PB $29.50x